LABOR PAINS

*A Tale of Kicking, Discomfort, and Joy on the
Broadcasting Delivery Table*

JEFFREY RUTHIZER

Archway Publishing books may be ordered through booksellers or by contacting:

Archway Publishing
1663 Liberty Drive
Bloomington, IN 47403
www.archwaypublishing.com
844-669-3957

ISBN: 978-1-6657-0678-0 (sc)
ISBN: 978-1-6657-0677-3 (hc)
ISBN: 978-1-6657-0679-7 (e)

Library of Congress Control Number: 2021909091

Print information available on the last page.

Archway Publishing rev. date: 8/24/2022

CONTENTS

INTRODUCTION

Mine of course were of a different variety, but labor pains they were nevertheless. Sometimes excruciating, these pains featured all of the initial excitement, accompanying nausea, periodic discomfort, frequent medicinal relief from heartburn, and more than occasional kicking.

Stretching out for more than four decades, they also encompassed the ultimate, rhapsodic joy of a series of difficult but yet splendid births on the broadcasting delivery table. There were many hundreds of these extraordinary moments until one day the labor pains miraculously disappeared upon my retirement from The Walt Disney Company in 2009.

Suggested to me over the years by others patiently listening to my labor tales as a possible title for my life experiences, this memoir got kick started in 2019 with the publication of a non-fiction book. *In Hoffa's Shadow,* authored by Jack Goldsmith, dealt with '75's mysterious disappearance and murder of the legendary Teamster leader Jimmy Hoffa. The work featured as one of its central characters a Detroit Teamster official named Chuckie O'Brien. At one point in the investigation into Hoffa's disappearance, as related by Goldsmith in this book about his stepfather, O'Brien was fingered as the chief suspect. Never charged by the authorities with any crime, it was clear that O'Brien was nevertheless no ordinary union official.

This particular book got my rapt attention when I read its review because I had known O'Brien. He and I once had a near physical altercation during one of my earliest bouts in the labor arena. That was a half-century ago, in 1971, during a strike involving our performers at ABC's broadcasting stations in Detroit, Michigan. While I was a young lawyer representing the company, Chuckie was a young Teamster official who had somehow gotten himself enmeshed in another union's labor dispute.

Having told this particular story many times over about our almost coming to blows, I felt destiny was directing me to write my story. As I started doing so, I began adding a number of other accumulated labor pains over my 45-year legal career.

My commitment to writing these assorted tales was considerably strengthened with the 2019 release of Martin Scorsese's Oscar winning movie, *The Irishman*. In that film, O'Brien again appeared as a real life character prominently involved in Hoffa's life and disappearance. If it is good enough for Scorsese, Al Pacino, and Robert De Niro to hang out with Chuckie O'Brien, I reasoned, it was good enough for me to tell the story of our almost coming to blows.

As perhaps another sign of destiny, I was to learn that O'Brien had retired from his Teamster position and moved with his wife in later years from Detroit to Boca Raton, FL. That's a town close to mine. So, I asked myself, why not a lunch between former adversaries and recount old tales of labor pains long forgotten. It was, however, a bit too late because his phone was disconnected when I found his number and called. Shortly later in February 2020, his obituary appeared in the pages of the *The New York Times*.

PROLOGUE

"Captain Nathan Brittles"

Most readers are unfamiliar with labor negotiations except through what might be picked up from TV news reporting, movies, descriptions in newspaper accounts, and anecdotes to be read in this and other books. What goes on and how deals are actually crafted, neither exactly an art nor a science, is a complicated and often bewildering subject. This was particularly true in the entertainment industry where we had so many unions—performers, writers, directors, technicians, and stagehands, not to mention musicians, editors, camera operators, makeup artists, and hair stylists. Even truck drivers, motorcycle couriers, and a lonely projectionist or two.

Yes, there is, as I discovered from many hundreds of experiences over a lifetime, a great deal of kicking and discomfort on the delivery table before any of the ultimate joy can ever be felt.

Not only is the making of a labor deal often a difficult task, equally challenging is the daily living. Occasionally in hot combat with one, we were always getting ready for talks with another—or several. It was a never-ending demonstration of problem-solving at the highest, often most intense levels. And it displayed the frequent inevitability of human conflict. These pages will draw the reader's attention to only some of the highlights and low points of my career while first gaining experience as a young government lawyer and then in the far more challenging and disruptive corporate labor relations world in the volatile entertainment industry. In four major test kitchens I labored over hot stoves—learning how labor chefs went about trying to make tasty dishes that sometimes though just came out hash.

When that career ended in 2009, I went riding out into the retirement sunset. It was much like one of my most favorite movie characters, Captain Nathan Brittles, from RKO's and director John Ford's 1949 western classic, *She Wore A Yellow Ribbon,* starring John Wayne. Part of Ford's and Wayne's "Cavalry Trilogy," the year is 1876. It's right after General George Custer's 7th Cavalry defeat at the Little Bighorn 800 miles distant in the northern Montana Territory. Near the end of the movie there's a touching scene when Captain Brittles, played brilliantly by Wayne, has just led his young lieutenants, John Agar and Harry Carey Jr., in a victory over the restless Native American tribes. It never fails to bring a tear to my eye.

At that moment of victory, Brittles looks at his brand new, silver pocket watch retirement gift, with its bland but at least to him emotional sentiment—"From C Troop, lest we forget"—inscribed on its back. Its hands tell him he has just officially, at two minutes after midnight, retired from the US Army. Brittles is then seen after his long and successful career as a captain of cavalry riding off into the sunset for his final retirement days in California.

Such a great movie, I could talk about it at any hour and sometimes did during long breaks in negotiations when we played movie trivia late into the night. I actually learned a few lines from Wayne's Brittles that helped in my negotiating career. One that stayed with me was, "Never apologize, it's a sign of weakness." I always tried to follow Wayne's sage advice whenever I could when I was deep in my own cavalry battles across the bargaining plains.

The Brittles role always resonated with me. It did so particularly after my own retirement and ride not out west to the new frontier settlements in California but rather my drive south to the new retirement developments being built in Florida.

A retired captain myself in the US Army, I was certainly no Captain Nathan Brittles. I sometimes fantasized though over the decades of my career that I had a loyal troop of rugged, blue-shirted cavalrymen riding right behind me and following my every order. When I became a retired captain of cavalry of my own—only the third such commander of ABC's labor relations forces in the storied 75-year history of the company—my place was taken by a new regimental commander. I had selected him for his good horsemanship and savvy instincts nearly 20 years previous.

Keeping busy with some voluntary work and consulting for The Walt Disney Company and others after my retirement, that helped to keep intact the scalp of this retired cavalry officer. Doing so helped me preserve a sharper mind than what would have otherwise happened just sitting around the barracks waiting for my final mustering out and watching my silver pocket watch tarnish. The result of that enabled this memoir ultimately to be written from clear mind and careful memory.

The nearly five-decade story beginning in my law school days recounted in *Labor Pains* tells of some of the most memorable labor experiences of my life and times. Relating stories from my past while deep in the trenches of human conflict at the bargaining table or at other contentious moments with many unions, it speaks to events and occasions at the four broadcasting and entertainment companies for which I worked during my career—ABC, NBC, RKO, and Disney. It's interlaced with some historical moments and other stories, which are nothing more than interesting anecdotes of personal encounters or experiences along the way which were mixed in among the many labor pains. Those events made the heavier moments on the broadcasting delivery table much more bearable.

A friend of mine who read some advance copy of these pages

told me I should apologize to women for the temerity of borrowing my title from the intense pain of true labor. This will serve as that apology for hijacking both the pleasures and pains of those moments into the title of my transferred labor experiences.

In the course of writing this book, there are stories I describe about many prominent figures. Among the legendary entertainment titans are Disney's Bob Iger, Michael Eisner, and Michael Ovitz. ABC leaders Tom Murphy, Dan Burke, Roone Arledge, and Leonard Goldenson also figure prominently as also do a few chief executives at NBC and RKO. A number of the names sprinkled throughout are not on everyone's lips today but their presence was once mighty.

Also recounted are experiences with famous individuals I met and shared some time and space with along the way. Included in the potpourri of notables are President Ronald Reagan, the Four Tops, the 2000 Year Old Man Mel Brooks, Mrs. Douglas MacArthur, and Henry Kissinger. Howard Cosell, Bernadette Peters, Rudy Vallée, and Eartha Kitt also get featured appearances. There's a peek at NBC legendary talk show host Johnny Carson and a much longer look at the grandaddy-host of them all, Joe Franklin. Episodes with actors Peter O'Toole, Gordon MacRae, Jerry Orbach, Jason Robards Jr., and Telly Savalas are also related. There's even a story or two with Mark Hamill's Luke Skywalker, James Gandolfini's Tony Soprano, and the dancing duo of Fred Astaire and Ginger Rogers.

My bayonet instructor during basic training at the US Army's Ford Ord, while preparing my unit for possible combat duty in Vietnam, unforgettably told us in 1967 that there were only two kinds of bayonet fighters—the quick and the dead. That was an excellent life lesson 54 years ago necessary for survival on battlefields of every description—including most definitely the labor arena. If the US Army gave out grades for bayonet training, as the following pages hopefully will make clear, I got an A+ in that course.

1
CHAPTER

Pains Out on the Horizon

Columbia Law School in the 1960s had a Mount Rushmore-type faculty. Among the giants were two professors with whom I was fortunate to study labor law. Judge Paul Hays, sitting on the Second Circuit Court of Appeals, taught the basic, introductory course that I took in my second year. It captivated my interest. In my third year, after I had decided that labor law was the field in which I wanted to specialize, I took the advanced, small seminar taught by Professor Michael Sovern. If Hays himself did not reach Mount Rushmore status, Sovern's chiseled image—high up and prominent on that mountainside—is there forever.

A Columbia College and Columbia Law School graduate himself, Sovern had become in 1960, shortly before I entered, the youngest full professor in the long history of the law school. Mike went onto an illustrious career at Columbia. He became dean of the law school in 1970 after the disastrous '68 college campus disturbances and then some time later the president of Columbia University itself. With his considerable stage presence and somewhat more than modest ego, like so many of the other great law professors, he enjoyed every minute of teaching, with all of its necessary theatricality. Always inspiring, he loved to pepper us with questions about the cases we were examining. While carefully constructing hypotheticals, he was constantly testing our self-assumed intelligence while simultaneously displaying his own, true brilliance.

After graduation and in the days long before email, I was fortunate to have been able to stay in touch with Mike through the US Postal Service. As my broadcasting labor relations career advanced, I'm positive from our exchange of notes that he took more than just a small piece of the credit for my promotions. At one point in his Columbia deanship days and my time at NBC, we shared with our spouses a very special dinner table at a mutual friend's country kitchen in his Greenwich Village townhouse. After an evening of simply stunning discourse in the noted arbitrator's home, Sovern dropped Monica and me off at our New York apartment on his way back to their upper west side apartment. Over the last decade, we communicated periodically through another mutual friend who sat with him—so well-suited for his thespian personality—on the board of the mega-Broadway theatrical producer and theater owner, the Shubert Organization. Mike died in 2020 shortly after we had spoken one last time through our friend, Elliot Greene, Shubert's COO.

What I found most intriguing about labor law while studying at Columbia under Hays and Sovern was that it was not just the mechanical application of some body of boring law. It was not at all like tax, trusts and estates, commercial transactions, or antitrust. Rather, it represented the dynamics—the constant push and pull of people, unions, and companies interacting in the workplace. Like giant tectonic plates, unions and employers were constantly grinding against each other, preparing for some inevitable earthquake and then living through the consequences. It was though more than that. It was a constant battle for respect, control, and dominance. Most importantly and in its essence, it was about workers' economic futures balanced against a company's striving for efficiency and maximum profit under the American free enterprise system—and the legal system built up around that struggle.

For me, this challenging mix of the people and the law was unique and exciting. I found it also in criminal law, which has considerably more of the same people factor but in a wholly different legal setting. I discovered and also liked admiralty law, the law of ships and the seas, but it had no people factor whatsoever other than captains and mates and was considerably more dry despite its inherently liquid nature. Criminal, labor, and admiralty—these were my three possible career paths before I zeroed in on labor law.

Some who took Judge Hays' basic labor law course had a philosophical bent favoring unions. While largely ceremonial, a number decided they wanted to sit on the left side of his labor law classroom. I didn't care where I sat. My father had not been any kind of a tycoon or anything approaching but had just been a small businessman owning a hardware store on Long Island employing a few people. It's possible he may have been a union member when he worked on battleships like the USS *Missouri* during the Second World War at the Brooklyn Navy Yard. Unions though were not a big thing in my family or part of my upbringing. I just somehow saw myself on the management side of the table right from the start.

At the time of my graduation from Columbia in 1965, the Vietnam War was raging. No employment was possible for an unmarried, male lawyer like myself until one's military status could be better determined. Like George Bush the younger in Texas, I set out to avoid the draft and probable Vietnam duty by getting on a National Guard waiting list. I soon found myself being sworn in as a reserve army infantryman in the famed 42nd Infantry Division of the New York State National Guard. Shortly after, now employment-eligible, I was hired by my employer of choice, the

National Labor Relations Board, or the NLRB. It was and remains the US government's premier, administrative agency charged with enforcing the nation's federal labor laws. It is also referred to as the "Board."

There would be a long wait before I and many tens of thousands of other new National Guardsmen would be shipped off to basic training. We were low priority because all of the US Army training camps across the country were filled to capacity with draftees going off to fight the quickly escalating war.

The Board, I had decided, was the perfect starting place for a career in labor law. There I would learn the rudiments of how federal labor statutes, rules, regulations, unions, companies, and case law came together for both employees and employers in the large, unionized segment of the American workspace that then existed.

With regional offices all over the country, I wanted to work in the New York metropolitan area where I had grown up and was living. Applying for a position in the New York, Brooklyn, and Newark regional offices, I was hired and assigned to the Board office in Newark, New Jersey. Region 22 covered a highly populated, big geographic area slightly more than the upper half of the state. Residing in Manhattan, I'd reverse commute by train each day for an hour under the Hudson River.

Most of the 30 or 35 labor relations professionals in the office were lawyers. And it was in those days an all-male, mostly white group. The regional director was John Cuneo, a seasoned NLRB official of many years standing with a somewhat gruff exterior. That way with many, for some reason I could never quite understand he was decidedly less so with me. Often distant and disagreeable, Cuneo's personality and his running of the office were so bad that the staff had decided the year before I arrived on the scene to join a government union to protect themselves against his excesses. The National Labor Relations Board Union, as it was called, or the NLRBU, was not particularly strong or effective.

That was the only time in my life I ever was in a union. But later on I would try to capitalize on that membership by telling union leaders across the bargaining table of my NLRBU membership. Looking back, it was a clumsy attempt to present some sort of commonality with their cause. The more savvy unions though probably saw right through my professed kinship.

Cuneo was famous for his annual Christmas staff luncheon and gala Christmas party. Highly unusual, it was an "Uncle Sam wants you" kind of thing. The arm was put on all the unions, big and medium size employers, and law firms who regularly did business with the NLRB in northern New Jersey. As an equal opportunity schnorrer of the highest magnitude, Cuneo's motto might have been "go out and buy it, if you don't make, bake, or cook it yourself, and provide it to my government agency at holiday time for us and the many hundreds of guests to eat, drink, and enjoy." It gave the term "BYO" a whole new meaning.

Platter after platter of the finest deli meats like carved turkeys, hams, roast beefs, pastrami, and corned beef were offered. Quite probably there were some hot dishes too, like trays of lasagna. There were giant bowls of tuna, potato, macaroni, and shrimp salad. Bakery goods stretching from loaves of bread to cakes, pies, and trays of cookies filled the tables. A giant display of cheeses was the centerpiece. It was a feast, a huge groaning board.

Perhaps upwards of 500 people were going to be fed and boozed at our offices in a giant, open area, cleared of all secretarial desks on the day of the party. Picture a row of tables with white linen table cloths, both similarly procured, running the length of the room. It was easily 40 feet and piled long, deep and high with all these comestibles. With a well-stocked bar of contributory liquor on the opposite side of the room, where the newer staff was expected to take turns as bartenders, no catering hall could have provided better. The only thing missing was a small band.

Never-ending columns of trucks pulled up the morning of the

party to the delivery entrance at the 744 Broad Street building. Large boxes and cases were continually unloaded. Cuneo had requisitioned one of his senior supervisors, Arthur G., to manage the logistics for the party. One of the more knowledgeable agents in the office and mentor to many, Arthur was a sweet guy—the most likable person anyone could imagine. In his 50s, suffering we had heard from some mild heart disease, and terribly overweight, he needed help. A few of us younger guys gladly came down to assist him in moving the delivered goods through the lobby and into the freight elevator for the trip up to our offices.

Picture this large man in his white shirt, with tails hanging out over his trousers, slowly pulling, with thick ropes around his shoulders, the laden down trolley cart. His leaning heavily into it and sweating profusely were highly reminiscent of Tevye from the few years earlier Broadway musical and later film, *Fiddler On The Roof*. But the difference was that our Tevye was not playing any violin or singing catchy tunes. The whole time he never uttered a single a word of complaint, not to God, or anyone, about this work that clearly was not in his official US government job description. Tevye for several years, Arthur was to die a relatively young man the following decade after I had already left the agency. Friends at the time wondered if there was any connection.

Then there was the "donated" alcohol. Case after case of liquor, wine, and champagne were delivered and many liters were consumed. What bottles went unopened would be stashed away in the director's office and went home with him and his chief assistant for days after the party. Shortly before the normal 5 P.M. closing hour approached, we'd see the pair sneakily walk the long hallway to the suite's exit on the way to their getaway cars. Both arms of each were weighed down by briefcases that we just knew were brimming with booze.

One year there was a serious logistical error. A case of Dom Perignon champagne—only the finest and sent by a prominent union or its law firm—was delivered to the Board's offices. Apparently in prior years, the office had gotten a case of scotch and the champagne went to Cuneo's home. But not this time. The scotch went to Cuneo's home and the champagne arrived at our offices—just in time for our Christmas staff lunch. As word spread of our good fortune, drinking each glass at our lavish luncheon before the party began became even more enjoyable. Some thought they could detect Cuneo fidgeting each time there was a decidedly loud pop of a Dom cork.

The party ran for hours and well into the evening. The hundreds ate, drank, schmoozed, and seemingly never left. Included among the guests were numerous NLRB alumni from companies' or unions' legal staffs, union officials, and lawyers from firms representing either unions or employers. Many there had probably not seen each other since the last Christmas bash. My recollection is that it was primarily the more gregarious union business agents having most of the fun. And drinking most of the booze. Board lawyers came from the nearby NLRB regions in New York and Brooklyn. A few even took the train from the more distant Philadelphia office.

Colleagues looking to leave the agency used the party as a great opportunity to mix with and impress visiting partners from major law firms. I'm sure that over the years many jobs were landed. It was at one of these parties that I first met returning Region 22 alumnus, Al DeMaria. Going on to become a good friend, Al and his firm later did some work for me in my subsequent career.

Such were the ethics of the time. Today I am fairly certain soliciting or accepting platters of food and cases of booze from unions, employers, and law firms for a festive party run by a governmental agency at Christmas time might run afoul of the law. It was probably justified in the Regional Director's mind as just a public relations/goodwill gesture for his many and varied "clients." Even with no quid pro quo demanded or expected from the donors, soliciting and accepting gifts like this surely would not cut it today.

The impropriety of keeping his home liquor cabinet overflowing probably never entered his mind.

When it wasn't party time, the NLRB was the excellent place I thought it would be to learn the underlying body of Board labor law. Sometimes even into the evening hours we'd knock on doors. Looking for witnesses and identifying ourselves as "federal agents" by flashing our badges" or just in our offices or on-site visits interviewing employers, employees, or union business agents, it was a constant search for the facts. And then we'd apply the law, which I was rapidly learning, to remedy alleged possible wrongs.

New Jersey was loaded with manufacturing plants and industrial facilities. The union movement had not dropped off much from its post-Second World War peak and still represented by 1968 over a third of New Jersey's workforce—one of the highest in the nation. Yet new businesses were always opening and union organizing remained a very big deal. Employer resistance was strong. Organizing led to elections but also brought on allegations of unfair labor practices. It could also lead to strikes and lockouts.

There were all sorts of things that could result in unfair labor practice charges. Employees were fired or threatened because they wanted to bring in a union. Supervisors told employees to stay away from unions or they asked improper, interrogating questions. Businesses were shuttered or relocated to avoid unions, or such actions threatened. Maybe there were sudden wage increases granted during an election campaign, or benefits long enjoyed by employees taken away. Someone could have been asked to spy and report back to management. Perhaps employees were promised some financial incentives if they voted against the union. A union or company might be accused of bargaining in bad faith at contract negotiations time, or an employer of locking out its workforce unlawfully. Most of the unfair practice charges we investigated were brought by unions against employers, but the law also covered unions. Charges were sometimes brought against them, too.

The other big thing that the NLRB did was run elections. Once a union filed a petition announcing it had gathered enough signatures from the employees of any particular business—small, medium, or huge—the Board would spring into action. Many secret ballot elections were held to determine if these employees wanted to bring in a union or remain non-union. Elections at factories and other businesses were conducted by all of us—at all hours convenient to the working shifts. The elections were frequently fever-pitched campaigns fought by both parties over each of their economic futures.

If a union was voted in, then negotiating would normally begin for a contract. But often there were hearings we conducted to determine election issues. Often drawn-out and contentious, contract bargaining is where labor lawyers on both sides made their real money. Instead of a deal, after many months of talks, strikes or employer lockouts could result. More unfair labor practices might be filed by either side against the other during negotiations, which required more deep and lengthy investigations.

Investigating unfair labor practice charges wasn't always so black and white though because facts, as we all have come to learn, are sometimes slippery things. So learning how to do a proper investigation, and make credibility findings where necessary—because people despite sworn affidavits are not always telling the truth—were important parts of our training. I know I did my work and surmised others did their's without any regard to our own individual pro-union or pro-management sentiments. Because it was well-known at the time that our region was always applying the facts and the law straight down the middle in conducting investigations, running elections, and making our decisions, what we decided was largely respected by all. I assumed it worked that way everywhere at other NLRB offices.

As an invaluable side benefit from working at the Board, I developed a knowledge of how to deal with unions, speak with their leaders, and begin to understand union thinking. At the time there was a great deal of organizing going on by aggressive unions intent on gaining members at the considerable number of both new and established non-union facilities dotting the New Jersey landscape. There were lots of different unions representing the various trades—all with their own little niche—and many business agents in their numerous locals.

Their motive was, I have to believe, mostly for the genuine well-being of the workers. I'm certain many union officials philosophically supported the union movement. But at the same time, this was the business they had chosen and how they made their living. Through membership dues and initiation fees gained from representing employees, union officials ran their businesses, enhanced their own personal financial circumstances, and raised their families.

One union official frequently using our services was the head of Local 560 of the International Brotherhood of Teamsters, Tony Provenzano. Also known as "Tony Pro," Tony was another character who figured prominently in the story of Hoffa's '75 disappearance, as portrayed in the Scorsese 2019 movie, *The Irishman*. Tony's brother Sal, another frequent visitor, was also a character in the movie.

As time went on, in order to make myself better-rounded as an experienced labor attorney and attractive to a prospective employer, I needed trial experience. There was, however, little to be gained in Newark. Very risk averse, Cuneo did not allow many cases to go to trial because losses would show up in his statistics and cast, he thought, an unfavorable light on his administration of the region. As the result, he was prone to settle most cases where he had issued an official unfair labor practice complaint after an investigation.

His reluctance to try cases created a frustrating dearth of opportunities for the younger attorneys like myself. Whatever few trials there were after formal complaints were issued, they usually were assigned, and appropriately so, to the more senior, experienced attorneys. Hardly any were ever given to the rookies who were all clamoring for the same opportunities to gain experience and leave the agency.

It became such a concern that I went to see Cuneo seeking his assistance in getting a trial elsewhere. For some reason—perhaps it was our common taste of Dom Perignon—he liked me. Whatever it was, he arranged with his Washington bosses for them to assign me to an upcoming out of state trial. It was to be in rural Arkansas.

The NLRB's regional office in Memphis covered not just all of Tennessee but also the neighboring state of Arkansas across the wide Mississippi. The Memphis office had issued an unfair labor practice complaint against the Ottenheimer Brothers division of Kellwood Company after the Board had conducted its investigation of the charges brought by a union.

Kellwood was a major wearing apparel manufacturer in the south with one of its 36 plants in Lonoke, AR. The US government's allegation in the complaint was that Ottenheimer acted illegally when it granted wage increases during a union organizing campaign to keep the union out of its Lonoke factory, and fired some employees who were active in the attempt. If the government could prove its case before the Board judge, the employees would get back their jobs. I was to be, in effect, the prosecutor representing the US government.

In the winter of '67 I flew down to Memphis, met with the regional officials, and familiarized myself with the case coming up for trial. Driving over the Mississippi River bridge and 150 miles deep into Arkansas in my rental car, that trip and the next week or so would be a whole new world for me. Staying for a while in a Little Rock hotel, I'd travel out daily the half-hour or so into the countryside around Lonoke to interview witnesses and prepare them for trial.

Called a city, Lonoke was more like a small town. With a

population of around 3,000, years later it would gain some fame for being the home of Paula Jones—one of Bill Clinton's main accusers. Its county courthouse was to be the site of the trial. And one of its motels would be where I would move into shortly before the trial began.

The plant where the women worked was nearly all-female on the production line. And mostly if not entirely, as my recollection tells me, white women. The union involved was the International Ladies Garment Workers Union. Known as the ILGWU or simply the ILG, it was powerful throughout its decades'-long existence. Then representing nearly a half-million textile workers, it was busy at the time of my arrival in organizing new garment manufacturing plants springing up all over the South that had fled heavily union-represented New England in search of much cheaper non-union labor.

The union assigned a business representative to work with me on behalf of the fired women. We'd arrange by phone to meet up at some location in the area, usually in a Lonoke cafe, and drive around together meeting with the witnesses. The US government provides a per diem expense allowance for traveling employees to cover room and meal expenses while on the road. In 1967, as difficult as it is to believe a half-century later, that figure was $16. It was most definitely not a problem in Arkansas where a hotel or motel room might be a few dollars a night and meals about the same. Finding the foods I was used to though was another story, and getting proper nutrition.

The fired Ottenheimer factory workers had been paid under the piecework system common at the time in the textile industry. Pay was for each "piece" or garment they completed at their sewing machines, which garment later would be sold at Sears, Roebuck. At the time, the federal minimum wage was $1 an hour and Arkansas' was probably no higher. It was a combination of the low hourly wage and their meager piecework earnings that was the driving force behind the union's organizing efforts.

The women lived with their families in the surrounding rural areas near the plant in whatever housing their low wages could afford. Small, one or two room houses perhaps more appropriately called shacks, some lacked indoor plumbing. Once when I was in one of these modest homes, I had the impression that the kids, of which there seemed to be many, slept together in one or two cramped beds. My first and only exposure to Appalachian-style, white poverty, it was eye opening and would have a profound effect on me for some time to come. Familiar a bit with black poverty from driving with my parents though the '50's rural south on vacation trips to Virginia, I had never before seen white poverty.

The overall situation predated Sally Field and the Academy Award-winning movie, *Norma Rae,* by about a decade. When that film came out, its central theme of low-wage women working under difficult conditions at southern sewing machines and wanting a union in their factory brought back memories of my Arkansas experience. Ottenheimer's defense was that the women were just bad workers under the piecework system and had not produced daily the right amount of properly finished goods. Further, it argued the wage increase was long-overdue and had nothing do with keeping out the union. It was my job to establish these defenses were not true—just a giant pretext—to get rid of these trouble-making women and keep the plant non-union.

Getting deeply involved with these people while preparing my case, it became probably the most emotional experience in my 45-year legal career. And when we would go on to win the case before the NLRB judge, it also became one of the most rewarding.

I had this feeling soon after I arrived—call it a sixth sense—that the town didn't care much for unions. Both local officials and merchants in places such as Lonoke often feared that a successful union organizing campaign might drive a company to close the factory. Not so-veiled threats by employers of shutting down after victorious union elections hung in the air, and not just in the south.

Employing several hundred or more workers, a plant's closure could destroy a small town's economy overnight. Part of my worry was that normal "southern hospitality" might not extend to suspected union officials and those seen dining with them in local cafes. The trial was no secret. Word surely had gotten around that the plant's future might be in doubt. Maybe it was just my normal attorney paranoia, but I always felt townsfolk who were suspiciously eyeing two strangers the moment we walked in the cafe's door had already figured out who we were.

One day over a $1 or less breakfast the union business agent warned me quietly, "Check your car every day Jeff. I mean under the hood," and "take this seriously, as I check mine." I thought at the time she was surely exaggerating any danger I might be facing. While I never did look under my hood, her warning scared the heck out of me.

One crisp, late winter morning, I was standing on the hardscrabble ground outside one of these modest homes. After interviewing one of the fired women, I started talking to one of her poorly-clothed children and asked her what she wanted to do when she grew up. She must have been no more than a 13 or 14-year old, quiet and shy. After having just seen their living conditions and knowing her mother's economic circumstances, I was trying to build up some hope and confidence about her own future and what she could achieve in life.

An airplane flew overhead. I looked up at the engine noise, pointed, and said, "Hey, maybe one day you might want to be a stewardess." Today in 2022, that question might have been "how about becoming a pilot?" She looked at me, with kind of an empty expression I can still recall. Her look did not change when she hesitated for a moment and then said, "Naw, I just want to grow up to be like my ma." It was the ultimate disappointment. When it sunk in that the next generation of these children might very well grow up with the same hopelessness of their parents, it was a staggering message.

Gathering statements and preparing witnesses, I wrote my brief back at the Lonoke motel where I had moved into for the trial. After perfecting my arguments and practicing my presentation before the bathroom mirror late into the night, then came the trial. A lawyer always remembers the circumstances of the first time before a judge as if it were yesterday. Unsupervised and on my own in a far-distant town in the middle of rural Arkansas, more than a half-century later, I recall it in vivid colors.

Conducted by an NLRB judge sent out from Washington, the trial lasted several days. My opposite counsel representing the clothing manufacturer was a tough and experienced trial lawyer from one of the premier union-fighting firms in the south. Very good at his trade, here was I—this newbie—slowly navigating my way. The judge though recognized my inexperience and was patient, trying to go a bit easy to help me, as he must have done on countless occasions with other first-time, government lawyers.

Later that winter back in Newark after the trial was completed, I was writing my brief when my military papers for basic training finally came through. I was ordered to report in late March to Fort Ord, the sprawling US Army base on the California coast. Having waited 16 months since I had joined the National Guard, my time had finally arrived. In a few days I'd be departing for four months of basic and advanced infantry combat training at this huge army base, two hours south of San Francisco on the Monterey peninsula.

Deciding to seek a delay in order to complete the post trial brief, I sought Cuneo's help. But in seeking his assistance, I drafted a letter at his request to the US Defense Department asking for a deferment and chose poorly with one particular phrase. When I wrote, "Ruthizer is indispensable to the government's case," it did not sit well with Cuneo. Suddenly his gruff personality emerged and he had me in his sights. Shortly after receiving my draft, Cuneo swiftly walked the hall to my office while shouting along the way for the entire office to hear—"Indispensable, indispensable, nobody is indispensable around here. Not me. Not Ruthizer." A few days after he angrily threw the letter back at me and stormed out of my office, I shipped out to Fort Ord as ordered on a United flight to San Francisco.

Away at Fort Ord for four months, learning at age 26 how to be an infantry soldier, I went though the same rigorous, live ammo combat training as did the young draftees all around me going off to fight and possibly die in Vietnam. There were a couple of other lawyers in my unit and we, the older, wiser guys, naturally bonded. One, a Brooklyn assistant district attorney, remains a friend to this day. It was the summer of the destructive '67 riots in many cities across America, including Newark and Detroit. I learned about the riots back in the barracks while listening on a tiny transistor radio my dad had sent—my only source of news and connection to the outside world for much of the training.

Newark, as I was to hear on the radio and later got confirmed, was especially bad. The New Jersey National Guard had been called up. Many people died, hundreds were shot or otherwise injured, and 1000 or more were arrested. In certain neighborhoods, whole blocks of houses and stores were burned-out. The city I returned to from California in late July was a much different place from the one I had left in March. In many parts of the already decaying city, Newark had become unrecognizable. Not particularly warm and inviting to begin with, it was now even less desirable. Fortunately, I only worked there.

While I was gone, the judge issued his decision in the Ottenheimer case and we won. I felt even better when we subsequently prevailed in the appeal before the NLRB Board. Making an excellent addition to my resume, the trial experience I gained I felt would surely boost my chances of landing a job in a corporate legal department.

A month or so after my return to Newark, Cuneo called me in and asked if I would like a temporary, three-month assignment to the NLRB's office in Detroit. It seemed that the Board region there needed some additional help during its extraordinarily busy time handling the big UAW and Ford Motor strike. Washington was offering this assignment to a few of its best, most promising attorneys, said Cuneo, and with me a bachelor and easier to be away for this stretch of time, he had suggested my name. Flattered, I quickly said yes.

Packing a bag, I drove the 700 miles out to Detroit where I had booked a room at the downtown, long-stay, Leland House hotel. Getting a giant discount at the special US government rate, it was $100. That's per month—not per night. Of course, that was 54 years ago, but the government rate was an extraordinary reduction even at that time. Perhaps the regular rate at this second tier, business hotel would have been around $15 or $20 per night. Staying in this still decent area not affected by the summer riots, I was there for the length of the assignment. Some players from the Detroit Lions football team, who I ran into on the elevators from time to time, were also living at the Leland House. So I knew it would be comfortable if not exactly luxurious. But who knew from luxury in those days.

The government's per diem expense rate to cover my hotel and meals was the same $16 a day that had sustained me in Arkansas. But Detroit was no Lonoke. Despite my initial worries that this paltry sum would not cover Detroit's much higher living expenses and particularly dining costs, it worked out fine. Some days, unbelievably so as I look back, I actually walked away with a dollar or two excess in my pocket. Breakfast in those '67 days was $1 to $1.50 at most, lunch was perhaps $2 to $3, and a three-course dinner at a very respectable restaurant was no more than $7 or $8—maybe $10 with tip.

While it was the same meager amount, the food, thankfully was a lot more recognizable and enjoyable. Downtown Detroit then still had many good restaurants, including popular steakhouses—such as Carl's and Berman's. There was also an excellent Italian eatery called Mario's and a pretty good fish house.

The hotel cost of $100 per month worked out to less than $3.50 a night. It's nearly impossible for someone reading these pages in 2022 to believe these were the actual food and hotel prices in 1967. But of course, salaries were also dramatically less. Inflation since that time has been an astounding 665%. The special government hotel rate of $100 a month in today's prices would be about $775. For a month's stay, it would be still be an unbelievable bargain when a decent Detroit hotel room in 2021 goes for several hundred a night.

Detroit's downtown business district had not been scarred by the recent summer riots that had destroyed other parts of the city so it was still livable. The mainstay Hudson's department store remained an anchor for downtown commerce, many movie houses still existed, as did the live Fisher Theater and the concert hall where the Detroit Symphony performed. Detroit was a great sports town with its professional baseball, basketball, hockey, and football teams. Ann Arbor and East Lansing—where Michigan's two great, rival universities played Big Ten football now that the fall season had begun—were each only about less than an hour's-drive away.

But I had a day job. Conducting investigations, holding hearings, and the entire time gathering a lot of experience dealing with unions and union officials, I worked on numerous and varied assignments throughout the state. There was even one matter I had with a young labor lawyer named Jimmy Hoffa Jr., representing his father's Teamster union. All in all, it was a valuable assignment. Before Thanksgiving, mission accomplished, I drove back to resume my commuting life from Manhattan to the NLRB in Newark.

As the national debate and resistance to the Vietnam War intensified, that year spilled over into 1968. With the nation reeling from the surprise of February's Tet offensive, CBS' Walter Cronkite pronounced on air that the war was unwinnable, a big mistake, and the US should pull out. Shortly after that shockwave, LBJ announced he wouldn't run for reelection. In the spring,

Martin Luther King Jr, was assassinated in Memphis and race riots exploded across America. A few months later, Bobby Kennedy was killed in Los Angeles while he was campaigning for the Democratic nomination to succeed Johnson. Later that summer was Chicago's calamitous Democratic National Convention. The year 1968— the year of assassinations, political recusals, riots, and raucous demonstrations—was like none other that most Americans had ever experienced. The entire nation was on tenterhooks. We all felt '68 very personally because America's future looked so uncertain.

With riots breaking out every summer in cities across America, my National Guard battalion was trained for possible duty in the Black neighborhoods surrounding our Brooklyn armory. Thankfully, we were not given any live ammunition. Better yet, the 106th Infantry was never ever actually called out, but we had our empty rifles at the ready and were fully prepared. The 12,000 men of the 42nd Division throughout New York State were also poised for possible call-up for the intensifying Vietnam War.

Most of us, however, never thought that the Pentagon would activate an inadequately trained, badly equipped, and non-professionally led National Guard division. Convincing ourselves even more of this after hearing the legend of the ill-trained and poorly prepared Hawaiian National Guard division that had been called up during the Korean War and suffered huge casualties, we were very fortunately proven to be nearly 100% correct. Very few army National Guard units, as it turned out, were ever activated for Vietnam duty.

LBJ came to Newark one day that summer of '68. After the disastrous Chicago National Democratic convention, he was there to push his veep, Hubert Humphrey's candidacy. Announced with a few days notice, the entire federal government workforce, including the NLRB lawyers, were given a few hours off to help line his motorcade's expected route along Broad Street. The streets were crowded with many thousands of people jockeying for a good position to see the presidential motorcade and perhaps catch a glimpse of LBJ himself.

Somehow a group of us from the Board had secured a good spot right at the curb in front of the new Federal Building into which we had moved the year before. Much to our shock and amazement, that is exactly where the President's "Queen Mary" armored limousine stopped—directly where we were standing. A Secret Service agent jumped out from the front seat, opened the back door, and out popped LBJ to shake the hands of the loud and cheering crowd. With his left and right hands constantly moving to work the crowd, in the well-known LBJ manner, he grabbed my extended right hand as he began to move down the line, accompanied tightly by his agents. At the time, I could not help but think of the JFK assassination in Dallas during my law school days just a few years earlier when Johnson had become President of the United States.

The move into the Federal Building earlier that year had been an interesting experience in dealing with unions. For some reason lost to memory and history, Cuneo asked me to take responsibility for supervising the weekend move. The GSA had hired a union moving company but there would be several trades, all union to be sure, involved at both ends of the move. The several unions would go on to present competing jurisdictions that would need resolution. When that later occurred, it became my job to sort out the mess.

The mover's Teamster union had jurisdiction over loading and unloading the trucks and bringing the furniture and files from our old offices up the ramps of the new Federal Building and into the building's elevators. Another union had jurisdiction within the Federal Building to take the furniture and files, once in the elevators, upstairs and move them into the new office space. It wasn't long that weekend day before a question arose over which union had jurisdiction concerning one highly technical matter— hitting the elevator buttons. A brief stalemate shut down the move until Solomon-like Ruthizer appeared on the scene and worked out an acceptable resolution. True brilliance intervened. Clearly not anything I had learned in law school dictated it should be both workers from each union hitting the button simultaneously. Problem solved. Once again, although ridiculously simple, it was another invaluable lesson about dealing with unions.

Later that same '68 summer, during the final months of the Johnson administration, word got around that the NLRB chiefs in Washington found themselves with a little budget surplus. They decided at the last minute to burn it off with a series of training conferences and chose Miami Beach. Flying in the entire group of professionals from the 30 or so regional offices around the country, maybe as many as 1500 to 2000 people, they broke it up into staggered groups of perhaps four or five regions at a time. Region 22 was off to Florida for a few days of training and some time in the surf, sand, and sun. A couple of our new Newark lawyers whose first day on the job was that Monday could not believe their good fortune when they were told to pack bathing suits when handed tickets to Miami.

I was recommended to Washington by Cuneo to lead a major study group of 100 or so lawyers on the subject of union representation elections and potential reform. Somehow, Cuneo believed that I had gained some special expertise in this area of the law, or perhaps he saw something in me that made me worthy of being a group leader. While I had conducted many dozens of union elections, just as had most of my colleagues, I did not possess any special knowledge. After our morning discussion, it was my job to present our group's recommendations at the afternoon's plenary session to be presided over by Washington's senior NLRB officials.

In my presentation outlining the group's conclusions, I included as a relatively minor point our negative assessment about attorneys themselves conducting elections rather than hiring true election specialists. That aspect of my report did not sit well with the assistant general counsel, so when he took the rostrum after my remarks, he gently reproached me. Saying that he was proud to have given out Board election ballots to Black workers at southern factories long before they were permitted to vote in local, state, and federal elections, he could not understand how NLRB lawyers could be critical of a lawyer's role in the union election process.

By that time, I had been getting a little tired of the routine of reverse commuting to a declining Newark as well as my overall NLRB existence. After the Miami Beach conference, and having seen so many of my friends and other colleagues leave for jobs in corporate America or with law firms, I had a renewed interest to start my own job search. I wasn't looking for a law firm. Earlier that year I had been offered but turned down an offer by one of New Jersey's leading, management-side labor firms. Instead, I had become convinced I wanted to work in corporate America.

The normal rule that Board lawyers followed was that unless one left the agency by the end of the second or third year, one would probably never leave and would thereupon become a "lifer." I had no desire to spend the rest of my legal career working as a labor lawyer for the federal government, although a number of my friends did just that and quickly rose in the ranks to high position.

As that three year measure for becoming a lifer was drawing nearer, I picked up the pace of my search for a corporate labor attorney position in New York where I lived. When the opportunity arose to leave the NLRB in the late fall of '68, with two simultaneous job offers, one from an airline, Mohawk Airlines, and the other from a broadcasting company, the American Broadcasting Company, I was ready to make my departure.

2
CHAPTER

My First Tour of ABC Duty Begins

So I had these two choices as I was deciding to leave the NLRB and Newark far behind—Mohawk Airlines or ABC.

Mohawk Airlines was a small, regional airline that serviced primarily New York state, Pennsylvania, and other parts of the Middle Atlantic region. Regional carriers at the time were prevalent throughout the US airline system and filled a need that the bigger coast-to-coast airlines didn't yet provide. Since that time, however, starting with the Airline Deregulation Act of 1978, regional airlines went through a gradual process that began with consolidation and eventually led to just about all being swallowed up by the few remaining major carriers.

Interested in the Mohawk job, I learned I would be based at its Rome, New York, airport headquarters. I would be handling all of the grievance and arbitration work with the pilots' union, the flight attendants' union, and a handful of other service unions on the ground, like baggage handlers and ticket counter people. I'd also be able to slide right into Mohawk's NLRB work when some of that might materialize.

There would also be, I was told, the opportunity to go to the table with the company negotiators. It sounded like an exciting job, and a good entry into the airline industry. With its expanding traveling base, tight government price regulation, and solid revenue stream, the industry was at the time red-hot. Mohawk, I learned upon a bit of investigation, was a sound, well-run company. Perhaps, I imagined, I could use Mohawk as a stepping-stone to the giant TWA for a better labor position with a more popular airline, or to my dream airline, the even bigger and more prestigious Pan Am.

Rome was a small industrial city almost exactly in the middle of New York State. Still a bachelor enjoying the Manhattan life, I was not particularly enthralled about relocating. Clearly for me, all roads did not lead to this Rome. The salary was pretty good though, and the airline held out a special perk of free air travel for myself and my family on any domestic carrier. I could also get to Europe on TWA, or even on Pan Am, which I was told were also covered by the inter-airline free-travel arrangement.

After considering the offer for a while, I decided that Mohawk had made me an offer that I could easily refuse. It turned out to be a smart move. Mohawk Airlines was to go out of business after only four years when in '72 it fell victim to acquisition by another regional carrier—Allegheny Air. Allegheny itself was swallowed up later by Piedmont and Piedmont in '89 merged into US Air. US Air, nearly a decade ago in the early 2000s, disappeared when it merged with American Airlines.

Mohawk Airlines a half-century later figured prominently in an episode or two of the *Mad Men* cable television series. It was when Don Draper had to tell the Mohawk advertising executives that he was dropping their business when he believed he was getting a much more lucrative account with the considerably larger American Airlines. Mohawk's anger and dismay turned into glee when Draper never got the American account. Watching his anguish on AMC in losing both accounts about a decade ago, it brought back memories of what could have been for me a very unpleasant Roman holiday.

I carefully checked out ABC, which was known at the time as the "third" network. That's a kinder way of describing what many considered to be ABC's "half" in the two-and-a half network television landscape. Also sometimes referred to as the "Almost Broadcasting Company," it was a pejorative no one working there could have very much appreciated.

ABC had a mixed need at the time for a new labor position at its New York headquarters. I was told it was going to be a blended job of both labor lawyer and labor relations executive. I wasn't quite sure what the distinction meant, if it had any significance, but it sounded interesting. Turning out to be a unique position at the time in the broadcasting industry, it presented an exciting opportunity. It was also for me an entry into the wider field of entertainment since ABC, as I was to learn, had recently expanded its Hollywood movie production operations through its ABC Pictures subsidiary. The movie *Charly,* for which Cliff Robertson won the best actor Oscar, and the Oscar-winning *They Shoot Horses, Don't They?,* starring Gig Young and Jane Fonda, were just two of its recent film productions. After my interview and ABC's job offer, I said yes.

A big part of my assigned duties was to have responsibility for union relations at our TV and radio operations in ABC's Midwest—Chicago, Detroit, and the city in the westernmost part of Pennsylvania, Pittsburgh. Requiring a considerable amount of travel, I'd be responsible for negotiations, the occasional NLRB matter, grievances meetings, and arbitration hearings.

At roughly half of my blended job, the other part was to be the second lawyer assisting with the Company's arbitration caseload in New York and Washington, DC. The load had been growing and had become too heavy for ABC's lone labor lawyer to handle on his own. Mostly arbitrations with the National Association of Broadcast Employees and Technicians, otherwise known as

NABET, the union represented thousands of ABC's employees and was to take on a major role in the rest of my career. Much will be written about it further in these pages.

Enjoying the single life, spending roughly a week a month on a regular basis in a vibrant city like Chicago was appealing. Far less inviting was my spending much overnight road time in Detroit while Pittsburgh held no such attraction whatsoever.

In those days, air travel was far more enjoyable than today. It was actually fun, with no security concerns, to get on a plane and fly anywhere. Part of the enjoyment was the service, and that was graciously provided by the flight attendants—then an all-female group. With standards and qualifications other than basic competence different in 1968, they had to be young and quite pretty—if not downright gorgeous. Once flight attendants reached a certain age, became pregnant, or did not maintain proper weight standards, under the terms of their union contracts, and as permitted by federal law at the time, they could be terminated. Beauty and physical appearance were vital factors in those days for an airline hostess job in order to attract the mostly-male flying audience. Also attire. One airline went to extremes by famously dressing its air hostesses in hot-pants and go-go boots.

Most passengers were men. Hanging around galleys on United's, TWA's, or American's Boeing 727 flights was the dream of many—whether single like myself or married. Quite a few of the stewardesses, called even by themselves "stews," didn't seem to prefer one kind to the other. A lot of virtual elbowing would ultimately take place outside the galleys to get names and numbers once the unbuckle seat belt sign went on. The stews, while dodging unwanted ambushes, managed to serve hot meals in those days, even on shorter flights such as Detroit.

My initial day on the job was in November of 1968 right after ABC's Mexico City Olympics. In what was to become an act of great symbolism, I had to walk that morning through a union picket line set up by the striking musicians union, the American Federation of Musicians. It would be my first. Right in front of me as I was crossing the line with hundreds of other employees was the legendary ABC Sports broadcaster, Howard Cosell.

Exchanging a few words while walking in together, I introduced myself and told him it was my first day on the job as ABC's new labor lawyer. Surprisingly, he answered while welcoming me to ABC that he himself had once been a labor lawyer. When we'd run into each other at future ABC events or industry functions, Howard, when prompted, always remembered our first chance encounter between a once practicing labor lawyer and a real one.

A few days later, I had my first dose of negotiations when my boss brought me along to assist in the AFM settlement talks. All foreign and a bit bewildering, that first time at the table is something a new labor lawyer never forgets.

My initial trip to Chicago was a few weeks later in early December for my first arbitration case. It was before a nationally known arbitrator named Burt Luskin. Involving the termination of a radio news writer at our WLS-AM radio station, it was a silly dismissal for his having used the company Xerox machine to copy a few personal papers. Convinced it was a crazy basis for any discharge and despite the best case I might be able to present, I saw no way Luskin would agree with the Company's position that this met the legal definition of "just cause." Even though I informed the news director of our certain loss, he disliked this individual intensely because he thought him to be a terrible news writer and decided nevertheless to proceed.

NABET's workforce nationally was mostly engineers. But in Chicago it also represented our news writers. The case is notable for two reasons. Not only was I concerned it would turn out to be my first loss—never a good thing to blow one's first case—it would also be my initial encounter with this union and my introduction to its two local leaders. Its president, Dan Delaney, and his chief lieutenant, Ray Taylor, showed up that morning and stayed around for decades.

Despite my arguing the discharge's justification, the union lawyer would have no trouble convincing the arbitrator to see right through the station's flimsy case. Luskin asked me during a break where I was dining that night. Since it was my first trip to Chicago, I knew little about Chicago restaurants and answered unwisely. When I responded it was the George Diamond Steak House, recommended to me by my father from one of his business trips to Chicago, Luskin responded, "Young man, if you ever want to win a case before me, never tell me you intend to dine at George Diamond's."

Even though he ruled against us a few weeks later, the case was so weak I am sure the arbitrator did not have the slightest inclination to hold my poor restaurant choice against us. That would be reserved for a future case. It was though a lesson silently learned and long remembered—to be a bit more circumspect in idle chit-chat with arbitrators. It was also a message to improve my choice of restaurants.

Chicago was very cold that December, as it was all Decembers. The wind would come whipping in off of Lake Michigan and there was always plenty of snow in the air and ice on the streets. Some of the older hotels did not have great heating systems and rooms could be chilly. The best Chicago hotels a half-century ago, like the Continental Plaza, the Executive House, the Palmer House, or the Drake, then averaged around $30 a night. I distinctly recall the hotel prices because my boss once gently admonished me when I submitted an expense report showing I had spent "$31 of the Company's hard-earned money," as he called it, at the Continental Plaza, later to be changed in name to the Westin. After all, he said, on my last visit I had stayed at the Executive House—for only $27.

Chicago had many good French and Italian restaurants and more than a few very decent German ones. The city of the old stockyards, it was well-known for its excellent steakhouses. George Diamond's, as I had learned, apparently did not make the list. Like Detroit, except with better restaurants, one could easily have a very good three course dinner for $10 or less. With a drink or two—then maybe 75 cents each—and tip, the whole meal might come in at no more than $15. Chicago was a great town not only for restaurants, but also bars, and Rush Street was packed with all kinds of joints.

All in all, with the Company picking up my traveling, living, and dining expenses, it was a great life for a 27-year old bachelor. A year before, I had been working as an attorney for the federal government, restricted to $16 a day for daily expenses, and eating bad food at strange cafes in rural Arkansas. Now, I was in Chicago and dining at some of its nicest establishments. With ABC reimbursing me for what I actually spent, as long as it was reasonable, and allowing me to entertain union officials at lunch, dinner, or over drinks, it was an entirely different and very welcomed world.

At that time in 1968, ABC's legal department, of which Labor Relations was a part, had stolen me away from the NLRB by paying me the munificent sum of about $14,000 a year—about $4000 more than what the government had been paying. The next year, however, ABC's general counsel, Ev Erlick, approved a big increase to about the $20,000 level when he realized he had gotten me far too cheaply. To give salaries back then some needed context, it's my strong recollection that long before the late 20th century's huge escalation in executive compensation that took place across corporate America, ABC's general counsel himself around 1970 was only paid a salary of $75,000.

At Christmas in those early ABC years it was customary and considered generous that all lawyers at my level would receive an end of year bonus of two additional weeks of pay. As another gesture to which we all looked forward, CEO Leonard Goldenson and Executive Vice President Si Siegel's would visit every floor and each employee in the 1330 Avenue of the Americas headquarters building, shake hands, and wish all a merry Christmas or happy holidays. Leonard's and Si's visit was a remnant of corporate America's warm and friendly past as well as a nice example of the small company atmosphere that prevailed at the old ABC.

The normal routine I followed for about four years was to travel monthly from New York's LaGuardia airport to Chicago's O'Hare. It was generally for about a week at a time. I would also hop a plane every second or third month to Detroit for a day or two but Pittsburgh trips were rare and usually only at negotiations times.

The broadcasting industry had been highly organized by a number of different unions. ABC had across the board, often many-page contracts—over 100 in number—that mostly dated back in their origins to the pre-television days of the 1930s. Most of our union-represented employees were engineers—thousands nationwide. In Chicago alone, NABET represented several hundred engineering technicians at our TV station and news writers in both television and radio. In Detroit radio and TV, as well as Chicago radio, the engineers were represented by a different technical union—the International Brotherhood of Electrical Workers, referred to as the IBEW. Pittsburgh radio had still a third engineering union—the International Alliance of Theatrical Stage Employees, also known as IATSE, or sometimes just the IA.

The American Federation of Television and Radio Artists, or AFTRA, represented tens of thousands of radio and TV performers at stations and networks across America, including all of ABC's properties. Specifically in Chicago and Detroit, AFTRA had our TV and radio broadcast journalists, radio disc jockeys (DJs), show hosts, and announcers. Pittsburgh radio was DJs and news people. A number of different IA locals held contracts in all our cities for hundreds of other television workers, including stagehands, news film cameramen, and many other crafts. The Directors Guild, known as the DGA, represented the directors, associate directors, and stage managers in Chicago and Detroit as well as at our other station and network operations. We had Writers Guild (WGA) contracts, but none at our midwest properties.

There was even a contract covering AFM radio "record spinners" at our market-leading, Top 40, Chicago station WLS-AM. Its origins are interesting. A bit murky, it was a throwback to the early days of radio when the growth of recorded music threatened live music and the gainful employment of professional musicians.

James C. Petrillo had been the AFM's national president and Chicago was his base. And very powerful. For two years during the '40s, every musician member in America, on his orders, stopped making records in a dispute over royalties for recordings played on radio stations and the resulting reduced work for live musicians. The record industry was shut down completely since without musicians, vocalists like Bing Crosby and so many others, were unable to make records. At the time, many big city radio stations, including WLS, had house orchestras that played live on-air and these continued to perform during the recording ban. When that ban ended, there was a price to pay at some radio stations— particularly in Petrillo's home city of Chicago. To help cure the growing problem of musicians' unemployment brought on by the huge growth of the record industry, and as house orchestras were dismantled, many stations were required by the union to engage musicians as record spinners.

That accounts for why Chicago's WLS, when I first arrived, had three employees in the small radio studio. On one side of the glass partition sat the AFTRA-represented DJ who'd deliver his unique patter in mellifluous tones to his listening audience. The IBEW engineer operating the control board and the AFM record spinner playing the selected records sat on the opposite side. It was only records in those days— long before cassette tapes and CD's would enter the scene. Three people did the job that really required only one. It would take years as both technology and labor relations common sense advanced before the DJ would do it all himself.

When that happened in Chicago, the record spinners would be the first to go. The engineer soon followed when the station went "combo"—and the DJ began operating his own board.

Petrillo's office, which I visited, had legendary, bulletproof glass windows looking out onto the street below and six-inch thick, solid wooden doors separating his office from where the bodyguards sat on a bench outside.

Our TV station located in the heart of downtown on Michigan Avenue in the area known as the "Loop" was the powerful and successful WLS-TV. Channel 7 dominated the local news ratings at both 5 and 10 P.M. with its popular "Happy News "format and its famous anchor team of bow-tied, local news legend Fahey Flynn and his equally renowned partner, Joel Daly.

For a moment that stretched far too long, WLS-TV achieved some unwanted notoriety. It happened when a group of visiting Japanese legislators on a US State Department sponsored tour was hosted by the station. The delegation included one distinguished member of the Japanese parliament who had been the pilot who famously lead or played a major role in the December 7, 1941 Pearl Harbor attack. The group was welcomed warmly by station officials, got its tour of the studios, and all apparently seemed to go well.

NABET had its own national monthly newspaper called the *NABET News.* It was published out of Chicago and edited by a locally based, NABET-represented employee whose day job was writing for WLS-TV's newscasts. Most of us knew this guy was more than just a little quirky.

Imagine the horror of many who opened the *NABET News* one day a month or two later and read an ill-advised front page headline. In huge, bold lettering, it pretty much said: "NABETs MEET JAP KILLERS." Shock waves must have descended upon the US State Department. It was a moment of shame that such a hateful headline could have been written by any television journalist—let alone an employee who worked for ABC at WLS-TV.

Amid the uproar, NABET local president Delaney, who had appointed the editor, abruptly fired him. Not much better as a writer for the station's evening newscasts, somehow he would go on to survive many termination attempts only because of the contract's complicated discharge procedures. Both Company and union officials would go on for decades to share many a laugh, as well as tears, over this individual's performance and odd behavior.

My main monthly job in Chicago was to deal with NABET grievances. I had no idea how many there were until I started my regular visits and got into the records. When *Dracula's* Renfield said—"Master there are hundreds of rats, thousands of rats," he had nothing on Chicago's grievance situation.

There were hundreds of grievances in a huge backlog, maybe even a thousand. Like Renfield's rodent, they were sometimes mean and dangerous in their scope, breadth, and potential impact on operations and cost. ABC's nationwide NABET contract had progressively grown in granularity over the decades of successive renegotiations. With many hundreds of difficult to manage provisions and work rules buried among its voluminous details, a grievance mentality took root. It became a pervasive culture not just among the Chicago workforce but also in every other city where ABC owned stations under the NABET agreement.

The exceptions were Detroit and Pittsburgh—where we had the two other engineering unions. In those locations, the IA and the IBEW did not share NABET's underlying grievance philosophy. In sharp contrast even within ABC's Chicago, the grievance culture did not exist just down the street at our WLS-AM radio station where we had IBEW engineers instead of NABET. The Chicago grievance backlog had not been dealt with properly and had been growing. At perhaps a pace approaching 50 or more new ones a year, it was a veritable grievance factory. Soon later that factory, like everywhere we had NABET, would surge into an entire cottage industry.

A few local station officials, including the station's chief engineer and the general manager's chief lieutenant, would join me for about a week each month discussing grievances with the two major NABET officials, the Irishmen Delaney and Taylor. We'd argue all day long back and forth for hours over the facts—most often long forgotten— and the contract's proper meaning. Always looking for a reasonable settlement wherever possible to clear the logjam, we had a sign virtually hanging over the conference room entrance that read, "The rule of reason shall prevail." The good news was that sometimes reason— helped along by some humor and I'm sure a little fatigue, actually ruled the day.

The burgeoning industry was gradually sapping the strength and energy of all on the Company side. It was to happen to all of us—lawyer and station operator alike—particularly those whom I had dragooned into these meetings. This weakened state of existence would continue until we were finally able to break out of the grievance culture much later in the 1990s. Lots of issues were settled. But the meetings were often frustrating experiences. In addition, new grievances kept washing up onto our Lake Michigan shores that took the place of the smallest particles we had succeeded in putting out to sea. Unsettled grievances could lead to arbitrations, although Chicago's situation under Delaney was far from New York's or LA's.

It was, however, while frustrating, also enjoyable. I genuinely liked these two decent and interesting Delaney and Taylor guys with whom I was dealing. And I always had the feeling the liking was mutual. I learned a great deal from them—in more ways than what the contract instructed. There was an expression at the time— never trust anybody over 30. So when I would go on to cross that threshold, I knew I was in trouble with these two.

The real benefit I derived from the endless discussions was learning volumes about the deep intricacies of the agreement. We'd go on gently hammering each other for days on end during my monthly visits. Exploring in detail, it seemed, each and every clause in that several hundred page contract, both sides would argue our different positions on each specific grievance. My mastering the hidden secrets of that highly complicated book would go on to serve me well in the decades ahead after I gained my sea-legs. But it also served to begin my stargazing as to why so many of these restrictive provisions were there in the first place. And my conjuring up future reforms.

Many times it was just simple room service that night back at the hotel after the exhausting grievance meetings ended. Once or twice each week, however, we'd go out together to dinner at one of Chicago's better restaurants. It was always the Company's treat. Over more meals of the then popular Beef Wellington or Steak Diane than I can today imagine, and frequent drinks, we'd continue discussing in a more light-hearted vein some of the same subjects we thought we had left behind on the conference room table. Occasionally we even made it to the famed 95th floor restaurant of the recently completed John Hancock Tower—the second tallest building in the world when it was built. The views were simply stunning.

There were so many grievances pending that on a few occasions I tried settling whole rafts. Like what we called the "baseball grievances." When ABC Sports had started in the early '60s broadcasting national Major League Baseball weekend games, the work was all done, as would have expected, by an experienced, New York-based regular sports crew. However, under the difficult and rigid language of the NABET contract, the work in the Midwest should have been originated by the nearest engineers—the Chicago-based ABC engineers working at WLS-TV. The agreement called for them to have been assigned even though most of them were totally unqualified for sports events. A host of these technical-violation baseball grievances just hung around unsettled for years. A big chunk of money had to change hands if we were going to settle and avoid a sure-loser arbitration, with even heavier potential liability—unless, of course, creativity found another solution.

I thought I had stumbled across one. It was around the time of *Apollo 11* when our CEO Goldenson had declared a special holiday and given all of ABC's non-union employees a day off. I had come in that day anyway to watch on the big set in our conference room Neil Armstrong's epic moon walk, then followed by Buzz Aldrin's. July 20, 1969, was no ordinary day in the life of our nation as 53 million households tuned in to see the amazing coverage on all three networks.

Capsules for returning-to-earth astronauts on space shots were always recovered at sea by US Navy carriers and their helicopter crewmen. Network news crews were assigned aboard the ships to shoot the recovery story. Generally, technicians had a fairly relaxing week or longer in the Pacific or the Caribbean while awaiting the splashdown. The three networks always rotated the carrier assignments, so ABC had roughly one third of them.

I had the brilliant thought one day to wipe out all of the Chicago MLB baseball grievances and save the Company a bundle of money by giving the next ABC News splashdown assignment to some of the station's technicians. Knowing it was a long-shot because the work had been handled for a long time by a team of New York-based, Network engineers, who had become extremely proficient at it, nevertheless I sent the idea on to my bosses. With no traction whatsoever from Network engineering and news management, my first try at real creativity failed miserably. The fat settlement check was soon delivered.

One year I was in Chicago at Christmas time for my usual monthly combat. The WLS-TV general manager was taking his department heads out for his annual Christmas luncheon and he invited me as the visiting lawyer from New York to come along. With about a dozen of us, all male, sitting around a square hollow table in a private dining room at his favorite restaurant, it was a festive holiday mood. Booze was freely flowing both before and during lunch.

After the dishes were cleared, the GM stood up and began speaking. Addressing the successful year the station had just enjoyed, he went around the table in his own style praising each of his staff individually for their achievements.

Comments flowed to his news director—"Super job in making Eyewitness News Chicago's number one news program." Then followed a heaping of praise on another, "Great job because you made our morning show, *Kennedy and Company*, the top rated morning talk show in Chicago." Continuing around the table, his laurels landed on still one more department head—"The best thing you did this year, the very best thing, was to get rid of that big-titted kike."

The room went silent for a moment that seemed to last forever. While the GM kept talking, I felt in my imagined silence that all eyes turned to me—the only Jewish person in the room. A few at the lunch knew I was of the Jewish faith, and perhaps even the GM. I just sat there and said nothing, in shock and pain from the GM's, intended or not, anti-Semitic trope.

Maybe he regretted it the moment it came out of his mouth, but he seemed totally unaware of the huge insult he had just thrown at Jews in general. Although I had no idea to whom he was referring, his explosion of anti-Semitism was deeply troubling. After the luncheon ended and we were exiting, some of his staff whom I knew best came up to me and apologized for his behavior. The GM, however, never said a word.

What really bothered me about this incident was my youthful inexperience—I just didn't know the proper thing to say or do. I had come across anti-Semitism before in my personal life. But this was my first time in the workplace that I witnessed religious bigotry first hand. Certainly I had heard about it from others, and this was the America of the '60s. When it happens though directly like this, it's startling. In my opinion, he was a great GM, one of the best I ever knew. I asked myself whether he just a bit high from the drinks, secure and safe in the midst of his closest staff, and this slur, forgetting I was in the room, just slipped out. I had no idea what was in his mind or heart, but the shame in witnessing this and my resultant silence were disturbing. Years later in my executive development, my reticence to say something would have been far different.

When I came back to New York from Chicago, I went to see my boss, Dick Freund, the long time head of labor relations. Freund, himself of the Jewish faith, was equally outraged. So he took me by the hand and we went upstairs to see ABC's CEO and founder, Leonard Goldenson. Also Jewish, Leonard was a prominent philanthropist for major Jewish causes and a strong supporter of the State of Israel. Expressing outrage at this display of anti-Semitism, he offered me his apologies for what the GM had said.

It's an interesting historical footnote to note that a half-century ago, putting aside the religious bigotry for the moment, commenting about a woman's physical appearance in these outrageous terms in the workplace did not hit anyone's radar other than just an act of boorishness and extremely bad taste. Even if the GM had made this comment directly to a woman and she had taken offense, this was not yet viewed seriously in American businesses at the time as something legally improper or worthy of punishment. It was a different era and an entirely different culture. Legal sensitivities and court developments dealing with women's rights and sexual harassment in the workplace, where few women in any industry were working, still were years if not decades away.

The Goldenson whom Freund and I went to see about this incident was a strong leader among the American Jewish community. A major supporter of the State of Israel, he was often visited in his ABC offices on their trips to the United States by its prime ministers. Goldenson was personally close to Israeli prime minister Golda Meir. When she visited the US in around 1970, she came to see him. I'm not certain how there was a security breach, but when word spread throughout the building that Golda Meir was coming, hundreds of employees crowded into the ground floor lobby of our headquarters building awaiting her arrival.

When she entered, a cheer arose from the assembled group. There she was, this famous tiny but strong like-steel woman, dwarfed by the protective height of her surrounding American and Israeli security detail. Meir walked in through a cleared path, smiled, did a little wave to the crowd, and disappeared into Goldenson's private elevator that whisked her up to his top floor offices.

Such was the reputation, power, and strength of this man in the Jewish and international community who had apologized to me for the religious slur and boorish behavior. What I recall was that his focus was on the anti-Semitic comment. I do not know what if anything was ever said to this individual or what action Leonard might have taken behind the curtain. Today, with the necessary developments in workplace law and the rise of employer's sensitivities to lawsuits and monetary damages, he unquestionably would've been severely chastised if not immediately terminated for his highly improper words regarding both religion and sex.

I was in Chicago so often that it became both a sword and shield. It was a sword when going into battle with NABET or any other union, and a shield when I needed something Kevlar-like to protect me from imminent danger.

In March of 1970, such a danger suddenly erupted. It was brought about by an illegal, wildcat strike by US postal workers that broke out in New York and rapidly spread to other parts of the nation. Ultimately over 200,000 mail carriers were involved—the first and only mail strike in the history of the country. The entire flow of national mail and packages would be seriously disrupted. Decades before email, hand-written or typed letters delivered by the US Mail service was the only way people communicated with each other other than over the telephone. Moreover, mail was the means by which much domestic and international business was conducted.

The delivery of letters and packages through a working postal system was essential to the proper functioning of the American economy. So at the time it was a very big deal—nothing short of a national crisis. The New York Stock Exchange reacted and suffered a quick, dramatic fall. President Richard Nixon took to the airwaves and addressed the nation. In that speech he announced he was calling out National Guard units in many of the affected parts of the country to take over post offices and get the mail delivered again.

Since the eye of the wildcat action and ensuing disruption was in New York, Nixon's order meant for sure that New York's 42nd Division would be activated immediately. Still an enlisted man in the National Guard for another two years until my six-year term expired, I was totally vulnerable to this call up. But I was not in New York at the time. I watched Nixon's speech from my Chicago hotel room. Immediately the wheels began churning how I might be able to use my out-of- town status to avoid wasting many days of my life. Out of my suitcase came my kevlar shield. It was actually a solid and, I thought, fool-proof plan to avoid flying back to New York and becoming a temporary mailman.

My purpose in Chicago that week was at the negotiations table. It was with our stagehands union—IATSE Local 2—which represented about a dozen stagehands at WLS-TV. We were deep in talks when the mail strike took place and Nixon ordered the call up. Through my boss Freund, we immediately got Ev Erlick, ABC's general counsel, to send a telegram to New York Governor Rockefeller's head of the National Guard. The telegram to "Rocky's" general asserted that my presence in Chicago was vital. A work stoppage, said the GC, could adversely affect the delivery of television news in the nation's third largest city. Erlick submitted, as Freund and I had formulated, that it was more in the national interest for Ruthizer to remain in Chicago than my putting a mail bag over my army uniform to trek though the streets of Brooklyn and shove bills and letters into mail boxes.

It was only a bit of an exaggeration of my importance and the seriousness of the talks—where there was no strike threat. But it sounded good and was what the New York State National Guard general needed to hear to grant a waiver of the call-up order. Sure enough, it worked and I got my reprieve. But for proof that I was really in Chicago, the general ordered me to show up every morning during my Chicago stay at the Illinois National Guard armory on Michigan Avenue at 6 A.M. and get on the Army's official "morning report." Reporting every morning was easily accomplished since the Continental Plaza hotel was only a few blocks from the armory.

So, it happened that I hung out in Chicago for the week it took for the mail strike to be settled. The Local 2 IA officials were decent guys and very accommodating. Talks were uneventful and just dragged out a few extra days. Each day I'd report to the armory at 6 A.M. and sign in. My federalized Brooklyn based battalion was called up but was never actually sent out to deliver mail in the surrounding neighborhoods. The 600-strong, 106th Infantry Battalion just hung around the armory all day in uniform. Doing nothing more than cleaning weapons, waxing floors, carrying out other make-work army tasks, and eating miserable lunches prepared by National Guard cooks, they went home each night. Thankful I had avoided a lost week of my life, It was even worse than the complete waste I had first imagined.

My National Guard friends who had been activated were upset I had not joined them in their week of postal-strike misery. Upon my return to the Brooklyn armory at our next drill, it was nothing but good-natured, constant abuse for my having found a seemingly valid reason to avoid their pain and suffering.

Imagine their collective glee some time later when Rockefeller

made a surprise announcement. Every guardsman called up—
regardless of whether any mail had actually been delivered—was
to be given a one year reprieve off of his six year National Guard
reserve commitment. A little-known provision of applicable law
dealing with soldiers being federalized, it was wonderful for them
but what about me?

After all, I had been ordered to appear every morning at the
Illinois National Guard armory and get on the army's official
morning report. I wrote to Rockefeller equating my orders to show
up at 6 A.M. to my army pals' having been activated and sitting
on their backsides at the Brooklyn armory. His military officials
though wouldn't buy it. My cleverness that week when I stayed in
Chicago, using Local 2 stagehand talks as a shield, cost me a year
of reserve duty. My friends, who now had the last laugh, could
not have been any happier now that my imagined kevlar vest had
imploded.

Facing a one-year longer term in the National Guard without
most of my army buddies who would be leaving, I decided to
transfer and apply for a direct commission as an officer in the
United States Army Reserve Judge Advocate General's Corps.
Having practiced law for well more than two years, I was eligible
for a direct commission as a first lieutenant. Quickly accepted into a
New York City-based JAG unit, I finished out my remaining term of
military service as an Army Reserve lawyer in the 4th JAG, USAR.

It was a very distinguished group of New York's finest lawyers,
both officers and enlisted men, that I was privileged to join. Some I
ran into years later in my broadcasting career. The future TV news
anchor and later popular entertainer, John Tesh, was in the same
detachment. Because of my ABC Network background, the colonel
somehow thought he could use me more effectively by appointing
me as the unit's public information officer. Shortly thereafter I was
promoted to captain and shifted from legal affairs dealing with
courts-martial and procurement to my new PIO duties.

In the finest traditions of the the US Army Reserve JAG Corps, my unit was shipped off to two weeks of summer training exercises on the campus of the University of Southern Mississippi in Hattiesburg, and nearby Camp Shelby. While there, I arranged—with the help of ABC Radio—a meeting and then dinner at his country club with the owner of the local ABC radio affiliate. Taking me the next day to the monthly, well-attended Rotary Club luncheon, he introduced me as his "good ABC lawyer friend from up there in New York City"—followed by the traditional "Hail Rotarian!" bellowing reception.

Having asked me at his house while shooting pool the night before about my ancestry and "what kind of a name is Ruthizer," dinner and the Rotary luncheon were very warm displays of true southern hospitality. The whole time in Hattiesburg—just as any proficient JAG PIO would be doing—was spent supervising my writing staff and serving as the publisher of the unit's pretty decent, 20-page internal newspaper. It was far better than the summer-training, infantry field exercises at Fort Drum I was accustomed to from my prior National Guard days.

3

CHAPTER

Growing Into the ABC Job

It was Dick Freund who had hired me in 1968. Clearly, our common Columbia Law School backgrounds two decades apart had not hurt. The head of ABC Labor Relations since the mid-'50s, Freund was not only smart but also clever—a solid pro and a storied negotiator. Like other great ones, he had a strong memory for details both large and small. He had come up through the labor relations ranks with progressively more challenging law firm and corporate positions.

He was himself the expert draftsman of many clauses in the multitude of contracts to which ABC was signatory. I liked him a lot, and he was a great mentor and boss. Ironically, I was to take his place as corporate head of ABC Labor Relations 20 years later in 1987 when he retired from the CapitalCities/ABC Inc. after Tom Murphy's and Dan Burke's acquisition of ABC.

Freund's group on both coasts negotiated and administered the 100 or so labor agreements in our seven cities—New York, Washington, Chicago, Detroit, Los Angeles, San Francisco, and Pittsburgh. The main contenders we dealt with were NABET, AFTRA, WGA, DGA, AFM, NABET, SAG, plus a host of IA locals.

The IATSE local unions were broken down into numerous specific crafts and trades in each city or section of the country in which we operated. Its representation was vast across the spectrum. IA stagehands, hair and makeup artists, film processors, film editors, projectionists, wardrobe attendants, graphic artists, news crew cameramen, and news crew sound or lighting technicians roamed our corridors and worked our streets.

Some of the main contracts were national in scope, like NABET, while others, such as AFTRA, had separate network and local agreements. Some contracts were solely for staff employees and a few like AFTRA, WGA, and DGA had both staff and freelance components.

Common throughout broadcasting, unions, especially NABET, were always trying to organize other unorganized parts of the Company. My job, along with that of the other New York labor attorney who I had been hired to assist, was to deal with those efforts, too, including organizational campaigns NABET or any union might launch, NLRB election proceedings, and any unfair labor practice charges that could result.

There were five of us in New York after I joined and another four on the West Coast. When I was to return nearly two decades later to head labor relations, there had been so much more additional work piled on that the group would grow to 14—eight in New York and another six in LA.

There was once a time in the early '70s that the ABC TV Network was broadcasting the *Grammy Awards* from the Felt Forum in New York's Madison Square Garden. The live show was to be hosted by the popular entertainer, Andy Williams. Freund called me into his office and told me to get down there. Apparently there was a fight brewing between our NABET crew doing the pickup and the house IBEW union over whose workers would strike the mic on the stage. "Striking a mic," before the days of high technology, meant physically carrying the microphone on its stand on and off the stage for a performer or group to use as part of the act. He wanted me to investigate and decide whose work it should be.

I went down and spent a few hours examining the two competing contracts and interviewing the various players involved in the jurisdictional dispute. Concluding that this was properly "house" work under the Garden's IBEW contract, I told this to Jim Nolan, the president of the New York NABET ABC local whose members were doing the pickup.

Nolan responded immediately with, "If you give them the work, the show goes dark." With this strike threat for a live broadcast only two days away, I ran to a pay phone in the lobby and called Freund.

Freund told me to call the contract arbitrator, Ben Roberts, and get him to agree to give ABC an immediate, next day hearing in a bid to enjoin the *Grammy Awards* strike Nolan had just threatened. The facts being what they were, it did not seem all that difficult a task to establish the threat and enjoin the strike.

When I called Roberts in his office and told him we needed to see him the following morning about a strike threat, he said he couldn't do it because he had another arbitration hearing that next day with NBC and NABET. But he said he would be willing to cancel that hearing and give the date to ABC if both NBC's head of labor relations, Dick Goldstein, and the NBC NABET local president agreed. I called Goldstein who I knew and could see though the phone doing backflips in his sheer joy of giving up an arbitration date.

Calling the union president, who I did not know, I introduced myself as an ABC labor relations attorney, told him about the strike threat, and asked for the date. After I related what Roberts had said, and that Goldstein had already agreed, he also agreed. Calling back Roberts, I then called Freund to tell him we were set for a hearing at the arbitrator's office the next morning at 9 A.M. That night was spent preparing our case.

When we arrived at Roberts' office the following morning, the arbitrator quickly pulled me aside and asked, "Did you tell the NBC president yesterday when you called that you were an ABC NABET shop steward?" I told him not to be ridiculous—"Why would I ever do that?" He replied that this is what the official, who was sitting in the adjacent room, had told him about our brief telephone conversation. He had related to Roberts that the only reason he had given up the date was because he was under the mistaken belief that I was a shop steward and was speaking for ABC's Nolan in requesting a hearing. It was totally nuts how he could have so misconstrued my call.

As it turned out, Nolan was upset that the NBC union president had gotten it so wrong. By agreeing, he had allowed ABC an opportunity to show up at the arbitrator's door and seek injunctive relief. Freund and I had a good laugh over this comedy of errors, as did Nolan later on after the arbitrator heard the case and enjoined the strike. The *Grammy Awards* show went off without a hitch— with the IBEW doing the microphone striking.

Freund over the years was a great teacher, and I learned much from him in the art and science of labor negotiations. Both in careful preparations and at the table, he paid acute attention to detail, thoroughness, timing, pacing, phrasing, arguing, and maybe even some acting. Yes, a little thespian ability from time to time is never a bad characteristic for a serious labor negotiator. Many labor talks have dramatic moments. It's like what distinguishes a good trial lawyer from a great one. Or an average news anchor from a Peter Jennings. It all has to do with developing a strong presence at the table. Call it gravitas, believability, and persuasiveness. Remembering that there are never any do-overs, the best union and management negotiators both have it and know how to use it. It's learned, shaped, and sharpened along the way. Of course, one's underlying personality, and negotiations persona, dictates both its frequency and effectiveness. And it has to be live—not on the phone, or in a modern era Zoom call.

Freund also taught by example the importance of developing personal relationships with union leaders. It had to be across the many spectrums of our labor contracts, even those with whom one is not so crazy. Lunches are usually the most important vehicle to kindle a flame and keep it burning. Maintaining critical relationships proved crucial in my career and yielded results for my companies—sometimes when least expected.

He once had travelled by subway out to Queens in a blinding snowstorm to attend the funeral of an IATSE official's wife. It was so much appreciated that this person went out of his way to do things for Freund, and ABC, when otherwise he could have been negative or even obstructionist. I learned about Dick's act of kindness from the union official involved, never from Freund. This official went on to tell me he would never allow anything bad to happen to ABC.

Freund gave me opportunities over the years that allowed me to sharpen the skills that I would need to move ahead within the Company and industry. When thin, round, black plastic discs called records were still king, ABC Records, one of our subsidiaries, was a major record producer. Its labels included famous Dunhill Records. Some of Dunhill's most noted recording artists were The Mamas & the Papas, Three Dog Night, Jimmy Buffett, and Steppenwolf. ABC Records had a big record pressing plant where long-playing recordings ("LPs") on many different labels were daily manufactured in the tens of thousands. The Long Island plant employed about 100 workers and had a labor contract with a Teamsters local.

One day Freund called me in and gave me the assignment for the upcoming pressing plant negotiations. The first of my many Teamster negotiations, it was a bit unusual because the workers were almost entirely all part-time housewives. The male business agent had his own ideas about not only how to make the deal representing these women but also how to make it stick. It was therefore necessary to arrange in the parking lot during a break a little stage choreography that included some across the table shouting as well as lesser dramatic moments. Over a number of sessions during a few days with a handful of ups and downs, the deal was done. The contract was roundly ratified—with no sound distortions, skips, scratches, and at perfect volume.

I walked away from the factory with a heavy, thank-you carton of ABC Records' finest LP's for my home turntable. There were several of its best albums that I hung onto for many years, but it was mostly second and third tier recording artists pressed for different labels. Some friends though to whom I gave them were thrilled.

At the time I was hired in '68, ABC was still, with some degree of justification, referred to as the "half" a network. Or the "A" to "Almost." CBS and NBC, on the other hand, were long-term and well-established networks. Each was a full-service television operation, making a great deal of profit, boasting a big tent of affiliates, and drawing down consistently high ratings. In many weeks, year-in and year-out, CBS and NBC would have between them all of the ten top-rated programs. ABC's shows were generally not even close and hardly ever cracked the top ten—or even the top 20. Both CBS and NBC had powerful, well-funded news divisions, with stables of star anchors and renowned correspondents.

ABC was the relative new kid on the block. It had been the last to convert to color and had the oldest cameras and other equipment. Founded by Leonard Goldenson when he took over earlier pieces of records, theaters, and broadcasting, he had forged them together into ABC in the mid-'50s. It had the fewest number of local affiliated stations, which hurt its ratings. For example, for a number of its early years, even when I was there, ABC lacked television affiliates and consequently potential viewers in parts of the state of Ohio.

ABC's news division had struggled along with vast underfunding and a much smaller staff than the other two networks. Led by its

Labor Pains

president, Elmer Lower, he had discovered a 26-year old talent from Canada by the name of Peter Jennings and in 1965 put him in the anchor chair. Peter though was not yet ready for prime time and did not last long as chief evening news anchor. Soon back to being a correspondent, he would have to wait a few more decades to return to the anchor chair. Blessed with a nose for talent, Lower also brought in Sam Donaldson, Ted Koppel, and Frank Reynolds. Reynolds—along with Howard K. Smith, who had come over from CBS News, were two solid pros who co-anchored our evening newscast when I joined the Company. It was a good product but its ratings were a constant third.

However, ABC had a strong and ever-growing more popular sports division under its legendary leader, Roone Arledge. ABC Sports' growth and esteem helped substantially in subsequent years to build the entire Company's reputation. Our coverage of the highly rated '68 Mexico City Olympics shortly before I arrived was outstanding. *Wide World of Sports* had established new standards in sports broadcasting. I got to meet Roone around the time ABC Sports acquired the National Football League broadcast rights and in '70 began producing the very successful *Monday Night Football*.

A trip down to Philly that first season with two other ABC lawyer friends was to watch the Eagles defeat the Giants. It was the game where Howard Cosell got sick and famously vomited in the announce booth on Don Meredith's cowboy boots. Tickets and credentials for many ABC Sports' NFL and NBA productions were not only great perks but also excellent learning opportunities.

I was well aware of the Network's weaknesses at the time I turned down Mohawk's offer and joined ABC. However, over the nearly four years that I was with ABC in my first tour duty, its competitive posture changed considerably—with ever increasing speed. At some elusive point we stopped being considered the "half," found the missing piece, and lost that monicker. Most people in the know attribute it to when Goldenson had the wisdom to bring in

Elton Rule from his post as GM at KABC-TV to serve under him as first the Network president and then corporate president and COO. Rule in turn would bring in Fred Silverman to run Entertainment. That milestone event, which turned around ABC, would not be until after I had already left the Company. Its big hit of *Happy Days* wouldn't happen until 1974.

At the same time as the TV Network's general prime time weakness, ABC owned five strong, highly-rated, and profitable local television stations—in New York, Los Angeles, San Francisco, Chicago, and Detroit. Strong, dominating local news programs made the difference. It also owned the market-leading, iconic, Top 40, AM music radio stations, with legendary disc jockeys, in those same cities plus Pittsburgh. FM radio was just beginning its long climb to eventual dominance over AM. And ABC Radio, clearly seeing its future, was investing heavily to build the FM brand.

At the time though, WABC-AM and its acclaimed program director, Rick Sklar, still ruled the roost in New York with *Music Radio 77 WABC*. Its famous DJ team that became household names was led by Dan Ingram. Later in the '70s, Ingram would be joined by "Cousin Brucie" Morrow. It and its burgeoning sister FM station between them employed close to three dozen NABET engineers on top of maybe a couple of dozen DJs and news voices.

ABC also operated out of New York and Washington a successful Radio network. Shortly before I arrived, it had been reorganized into four separate news programming arms. Each of the four— also called "networks"—had hundreds of separate affiliates and a host of all-male, AFTRA news and announcing voices. Dozens of engineers were also engaged, as were numerous WGA news writers and editors. It no longer featured full-length dramatic and other entertainment programs as it had in the earlier decades of radio's popularity before television's arrival. Network Radio had become instead an hourly news and commercial delivery service. The Radio network's star news announcer, Paul Harvey, for decades delivered his popular and highly profitable daily newscasts from the Radio network's Chicago studios.

Technology was always shifting and causing union upheaval. Until the mid-'50s when video tape was invented, TV's primetime entertainment shows were either shot on film, under the jurisdiction of another union, IATSE, or were broadcast live.

The technical unions' ability to disrupt live programs, with threats of strikes over contract disputes in the live television days, was the source of their power. The introduction though of video tape technology in the mid-'50s allowed entertainment programs to be shot and recorded in advance of their air date, edited, and put in the can. Safely awaiting broadcast, video tape largely insulated TV against its former susceptibility to live programming's sudden labor disruption.

NABET had struck NBC in 1959. And ABC in '67—the year before I arrived on the scene. The 1960s witnessed other serious industry strikes. A 1960 Hollywood producer and network strike by the Writers Guild affecting Hollywood film and primetime entertainment product lasted three months and badly hurt the networks.

In 1967, there had been a short, but powerful, 13-day, three-network strike by AFTRA over network correspondents' issues. That work stoppage also took all other AFTRA performers, including announcers, network sportscasters, soap opera actors, newscasters, and our local stations' newspeople, out on the streets. Even star network news anchors—such as CBS' Walter Cronkite, ABC's Howard K. Smith, Frank Reynolds, and Bill Lawrence, and NBC's Huntley and Brinkley—walked the picket lines in support of their union's demands before a settlement was reached.

Walter Cronkite's temporary strike replacement at CBS News was an executive by the name of Arnold Zenker. He introduced himself on air each evening by saying—"This is Arnold Zenker sitting in for Walter Cronkite." He became famous overnight when Cronkite returned after those 13 days and said, "This is Walter Cronkite sitting in for Arnold Zenker." While his name was on everyone's lips, what was little known was that Zenker had previously worked at ABC in a labor relations role under Freund just a few years prior to my arrival.

ABC's "halfness" before but even after it was shed meant that it earned considerably less money from commercials than did our two, full TV network competitors. Consequently, our ability to meet the common, expensive pay terms of our shared labor contacts was that much more difficult.

Decades later, I marveled at what Fox, when it was a startup as the fourth TV network in the 1980s, had been able to achieve. It had convinced the talent unions to grant it a number of concessions not enjoyed by the three other networks. We had no "Fox exception" decades earlier when ABC in the '50s and '60s really could have used one. I sometimes wondered what would have happened if ABC had been more aggressive with these same unions in seeking lesser terms during its fledging "half network" days.

When I arrived at ABC right after the Mexico City games in the fall of 1968, one of the first things I learned was that the ABC and NBC contracts with NABET were basically identical. It was due to the fact that ABC had been born out of the NBC mothership. In the radio only, pre-TV days of the early '40s, the federal government had ruled NBC Radio was a monopoly and forced it to break up its two networks—the Red and the Blue. NBC disposed of the Blue, the weaker of the two. That entity eventually became ABC Radio. The new radio company that emerged, and later developed into television, inherited as a matter of law NBC's old NABET contract.

As radio continued on and television grew, ABC and NBC bargained their NABET contracts side-by-side at their common expiration date. Changes negotiated applied equally. In 1967, there was a temporary breakdown of that twinning arrangement when NABET struck ABC over something NBC had accepted but ABC rejected.

When the strike was finally settled and that issue resolved, both contracts were back matching each other except for their expiration dates. That meant that when ABC's agreement with NABET was to expire in 1971, ABC would do that negotiations on its own.

San Diego was chosen and Freund wanted me there as a member of the ABC bargaining team. It would be this 29-year old lawyer's introduction to "big-table" collective bargaining. With lots of moving parts, many nuances, and numerous players, neither side came in wanting to see a repeat of the '67 strike. Ed Lynch, NABET's president, was the union's chief negotiator and head of its bargaining team. Jim Nolan, the powerful leader of its biggest and most influential New York local, though was the real power sitting by his side.

Not in San Diego to help on tactics or strategy, nor generally expected to speak across the table except on perhaps a Chicago labor relations issue where I had some real familiarity, I was neither ready nor comfortable in doing either. That was Freund's job as chief negotiator. And his chief lieutenant's, Irv Novick. While I was there chiefly wearing my lawyer's hat to assist in drafting and help on other legal issues, I was also soaking up as much as I could about how big-table talks were planned and executed—learning how Freund organized his team and how he handled himself at the table. It was the early discovery stages of how to become a skilled negotiator. In that process I would soon go on to develop a point of view of my own and begin to question why things were the way they were. How, I kept asking myself, had the NABET contract developed into this terribly restrictive agreement. 1971 was my first lesson in living history.

A skilled negotiator quite obviously does not spring forth suddenly as a fully formed and functioning vessel. It takes lots of time, stumbling, failures, and many both good and bad experiences. Roots have to be well and deeply planted. It's a rolling combination ultimately of developing and building strong confidence in oneself as well as mastering the subject matter, studying sea charts, learning how to handle the navigation and sea-lanes, and getting along with the rest of the crew.

In Nelsonian naval terms, I was in San Diego more as a midshipman. I was there to watch how the ship gets rigged for both smooth and rough seas and getting ready to fire only on the up roll. Midshipmen normally progress slowly up a long chain of naval command. At some point, if one survives all the sea battles, with all limbs intact, one wakes up as a captain of his own ship. That was the day of which I was imagining.

What I was observing, which at the time was normal in American labor negotiations, was that most of the bargaining effort was devoted to the union's proposals for change and improvement. Like more holidays, better vacations, more pay, improvements in this area, improvements in that area, improved language here, better language there, always something else. ABC, like most employers at the time, had to give and keep giving.

Hardly any focus or serious attention as I think back, was devoted to what ABC proposed, as insignificant, in retrospect it might have been at that moment in history. Nothing we sought, from the retrospect of a half-century later, had been bold, daring, challenging, threatening, or delimiting in its effects and impact. Nothing was designed to change any of the provisions or work rules that operators were telling me, on my visits to Chicago operational areas, were hampering their ability to manage their workforce. The intrinsic hardship of so much in the contract was not yet understood at the higher levels and therefore was not reflected in our proposals.

Many of the individual rules and restrictions probably made a lot more sense when first negotiated years earlier, but their cumulative impact was not properly appreciated. In many respects not quite comprehended at the time, they were beginning to outgrow the Company's operational comfort zone. One day in the not too distant future there would be an awakening.

These talks were over a half-century ago and nearly 40 years before I retired. Mostly what we did was resist further union advances. If we had been more bold and aggressive, with the prevalent attitudes of the time, it undoubtedly would have led to another long and bitter strike because the times in 1971 were just not yet ripe for any such employer proactivity. Most of our proposals, and certainly what we achieved, were small pieces of improved or clarified language, and even these were difficult to achieve.

There was, however, a new subject introduced that our MIT-type professional engineers told us had to be tackled. Hardly any of us understood the first thing about it but it was the first baby step in addressing the coming age of computers and computer assisted technology. At the time, our term for it was "process control computer." No one other than the handful of true, professionally-educated engineering gurus had a clue what the term meant. Nor did any of us in labor relations have any idea of what changes computers would ultimately bring to the television industry. Remaining mostly a little used provision, it would be much refined and considerably expanded in future contracts beginning in the early '90s as the struggle over computers and keyboards would be heating up into finally a firestorm.

Our company's engineering was coming into the modern era as broadcast technology was on the verge of even more seismic shifts. Strangely, the concept of automation had always been accepted under the NABET contract. One NABET negotiator, Tom Kennedy, and more about him in later pages, always said, "I don't give a shit about how many NABET jobs get lost though automation, but the last person standing to hit that button to turn on that automated equipment and run the studio has to be a NABET." Over the years Kennedy would become famous for uttering many memorable lines like this.

BOE, standing for Broadcast Operations and Engineering, was ABC's technical arm. Led by Julie Barnathan, it was responsible for managing the technical workforce and operating our studios. On the San Diego team for the duration, Barnathan was second in importance only to Freund. At the time, BOE had facility operational responsibility and control over people nationwide for both the television and radio networks as well as the owned TV and radio stations. With his grip over managing 2000 engineering jobs in studios everywhere, Barnathan led a powerful and influential group within the Company.

A colorful character—brash, and outspoken at the table—he was constantly getting exercised over various union proposals for further incursions. Arguments only provoked him further. He talked a lot and had a lot to say, even in our own caucuses. His near blue collar nature and very much down to earth personality held out great appeal to the union side who liked and greatly respected "good old Julie."

There's a great scene in one of my favorite movies, 1986's *Top Gun,* where Tom Skerritt tells Tom Cruise's Lt. Pete Mitchell about serving with his dad on the USS *Oriskany* in Vietnam waters during the war. The Vietnam war was still raging in '71. In real life, Senator John McCain flew off of that carrier. The *Oriskany* was back in the San Diego naval shipyard for refitting the month we were there before it would be redeployed back to its combat station in the South China Sea. ABC News made arrangements through its Pentagon contacts for Freund's team to get a private tour of the carrier on one of the weekend days we were not working.

With the crew mostly on leave and off the ship, and the command bridge vacated, we were allowed turns sitting in the captain's big chair. His map case was attached to the side. When it came my turn, for some reason lost to memory and logic I decided to reach into the case to pull out a war map. Much to my amazement, I came up with an issue of *Playboy* magazine. As we all had a laugh, it was clear that even the captain from time to time needed a bit of his own R&R.

There was neither a deal nor a strike during our five weeks

San Diego stay when the contract expired March 31. With both sides trying to avoid another '67, a traditional extension agreement guaranteeing wage retroactivity conditioned on a peaceful settlement was signed. Both parties were content to adjourn and resume in Washington sometime later that year. When bargaining resumed, a deal was reached—but only after some tense moments. With its many pages, there were lots of improvements for the union, but hardly anything good for the Company.

For me, I had seen up-front and personal the intricate rules and serious problems operators had to deal with during my grievance education in Chicago. I thought I knew the contract well from the constant arguing over what so many of its many clauses meant. But nothing educates a person more about a contract than sitting at the table for five weeks listening to arguments back and forth about its deeper meaning.

That was when I, the new kid on the block, first started thinking that a manager could not walk into a NABET facility anywhere in the country and say "Good morning" without somehow violating a provision of that highly detailed document. In later years when I was in the command module, I used to make this comment often across the table. To jeers from the other side, I'd then add that "It's a virtual *Hammurabi Code*."

What I of course meant was that its tight strictures on what management could or could not do to operate its business in a reasonable and intelligent manner was akin to the 228 strict rules that the ancient Babylonian king had set down 4000 years before to provide order in his realm. At our time in 1971, no one on our side was thinking of how to get rid of Hammurabi, if they had any idea whom he was. Indeed, Hammurabi himself might not have liked his name being taken in vain.

The kind of contentious and grievance-cultured relationship that we had with NABET everywhere we thankfully did not have with our engineering union in ABC's fifth television station city—Detroit. A market in considerable economic flux and demographic change by the time of my first visit in '68 and dating back to even before the riots, its slide would only accelerate over the succeeding decades. Still then the US's fifth-ranked city by population, today in 2022 its greater metropolitan area size has shrunk to 13th.

Visiting Detroit much less frequently than Chicago, I soon appreciated the joy of operating a broadcasting property in a far less adversarial atmosphere. The 150 to 200 TV, AM, and FM technicians were represented by the IBEW, with whom I had negotiated relatively smoothy a new contract early-on after my arrival. With grievances hardly ever filed and arbitrations non-existent, it was a universe far, far away from NABET in every measurable characteristic.

We had few grievances because we had a markedly reduced and much less restrictive contract. It's impossible for employees to cast allegations of violations and file grievances when the underlying document does not have the multitude of highly detailed rules and restrictions, easy to trip over, that our Hammurabi friends embraced. Yet, our Detroit IBEW employees were well-paid, satisfied, and content in their contractual relationship. The culture meant an entirely different daily stress level for our managers and myself when visiting.

The stations were not actually in Detroit since they had moved years before the riots from downtown to the middle class suburb of Southfield. The property was on Ten Mile Road, set back maybe a thousand feet and situated in a red brick, colonial style building. When I first started my visits to Detroit for ABC in the late '60s, I would stay at the better downtown hotels—such as the Sheraton Book, the Pontchartrain, or even the St. Regis across from the GM headquarters building. It was an easy, half-hour drive in reverse traffic to the stations.

Downtown Detroit was an enjoyable area in which to stay

because it had a variety of good restaurants, some of which I remembered from my prior year's NLRB visit. Whether it was the French restaurant Pontchartrain Wine Cellars, right next to the hotel of the same name, or a plethora of famous chop houses like Carl's and Berman's, there were many. There was even the legendary London Chop House, with its walls filled with celebrity caricatures, that I, no longer bound by the $16 federal government spending constraint, occasionally could experience.

But the town was changing at a fast pace following the 1967 riots. Crime was getting so bad that a hotel bellman once advised me after I was taken to my room, as an extra precaution not to leave. "Not leave the hotel, I asked incredulously," as I was thinking of going just next door to the Pontchartrain Wine Cellars restaurant. "No," he responded—"I mean don't leave your room. Order room service." This scared me so much I decided it was time to reconsider downtown Detroit.

The Northland Inn in Southfield's Northland shopping mall was a decent hotel, perfect for a night or two stay, and only a few miles from the stations. In addition, the mall had a nice Scotch 'N Sirloin restaurant where I could dine by myself, with a manager from the stations, or union officials. With other decent restaurants nearby and Detroit, despite its fine dining places, now off limits, the Northland Inn it would be.

4

<u>CHAPTER</u>

Detroit Is More Than Making Cars

We had an AFTRA performers' contract in Detroit at our three stations—WXYZ-TV (Channel 7), WXYZ-AM, and our FM station, WRIF. Due to expire in the spring of 1971 and applying to both journalists and DJ's, the agreement covered around 60 people. But the preponderance was clearly on the television side with its large number of anchors, reporters, and announcers. It was around this time that the station's premier news anchor for many years, Bill Bonds, first joined the *Action News* WXYZ -TV staff.

Handled by Irv Novick, my immediate boss and ABC's director of labor relations, the talks dragged on for several weeks. Irv held the number two position in the department and was an experienced negotiator. Going on to learn much from him while second chairing, I was then a 29-year old lawyer working in the third year of my first tour of duty at the alphabet network.

Led by its local executive secretary, the AFTRA bargaining team was joined at the negotiating table by a number of the radio and television personalities when their on-air time and other duties permitted. On our team, we had the stations' program directors, news directors, and a few financial people. While engaged in the preparations for the talks and monitoring from the sidelines, the three stations' general managers didn't generally show up at the table.

AFTRA came in with a startling proposal. What it wanted was to gain for its TV journalists a system of lucrative on-air performance fees on top of their already high weekly salaries. Arguing that all four other ABC-owned TV stations in our major markets of New York, Chicago, Los Angeles, and San Fransisco paid these fees, it demanded Detroit do the same. It was one of those frequently-heard "we will no longer be second-class citizens" arguments. While the statement about fees and salaries was indeed true, the underlying circumstances in those four cities were entirely different.

A broadcaster, or for that matter any employer, can never pay far in excess of its major competitors. While it was a fact that we had the salary plus fee system that the union wanted in place in those cities, so did our CBS and NBC TV station competitors in those very same cities. In Detroit, however, no other TV broadcaster paid both fees and salaries. While we made it crystal clear from the outset that we would never agree to their proposal, their constant refrain was, "What's good at the other four owned ABC television stations is also good at its fifth." Expecting to break new ground in the Detroit market, they could care less how other local TV stations paid their performers.

But ABC cared. Neither TV GM Don Keck nor his labor relations lawyers were remotely interested in adding on a huge amount of extra cost that our competition did not share. CEO Leonard Goldenson and Freund, were brought up to speed, so we knew we had the Company's support. As the negotiators, it was Irv's job and mine to disabuse AFTRA of any notion that their proposal was even remotely possible. The AFTRA official in charge listened politely but told us the talent felt so strongly about it that it could well be a strike issue. While we did not necessarily believe such blustering, we always took statements about strike possibilities from union officials very seriously.

Going into the talks, as we normally did, the stations had developed a strike contingency plan. Now we ratcheted it up a few notches since we were hearing the performers might actually go out over these impossible demands. While no one in management wanted a strike, there was no backing down on an issue of this critical importance. While threats of AFTRA strikes weren't exactly rare, actual performers' strikes though were. With emotions running high, as often happened in these talks, we could take no chances that reason would ultimately prevail.

It was a good thing we prepared much better because one day in June, after the contract expired and talks had broken down completely, AFTRA decided to walk. A few of our local managers and producers with prior on-air experience stepped in immediately on-camera and behind the mics. So did our trained replacements, supplemented by other managers with on-air experience quickly flown in from nearby Chicago and New York, as well as our other stations.

Adjusting to daily routines in the studios and out on the streets with an entirely new set of replacement talent, the three stations settled in for what could be an extended strike. Not surprisingly, the other unions with firm no-strike clauses in their contracts, and happy to have paychecks, refused to support AFTRA. Driving their cars daily through picket lines, hundreds of the three stations' IBEW, DGA, and IA-represented employees, as well as our large non-union workforce, continued to perform their regular duties.

The strikers' picketing at the bottom of the stations' long driveway entrance went on for weeks. But it was unsuccessful in inflicting any damage on the stations' operations, advertising, or audiences. To the contrary—the performers' strike actually seemed to cause a surprising uptick in our ratings.

Curiosity abounded as news of the performers' strike spread. Detroit's audience wanted to see and hear the new talent taking the place of the familiar faces and voices as viewers and listeners first tuned in and then hung around. Sitting in their living rooms watching the local evening news, very few viewers seemed to care that their favorite Channel 7 anchors or street reporters were AWOL.

Many were loving the mostly non-professional TV replacements— usually the handsome and extroverted sales guys— with their effusive and jocular personalities. Often flubbing lines, they'd laugh it up while trying to deliver news stories in their own, distinctive styles but with an air of imposed, journalistic seriousness. Added to this mostly male mix were some gorgeous station females of somewhat dubious talent from the secretarial ranks—usually the only positions where women worked at TV stations in those days, other than a reporter job or two. But their presence was carefully calculated to keep at least the male eyeballs glued to Channel 7—and their errant fingers far away from the remote control.

The two radio stations carried on equally well, perhaps with a lesser degree of complexity, while their disc jockeys were out walking the pavement in support of their television brethren's issue. A number of former DJ's at ABC's other successful radio stations who had been elevated into management ranks—especially program directors—were flown in to take over air shifts. Bringing with them different announcing styles, voices, and names, as long as the music was the same, Detroit's listening audience generally didn't seem to care that much. Hearing cool and appealing chatter in mellifluous tones and their favorite recording artists, it didn't matter, at least in those early rating books, that their favorite disc jockeys—Dick Purtan in the morning, or Johnny Randall in afternoon drive-time—were off the air.

It had to be a blow to the striking performers walking those endless picket lines that their job action, involving the surrendering of paychecks, was so ineffective.

As a matter of historical record, the '71 strike was the second of only two strikes that AFTRA ever called against ABC in the long, conjoined history of both organizations dating back to the earliest days of radio. And it was ABC's only station strike ever. To this day in 2022, as this book is being published, a half-century later—AFTRA (now SAG/AFTRA) has never called another strike against ABC. This fact alone speaks volumes about the successful labor relationship between ABC and AFTRA. Several decades of that 50-year, well-managed peace took place during my watch.

Novick had earlier advised me that he had a long-scheduled, month's European vacation set for July, but I had not taken him seriously. As June dragged on with no sign of settlement, much to my shock one day he told me that he had decided not to postpone the trip. Leaving as he said he would, Novick departed for Europe at the end of June and put me in charge.

When I discussed this with Freund, he told me to monitor the strike on visits as often as I needed. But I had to be available to be chief negotiator if and when AFTRA showed any desire to return to the table if Novick's European vacation had not yet ended. Despite the show of confidence, I was more than a little nervous because not only was it my first actual strike, it was also an extremely high profile one. With my limited negotiations experience, I was hoping the performers would stay out as long as necessary and not return until Novick was back.

Both sides settled in for the long haul. As the bothersome but totally ineffective strike and picketing were still going on after about a month, the July 4th holiday weekend approached. I happened to be in Detroit the previous week on one of my frequent monitoring visits. Calling Freund, we discussed the upcoming three day, holiday weekend and my intention to fly back east. My plans were to go to my summer beach house which I shared with a group of other

ABC New York-based, bachelor lawyers. Freund though strongly suggested I stay in Detroit. Probably to make me feel better, he threw in a hunch that something big might happen and he wanted me there. Rarely in the course of intense labor pains, as later events were to make clear, has such a spur of the moment gut-feeling ever proven to be so remarkably prescient.

Following Freund's orders, I hung out in a boring weekend at the Northland Inn. Spending the days lounging at the pool, I ate more than I should have, undoubtedly did too much celebratory drinking, and watched some baseball as well as that night's patriotic fireworks display.

Early the morning after the holiday weekend, I was awakened in my hotel room shortly before 6 A.M. by a call. It was from Keck. In a voice laced with panic, the TV station's GM told me that Channel 7 was off the air. Hundreds of union "goons," as he called them, were blocking the driveway's entrance where for weeks the handful of AFTRA strikers had been peacefully picketing. Keck went on to relate that they were attacking any car attempting to drive in. Hardly anyone like himself, and maybe because he was the GM and they went easy on him, had managed to get through successfully. Most employees had given up once they saw the raucous crowd blocking the entrance and what was happening to the cars that were attempting to run the blockade.

The station had signed off its previous broadcast day at 1 A.M. earlier that same day in the normal ritualistic way—common in those days—of the "Star Bangled Banner" playing while the American flag waved in the background. At 6 A.M., as everybody had been thinking, the station would be going back on the air.

The mass picketing though that Keck was screaming about had prevented that from happening. The morning shift of IBEW technicians and all the other necessary union and non-union personnel, including replacement on-air talent, just couldn't get in. Engineering switches had to be pulled, dials set, and buttons pushed to get the TV station, its studios, and transmitter back on the air. But now there was no one qualified inside to do it.

Keck implored me to get over as fast as I could. As we were talking, I turned on the set in my room and sure enough Channel 7 was off the air. That was probably the first and only time in the station's long history, then or since, that this had ever happened. It is rare indeed in the history of American television.

Fortunately, the two radio stations never signed off and went all-night with a mix of mostly syndicated programming. With their relief column the next morning blocked from proceeding up the driveway, radio was still flying, but it was just for the moment—and with only one wing.

Showering and dressing as quickly as I could, I drove my Hertz rental at ridiculous speeds the few miles up Ten Mile Road to the stations' driveway entrance. I was extremely fortunate there were no Southfield police on the road to stop my vehicle. As it turned out, they were at the rear of the stations' parking lot taking statements from Keck and the valiant few who managed to drive, relatively unscathed, through the picket lines.

Nothing that I had or would ever experience in my years as a labor lawyer prepared me for what was about to happen. It was far worse from what I was expecting when I hung up with Keck. Making sure my windows were closed and doors locked, I slowly made the left hand turn and attempted to navigate my way up the driveway. I was pretty much stopped within a few feet of making the turn by a massed crowd blocking my path forward. It was a group of between 75 and 100 angry, shouting, mostly males carrying picket signs with names I could make out of AFTRA and Teamsters. Some in the crowd were holding baseball bats. Rocking and attacking my rental vehicle that was still slowly creeping forward, it was a scene right out of some easily recognizable news footage. It could have been picket lines from years past nasty automotive strikes in Detroit or steel strikes in Pittsburgh.

The windshield was attacked and cracked, but miraculously it did not shatter. Still seeing in my mind's eye, 50 years later, not only the face of the person who hit it with a bat but also the deep, blue color of his work shirt, I can almost hear the jeering crowd. Somehow, and to this day I do not know where it came from, I managed to keep control of the car. Partially covering my eyes with one hand for protection against any possible flying glass, I pressed the peddle and the car moved forward. With that, the crowd separated a bit creating a space just wide enough to pass through. While they were still beating on the car, it was a miracle I maintained control and did not run over or injure anyone.

When I arrived at the back of the station, I found a few Southfield police officers interviewing the brave few who had preceded me safely through the mass of violent picketers. Several people later told me that in my excitement and high emotion, I jumped out of my car and began screaming at the police, in a high-pitched voice. My adrenaline was demanding answers why they were not up front at the driveway entrance controlling the crowd and protecting those trying to get through.

Now after a half-century, I can honestly admit it. This was the only time in my four-decade career in labor relations, living through many very high stress situations involving my own personal safety—with some tough and mean characters—that I was ever so truly scared.

Quickly recovering my composure, I soon found a slightly more calm Keck than the one I had spoken with earlier even though his station remained off the air. Together, we went over a variety of mostly non-sensical ideas. One suggestion we rolled around for a minute or two was to hire a few big trailer trucks. We'd load them up off premises with the vital, non-striking employees. With private guard and police escorts, we'd force our way through the blocked entrance and get WXYZ-TV back on the air. Both of us pretty much at the same time rejected the heavy-handed approach as ridiculous and not even remotely feasible.

Sharing some intelligence that he had picked up earlier that morning from his news director, the GM explained the Teamster's presence. It seemed that a few of the striking news talent had become frustrated with AFTRA's inability to change anything during the month of stalemated talks and the weeks of inconsequential striking. Like most American workers, many television journalists and radio DJ's lived from pay check to pay check. Savings in some cases had been exhausted and a good number of them had to be hurting badly. Disappointment that they had not been able to hurt the stations sufficiently to force the Company to accede to their fee demands had led some, in their desperation, to turn to the normally more aggressive union—the Teamsters.

It was, as I was to learn, not just any Teamster local. The crowd blocking the driveway that morning and creating the havoc was carrying Local 299 picket signs. They were from the Teamster union involved over the years in many legendary Detroit strikes and other major labor actions. Until he went to jail, it had been led by the well- known labor leader, Jimmy Hoffa. It was his base and source of national strength when he served as International Teamster president before his 1967 sentence for jury tampering. At the time he began serving his seven year term, Local 299 was perhaps the most powerful Teamster local in the country. Four years later and with him still in federal prison, it probably remained the most powerful. His handpicked successor, Frank Fitzsimmons, out of the same local, was now International president.

As a needed footnote, weeks after the strike ended I received some intelligence from a credible but unconfirmed source. Apparently one particular sports commentator who worked for Roone Arledge's ABC Sports' operation out of New York was the person responsible for bringing in the Teamsters. Residing in Detroit when he was not on the road for *Wide World of Sports,* and supposedly good friends with a number of fellow Detroit WXYZ AFTRAns, he suggested they call some people he knew personally at Local 299.

Before my mad drive to the station, I had called Freund at his Long Island home and got him before he left for the office. Shocked at the news, he told me to call National AFTRA Executive Secretary, Bud Wolff, the head AFTRA official. Somehow, Freund knew that Wolff was then in Louisville, KY, about to start his union's annual national convention. He also provided me with the name of the hotel where the convention would be taking place and where Wolff was probably staying.

Wolff and I knew each other from previous AFTRA negotiations in Chicago. Once I arrived at WXYZ, I tracked him down at his Louisville hotel before he left for breakfast. Expressing shock at the picket line violence, my own narrow escape, and AFTRA's losing control of the unit, he told me he was putting his convention on hold and getting the next flight he could to Detroit. Before hanging up, we agreed to meet at the Northland Inn after his plane landed.

Before he left Louisville, as I later learned, Wolff set his counterinsurgency plan into motion. Reaching out to a senior ranking national Teamster official he knew through some high level AFL-CIO contacts, he asked him to call Teamster president Fitzsimmons. Wolff urged his contact to pass along a message from one major union leader to another—Fitzsimmons should order Local 299 to back away from interfering in another union's jurisdiction and its labor dispute.

The Northland Inn, just down the road from our stations, was where we set up our emergency headquarters to coordinate our rescue and recovery operations. A few hours later when I left Keck and the Ten Mile Road property, it was easier getting out but cars were not getting in. WXYZ-TV was still off the air. It was quite a scene upon my arrival at the hotel. The parking lot and public areas were packed with the dozens of union and non-union television and radio station employees who had been blocked from entering the property. Many were just hanging around waiting for information. As soon as I arrived, local IBEW and IATSE union officials sought me out in search of answers that I could not possibly provide. High on their list were questions about lost pay, and, of course, considering what had just happened down the road, their members' safety.

Wolff's flight after some connections did not land until around noontime. We found a room as soon as he arrived and it might well have been my own. Followed into the room by a tough-looking stranger who pushed his way in before we could shut the door, I demanded to know who he was and what he was doing in our room. The intruder somehow knew who I was but not Wolff until Bud identified himself as the head of AFTRA. Proceeding to tell us he was Chuckie O'Brien, that name meant absolutely nothing. But then the stranger added he was a business agent from Teamster Local 299. And he was on the scene because the stations' on-air talent, fed up with AFTRA, had come to him for assistance.

With his barging in like this, the atmosphere had become pretty heated. Not surprisingly, as our mutual adrenalines were racing, there was a lot of shouting back and forth. I was insisting that his presence was uninvited and I demanded that he should leave the room at once. The exchange basically went—"I don't care who you are. Get the hell out of the room that ABC is paying for and not you." O'Brien flat out refused. It was something like—"No fucking way. These people want me because AFTRA is doing shit." Wolff began shouting at O'Brien that he represented the striking talent— not Chuckie and the Teamsters. With our three near-exploding faces quite close, it was fast becoming a tense and agitated standoff that could easily have gotten out of hand.

Not having grown up as a street guy nor, in fact, ever having been in a fist fight during my entire life, I knew if this confrontation had turned physical I would have gone down fast—and for the count.

Chuckie looked like a guy who knew how to handle himself. But this was new territory for me, and I imagined for Wolff, too. Back at Fort Ord in 1967, I had US Army training at bayonet practice, tossing live grenades, and shooting my .45 revolver. But nothing in actually throwing punches or engaging in hand-to-hand combat. I suspected Wolff, another lawyer, maybe by that time 20 years my senior and in his late 50s, couldn't throw a punch either and would have gone down just as quickly—if not faster.

I had developed since a kid certain skills and one of them was my verbal ability to talk myself out of physical fights. Wolff's normal abilities, I imagined, ran in the same direction. His and my usual displays of toughness were limited to sharply raised voices, arm-waving, finger-pointing, and occasionally slamming the table.

Later on, when we learned more about O'Brien's reputation after his name periodically made the papers, and usually in the context of rumors about Hoffa's disappearance, we were much relieved our screaming had not led to a physical altercation. The feeling of relief became even more pronounced a half-century later after I read Goldsmith's 2020 book about his stepfather and saw O'Brien's depiction in Scorsese's *The Irishman*.

Getting nowhere with O'Brien, Bud and I moved very quickly to bolt. Surprising O'Brien who was momentarily distracted, we raced a few steps ahead of him, found another room down the hall, and locked the door. Seeming to have lost O'Brien, at least momentarily, Wolff made a call from that room's phone to his contact in the national Teamster hierarchy whom he had reached earlier from Louisville. The person must have already relayed Wolff's message to Fitzsimmons— because it wasn't too long before, or so it seems a half-century later, O'Brien stopped wandering the halls looking for us.

At that time many decades before the invention of mobile phones, it's difficult to comprehend how Fitzsimmons so quickly was able to track down O'Brien to deliver his back off message. But

Teamster power has its ways, and O'Brien stood down. Despite his seemingly no longer looking to insert himself into the talks or take over the AFTRA unit, he still hung around the hotel corridors for a while longer bird-dogging Wolff and myself and trying to play a role in the final deal.

When Wolff and I met alone, in consultation with his local AFTRA leader who had accompanied him from Louisville, he withdrew the performance fee proposals that had triggered the strike. With a deal quickly hammered out, the strike was over—at least in principle. So I called Freund and the three of us, hugely relieved, probably talked together. Wolff and the Detroit AFTRA leader were able to regain control of the renegade unit. Later that afternoon, the two of them together mustered enough influence and votes to convince the bargaining unit to accept the settlement and return to work. The next day Wolff flew back to his convention, I left for New York, and normal life at the stations resumed.

As an interesting aside about Wolff, he and I had first met in Chicago a few years earlier. It was shortly after I had started with the Company and was in town negotiating the stations' AFTRA contracts. Improvidently, out of my inexperience, I foolishly said across the table that "WLS-TV was not afraid of and totally prepared for a strike." It was just a little over-blustering by a still learning and youthful negotiator. Wolff, the experienced lawyer and national head of AFTRA, called me out into the hall. He cautioned me—"Jeff, I like you and you have a big future in this business, but take some advice from me. Never mention the word strike until it's first brought up by the union." It was a well-learned lesson that stuck with me for the rest of my career about needlessly and prematurely using provocative terms.

Sometime later I found out that Wolff had called Freund and told him about the incident. In that conversation as Freund related it, Wolff went on to commend me as a lawyer he saw with a big broadcasting future. Bud and I were to remain close acquaintances for the rest of his AFTRA career, which ended a few decades later. Several times we again talked about Chuckie and that Detroit experience.

During that time of our continued relationship, he also taught me another valuable lesson—of rebuilding collapsed bridges. Once after I had gotten into a major dispute with one of his New York local AFTRA leaders, Bud went out of his way to repair the damage. He took the two of us to lunch at his favorite New York restaurant, and soon to become mine, the Italian Pavilion. That lesson stayed with me forever.

The WXYZ strike had ended because the reporters, anchors, and DJ's had had enough. Apparently many if not most were appalled and shaken at the violent picketing, carried out their name, they had witnessed. They simply were through with the Teamsters and Chuckie O'Brien. He disappeared. The Detroit stations never heard from him or the Teamsters again. The fees the TV newspeople had been seeking were never again sought.

When I got back to ABC's New York City headquarters, I wrote a report for Freund. At his request, I copied Leonard Goldenson and we later met in his office. The memo caused a high level of concern for some time thereafter.

As a footnote, Jimmy Hoffa Sr., was given a pardon by President Richard Nixon in late '71 and let out of prison. Returning to Detroit, he immediately, with the help of Chuckie O'Brien, attempted to regain control of the International Teamsters union. After several years of trying to get back into the game but never successful, he mysteriously disappeared in 1975 on his way to lunch at a now famous Detroit-area restaurant, Machus Red Fox.

Press accounts exploded. Speculation and rumors abounded—then and for decades thereafter. According to legend, the Goldsmith book, and the Scorsese movie, Chuckie O'Brien was somehow involved in his disappearance. It was always denied by O'Brien and nothing was ever established by any investigating authorities.

5
CHAPTER

The Peacock Network Flies High

Dick Goldstein was the vice president and head of labor relations at NBC. I had the privilege of working for Dick at NBC after he lured me away from ABC in 1972. The National Broadcasting Company, or NBC, at the time was a subsidiary of the formidable industrial giant, the RCA Corporation.

Both of my first two broadcasting bosses named Dick—Freund and Goldstein—had first class minds. Brilliant negotiators, they led their departments with distinction for decades. Together, and particularly when they were joined at the table by CBS' equally strong labor relations chief, Jim Sirmons, they were an unbeatable team. All three had characteristics common to all great negotiators in displaying intellectual stamina, creativity, fortitude, humor, a little acting ability, some humility, and a considerable capacity to both galvanize and portray strength. Quite obvious to many, the NBC and ABC Dicks also demonstrated the common virtues of intelligence and wisdom— when sometimes making certain hiring decisions.

Both companies enjoyed another common denominator. Goldstein was able to attract me to NBC with promises of even more love, warmth, and affection from NABET than the union had given me at ABC. Because the alphabet network had been born out of the old NBC radio company in the 1940s, as described earlier, it had inherited as a matter of law at its birth the same NABET labor contract to which NBC was a signatory. The union had actually been started by NBC's parent, RCA, under a different name during the 1930s as a company-dominated union. At some point though it later changed its name, turned on its creator, and shed its pro-management skin.

By the time I arrived on the scene, NABET had grown into the most aggressive and litigious union in the broadcasting industry. I was to soon learn that this was even more true at NBC than what I had experienced at ABC. And it was light years more difficult to deal with than its two chief broadcasting rivals also representing technicians—the IBEW and IATSE. At the time I joined, NABET represented thousands of mostly engineering technicians at each of NBC and ABC. Through shrewd negotiating in applying its aggressive labor movement philosophy in calling strikes and making threats, it had gained for its members at both companies the most stringent and restrictive engineering agreement in broadcasting.

As recounted in previous pages, ABC and NBC jointly bargained their nearly identical contracts at their common expiration date. The last time this joint bargaining had taken place was 1967. In that year, NABET struck ABC after NBC had caved in near the very end of talks to NABET's key demand. When ABC stood firm and wouldn't agree to shorten the work day from nine hours to eight, with its paid meal period, NABET struck ABC.

I recall the story vividly, as described in perfect detail and separately corroborated many times over by both Freund and Goldstein. The final phase of the '67 negotiations was being held at a Miami Beach hotel. It may well have been the fabled Fontainebleau. Federal mediators had been called in. Towards the end of the scheduled talks, when the companies had to give their final response to NABET's key demand of a shortened workday, NBC decided, at the last minute, to agree. How that message was delivered to ABC became the stuff of industry legend.

During a break in the talks one afternoon, as they were getting down to the climax, Freund went for a swim to relax in the ocean off the hotel beach. Dick Goldstein waded into the surf and swam out to join him. When Freund would tell the story in subsequent years, he would love to flap his arms around to show Goldstein, the great athlete, swimming with his fast stroke over to him. As he got closer, he could hear Goldstein yelling, "Dick... Dick, I have to tell you something." Goldstein, proceeded to tell him that he had just gotten orders from his NBC bosses and parent RCA management to agree to NABET's workday demand. Freund, believing they had a blood pact not to give in, and knowing it meant a certain strike for ABC, was furious at what he saw as NBC's betrayal. Most probably nearly drowning from taking in too much water while receiving the startling news, Freund swam in to shore. From his room he called ABC chief Goldenson to tell him about NBC's defection—and the probability of a strike.

NBC made its deal and ABC had its first NABET strike. With trained management replacements, it held its own in its studio and remote pickup operations. But it couldn't sustain a long strike and after nine weeks out, it decided to settle—on the same terms as had NBC. ABC managed though a slight delay in the implementation of the shortened work day change. It also got its different 1971 expiration date.

During the nearly four years I had worked for Freund at ABC and our departments worked closely together, Dick Goldstein had gotten to know me. Apparently liking what he saw, in early '72 Goldstein approached Freund and told him he was going to offer me a new position he was creating. Needing help in managing his department, heavily invested as it was in a mounting NABET work load, I was to be his director of labor relations, a new position and the number two labor job in his New York office. Freund called me in to give me the news and advise me to expect a call from Goldstein. Telling me it was a great opportunity and that he hated losing me, Freund added that at least there was comfort in knowing I would still be around in the industry and working closely with him in our many joint negotiations.

Ev Erlick, ABC's general counsel, had taken a liking to me and invited me up to his office to review my options. I attribute that reach out to the fact that he had once asked me to help with a personal legal matter. That's where he got to know me better than most of the other young lawyers.

Seeing too many senior lawyers in front of me impeding promotion to the director of labor relations level, he said he would be sorry to see me go but thought that I should take the NBC offer. Prophetically, he told me that ABC would soon gain some big programming and ratings improvements and begin to catch up with NBC. His predictions proved true when a few years later the programming guru, Fred Silverman, was hired by ABC's COO, Elton Rule, as the new head of Entertainment.

As I write these particular pages in February of 2020, Fred Silverman has just died. Long-retired from the networks, he worked miracles in those ABC years and later went on to become a legendary Hollywood producer. I got to know Fred early-on during my retirement when we were working together around 2011 on a business deal, along with my good friend, Paul Rauch, the noted serial producer. The deal was acquiring the rights to produce some hour-long soap operas that had just been kicked off all three networks' air because of failed ratings, shortening the new productions to half hours, and distributing them on different platforms such as Hulu. I was their labor partner. We were all set to launch when the market for soaps really tanked. Paul was later taken from us, much too young, a year or so later after the venture had died.

Goldstein took me to lunch at his Rockefeller Center club where he made the offer and then I met with the NBC HR people. Its HR department was then called "personnel," the same as at every other company in America. The money seemed right and the deal was done. I was told by the personnel manager that at age 31, I was the youngest director level executive anywhere in the Company.

My new, spacious office in the labor relations suite on the 15th floor of 30 Rock where NBC was based overlooked the Rockefeller Center skating rink. Our suite was next door to Johnny Carson's offices when *The Tonight Show* was still in New York. I saw a rather taciturn Carson any number of times at the elevator before his show moved to the West Coast a year or so later. We'd usually just nod at each other. With Johnny's constantly giving off negative vibes, I never gathered up the courage to engage in any kind of conversation.

Oh, how I longed to talk to him about my favorite *Tonight Show* of them all that I watched in my law school days. That was the debacle when Bert Parks, of *Miss America Pageant* broadcast fame, was the show's street reporter for 1963's live remote opening of the movie, *Cleopatra*, starring Elizabeth Taylor and Richard Burton. So many lawsuits had been threatened over that show's content that NBC basically had pulled it from its available tape library and never allowed any replays. I had roared hilariously at Parks' irreverent commentary about the movie's stars and his incredible dialogue with Carson back in the 30 Rock studio. In addition, a couple of performers who had become friends had appeared on his show, so I had a line or two about them ready for delivery, too.

His coolness, perhaps shyness, was consistent with everything ever written about Carson's not being a very affable fellow once off-camera. I was a bit surprised, however, that his reticence to chat even extended to his 30 Rock, next-door neighbors, frequently standing shoulder to shoulder, at or in the NBC elevators. Even making eye contact was difficult. Forevermore, I was to regret my reluctance in not engaging Carson a bit more aggressively. The following year any opportunity was lost when the *The Tonight Show* relocated permanently to our Burbank studios.

My job reporting to Goldstein was to head a team of four lawyers who functioned as either labor lawyers or labor relations executives in our multiple dealings with our many unions. We, like ABC, still had that distinction. All of my favorite players from ABC were in the mix—NABET, AFTRA, DGA, WGA, SAG, and of course IATSE in its many iterations. The gaggle of IA locals once again included stagehands, film cameramen, sound and lighting technicians, film editors, and film processors. IA also had the makeup artists, hair stylists, and graphic artists. The other usual suspects included the Teamsters and a little bit of the IBEW for NBC's 30 Rock house electricians. We also had a contract with the the AFM, for our live musicians in Johnny Carson's *Tonight Show* Doc Severinsen band.

Mostly the same leaders that I had been dealing with during my ABC time, it was all very familiar territory. Goldstein had checked me out with a number of them before hiring me. Apparently, they had nothing bad to say—at least for those whose opinions most mattered.

The NBC TV Network was big, powerful, and dwarfed ABC in ratings, revenue, and profitability. It was part of the giant electronics, book publishing, appliance, phonograph recording, and radio and television set manufacturing company that RCA was at that time. NBC's technical broadcasting facilities, not surprising considering who was its parent, were top-notch.

With its ample financial resources, and in order to help it sell millions of new RCA color television sets coming off its assembly lines, RCA had made sure its NBC subsidiary had converted from black and white to color transmission at the earliest opportunity. When that early color conversion happened, NBC became known for a while as the "Color Network." With its multi-color, exotic-plumaged, peacock logo, it also was known as the "Peacock Network." Milton Berle had been its entertainment star when I was a kid growing up, and later it was Sid Caesar. Now it was Rowan and Martin's *Laugh-In,* Bob Hope's popular *Vietnam Christmas Specials*, and *The Dean Martin Show.*

NBC News, with lead anchors Chet Huntley and David Brinkley, and a team of strong, well-known correspondents and bureaus stretching around the world, was always at the very top of the network news ratings—neck and neck with CBS's Walter Cronkite. While its owned radio and TV stations were successful, radio was not doing well having slipped far behind ABC Radio at both the local station and network level.

Its NBC Sports was a top contender with one half of the Sunday NFL package, major league baseball, and many other sports. It had just broadcast the '70 winter Olympics from Japan and soon would be on the verge of taking away from ABC the rights to the '80 summer games in Moscow. Some of its senior executives who I got to know would within a few years leave to develop ESPN into the sports behemoth that it later became.

Overall, NBC was a first-rate, well-established and highly respected company—a great deal more prestigious at the time than ABC. I was happy to be there and working for Goldstein. A good boss, he was well-respected both within and without the Company. Going on to give me great independence and support, Dick was extremely knowledgable in most of NBC's many contracts. I would learn much by observing his style—particularly in preparing for negotiations and at the bargaining table.

One of the lawyers whom I hired shortly after joining the Company was Alan Raphael. With me a few years before moving to a labor relations position with NBC on the West Coast, Alan soon thereafter joined Warner Brothers where he became a vice president and its long time head of labor relations. We remain good friends in 2022.

Raphael would become one of the eight or nine labor lawyers who I hired during my career at NBC, RKO, CapitalCities/ABC, and

Disney who would go on to achieve vice presidential or higher rank and major success at their respective companies. The list includes CBS, Disney, Warner Brothers, Fox, ABC, Dow Jones, the Museum of Modern Art, Sony, and NBC. One of those I hired shortly after I joined the Company was Day Krolik. Years later, Day's skills would take him to the chief NBC labor job where we would work closely together for decades upon my return to ABC in 1987.

At the time I joined NBC, NABET was the same strong and powerful international union I had known at ABC. But in New York I would be dealing with its sister local—separate and distinct from the ABC local I had just left behind.

While all labor contracts in America are nothing more than a body of rules and regulations governing how the employees in the workplace are to be treated, the NABET contract at both networks took this to new heights. Both the NBC and ABC books, largely identical, contained—as I had learned at ABC—a frustrating set of work rules and restrictive jurisdictional provisions. By their very nature, work and jurisdictional rules often fly directly in the face of efficient management. It was only as time marched on, however, as technology was massively changing, that management would fully grasp the damage that crippling work rules and rigid jurisdictional boundaries had inflicted.

There was a lot of NBC history to learn and I soon heard the legend of the 1959 strike. It was a galactic struggle involving *The Today Show*, NABET, and Paris. It erupted when the popular morning show, then hosted by Dave Garroway, announced with great fanfare that it was going to originate a week of programs from the French capital. NABET officials immediately demanded the work overseas—sending the same studio crew that normally did the show from 30 Rock. Having decided it would be far more efficient to do the five, two-hour shows with locally hired French technicians than fly over the regular crew, NBC refused to do so.

With no live broadcast through satellite transmission yet

possible, shows were going to be recorded on video tape in the Paris studios and flown back to the United States for broadcast. Video tape was a huge technological breakthrough that had come into use just a few years earlier and would allow this delayed broadcast of the normally live *Today Show.* Both ABC and NBC had negotiated with NABET in the mid-'50s at the time of tape's birth and given the union—because it was just an extension of live broadcasts— exclusive jurisdiction over video tape program production. But the NABET agreement expressly provided that the union had no contractual jurisdiction whatsoever—live or tape—over programs originating outside of the United States.

The union contract clearly said "no" to foreign pickups, but that did not stop NABET from trying to muscle the work for its members. Lots of heated discussion ensued. Finally, to avoid a major dispute and a possible job action, Mack Clifford, the senior NBC executive who oversaw labor relations, offered a compromise— half of the crew in Paris would be NABET. Half meant sending roughly a score of NABETs over to France instead of the perhaps 40 upon which the union was insisting. But 20 was a score more technicians than what NBC had originally been prepared to send.

NABET though still resisted. In one of the great miscalculations in its history, then or since, its leaders insisted it had to be the complete crew. So Clifford, with NABET now overplaying its hand, stood tall and said that it was going to be zero. As the result, no NABETs walked the streets of Paris or sat in cafes on what could have been a very plush, week-long assignment. With Clifford's pronouncement and NABET's expected reaction, NBC prepared for what could be a potentially disabling, nationwide strike. As one NBC NABET leader famously used to say to justify its responses in situations such as this, "When NBC acts, NABET reacts."

Garroway's Paris *Today Show* went ahead as planned. Shot in the studios by a French crew, the tapes were flown back to New York on the long transatlantic journey—quite possibly on one of the new Boeing 707 jets that Pan Am had recently put into service. The tapes were picked up by an NBC motorcycle courier at New York's Idlewild airport, soon to be renamed JFK, and whisked to 30 Rock. When they were brought into the building and NABET technicians ordered to put them into the video playback machines for that day's broadcast, all NBC NABET employees nationwide dutifully followed the union's orders and walked off the job. Thousands of employees at the five owned TV stations, a dozen or so radio stations, the TV network, and the radio network were striking. Studio shows, news events, and sports remote coverages would be extremely challenged and could be potentially disrupted.

The union's leaders thought the strike surely would bring NBC to its knees. But NABET had grossly underestimated NBC's preparedness and misunderstood its resolution. Two weeks later, with NBC not having missed a beat due to well-trained replacements and RCA's assistance, NABET tried to limp back in and begged to make a deal. Its members had lost two weeks of salary in this power grab and fruitless tilting at windmills.

As a condition of ending the strike and letting its NABET employees return to work, NBC required the union to sign a strike settlement agreement. The pact covered a number of new flexibilities that NBC had long relished, like the right to suspend employees for just cause and not just to seek their discharge. Most importantly, it contained a commitment not to strike during the term of the agreement, as this strike over Paris had been. NABET's international president—who had been the mastermind behind the *Today Show* miscued strategy— had no choice but sign the surrender document. Soon thereafter though he was kicked out and a new regime took over. It was the lowest point in its history.

As an interesting aside, the NBC executive named Clifford who made this fateful decision was the father-in-law of Frank Jordan, NBC's News Bureau Chief in Washington, DC., during the '70s. I had gotten to know Jordan well. An interesting character in his own right and great raconteur, Frank in buoyant animation one night over drinks at his favorite Washington watering hole related the *Today Show* story.

NABET rebounded from its '59 low. While not giving up on aggressive bargaining tactics, a major ingredient of its reemergence centered on a new found preference for the grievance procedure and the arbitration process. Litigiousness became an obsession and a grievance culture high on steroids took firm root.

NABET became protective in guarding its work jurisdiction by filing voluminous grievances over a myriad of issues. Some arbitrators provided a big assist in that effort. One particular NBC arbitration that was decided in the late '50s around the time of the *Today Show* incident became an extremely harsh precedent for many decades to come.

That decision held that any work NABET employees were assigned to perform—regardless of whether it was within their specified and express contractual jurisdiction of "operating" technical equipment— could not thereafter be taken away. The example from the particular case involved a NABET employee who had been assigned to operate in the studio a rear screen, film projection system. It was a device clearly not "technical equipment" within the terms of the NABET contract. Nor was it controlled by any other labor agreement. Once, however, given to them exclusively, said the arbitrator, this work—not in their express jurisdiction— became their's and could not thereafter be taken away.

This interpretive addition to NABET's work jurisdiction, imposed by an activist arbitrator, and never agreed to by the parties in bargaining, became enshrined. It was a major expansion and restriction of management prerogatives that was to haunt both NBC and ABC in a wide assortment of ways for decades to come. What lesson this decision taught operating management was simple. No more would we give to any NABET employee anything not expressly in their contractual jurisdiction because if we did, it might become their's forever.

Grievances inevitably meant grievance meetings, in an ever increasing multitude, the same I was accustomed to from my Chicago-ABC days. They were nothing more than extended, often heated arguments over who was right about an alleged contract violation. Just as at ABC, many hundreds if not thousands of hours of labor relations lawyers' and operational management's cumulative time were spent on this process. Thriving on this strategy while management silently suffered, the grievance and arbitration culture had become even more pronounced than ABC's.

At one point in the mid-'70s, NBC had hundreds of arbitration cases in its backlog or on the docket to be tried, with a hearing or two a week in both New York and Los Angeles, plus others in our other cities. Since our designated contract arbitrators ran out of possible hearing dates, NABET went to the American Arbitration Association for additional dates—and more arbitrators to hear the cases. The lawyers I was supervising were so wrapped up in these cases that we had to borrow a few litigation attorneys from NBC's legal department for the overload. When that proved to be an insufficient resource, we were forced to outsource a number of cases to law firms.

The New York management-side, labor law firm known as Proskauer had represented NBC for a number of years in mostly providing negotiating advice. We now began engaging it on a fairly regular basis to handle arbitration cases that our inside legal team simply was too busy to manage. Three of its best lawyers were assigned. Bob Batterman—the best of the best—who would go on to have a long and distinguished career at Proskauer, handled many of these cases. Bob and I, in our mutual retirements, have remained good friends until this day.

NABET had learned in the '60s, as the pace of arbitrations began to accelerate, that it could often gain more from grieving and occasionally winning claimed contract violations than it could achieve across the bargaining table. As any bargainer knows, contract language resulting from tense negotiations is often the product of drafting compromises. Compromised language, designed by its very nature to satisfy both parties, often brings with it a certain ambiguity that is susceptible to differing interpretations. Becoming the meat of many an arbitration, if the union only won a quarter of such ambiguous language arbitration cases, the union would be that much ahead of where it otherwise would have been.

By that time, a hundred or so arbitration cases had been decided by nationally known and respected arbitrators at each of ABC and NBC. Interpreting identical language, losses at one company would affect and similarly doom the other. Wins would also be equally applicable. Arbitration decisions filled many thick black binders in our law libraries and took on the force of contract law. In fact, arbitration cases in some instances were more powerful than mere contract provisions because the union was legally permitted to strike the Company if we violated an arbitration decision—willingly or even inadvertently.

In those days, we had an expedited arbitration provision for certain more serious alleged contract violations. Every Friday afternoon we waited anxiously for the arrival over the transom of a new "expedited" grievance demanding a "quickie" arbitration. Quickies frequently involved prospective live sports events such as our NFL games scheduled for that weekend where an operational decision of some kind was being challenged. The contract arbitrators were often on alert for one of these Friday afternoon expedited-missives. Arbitrations were sometimes tried over the weekend by one of our lawyers, with myself usually attending.

Soon after I came onboard and seeing all that was occurring with NABET that needed some fixing, I felt the need to summon the lawyers into my office for a serious conversation about resolve. I had talked this over with Goldstein in advance and he readily agreed a staff attitudinal adjustment was needed. So, I called my lawyers on relatively short notice into my office for a fairly stern talk regarding the necessity of showing greater fortitude and resilience in dealing with NABET.

Little did I know that one of my lawyers sitting in front of me had developed some sloppy, internal security habits. He had allowed NABET officials visiting him in his office to remain seated there when he was called away unexpectedly for what he thought would be a brief conversation with Goldstein or myself. No way could I have suspected that we had a potential security breach within the four walls of my own department—seemingly safe from the eyes and ears of our adversary—at the exact moment I called this quick meeting to urge additional vigilance and strength.

So I spoke comfortably—with my office door open—in what I thought was a secured space. Singling out one specific union official I said, "Never trust those bastards and particularly 'X.'" Sure enough, within a minute or two of my delivering this sharp directive, I saw first the head and then the body of this very same "X" come around the corner and into my door frame. With a big, sheepish grin on his face, "X" was alerting me to the fact that he had heard everything I had just said. His ability to show up in our suite and outside of my office door was symptomatic of the general, all-too casual attitude that I had been addressing just before that grinning face popped into view.

After his hearing "Never trust those bastards and 'X,'" needless to say the rest our time together at NBC was not the warmest. Allowing a roaming NABET body, our adversary, loose in our safe zone was unheard of. This episode was the end to security breeches in the very halls of our own office suite. With Goldstein's approval, I put measures into place to make sure NABET officials would never come in and hang around unannounced, undetected, and unwanted.

The '72 Democratic National Convention that would go on to

nominate George McGovern for president was scheduled for Miami Beach in July. It was just a few months after I joined the Company. Goldstein sent me down to supervise relations with the unions. That meant mostly NABET. In those days when perhaps 125 or more Network NABET technicians were assigned, political conventions were still a very big deal and covered "gavel to gavel." I set myself up at the NBC News headquarters hotel, the Fontainebleau.

It was at this convention that the miniaturized (for its time), shoulder mounted, portable, electronic cameras connected to hundreds of feet of cable were first introduced. Correspondents accompanied by NABET cameramen could now roam the floor of the Miami Beach convention center shooting with their light-weight cameras whatever was happening and of interest to the viewing audience. Since everything going on was now open for broadcast, the new portable cameras were dubbed by NBC's head of engineering, Bill Trevarthen, "creeping peepers," or perhaps his term was "peeping creepers." Whatever was its proper name, portable, electronic shoulder cameras were a major technological breakthrough.

NBC's senior engineering management people took me, the new kid on the block they were trying to inculcate with their aggressive labor philosophy, under their wing. For the several days I was there I was constantly taken around and force-fed by NBC engineering. That stuffing served me well in all my upcoming experiences. While at the convention center, of course, I frequently ran into NABET's "Don Quixotes" as they were off in their constant search for contract violations.

It was at the Miami Beach convention center while entering one morning that I met by chance and chatted with the former Disney "mouseketeer," Cheryl. This was the Cheryl from child-acting fame years before on ABC's *The Mickey Mouse Club*. Along with most American kids my age in the mid-'50s, I had so enjoyed watching it every day after school. Like so many, I had been captivated by the group of talented young performers ingeniously named by Walt Disney as the "mouseketeers." Well, little 12-year old Cheryl was now all grown up Cheryl—gorgeous, and famously married to the celebrated Grand Prix race car driver, Lance Reventlow, the son of the Woolworth heiress, Barbara Hutton. There had been a lot of publicity I had seen in the newspapers about their marriage about a decade earlier.

I instantly recognized the stunning blond the moment we walked in together through the press gate and I saw the name "Cheryl Reventlow" on her credentials. I'm not sure why she was there but it was either because she had something to do with Democratic party politics or perhaps was just a major donor. A lovely five or ten-minute conversation followed as we slowly made our way through the long security line while I told her what a big fan I had been. Just a week or two after the convention, I read the tragic news that her race-driver husband had been killed in a plane crash.

NBC was my first exposure to major, labor relations decision making at the most senior levels of any company. Goldstein started bringing me, his second in command, to a number of meetings with NBC chairman, Julian Goodman, and president, Herb Schlosser.

NBC operated under what I would today characterize as the committee system—at least for labor matters. Eight or ten group presidents from news, sports, stations, TV and radio networks, plus a few senior staff sat around a big conference room table. They'd listen to Goldstein present the major decision making matter under review—usually when I was there, a NABET thing. They'd debate it for a while. With Julian and Herb normally quiet, then after a round of opinions, Julian or Herb would jump in and decide or recommend the direction labor relations should follow.

Every company has its own internal governing process and this was NBC's. Being a subsidiary of the RCA Corporation, there was also the necessity of keeping the head of RCA's Industrial Relations, who had himself come from NBC, in the loop on anything significant.

The year after I began we had another NABET contract expiration. By this time in 1973, ABC and Freund had apparently made peace after their '67 Miami Beach divorce proceeding. Joint bargaining was to resume—but it was to be the last time.

Like monarch butterflies migrating back to the US after annually wintering in Mexico, both companies and NABET returned to San Diego. It was to be around five weeks beginning in late February and extending through the end of March. Each side stayed at separate but nearby hotels on Shelter Island. Ed Lynch was the International NABET president and once again its chief negotiator was the colorful network coordinator, Tom Kennedy. All of their NBC, ABC and joint local presidents were to be there—maybe around ten people. We probably had slightly more on our side from both companies.

I was a major yet still new to NBC player on that combined bargaining team. Joining my new NBC colleagues, it was also comfortable being back with my old ABC ones—especially Freund and Barnathan. Most of the time during these talks we fought hard to hold off further NABET incursions while seeking a few limited changes to increase operational flexibility.

One of the major changes we sought was lifting restrictions on the new generation of much smaller, video tape recording and playback machines that had recently been developed. It's a perfect example to illustrate the deep jurisdictional flaws nearly 40 years ago that would become so much more apparent as technology advanced and time went on. No longer big, bulky, and requiring an engineer to operate it in the industrial-type, 2-inch video tape machine recording and playback areas each company maintained, the new generation of now 3/4-inch Sony tape machines was a major technological breakthrough.

They were designed for simple operation in studios and editing rooms. But most importantly for us, they could be used in the comfort and privacy of executives' offices. Even homes. Everyone wanted one of these machines to record off-air or view program tapes sent in. No engineer was needed to hit the few, simple buttons on this vastly improved, close to consumer-type, piece of equipment that was to become so popular. In future years the tape itself and equipment became even smaller and much more consumer-friendly.

But the NABET contract, written in earlier days before these technological advances, made no distinction. It stated we had to assign a technician to operate any piece of technical equipment—no matter where it was located or how simple its operation. Whether studio equipment or new electronic recording and playback devices much more like what was emerging for home use on the purely consumer side, it all had to be operated by a union engineer.

The union resisted our proposal mightily because it would mean not assigning a NABET engineer up from the studios to the executive's office to slide in the tape, punch a few buttons and hang around for a while. And it was usually a team of two. Or sent out to the executive's home to operate this equipment—as NABET claimed and was even at one point arbitrated. Even dumb "suits" could manage to put in the cassette and hit the few buttons to play or record tapes. A great deal of NABET work would be removed if the two networks could achieve this—the beginning of a vast technological and operational revolution that both sides knew was coming.

The union reviled our proposal so much that its president referred to it repeatedly across the bargaining table in mocking tones as our little "rubber duckie." Lynch's snide reference to executives inserting tapes and hitting buttons on this device came from PBS' *Sesame Street* and its famous song about a child playing in the bathtub with the floating, rubber toy. Our "rubber duckie" though was gigantic and a portent of major changes on the horizon.

When it came, it and its digital age progeny would have a deep impact on NABET for years to come. Many hundreds of jobs would be adversely affected.

The talks did not settle by the March 31 contract expiration date. Being the customary practice of the time, retroactivity was promised as part of a short term contract extension agreement. A few months later joint talks resumed in Washington.

Under the best of circumstances, Washington is never very pleasant during the summer heat. While this summer was no different, the greater heat was coming from the congressional hearings taking place less than a half-mile away on Capitol Hill involving the Watergate break-ins. It was a fascinating time to be in the nation's capital.

After each morning's negotiations, we'd race back to our joint hotel suite to catch the latest revelations about Nixon's high crimes and misdemeanors. At the same time though, we had a job to do. Trying to fit in as much work as we could on pressing negotiations matters, we watched in stunned silence that day when Alexander Butterfield blurted out secrets about the President's hidden recording system. Those tapes, and the missing 18 minutes, finally ended Nixon's presidency the following year. The irony did not fail us that those recording machines were very much like the video ones we were busy negotiating. Nixon, known as "Tricky Dickie," as it turned out, was playing with his own "rubber duckie" well-hidden in the White House walls.

As the only sensible way, we'd take turns watching the proceedings in our joint suite one day on NBC and the following day on ABC. The hearings were produced under the special "pool" coverage provision of our NABET contract. One of the rare instances of contract flexibility earlier achieved, "pooling" allowed for only one technical crew from a single network to produce the technical coverage for all three networks' broadcast air. Whether

CBS, ABC, or NBC on any one day, the networks periodically rotated the pool assignments.

The few things that NBC and ABC managed to get from NABET at the end of the '73 talks that summer included some relief on the office video tape machines issue. And a minor change on sports remotes. Considered by us substantial at the time, those few gains were by our later standards embarrassingly modest. It has to be remembered, of course, that this was still nearly a decade before President Ronald Reagan took on the Air Traffic Controllers union in 1981 and changed forever corporate America's thinking about dealing with unions and restrictive contracts.

NABET, on the other hand, achieved once again more than it had going in. Better this, better that, better a third thing, it was always something better, or new. Incrementally over the decades of talks, at each negotiations, including the '73 one that had just been completed, NABET had demanded and gotten more. It was nearly all their agenda. Not that each item, in and of itself, was necessarily that significant, even though many were.

But the totality of the changes in this piecemeal approach over time had produced, from management's gradually growing perspective, an increasingly flawed and oppressive contract. This frustration was to become particularly unacceptable to both NBC and ABC in later years as rapid changes in technology, new platform viewing, and competition demanded increasingly more changes in the way we conducted our technical operations and employed our workforce. Office video machines, and this tiny piece on sports pickups, were just the beginning.

The two NABET contracts, already an inch and hundreds of pages thick, grew another millimeter or two in thickness and maybe another 15 or 20 pages in length as the result of the new deal.

The grievance situation though, already nuts, was getting crazier. One day we got a call from one of our studios. A soap opera was going to have a "nude bedroom" scene. Most likely, it was

How to Survive a Marriage that only ran for a season or two before it was cancelled. Relatively modest by today's standards, it was nevertheless to be a partially-clad nude-scene between an actor and actress—lots of exposed flesh for its time. The particular episode had been well-publicized for weeks in order to draw high audience ratings when the taped program was later to be broadcast—so the news had spread.

Consequently, to protect the privacy of the performers, the studio and stage were closed to anyone except the two actors and a limited crew of stagehands and technicians. There was a big sign hung on the studio door so advising everyone the studio had restricted staffing and was off-limits. One high NABET official though—perhaps it was even "X" himself—came aknocking. Surely, he arrived with the agreement in one hand and probably a grievance pad in the other. One can easily imagine his trying to peer in to see the action on the set when the door was opened a few inches. When I heard about it, the first thing that came to my mind was the head in my office door the year before. But here our Don Quixote was surely off in a quest for the unreachable heights of frontal nudity.

This errant knight arrived at the studio door, dismounted his steed, and with his lance banged on the door demanding admittance. "Hell no," was the studio manager's curt reply when he opened it a crack— "You're not essential personnel." So he slammed the door shut and locked it. Off goes our knight to the arbitrator to file an expedited arbitration to gain admission to the closed set. Why, one might ask? The answer is because the contract stated that the union had the right to show up anywhere and at any time to check for contract violations.

Contract violations? Clearly the inspection clause was not intended to satisfy some union official's interest in watching a nude scene. What a joke this was becoming within the Company and within the union. Pursuit of a little frontal nudity turned the serious grievance process into even more of a fiasco. This was, to the best of my recollection, one of the few times the arbitrator gave the union a big zero.

It was during my time with NBC that I began to serve on a number of boards of trustees for our industry health and pension benefit funds. These boards, consisting of both union and company officials, did important work in managing millions of dollars of assets to provide both medical and retirement benefits for union-represented employees not covered under the companies' own plans. Industry labor relations executives along with union officials were often asked to serve.

Over the decades, I was a trustee on many benefit plans, including NABET, AFTRA, AFM, and several IATSE national and local funds. Oftentimes important personal relationships were forged, benefiting both companies and unions, with the union officials sitting on the funds. On the AFTRA board when I was later to be a trustee, I became friendly with, among others, the famous radio, stage, and game show celebrity, Gene Rayburn. He was for decades the host of NBC's *The Match Game* as well as other shows.

Gene and I were once seat-mates on a particularly grueling, 15-hour Pan Am plane ride back from Hawaii where we were both attending a trustee benefits conference. Gene was easily recognizable and still in his advancing years a really handsome guy. The stews were never friendlier when they realized who this celebrity was. All the time I was entertained with many delightful stories of his showbiz days—but only after I took an oath of silence.

While generally a thankless volunteer job, these benefit plans normally did a great deal of good for entertainment industry employees. Employer contributions that consistently funded these plans were negotiated at contact talks and frequently were the subject of major battles. Over many decades and with careful investment, retirement plans grew into billions of dollars of assets for the benefit of plan participants.

Washington's AFTRA Executive Secretary, Evelyn Freyman, was another interesting character. She would go to become a good friend— saving my rear end numerous times. The lone female AFTRA local head nationwide for many years in a sea of men, Evelyn often referred to her stable of famous Washington-based network news correspondents at all three networks—whom she felt she was there to protect against the bad networks—as "my boys." Indeed, there were in those days no female network anchors and correspondents that she and AFTRA represented, whether in Washington or New York.

With a deep, southern accent and charm from her upbringing in Louisville, KY., and a strong presence from her stage days, she was always colorful and dramatic in her across the table presentations. Constantly lecturing us not to be so "damn amoral," she later journeyed up from Washington and gave a much-appreciated speech at my party in 1975 when I left NBC for RKO.

I had my trips to the Chicago that I knew so well to visit our WMAQ-TV and WMAQ radio stations. Whether it was NABET, AFTRA, DGA, or IATSE, it was comfortable dealing with the same unions and officials I had been arm-wrestling with when I was with ABC.

Work with AFTRA in Chicago was rewarding and successful with our local contracts covering news anchors, reporters, DJ's, and off-camera announcers. As an added aside, Amanda Jones, the daughter of Ray Jones, the local's executive secretary, achieved fame when she was crowned in 1973 Miss USA. Ray was proud of his daughter, Amanda. We could all say we practically knew her. Even though Ray was smart and a good-looking guy, he would have been the first to admit it was her mother's extraordinary looks and great talent that landed her the Miss USA title.

6

The Dying Days of News Film

NBC's fifth owned TV station—after New York, Los Angeles, Chicago, and Washington—was Cleveland. It was similar in many ways to ABC's fifth market of Detroit, also in the Midwest. But with Cleveland's WKYC-TV being a NABET station, we were not nearly as fortunate as ABC was in enjoying its more moderate IBEW relationship.

Cleveland's management was continually grousing over the fact that its technicians had to be paid and treated the same as the other NBC engineering employees in its much bigger and much more profitable markets. Cleveland ranked number ten among America's largest cities, but it was paying as if it was number one or two—the only station in town to do so. While management was entirely correct in its frequently expressed frustrations, NBC never had the muscle to break out of this unfair arrangement. Fortunately though, Cleveland's NABET grievance and arbitration culture did not resemble the toxic one at our other stations.

NBC's Cleveland also had a very strong IATSE presence. Adrian Short was the head of two different IA local unions.

The station's stagehands were in one local while its sound and lighting technicians assigned to news gathering were in the other. A genuine character the likes of which I had never met before or since, Adrian, known to all as "Junior," would go on to present a political challenge to IATSE's top national leadership. Years later though, Short was forgiven and would be appointed an International vice president.

Junior and I would frequently have dinner together on my occasional visits. He'd sometimes bring his wife and often an offspring or two. Once at one of his favorite Italian restaurants, Swingo's, we sat at a table next to famous songwriter, Sammy Cahn. Normally busy writing songs for Frank Sinatra, Cahn was singing his own tunes that evening at a local club to make a few extra bucks. That night we had a delightful conversation from our adjacent table. One of Short's two sons, Dale, who was to become a successful Cleveland attorney, joined us that evening. Junior had wanted me to meet Dale and later asked if I would write a law school recommendation, which I gladly did.

Short was the only union official I ever met who I know for sure carried a gun. I discovered this when he picked me up one day at the Cleveland airport and asked me to get something out of his glove compartment. Out tumbled a small gun. Later learning it was a Beretta, it shocked the hell out of me. I am fairly certain though that it was no accident because Short, as I was to find out, was normally too careful. I think he just wanted to check out my reaction.

His stagehands talks were always interesting. He'd normally bring along with him several of his other union officials—real characters right out of a Damon Runyon story. There was also an 80-something year old International New York IA rep sent by the International president to keep his eye on Short and the talks. After a Friday meeting, Short once invited me to stay over to attend his next day's annual membership picnic at a local park. The 80-year old was also there and that's when I discovered just how much he liked his booze— when he passed out and fell asleep in the back of a truck. Maybe the sauce had kept him alive all those years.

The octogenarian union official and I became friends despite the fact that he was twice my age. Most often over drinks, and never less than several, he would assure me that the International president would never give Short any authorization to strike NBC. Oh, how I loved to get that news. Occasionally on Fridays back in New York, the same rep would call in mid-afternoon and invite me to join him and one or two other industry negotiators at a bar near the IA offices for a few "pops," as he would call it, on my way home for the weekend. Such moments with the octo-guy were priceless.

Short went on to challenge NBC when we, like ABC, were just about ready to turn over to NABET the next generation of news gathering cameras. We had no choice because the new cameras were both electronic and video tape. Film, the basis for the IA's news jurisdiction, was going away. In a few years it would be gone. I'm sure all of us in senior labor relations management at all three networks would have preferred allowing the IA to continue doing the work with the new cameras, but the NABET contracts were clear and granted us no such option.

The acknowledgement of NABET's jurisdiction followed the huge technological change sweeping the broadcasting industry. The result nationwide only a few years later when the transition was completed would be the loss of many hundreds of IA represented news film workers at networks and stations throughout America. Short though was the only IA official in the country to mount a challenge to the loss of these jobs. Perhaps as many as a thousand or more excellent, high paying, IATSE represented TV positions in news film as cameramen, sound and lighting technicians, editors, and processors at ABC, NBC, and CBS would ultimately transition away from the IA. NABET at ABC and NBC, and the IBEW at CBS, were to be the beneficiaries of this sweeping change.

Short's grievance was filed on behalf of his few dozen sound and lighting technicians who worked for NBC in Cleveland and were soon to lose their jobs. It became a major issue and resulted in a monumental, multiple day, arbitration hearing in Cleveland in 1975 which I attended and where I testified.

NBC's case was presented by one of the lawyers I'd recently hired, Irv Brand. Irv, who shared my Lafayette College background, was a great piece of talent. Smart as can be, fast on his feet, and a quick learner, he never allowed anyone to take advantage. A smart litigator, Irv stayed with NBC for decades, rose to vice presidential rank, and achieved high prominence in the NBC labor relations department. Over the decades we did many cases and negotiations together. And we remain friends.

It was the craziest arbitration hearing that I, and probably 99.99% of America's labor lawyers, then or since, have ever witnessed. The union lawyer was a distinguished Cleveland practitioner. The lawyer however, as we were to find out, had a serious problem. He had a small bottle, or maybe it was a flask, hidden away in his briefcase on the table in front of where he was seated. Periodically, he'd open the briefcase and lower his head behind it to block our view of his frequent trips to that drinking vessel. At first, some of us thought it was maybe just mouthwash, but he wasn't spitting anything out after inhaling a mouthful. After the lunch break and as the afternoon wore on, his utterances became increasingly more unhinged as it became clearer what the lawyer was up to.

As his imbibing became more frequent, his slurring got worse. Whatever was in that flask was taking over. But before he put his head down on the table later in the day and passed out, he turned the case over to his second chair assistant, a stagehand from Short's other local union. "My associate Mr. 'Z' will take over from here," pronounced the lead lawyer in garbled words as he lowered his head to the table and closed his eyes.

Everyone in the room was in a state of astonishment. Even Short and his union cohorts were abuzz. The arbitrator must have seen what was going on but tried to keep some semblance of both order and distance. At one point before he took his nap, the lawyer had tried to light his pen that he put in his mouth when he playfully, it seemed, mistook it for a cigar. Waking up at one point as his surprised stagehand/lawyer associate was fumbling through their presentation, he loudly proclaimed "objection," before putting his head back down on the table and again going to sleep.

There were lot of job combinations in the broadcasting industry with which I was familiar, but stagehand/lawyer, however, was not one of them. Short had been proud in the lead-up to this case to tell me that this stagehand character actually had a law degree. I had no reason to doubt Junior's veracity, but strong legal skills were not exactly on display that day.

This individual, surely not expecting to become the main lawyer pleading the union's case but only serving as an assistant, or more appropriately a prop, took over in his totally inexperienced way from the passed-out lead lawyer. At one point in his attempted legal glibness and show of deep erudition he talked about the Supreme Court's famous trio of labor cases that any serious labor practitioner knew quite well. He, however, mispronounced it by calling it the arbitration "triology" (sic).

Adding to the surrealistic atmosphere of this hearing, the arbitrator, well-known himself in the field of labor arbitrations, had brought along his elderly mother and asked our permission to allow her to observe. The grey-haired lady, with hair piled up—in a scene right out of Grant Wood's *American Gothic*—sat behind him ramrod straight. With a constant, glowing expression on her face, she watched as her beloved son presided over the hearing and a passed-out, drunken lawyer.

After another day or two of hearing at which I testified and then briefs were filed, some months later we finally got our decision. The arbitrator, not surprisingly, found in favor of the company. Despite his loss, Junior Short is to be credited for his unique challenging of NBC's awarding this work to NABET.

The Cleveland arbitration smash hit was far funnier than any skit that ever would be written for NBC's new entertainment show that happened to be premiering that same year—*Saturday Night Live.*

We got a call one day in our 30 Rock offices sometime in 1975. It was from an NBC executive I had never heard of before by the name of Lorne Michaels. Lorne had a new programming idea to fill the time slot NBC was developing for its late night Saturday schedule. Not only was it a new concept, it was to be totally revolutionary—a live entertainment show of comedy skits, band instrumental and vocal music, and other features. Lorne needed to talk though his ideas with the labor relations experts. Intending to bring in a cast of little known television actors whom he was about to dub the "Not Ready for Primetime Players," he needed our help to sort through the various union issues he was facing in mounting such a live show. Nothing like this had ever been tried before.

Assigning one of my key people to do the bulk of the work, we approached the writers union—the WGA, and the actors' union—AFTRA, to try to negotiate some special deals to help bring down the hefty production costs. Applying the existing union contracts would have been far too costly for a startup show that might last only a few weeks. So we needed the unions to make some concessions. Thus the star-studded original cast of John Belushi, Chevy Chase, Dan Ackroyd, Jane Curtin, Garrett Morris, Laraine Newman, and Gilda Ratner was born. To be called initially *NBC Saturday Night* when it went on the air, the title soon morphed into *Saturday Night Live.* It debuted in October of '75 shortly before I left NBC. Little did we know that this temporary show would be a huge hit and survive—still under Lorne Michaels—for 46 years and counting.

As an interesting side note to the transition from film cameras to ENG, Junior Short's older son, Tom Short, had participated in the Cleveland hearing that confirmed IATSE's fate. He worked for NBC and was there as a member of the sound and lighting local union headed by his dad that was about to lose its work to NABET. That loss served to color his views of NABET forevermore. Short would soon leave Cleveland for New York. Rising up through the union's political ranks, he would first become International secretary-treasurer.

Later on in the early '90s, as *NBC Saturday Night Live* was still coasting along—with several dozen IA stagehands, as well as numerous IA hair and makeup artists and wardrobe attendants—Short would go on to serve as the International president of IATSE. Ironically, it was the same job his father had long coveted but never achieved. Tom Short served in that top position for nearly 15 years and left quite a record of accomplishment behind. For much of that time we were very good friends, based initially upon our Cleveland days and his father's relationship with me.

Before news film technology would be sent to its grave, there was one more round of national news film negotiations in the mid-'70s between the three networks and the IA. News crews normally had three people—a cameraman, a sound man, and a lighting man. Sometimes there was even a fourth when shooting a documentary with an assistant cameraman assigned. It was a time when technical jobs in the industry were almost entirely male and positions were called "men," as in "cameramen." Few women had these jobs and none certainly worked on IATSE film crews. Those film cameras were big and heavy. And the bulky lighting and sound equipment also took a great deal of physical strength to carry and set up.

"Camera" was the earlier set of these industry-wide talks and involved just the shooter on these camera crews that were represented by one group of IA locals. The other two crew members—the sound and lighting technicians—were represented by another set of IA locals and were to be involved in a second round of three-network talks the following year. ABC, CBS, and NBC negotiated both sets of talks together, and I represented NBC.

The camera talks took place in Phoenix with the three IATSE unions whose jurisdiction was divided up across the country into three large, contiguous slices—the New York, Chicago, and Los Angeles locals.

The New York camera local, the largest and most influential, experienced a change in its elected leadership shortly before the talks began. Its longtime counsel, Harold Spivak, admired by all parties, found himself on the outs with the newly elected leaders. Since Harold also represented the International IA union, which was in overall charge of these talks, it was a little awkward for the union side because he would be there regardless. Sidetracking Spivak, the New York local had gone out and hired a special labor consultant, the noted attorney and famed mediator, Theodore "Ted" Kheel.

Despite the contract's excellent pay and working conditions, the New York local was apparently dissatisfied and had brought in Kheel to show all of us, including Spivak, how negotiations should be handled. Up to that point though, Kheel had never been involved in any prior broadcasting industry labor talks. Unfamiliar as he was with the nuanced points and unusual provisions of the camera contract, as well as the basic operational elements of news gathering itself, Kheel needed to do a lot of homework to get up to speed.

Having heard the news the week before that he had been hired, all of us network negotiators expected Kheel would arrive at the table not only fully briefed but also fully ready to go into combat. Imagine our amazement when the Sunday night before the talks were to begin, a few of us on the company side were sitting at a table having dinner in the restaurant at the hotel where both sides were staying and overheard a conversation. There was a high barrier next to us separating our table visually from the table on the other side of the wall, and while we couldn't see anyone, we could hear voices.

It was a surprise suddenly to recognize Harold Spivak's voice and hear him talking to another person we soon realized had to Kheel.

Harold was giving him a tutorial on the key points of the contract we'd be negotiating the next day. It was like a rapid fire, cram course —Camera 101. Maybe ethically we should have banged on the wall and said something, but it was such a shock and so amusing to listen to that we just didn't. Remaining silent, within a minute or two of hearing Harold's voice and then what had to be Ted's, we picked up on the fact that Kheel had come in totally blind. Harold was reciting some of the most basic points about the camera agreement that Kheel surely should have learned well-before he arrived in Phoenix. It was nothing really confidential that we heard them discussing, but it was very revealing of how unprepared Kheel really was. Keeping our voices down while controlling our laughter, we left the restaurant after dinner unobserved.

Not surprisingly, Kheel's involvement was not a huge success. Despite his undoubtedly large paycheck, he hardly uttered a word the entire week. After Phoenix was over, he was gone. Spivak was soon back. Later making the deal in New York, it was to be the last camera negotiations before news film gave up the ghost. Sometime after the camera deal was made we all had a good laugh when in a moment of contrition we confessed to Spivak we had overheard him that night giving his tutorial to Kheel.

Six months later, the three networks moved into the second set of news film talks with the sound and lighting locals. Meeting in the giant conference room at the CBS building, we had with us locals from New York, Chicago, Los Angeles, and Washington. Headed up on its side by the IA assistant to the president, John Hall, the national table now also included Cleveland's Short. This may actually have been my first chairing of three-network talks.

Negotiations were proceeding smoothly when one morning the head of the Los Angeles local, with whom I had a good personal relationship, sat down at the table. He was sporting giant, *Top Gun* sunglasses. Not normally worn indoors and never at the table, our Tom Cruise did not remove them throughout the morning session. Rumors and speculation abounded one our side about why the shades. When I asked Junior outside in the hall after the lunch break what he knew, we got the full story.

It seems the night before the LA local leader had a great deal to drink and had gotten into an altercation with a stranger at a local bar near the Warwick hotel where the union people were staying. Blows were apparently exchanged. The result of that was the LA official banging on Short's hotel room door sometime after midnight.

In an unhappy mood at being awakened and probably half-groggy, he went to the door, asked who it was, and the LA official responded. Junior opened the door, took one look at this guy's swollen eye, and said, "Jeez, what the hell happened to you?" Our friend stepped into the room and answered, "I need to borrow your Beretta." After telling him why, Short retrieved it and gave it to him but probably regretted it the very next minute. As it fortunately turned out for all concerned, the bruised-eye LA business representative never found the other combatant and later returned the gun to Short. The shades were worn for a day or two and then disappeared from the table around the same time the deal was made.

The rest of the negotiations was relatively inconsequential compared to this high drama. But such was the stuff of some IA talks and certain IA players, unique among the many I knew in my career. Labor pains don't normally entail interesting anecdotes such as this, but sometimes it was all part of the joy on the delivery table.

Occasionally there were other joys, too. The IATSE International union had its headquarters early-on in my career in a midtown Manhattan office building overlooking the Radio City Music Hall. When negotiating there, we began to notice that the breaks were more frequent in hot and sunny weather. It turned out that the world famous, high-stepping, all-female, precision dance troupe, the Rockettes, would sunbathe on the Music Hall's rooftop between performances. Mostly attired in skimpy bikinis in open view just a few floors below our conference room, there were these several dozen, very attractive women. No breaks I ever took in my four decades of bargaining were longer, more enjoyable, or more welcomed than looking out from those windows.

The IA International president in those years was one day leading industry film talks in New York when he went completely off the rails. Known for bullying, he bellowed out a denunciation of management's chief bargainer, a good friend of mine. In the worst terms imaginable, he called him a "kike." The company side got up and swiftly left the room, vowing never to return without an apology. Several weeks later, this very same individual who had called the lawyer the most vile of religious slurs, was given the Humanitarian of the Year award by the prominent, national Jewish organization, B'nai B'rith. Quite apparently, the recipient of this good fellowship award had been chosen many months earlier. A number of senior labor relations officials from both sides attended that gala dinner. It included, I believe, the verbally-abused but probably by now apologized-to lawyer.

IATSE had a dozen or so locals in New York City representing thousands of film, Broadway theater, opera and dance, concert hall, and television workers. Mostly led by interesting characters, it seemed they were always having celebratory or anniversary dinners of one sort or another. Whether it was camera, sound and lighting technicians, stagehands, projectionists, hair, make up or wardrobe employees, graphic artists or film editors, there was always a gala event going on somewhere.

The broadcasting and film companies were always expected to buy tables for these normally black tie events usually held in hotel grand ballrooms or large catering halls. We labor relations executives sat through more dinners eating overcooked chicken, burnt but cold roasted potatoes, and limp asparagus than anyone could ever imagine. With a AFM band normally playing "Hey Look Them Over," or Freddy Mercury's "We Are the Champions," those of us labor chiefs and high union officials about to be seated on the dais would march into the room in a long, singe file. It was always good fun to be at these dinners with these interesting and very likable people.

My first date with my future wife was at one of these IA dinners. Monica and I have ever since had a good laugh about my taking her to that event—the first of maybe 30 or 40 such union galas we attended together over my four-decade career. We had met a few weeks earlier in an elevator in the Time-Life Building on our way to an event on its top floor that we were both attending. That first date a few weeks later was an IA local's celebration dinner at the old Terrace On the Park banquet hall atop the New York State Pavillon at the 1964 World's Fair site in Queens. I'm fairly certain it was the hair and makeup local, or maybe it was the wardrobe attendants.

Nothing very eventful happened at the dinner with two exceptions. Many of the IA officials who I knew and used to kid me, mostly out of envy, about my bachelor status, made a beeline over to meet Monica. They could not wait to tell her just how awful her date really was. At the dinner's end, the IATSE president—the recipient of the B'nai B'rith Humanitarian award only a short time earlier—came over as graciously as he could to hitch a ride with us in our rental vehicle back to Manhattan where he also lived.

One NBC union contract that became my special responsibility to manage was with Teamsters Local 817—the New York entertainment industry truck drivers union headed by the colorful Tommy O'Donnell. At NBC, Tommy represented a group of motorcycle couriers. Their job was to pick up news film shot at various locations around town or shipped into New York's airports from places all around the world and race it back to 30 Rock for processing and broadcast. He also represented the truck drivers who delivered scenery to the NBC soap opera studios in Manhattan and Brooklyn, but this was through a third party trucker where we were not directly engaged.

Tommy enjoyed flying his own plane—often promising to take me up with him but never did—and riding motorcycles. Formerly, as I was to find out, a Navy frogman, he relished big and very rare steaks accompanied by thick slabs of Irish bacon and a giant plate of hashed brown potatoes. In those days of the three-martini lunch so popular in broadcasting and so well-depicted in *Mad Men*, there was lots of serious Irish whiskey (while I was drinking my Bloody Marys). Tommy and I took took an immediate liking to each other that lasted until the day he died.

Maybe it was because of the extended, boozy lunches we lingered over, late into the afternoon, at his favorite steak joints. First, those were on 8th Avenue in Manhattan, later at Peter Luger's in Brooklyn, and finally at Lugar's branch on Long Island. He became a powerful figure on the New York labor scene as well as in the International Teamster organization where he was for decades a regional vice president.

Over the years, he was helpful in numerous matters for the simple reason that we liked each other. His sense of personal ethics ran so deep that he never allowed me or any other industry official to pick up the tab for meals. Funded by hefty employer contributions and renown for its generosity, his local's college scholarship fund was second to none. Annually hosting a holiday party at Long Island's Garden City Hotel, it was famous for its lavish buffet, free flowing booze, and interesting guests. Attendance was a must for any serious labor relations practitioner—management or union.

A few times years later he tried to twist my arm to accept summer jobs, real paying and working jobs, for my two sons, Josh and Alex, when they were in college. While the thought of them sitting in parked production vehicles at Manhattan movie locations, babysitting trucks being used in movie production and earning high pay was enticing, my high position and sense of ethics just wouldn't allow it. I'm certain though that others with different ethical standards accepted.

After these long, Manhattan lunches in my NBC days when I was living in Manhattan, he would have his driver drop me off at my apartment in the late afternoon. Claiming I was not in any fit condition to go back to the office and that he was only protecting me from Goldstein, he'd laugh and assert with a straight face that I gave away lots of concessions between drinks and red meat consumption. Could I be certain he was wrong and I did not sabotage NBC's interests at these lunches after my fourth drink, *Mad Men*-Don Draper-style? Absolutely I am sure. No contracts were ever changed nor side letters or writings entered into altering anything in our contract. Tommy just took particular delight in giving me these periodic ribbings.

7

CHAPTER

Rescue From Vietnam

Even though Henry Kissinger had received the 1973 Nobel Peace Prize for negotiating a settlement to the Vietnam War, the conflict did not end. While most American armed forces were withdrawn, the war between the two Vietnams, which had been raging for well over a decade during my time at both ABC and NBC, continued.

Since the war's beginnings in the '60s, the three networks had each sent over a succession of correspondents to work with locally hired, South Vietnamese film crews. It was still film in those days—the conversion to ENG cameras and satellite delivery transmission was still years away. Working out of bureaus located in Saigon's famous Caravelle hotel, NBC's correspondents and film crews, like their counterparts, hopped army or marine helicopters and were flown into danger zones to cover the many battles of the war. Whether it was Khe Sanh, Hamburger Hill, the My Lai village massacre, or the Tet offensive, raw film footage coming out of the villages, countryside, and cities of that war-torn country had to be hustled back to the Saigon airport for immediate transport to JFK airport on the first plane out.

Tommy O'Donnell's motorcycle couriers would take over at that point after the long, 15-hour flight from Asia. Perfecting the art of cajoling airport customs officials into releasing those film bags or boxes as quickly as possible, rumors circulated that little under the counter gifts or a bottle of gin could grease the skids. These guys knew all the tricks. The raw footage had to get back to 30 Rock for the immediate processing in the lab and editing before it was ready to be shown to the American public. What the viewing audience sitting at their dinner tables or living rooms each night saw were generals' pronouncements a day or two old and edited stories of battles mostly already won or lost. Electronic images and satellite transmission providing instantaneous pictures of war's terrible destruction were not there yet.

Whether CBS' Walter Cronkite, our Huntley and Brinkley, or ABC's Howard K. Smith and Frank Reynolds, the three networks were all in this race to make air, inform the public, and gain audience ratings. As one, infamous, American Civil War general on the losing side a century earlier used to say—we had to get there "the firstest with the mostest." To that end, these couriers drove big and powerful, company-provided, Harley-Davidson motorcycles. The bikes had the speed and maneuverability and the courier-cowboys had the skills. Swerving in and out of traffic through the 20 or so miles of crowded expressways, avenues, and side streets, they'd get back to 30 Rock's underground garage in record time.

After American involvement mostly ended in '73 and our forces withdrawn, the networks' news bureaus were slimmed down. But coverage continued to be a big deal since the war never ended. In the spring of '75, the war suddenly heated up when North Vietnamese forces rapidly and broadly advanced towards Saigon to take over the country. The South Vietnamese government seemed incapable of stopping the quick thrust as its forces just faded away into the countryside and entire divisions disappeared overnight.

As the South Vietnamese government was nearing a complete

collapse in late April, NBC News President Dick Wald and his senior executives were increasingly worried. Not only was it concern about the safety of the American bureau chief and his few remaining American correspondents, there was also deep worry about the fate of his Vietnamese film crews. Equally concerned for the same reasons were the senior executives at both ABC News and CBS News.

The crews had loyally worked for the three networks since the war's beginnings. With the imminent collapse of the South Vietnamese government and the North Vietnamese about to take control in Saigon, it was widely believed that our South Vietnamese employees would be viewed by the victors as allies of the hated Americans. Their lives and those of their families would be in grave danger. Needing to get our loyal, devoted, and now endangered employees out of the country quickly and safely, the networks made promises to all that they would have news film jobs waiting for them in America with our respective news organizations. With commercial flights and government charters soon ending, every resource was brought to bear to quickly get them all out of harm's way.

The three companies made hasty arrangements for the crews and desperate families, traveling light in many cases, with no possessions except what they could carry, to be evacuated by any means possible. Some missing the last commercial or US government-organized flights might have gone out on the final helicopters fleeing Saigon from the rooftops of the CIA Annex and the US Embassy to aircraft carriers at sea. The famous photos and footage of those days—culminating with Saigon's April 30 fall—so well-document the chaos and insanity of the evacuation. With our help, and that of the US government, the crews and their families were among the lucky ones. The 30 or 40, plus families, were flown to the United States to start new lives and jobs at NBC, ABC, and CBS as either film cameramen or sound and lighting technicians.

All seemed to be working towards a successful resettlement and jobs in the US but for an unexpected development—the IA and its film locals suddenly announced they were going to block the promised jobs from ever happening. For decades under an exclusive hiring hall arrangement, new or open news film jobs had been controlled directly by the IA locals themselves—not by ABC, CBS, or NBC. The process was now being used to prevent us from fulfilling commitments to the people who had just been rescued.

The way the historic hiring hall arrangement had operated was that the film unions dispensed open or new jobs to brothers, fathers, sons, male cousins and male best friends, or perhaps even male neighbors of IATSE members. It was only the male line back. Seeing our actions as a direct threat to their members' and families' economic futures, IATSE's local and international union leadership, while sympathetic to our cause and the plight of the crews, refused to budge.

The three networks jointly prepared for a full-throttled fight in both the courtroom and the court of public opinion. Legal papers were prepared while Goldstein and I on behalf of NBC, along with the other two companies' labor heads, had heated and angry conversations with the IA leadership and their counsel. It was a tense period but a proud moment for those of us working on this mission when a few days later IATSE's leadership dropped its opposition.

All of the South Vietnamese refugees following their tough journey were given news film jobs at our various operations in our different cities. Although there surely followed some difficult moments with some of their new fellow IA crew members, in time it all sorted itself out. As news film operations wound down over the next several years and news gathering shifted to electronic gear, the Vietnamese contingent, along with hundreds of other IA members, converted to NABET representation at NBC and ABC, and to the IBEW at CBS.

Absent the union twist, so much of what happened in Afghanistan in August of 2021—a year before the publication of this book—is so reminiscent of the US's withdrawal from South Vietnam 46 years earlier.

The last of the original South Vietnamese group retired from the three networks about ten years ago. One such individual still working at ABC Radio at around the time I was retiring in 2009 helped me years later in 2012 when my wife and I were making plans for a trip to his native country. Giving us as a precaution the name of a relative who was a high police official in Ho Chi Minh City, formerly Saigon, fortunately we never had occasion to call that number.

On a second trip to Vietnam in '17 more than four decades after the war had ended and diplomatic relations had resumed, Monica and I visited Saigon's legendary Caravelle Hotel. We were in search of the former network news bureaus and the many ghosts who roamed the halls. Although the famous rooftop bar where war correspondents gathered after hours still remained, the bureau space was long gone to renovation. Instead we found on the hotel's outside walls large, blown-up 5'X5' photographs of the networks' most famous correspondents who had worked out of the bureaus during the war.

I posed in front of one large photo of ABC's Peter Jennings as a young war correspondent in 1966 and his Vietnamese film crew. Later sending the photo of Peter along with a note to Disney CEO Bob Iger, Bob graciously responded what a great photo it was to see Peter so young. But he gently chided me for burying the lead of the story that I was in the same shot with our long-gone, renowned anchor. Seeing the photograph of ABC's '66 South Vietnamese film crew with Peter on the Caravelle's wall during our '17 visit drew me back to my 1975 involvement. It's quite likely the three networks probably helped a few of these very same crew members shown in the '66 photo and their families on their later rescue to safety and jobs in America.

It was around this time that I developed a strong relationship with two interesting, New York IA local union figures—both of Italian ancestry, very decent, and colorful. They were directly out of another Damon Runyon story. Officials with different locals, they had become good friends. But their physical appearances and personalities were like night and day.

One, the shorter of the two by far, a bit stocky, and with a deep, gravelly voice, once proudly related the tale that he had cold-cocked a management person during bargaining when things got a little rough. But he was always professional and kind with me in our talks. He once opened up with another revealing story. When his daughter's roommate's former boyfriend, who shared a room in their apartment, refused to leave after they had broken-up, she asked her father for help. He showed up one day unannounced at the flat, sat down in their living room, and simply placed a claw-hammer on the cocktail table where he was sitting with this young man. The formerly recalcitrant individual was packed and gone in a flash—proudly boasted my friend, the claw-hammer man.

A former Golden Gloves competitor, he had grown up tough and embattled on the streets of what became known as Manhattan's Spanish Harlem. Our backgrounds had nothing in common, but we genuinely liked each other and lunched frequently. At one point a number of years later, he started to become protective of me and my family when he heard that some troubling comments had been made against me.

The other, a tall, thin character with a long, craggy face, usually in a dark raincoat, and dangling a cigarette from his lips, would call my home at night. Very conspiratorially, he never identified himself except through his deep and distinctive, Queens or maybe Brooklyn accented voice. If it was my wife who answered, she instantly recognized who it was. "Oh 'Y,'" she'd say when he'd always ask for the "chief"—"I thought it was you." If I was not there, he'd give Monica short-clipped messages about things he thought

I should know or look into. It was usually about what NABET was up to, or threats against me he had picked up on the streets.

He was a key official with the stagehands union, IATSE Local 1. Preferring breakfasts more than lunch to conduct business, he was the only person I ever knew in modern times who still called a piece of danish pastry, at his favorite Wolf's deli on West 57th Street, a "bun." I laughed every time when he would order from the waitress a "cheese bun, dear." He had a summer "bungalow," as only he would call it, in the Massachusetts Berkshire foothills that with his stagehand's carpentry skills, it was said, he had built himself.

Contract talks with his Local 1 every three years were always interesting. Overall in our news or soap studios and carpentry construction shops, the union easily represented more than 100 department heads, regulars and extra stagehands. A very tight knit and protective group, several IA International presidents over the years would in only partial amusement refer to Local 1 as more of a cult. It was absolutely true its membership ties were strong and its leadership was devoted to members and families. With that extreme loyalty always impressing me, I knew several of its leaders quite well over the years.

Unlike the Broadway theaters or Lincoln Center, the networks aways had more success at stagehands negotiations in making changes from decades old, inefficient practices that cried out for fixing. A great deal was accomplished over the years in difficult talks to streamline our studio operations, and we did it peacefully through deal-making. As a demonstration of just how good, mutual labor relations can work, this union was the only one of the three networks' multitude of contracts that did not have a no-strike clause.

Both of these IA guys—the tall, thin one in the raincoat and the shorter, more stocky one—looked after me. Over the years, together and separately, in addition to being very decent and often helpful at the bargaining table on sticky subjects when I was involved in or supervised talks with their locals, we developed relationships that became friendships. This all proved Dick Freund's teaching many years before that real friendships truly matter in the successful world of broadcasting labor relations.

As we continued our friendship, years later the former boxer became concerned about my and my family's safety. Deciding I needed a gun at home if anything bad happened, he was adamant. Even though I told him not to pursue it, apparently I did not make it clear enough that I did not want a firearm. In the meantime though, he insisted that Monica keep his name and number on her bedside table for her to call him at any hour of the night if immediate help was needed while I was away. For many years, that piece of paper stayed on the table but thankfully, Monica never had to use it. There is no doubt in my mind he would have responded quickly in person or through a close-by proxy, of which there were several, at any time of night or day.

Then one day he called me for lunch and we met at one of my favorite Italian restaurants. I always ordered for the two of us. He preferred it that way—getting a kick out of hearing me order and then the two of us dining on Italian dishes he had never before heard the names of, or eaten, in his lifelong Italian upbringing. Even though I was always paying, on one occasion he took personal offense at the restaurant's $12 charge for a bowl of raspberries we each had ordered and consumed for dessert. Motioning over the waiter when the check arrived, he spoke in his best, claw-hammer tone. The server could not get the offending berries off the check fast enough.

On this other particular occasion he proceeded to tell me he had travelled upstate the previous weekend and had a "piece" for me in a bag sitting on the floor next to him. It was, he said, direct from someone he referred to as the "old man." A shiver went down my spine as I went on to tell him, as gently as I could, that I could not take it.

I was afraid of guns in the house and had not fired one since my army days. He got upset with me when I turned him down because, he said, he had gone to a lot of trouble, vouching for me to get this special "piece." Touched and thankful, I remained adamant, and he walked away unhappy that I had rejected his act of friendship. Over time, however, his anger subsided and we remained good friends. I never asked him what he did with the gun. But every now and then he would remind me of my serious error while asking if everything was okay with my family—particularly after he learned of death threats, and bodyguards protecting my home.

This former Golden Gloves contender was such a good friend that in later years he would travel by train for over an hour to Westchester County on a Saturday morning to give boxing lessons to one of my young sons. After I had shared at lunch one day a story of my son's nasty school experiences with bullies, the Golden Glove contender got upset and insisted on doing this. "Your son has to learn how to defend himself," he shouted at me in a crowded restaurant. It worked.

My wife and I attended his daughters' weddings, which the "conspiratorial" guy also attended and with whom we sat. I remained friends with both for their lifetimes. They came to my special birthday parties Monica arranged, also attended by some of my labor relations colleagues. When each passed in later years, just a few years apart from one another, Monica and I attended their services. It was with great sadness in my heart because I knew they were true and loyal friends.

As the end of '75 approached, I had just completed a negotiations in Cleveland with AFTRA involving our on-air television reporting and anchor talent at WKYC-TV. The talks had not gone badly, but at the end there was a small issue about which station management felt strongly. It flared up into a brief walkout at midnight before the strike was settled a day or two later. Those talks are memorable because a few days before the group walked, the AFTRA official in charge had stunned me when he asked that I not "throw a monkey wrench into the wood pile." Now nearly 50 years later, I am as clueless today what that term meant as I was the day he used it. Giving him the benefit of the doubt, it may have been a bargaining expression with perhaps deeper Cleveland meaning, but that's being very generous.

In late 1975, I was busy preparing for the following March's NABET talks when I got the headhunter's call. It seemed that radio and television group owner, RKO General, was searching for an experienced lawyer to become its new corporate vice president in charge of labor relations. My NBC years had been extremely busy and satisfying but the NABET situation had become a bit oppressive.

I had grown considerably within NBC as a valued labor relations executive. Gaining much experience, I had become under Goldstein a much more seasoned and savvy negotiator. At the same time, I was developing a point of view as to what labor contracts could be rather than just accepting the status quo of what they were. Even though I was relatively happy and not looking to leave, when the call came from the headhunter for RKO General, I was more than a little interested to hear some greater detail.

8
CHAPTER

RKO Enters Stage Left

Bob Glaser made the decision to hire me while we were in a yellow cab riding up the Avenue of the Americas. I sensed it at the time. It was since confirmed to me by Bob himself on a recent visit to Paris where Bob, now in his 90s and an expat, has lived for decades. We have been friends since that day. He was on his way to an appointment, or maybe it was his favorite watering hole, the 21 Club, and I was heading back to my NBC offices at 30 Rock after the job interview.

This happened in the late fall of '75. Bob was then the head of the RKO General TV station group and had just interviewed me in his New York office, located on Broadway, for the new vice president labor position that would report to him. We hit it off from the start, but he had to leave early to get uptown. In the cab while we were chatting, he mentioned a new book he was reading on Russian history. As it turned out, I had just finished reading a new book myself on Russian history, and I asked him if his was the work by the noted historian Richard Pipes. It turned out that it was. So we chatted about that coincidence for a bit while the cab rolled on. I had always loved Russian history—and apparently so did Bob.

A few weeks earlier, I had been contacted at NBC by a headhunter for RKO General in a search for its new head of labor relations. I had not been looking to leave NBC, having been hired just shy of four years earlier and relatively content despite the NABET situation. I thought I had a good future there and might one day take Goldstein's seat. Yet the RKO job intrigued me and so I had decided to pursue the opportunity.

Joining us over the phone the day of my interview from his Los Angeles offices had been Dwight Case, the head of RKO Radio. I was to have a dual reporting relationship to each of the division heads. Bob must have convinced Dwight that any labor lawyer with not only great credentials but also someone who could easily talk about Russian history was certainly good enough to work for them. So, I was officially offered the job as Corporate Vice President in charge of Labor Relations a few days later.

The money offer was fine. So I gave my notice to Goldstein and left NBC. Dick regretted my leaving, particularly on the eve of the next year's NABET negotiations just a few months away, but he completely understood the opportunity I had been presented. I had enjoyed working for him but RKO offered higher rank, wider opportunities, and the challenge to build something from scratch.

As a broadcaster, RKO was no NBC or ABC. I had no illusions about that. Having done my research, I knew it was a subsidiary of another industrial giant like RCA—the Ohio-based, General Tire & Rubber Company. I learned after some due diligence there were some ugly skeletons hanging in its closet relating to FCC allegations of financial and business irregularities committed by both General Tire and RKO. People whose judgement I trusted told me though that the worst case scenario of the FCC taking away RKO's broadcasting licenses would never happen. Since many at the time I spoke with both in and outside of RKO agreed with this assessment, I decided to get on the RKO express.

Like Metromedia, Capital Cities, Storer, Hearst, and Group W, RKO was a major group owner of broadcasting properties. It owned in its eight cities four TV and 13 radio stations. The TV stations were two "independent" stations in New York and Los Angeles and two network affiliates in Boston and Memphis.

New York's WOR-TV, Channel 9, under FCC license challenge, initially became famous in the mid-'50s because of it its *Million Dollar Movie* franchise. It had become the first TV station to broadcast Hollywood movies after General Tire acquired RKO Radio Pictures for $25 million. When that happened, it began playing on its air the huge "million dollar" library of old RKO movies. With its small news department, it churned out a modest news presence at noon and in the evening, featured lots of syndicated, off-network re-runs, New York Mets baseball, and iconic talk show host, Joe Franklin. Claiming to have been America's first talk show host, and perhaps he was, Joe had his daily *Down Memory Lane*. Interviewing by his own, surely exaggerated-estimate over 25,000 guests during his many decades on television, Joe was a living legend.

The Boston station, WNAC-TV, was a powerful and respected CBS affiliate in the nation's tenth or eleventh ranked metropolitan market. Its broadcast signal covered much of New England. Highly profitable, it was the station involved in the original and long-running license challenge that had hung since the '60s like a dark cloud over RKO's future.

As I was to find out after I joined the Company, it was a well-run operation, ably-managed by its GM, Jim Coppersmith. Coppersmith would later go on to a long and illustrious career. First at Metromedia in New York as GM of its WNEW-TV, after that it would be with Hearst where he ran its successful Boston TV station, an ABC Network affiliate, for decades. Jim and I are still the best of friends as these pages are being written.

The two of us fought together in the trenches of several union battles with the IBEW and AFTRA. At one point a new union appeared on the scene that presented some interesting challenges of its own. Boston-bred and calling itself "9 to 5," it later morphed into a *Nine to Five* movie, starring Jane Fonda and Dolly Parton. Coppersmith made local broadcasting history when he hired Boston's first $100,000 anchor, John Henning. With its five-year contract term, Henning also became Boston's first half-million dollar news personality. It happened I was in town the day Jim closed the deal, so he invited me along to the celebratory dinner with Henning and his lawyer. The lawyer happened to be an old friend from New York who represented both AFTRA as well as some of its performers.

Our Memphis station, WHBQ-TV, was an ABC Network affiliate. It had a smaller than normal transmitter coverage area because other ABC affiliates in neighboring cities outside of Memphis encroached on its broadcasting signal. It seems that years earlier, the ABC TV Network had gone to RKO and asked it to build a bigger, more powerful transmitter to expand its relatively weak broadcasting signal. RKO's senior management, however, declined to spend the money. Because RKO was just too cheap, ABC, as it had said it would, began seeking new network affiliates in cities surrounding Memphis. When that happened and their signals reached into the Memphis area, WHBQ's dominance and audience growth remained stagnant or declined. Short-sighted decisions like that plagued RKO for years.

The RKO Memphis TV station had another claim to fame. When ABC's Al Michaels made the famous remark that 1980 Sunday morning "Do you believe in miracles? Yes!!," it happened at the winter Olympic Games at Lake Placid. It was the hockey semi-finals against the Soviet Union. Everyone watching the *Olympics on the* ABC Network across America that morning saw the broadcast and heard that unforgettable comment—with one exception. The greater-Memphis viewing audience tuned to our station never got to see or hear that magical moment because WHBQ-TV didn't broadcast it. Its program director pre-empted the Olympic coverage because of a local church service the station regularly broadcast at that same hour every Sunday.

Blessed with no divine intelligence that this semi-final contest and Michael's comment would catapult the '80 men's hockey team into everlasting fame, he and the station's GM decided the church service was more important to their local viewers. Much to its embarrassment, it was the only ABC affiliate not to broadcast this historic game. So the men of that team like Davy Silk became famous, as did its captain, Mike Eruzione, but not that winter day in Memphis, at least not for WHBQ-TV viewers. Silk went on to an outstanding NHL career with the New York Rangers and other teams. Years later, when I met him through a pension fund on which I served, I told him the story and we both shared a good laugh over RKO's Memphis hockey mistake.

RKO's fourth television station, KHJ-TV in Los Angeles, was another "indie." It also had a small news department featuring a noon and evening news product, movies, and syndicated network re-runs. Its ratings and its revenues were usually last among LA's six commercial stations, much like WOR-TV's. Even the bottom though in television meant quite handsome profits. It produced a pretty good *Oscars* special each year. The station also featured *Elvira, The Mistress of the Dark* with Elvira as its famed horror movie host. Its location on Melrose Avenue in a carved out piece of the old RKO Pictures lot was directly across from the popular Lucy's El Adobe restaurant, a favorite spot for celebrities and politicians. KHJ-TV had another serious FCC license challenge hanging over its head that everyone also thought ultimately would be dismissed.

Led by Dwight Case from his base in Los Angeles, the RKO Radio group of 13 AM and FM stations in eight cities had a strong national reputation and was a major player everywhere we had a station. It was the day of the AM Top 40 rockers and FM was just beginning its climb to eventual dominance. Factory-equipped cars were still coming off the Detroit assembly lines without any FM band.

Unlike the television station business where owning a broadcasting station was a license to print money, even with second and third rate product, consistently yielding good profit in radio was a continual challenge. With a multitude of dozens of stations and different formats in each market, living from audience rating book to book, it was much more competitive.

Whether differing shades of rock 'n roll, blues or country western, classical, jazz, talk, or all news formats, achieving consistently high ratings and good profitability when there were dozens of stations competing for ears was tough. It was not only a matter of how profitable a radio station could be, station owners could actually lose money—something unheard of with television stations. Iconic DJ personalities at music stations were often more important than the exact music format, but the right combination of the two was perfection. To be a successful radio GM and generate large profits over an extended period of time required a whole different set of skills than running a TV station, and some luck.

RKO's AM Los Angeles rocker 93KHJ led the market. Its famous DJ's during its best years had outstanding, highly popular announcing voices and unique delivery styles. The very best were legendary names—such as Robert W. Morgan, "The Real Don Steele," Charlie Tuna, "Machine Gun" Kelly, and my good friend Charlie Van Dyke. Now decades later, Charlie, recording localized ID's and news headlines from his home-studio in Phoenix, is still the announcing voice for seemingly hundreds of TV stations across the country. When one hears "tape of mass murder tonight at 11," it's usually Charlie.

Quentin Tarantino featured 93KHJ's legendary jingles and famous DJ names and voices on the soundtrack throughout his award winning 2019 movie, *Once Upon A Time In Hollywood*. Visuals of logos and posters with the station's name, symbol, and DJ faces were sprinkled throughout in background shots. KHJ-AM must have been Tarantino's favorite radio station while cruising the streets and highways growing up in Los Angeles. It's the station that Brad Pitt is seen always tuning into on the radio in his big, white Cadillac convertible. Our other big AM rocker—500 miles up the coast—KFRC-AM, also led that market in very much the same way. My friend Pat Norman was the GM in its glory days of the '70s.

In Memphis, WHBQ-AM for a while had its own well-known DJ. Rick Dees had received big press and much fame for his earlier recording of "Disco Duck" that hit two million in sales. Dees later went on to a big career in Los Angeles radio. WHBQ-AM had a lot of connections to Memphis' famed Sun Studio recording studios where Elvis Presley and so many other major country and blues artists had recorded and much of rock 'n roll began. The station's former DJ and later program director, George Klein, was a good friend with and grew up with Elvis. Story has it that he was a pallbearer at Presley's funeral.

In New York City, RKO owned the legendary 50,000 watt talker WOR-AM. Its powerful signal allowed it to be heard in many parts of the United States outside of the New York area, particularly in the Midwest, when atmospheric conditions permitted. With lead talent John A. Gambling, the popular morning show *Rambling with Gambling* that he began hosting in '59 had for decades before been hosted by his even-more famous father, John R. Gambling. As we were considered and treated by its GMs as members of the greater WOR family from nearly the day I started, Gambling would later go on to announce on WOR's air the births of our two sons, Josh and Alex.

Saturday's overnight radio shift featured WOR-TV's cross-over talk show host Joe Franklin. He'd host his live, six-hour music and nostalgia talk show from midnight until 6 A.M. When my mother,

Ruth, died in 1982, Joe announced her death on the air—and in tribute played Al Jolson's "Mammy." Many condolence calls soon flooded in.

Joe Franklin remained a somewhat strange but dear friend until the day he died in 2014. His 42 Street office was legendary for its haphazard stacking of records, books, photos, and assorted materials on his desk or even floor—seemingly rising to the ceiling. Assorted trash was everywhere making it appear his office never got cleaned. Old coffee cups, some still with scummy-liquid inside like the one I once found under my chair, crumpled napkins, and paper plates lay strewn all over. Clearly not the neatest, the Board of Health would have had a field-day in his office. The mustard stains on his ties and jacket lapels, always far too-wide or narrow, depending upon the fashion of the time, bore witness to his sloppiness.

While a slob in clothing and office habits, he was a kind and generous soul. Whether it was complimentary, opening night tickets to many Broadway shows he had been given like *La Cage Aux Folles* or books he was always receiving from publishers and constantly giving away, his heart was pure gold.

His assistants were unusual characters themselves, direct from and redefining the term "central casting." Joe came to one of my sons' bar mitzvahs and gave as a gift a signed photo of Barbara Streisand that Joe proudly boasted was worth $1500. Years later, I found dozens of the same signed photo on eBay for $10. Like Joe's gift, they were all copies. Joe loved to tear off 50 cents coupons from his Nathan's restaurant coupon book and give them to waiters as tips when he'd leave restaurants. Waiters reciprocated by loving Joe. Passersby on the street would constantly accost and demand autographs and Joe, always needing fan adulation, never refused.

Joe called me in the office one day and invited me over to his Channel 9 studio across Broadway to meet some special guests who had just appeared on his *Down Memory Lane* show. Ten minutes later I was engaged in animated conversation and doing "YMCA"-routines with The Village People. As only Joe could, he had introduced me to my new best friends as someone only slightly less important than the president of the United States. A couple of choruses of "In the Navy" followed. Beverages soon were brought in by his central casting assistants as we virtually cavorted around the studio for a good half-hour with these unusual, "macho-men" characters.

Radio head Dwight Case out in LA always drove a white Cadillac convertible just like Brad Pitt's in *Once Upon A Time In Hollywood*, Always with the top down, it was one of those city block-long, heavily chromed cars from that era that got maybe eight or nine miles to the gallon, if one was lucky. It would not surprise me if Dwight may actually have been Tarrantino's model for Pitt. Seeing Dwight on most of my visits, he loved to take me to his favorite little French restaurants such as Au Petit Cafe in Hollywood and sometimes fancier ones. Authentically French and low-key with excellent food, Au Petit was soon to become one of my favorites, too.

A great radio man, Dwight gave new meaning to the term avuncular. Always inviting Monica and myself to his annual senior staff and general managers retreats at very nice resorts, he'd bring in, through the power and influence of his RKO Radio group, major recording artists to entertain us. Once Dolly Parton and her backup group gave 25 or so RKO senior executives and spouses a private concert. Another year in San Francisco it was a solo Melissa Manchester. After the concerts were elaborate cocktail parties where the stars in this intimate setting affably mixed with RKO's managers—the very people who had helped them achieve huge audiences and earn millions.

Most of RKO's TV and radio stations were unionized. Either the IA or the IBEW were just about everywhere. So was AFTRA. There would certainly be plenty for me to do in a constant flow of negotiations, discipline matters, NLRB actions, contract interpretation questions, grievance issues, and arbitrations. Additionally, I had to keep my eye on our few non-union properties in order to keep them out of the hands of unions.

It was mostly the same officials I already knew from my ABC and NBC days. New for me though would be the predominant IBEW presence with its locals representing engineering technicians in five of our cities. Dealing with some of its reputedly tough business managers, battle-hardened from their CBS network negotiations, would be different and challenging. I had some IBEW experience from my ABC Detroit and Chicago radio days, but now it would nearly across the board and far more challenging.

After experiencing first hand the unique NABET culture at both ABC and NBC, thankfully it was missing. My luck, however, was only good for another decade.

There was to be plenty of engineering action—with IATSE in New York and the IBEW in Boston, Memphis, Washington, Los Angeles, and San Francisco. A number of their business agents were interesting characters whose personalities carried over beyond deal making at the bargaining table. Like sometimes negotiating over drinks and grilled sand dabs behind the beaded curtains in the back room of one of our favorite San Francisco restaurants, Sam's Grill—just across the street from our KFRC studios. Or maybe gently arm-wrestling over pitchers of margaritas and platters of nachos at El Cholo in Los Angeles, only a short, ten-minute drive from the KHJ lot.

We had one news writers contract in New York with the WGA East and a few contracts with the DGA covering directors and stage managers at three of our TV stations. AFTRA's various locals represented on-air talent running the range of DJ's, anchors, reporters, show hosts, and announcers at 13 of our broadcasting properties in six cities.

Radio talks in our AFTRA DJ contracts everywhere were

frequently a challenge. But they became interesting when a smattering of the off-shift DJs themselves—all-male and often big names—would show up at the table to see what was going on and lend some support. Usually kept silent by their AFTRA bosses, the uniquely-voiced but always affable guys would sometimes join the banter. On the other hand, the news people, and they were mostly men, too, always played a more active role in helping their union push for its goals and resist ours. Most of the time, unlike with technicians' negotiations, and more so with the DJ group, it was normally just about money.

I soon learned the story of how my job had been created. A number of RKO's general managers had grown unhappy with the representation they had been receiving from a lawyer at a small, New York City law firm. Feeling that the individual did not know their businesses well-enough to represent their stations properly, a few of the most senior went to their leaders, Glaser and Case. They wanted instead an inside lawyer with knowledge of the operations and with better labor relations skills than the firm possessed or could ever hope to provide. Major group owners like Metromedia and Group W had been operating this way for years. It was much like the networks but only with much smaller departments. Bob and Dwight agreed and spurred RKO's senior management into making the change happen. The result was my yellow-taxi ride uptown with Glaser and being hired.

It was more than a little dicey though because the law firm whose work I would be replacing was, in fact, the firm where the RKO chairman's brother-in-law was the senior partner. Uncomfortable when I first found this out, the feeling soon disappeared as I learned more about the RKO way of doing business. The normal corporate rules I'd seen elsewhere about nepotism at the top and around the edges just did not seem to apply. The law firm's senior partner who was the brother-in-law took the lost work in stride since it continued to handle a great deal of RKO's other legal work. It was exciting to build a department from scratch and run it. While I had grown accustomed to hiring lawyers and having them report to me, here I would be both the hiring partner as well as the managing partner.

The Bob Glaser who hired me as the result of the cab ride is one of the great Renaissance men of all time. He is the most intellectual, genuinely smart broadcasting executive that I have ever known. An avid reader and student of history, there is no book ever written worthy of reading that he has never devoured. He knows huge amounts about great food and wine, restaurants, music, films, and plays. As best as I can gather, Bob has always been this way from his earliest days in Chicago working in sales for ABC at its Midwest regional office. It was a joy having Bob as one of my bosses all those years. This was particularly true when he brought me into his inner management circle, just as Dwight Case on the radio side. Bob was a guest at Monica and my wedding in 1976 and remains a dear friend.

The RKO job was a whole new thing for me because RKO, itself a subsidiary of General Tire, had its own subsidiaries. In my new corporate role, I had labor relations responsibility for all of these businesses, except for our successful Mountain States-regional airline that was wholly-owned by RKO—Frontier Airlines. This was the original, well-managed, and profitable Frontier out of Denver that Frank Lorenzo at Continental Airlines would go on to destroy through aggressive competition in the early 1980s. I had only a few interactions with Frontier over the years but one suggestion of lasting significance I had something to do with was getting the third person out of the cockpit. Frontier was the first.

RKO's two major business lines outside of broadcasting were our cable television systems company, Cablecom General, out of Denver, Colorado, and our Pepsi Cola bottling division headquartered in Fort Wayne, Indiana. I had little to do with non-union Cablecom General, which itself owned a chain of theaters and was eventually sold in the early 1980s to Capital Cities Communications. Bottling though was huge and soon was to become a major client.

We were one of the largest Pepsi Cola bottlers outside of parent Pepsi itself. RKO owned at one time as many as ten or so Pepsi bottling franchises—in Ohio, Indiana, Louisiana, Virginia, and West Virginia. We bottled not only Pepsi product but also a few other soft drink brands, such as Vernors ginger ale, that were locally popular in some of our regions. Delivering cases of bottles and cans to the shelves of supermarkets and convenience stores, and filling vending machines, was the job of drivers who were called route salesmen. Bottling, while not as good as broadcasting, was also a very profitable business.

Bottling is where I would meet up again with my old friends, the Teamsters. We had a number of Teamster-represented plants.

It was necessary to learn the bottling business from the ground up. I spent a lot of time early-on in several midwest plants talking to the GMs, observing workers on the bottling lines, and riding with drivers in their route delivery trucks on the way to super markets. It was fascinating to see thousands of bottles zoom through those high speed filling lines. In time, I learned the business almost as well as I knew broadcasting.

Roger Shook was its first head of bottling when I arrived on the scene. A bit odd and very chatty, most people who knew Roger would smile at the mere mention of his name. Despite his strange personality, Roger was likable and knew the bottling business inside and out. He found in me a lawyer experienced in the ways of labor relations and I found in him an interesting, knowledgable, and real character—someone who appreciated my work and was very supportive.

Based in Fort Wayne, Indiana, he loved to get in his car and tour his Midwest bottling kingdom. Driving another long, white Cadillac convertible like Dwight Case's and Brad Pitt's, he once or twice invited me to join him on visits to the Indiana and Ohio plants. Roger relegated his CFO on these trips to the back seat and insisted I ride shotgun. It was a hoot stopping off at some unusual places that Roger had found on his chosen backroads route. Roger made it a point though in his travels to stay as far away from RKO's New York headquarters as he could possibly manage.

Bob Glaser had no such option. He was not only in the same New York City headquarters building on Broadway as RKO's CEO but on the same floor. It was also my floor, on the opposite end from Glaser. And two doors down from mine.

9

CHAPTER

Tires, Tennis Balls, Rockets, Movie Stars, and Broadcasting

General Tire & Rubber, more commonly known as General Tire and based in Akron, Ohio, had three subsidiaries other than RKO.

The General Tire division, one of America's largest tire manufacturers, was also based in Akron—then considered to be the rubber capital of the world. The aerospace division, Aerojet General, was headquartered in La Jolla, CA. The third, Diversitech General, also out of that same Ohio city but with many plants in the US and abroad, manufactured industrial plastics, chemicals, wall coverings, and Penn tennis balls.

RKO's longtime CEO and chairman was Tom O'Neil. As did the three other subsidiary heads, Tom reported to General Tire's chairman in Akron. The difference was that the General Tire chairman just happened to be his younger brother, Jerry O'Neil. While this reporting relationship was rumored to be more on paper than real, brotherly reporting arrangements were surely not taught as preferred practices at the Harvard Business School, which Jerry had attended in the late '40s.

RKO's own subsidiary situation was itself also somewhat unusual. Tom O'Neil had run it for decades in a manner I soon noticed was more characteristic of an independent or even a privately-owned company. With its own small board of directors whom Tom appointed, on that small board of five or six sat his brother-in-law. It was his wife's brother—the very same individual who headed up the law firm whose labor work I had just taken away.

The RKO board, such as it was, held its meetings and performed its due diligence often from a spacious conference room on the same floor as my office. The room was jealously guarded over by an O'Neil longtime, very close lieutenant who never permitted its use for any other purpose between the occasional board meetings. Never once in over a half-decade before its conversion into more useful space was I ever permitted in that room.

The conversion would take place when years later there was an executive shuffle and Tom's son, Shane, took over running the Company. The underutilized space was redesigned into an executive dining room that while flourishing had a unique culture among American corporate dining rooms. Alcohol was both encouraged and flowed freely—first with cocktails before lunch in a back lounge area and then wine with lunch. And it was not just any plonk but usually pretty nice selections, with ample refills. When I at one point raised an objection that consuming alcohol like this might not be exactly the best corporate culture to advance, one of my fellow executives, who later rose astronomically in the corporate world, told me I could always put my hand over the wine glass resting at my dining place to refuse another pour.

In my dozen years at the company, just two doors down from Tom, I saw him on site on only a handful of occasions. It was never business but mostly for social events. The sole business exception happened in the mid-'80s after my responsibilities had been expanded to include PR oversight. Not counting our initial introductory meeting which surely happened upon my 1975 hiring, the only other time I know for sure that I saw Tom on-site, close-up and personal, was his standing next to me at the urinals in the floor men's room.

Never, I am sure, did he, the CEO of our company, in my 12 years at RKO, ever discuss with me any labor relations matter or any other of my later expanded, widespread, functional responsibilities—not a note, memo, or even a question about my work. It was Tom's management style not to get involved. Whether direct or indirect, in such important matters such as labor costs, bargaining strategies, strikes, or any other functional area within my domain having a deep operational impact on his businesses, there was this bizarre silence. Decision-making affecting these areas was handled by me and the divisional presidents or the COOs Tom appointed. Whether any of them ever went to Tom to discuss anything within my business realm, I have no idea. If they did, they never shared with me that experience, or his views about anything—other than, I had been told, he was not a big fan of unions.

In my 40-year career where I interfaced often with some great CEO's, at no time had I, or would I, ever experience a CEO with such a hands-off attitude. While empowering, it was also a bit unsettling. Thinking back on it today, his unique management style and unusual governance philosophy surely played consequential roles in determining RKO's ultimate fate.

Tom's father, William F. O'Neil, a former Firestone tire dealer, had broken away from Firestone. In 1915 "Bill" founded the company in Akron, Ohio, that soon changed its name to General Tire and Rubber. Initially just a small automobile tire manufacturing company, by the time of his death in 1960, especially due to enormous strides during and following the Second World War, it had grown a very large and prosperous footprint. The empire's operations were divided at his death between two of his three sons active in the business in accordance with his and the General Tire board's wishes. The third son got a high finance position.

Tom, the oldest, kept his broadcasting and entertainment businesses that he had been running and loved so much. Jerry, the younger brother, just over a decade out of the Harvard Business School, stayed with the industrial and manufacturing parts of the enterprise for which he had been trained. Bill's wishes, which the board followed, was to appoint Jerry the new CEO of the parent General Tire. So now Tom—as he had reported to his father, such as that had been, now reported to his younger CEO brother—such as that was to be.

Tom had been a young man in his early 30s, a dozen years before his father's death, when he had started putting together from scratch his broadcasting and entertainment kingdom that was to become RKO General. One of the things that I was to learn about Tom was his extreme loyalty to old friends and associates from his earliest days. As I was to discover years later in the '80s after my duties were expanded, there were maybe a dozen or two such people who had fallen on hard times. Some actually had jobs in the company but a number didn't. The payroll for those who didn't was discretely administered by a trusted individual in RKO's corporate accounting department.

One person on that payroll was an old friend on the West Coast who became a Beverly Hills car dealer. Another was George Murphy, the former Hollywood song and dance man and the movie actor who became a US senator from California. After JFK's 1963 assassination, his former press secretary, Pierre Salinger, (who I got to know in my career during my subsequent ABC days), was temporarily appointed by California's Democratic governor to the open US senatorial seat to fill out that deceased's senator's term. In the 1964 senatorial election several months later, retired movie actor George Murphy ran against and defeated Salinger. Murphy went on to serve in the US senate for six years before himself retiring in 1970. During his six year term as senator, his friend and former fellow actor, Ronald Reagan, was governor of California.

At what point the former movie star and US senator, George Murphy, went on Tom O'Neil's private payroll is not certain. Nor it is known how they had initially become acquainted and their friendship developed. But it should be noted that Murphy had starred in some RKO Radio Pictures films before O'Neil bought the studio from Howard Hughes in the mid-'50s. While the individual amounts for Murphy and each person on the private payroll varied and were not large, they added up to a considerable sum of money.

Attending once a meeting in Akron with Shane O'Neil when he was RKO's president in the mid-'80s, I was asked a question by the new CEO. Bill Reynolds had recently taken over from Jerry O'Neil as General Tire head and the company had by now been renamed GenCorp. Undoubtedly Bill was sensitive to the highly consequential General Tire overseas bribery and private slush fund allegations that were then swirling. So he inquired about the existence of any kind of irregular payrolls or payments of which we might be aware.

Remembering well George Washington's example and thinking it better to tell Reynolds the entire truth about the cherry tree, I had a duty to say what I knew about the private payroll. It was soon thereafter chopped down. Every time I see on cable TV George Murphy as "Pop," the grizzled old soldier in the riveting Second World War drama, *Battleground,* or his other movies with young Shirley Temple, I think of that cherry tree, the axe, and Reynolds.

All of this demonstrates just how loyal Tom O'Neil was to friends and associates who'd been kind or loyal to him over the years but who had fallen on difficult times or circumstances. He had a very big heart.

Tom O'Neil had founded General Teleradio in 1948 at the incredibly young age of 32. He did it with certain New England radio and TV properties he had begun to acquire with General Tire arranged financing. Then only six years later in 1954, he bought with more General Tire money the legendary RKO Radio Pictures studios and film library for $25 million from the magnate, Howard Hughes. It was such a big deal that Tom's face appeared on that week's cover of *Newsweek* magazine.

Legend has it that Hughes let Tom takeover midair flying his private plane from Las Vegas to Los Angeles. During that flight with Tom at the controls, the deal's final details were worked out. That same legend also says the contract later that night was signed—in a public bathroom—at the Beverly Hills Hotel where Hughes lived and kept his famous bungalow for entertaining starlets like Jane Russell. Combining the newly acquired RKO Radio Pictures into the General Teleradio broadcasting company that he was building, with first radio and then TV stations and regional networks in Los Angeles, New York, Boston, and other markets, Tom changed the name of the company to RKO General.

One of RKO Radio Pictures' last theatrical releases after Tom O'Neil had bought it from Hughes was 1956's *The Conqueror*. Starring John Wayne and Susan Hayward, it had been shot in and around the same Nevada desert where the post-Second World War atomic bombs tests had been conducted. While worthy of several rotten tomatoes as one of the worst movies ever made, it's most remembered for the fact that many if not most of the cast and crew, including Wayne himself, later died from cancer. It was supposedly due to their radiation exposure on location-shooting in the nuclear-contaminated, Nevada desert.

After a few other bombs, running the RKO Pictures movie studios proved to be unsuccessful. And in '57 O'Neil decided to cut his losses and sold it. Tom though kept the rich RKO film library, later the source of and title for *Million Dollar Movie*. The buyers of the movie studio buildings were Lucille Ball and Desi Arnaz—themselves former RKO stars, and their Desilu Productions. The deal carved out a small home on Melrose Avenue at the back of the new Desilu production lot for Tom's KHJ-TV.

Everything in Tom's story, past, present, and future, shouts out that he was a big picture guy. Adept at ideas, buying, and merging businesses, he was not an operator and certainly not an administrator. He left the actual running of his businesses and attention to details to a series of others he hired along the way and trusted.

To run those businesses, RKO had a complicated and at times bewildering, senior management structure. Former CBS TV Network president and Group W Broadcasting vice-chair, Frank Shakespeare, had been hired by Tom in 1975. Frank was president and de facto COO at the time I joined. Earlier in his career, Frank had been a CBS television station GM at WCBS-TV and ran the United States Information Agency for President Nixon. For a long time—up to and including working at RKO and long thereafter—Shakespeare remained well-connected within the upper echelons of the Republican Party.

The Company's three major operating units—Glaser's TV, Case's radio, and Shook's bottling—all reported to Shakespeare. But in an unusual arrangement for any major American company of similar size and stature, neither the chief financial officer nor its general counsel reported to the Company's president and de facto COO. The CFO instead reported to O'Neil directly. The GC reported to an EVP, Hubert DeLynn, who in turn reported to CEO O'Neil. Many have long felt that this division of responsibility—taking the COO out of any responsibility over financial and legal affairs and having these two officers report to CEO O'Neil, who was not by any stretch of the imagination a curious, detail-oriented or follow-up guy, played a consequential role in determining the Company's ultimate fate.

There was one other in Tom O'Neil's high executive suite. Jack Poor, a Harvard-trained lawyer and once RKO's general counsel, he had been at Tom's side since the late 1940s. For a number of years before Shakespeare had been brought on board, Poor had been RKO's president. Now he had the title of vice-chair but no real responsibilities any of us could see.

Frank's outgoing personality was in sharp contrast with both O'Neil and Poor's. Many felt his exuberance may have rubbed Tom the wrong way. Dynamic and a supportive leader, if left to his own devices, and absent any interference or the imminent threat from the FCC hanging over RKO's head, I am convinced Shakespeare would have made the Company into something truly special. Learning as I did that he had come on board as RKO's new president only shortly before I joined, that fact had encouraged me at the time that RKO's luck was about to change. If Frank saw nothing threatening on RKO's legal horizon, I reasoned at the time, why should I.

Inspirational, he knew, encouraged, and appreciated good staff work. Once in the late '70s, he surprised me and Glaser with a bottle of Dom Perignon in his office after my previous long day and night of successful IA negotiations. Having heard the happy news about our deal coming out of the talks, which he had closely followed, he wanted to congratulate me in person. A bit out of sorts from too much late night celebrating with the boys, I was not quite prepared to see him gleefully prancing around—offering champagne toasts—when he called me up to his office that morning. Five minutes earlier, my mind and body had been nicely at rest and recovering on the couch in my own office.

It had been a tough negotiations. IATSE at the time represented our entire technical workforce of perhaps 200 or more engineers at WOR-TV, WOR-AM, and our FM station then called WXLO. Coming in as we had days earlier with a list of critical demands, the union at the 11th hour accepted our final package. We had been poised for a strike, with our engineering supervisors and management replacements ready to move in at a moment's notice if the union had walked at midnight. Shakespeare, as were we all, was grateful it had not come to that.

Because of his CBS station GM background, his deep immersion in station operations taught him a thing or two about managing costs, including those from labor. Appreciating its nuances, he was knowledgeable about what sizable staff reductions coming from the radio "combo" change I had just negotiated would bring to RKO's bottom line.

However, Shakespeare's time as president came to an end in '81 when Tom O'Neil lost confidence in him and he was moved sideways and down into another vice-chair slot. Largely because of his political connections with a new Reagan administration in Washington, and the worsening FCC situation threatening RKO's future, he must have been kept on by O'Neil in this newly created role. But his new duties would be few, and internal visibility lean.

Frank was to hang around until '85 under this new arrangement. When he left after the RKO picture had considerably darkened, President Reagan appointed him first to be US ambassador to Portugal. A few years later, Frank, a man of deep religious faith, was named by Reagan to be the first American ambassador to the Vatican. As an interesting aside, Frank once invited Monica and myself to stay with him at the American embassy in Lisbon. To our everlasting regret, we never took him up on his invitation on one of our trips to Europe.

After his leaving the Company, with RKO's hopes for FCC victory considerably darkened and my own future so much in doubt, I would go on to reach out to Frank. Sharing with him that I was looking to leave the Company, he was kind enough to introduce me to his friend, Bill Simon, Nixon's former secretary of the treasury.

Simon and I both shared Lafayette College backgrounds, which Frank had discovered and helped cement an early meeting. Over the next year or so we met on several occasions at his midtown Manhattan foundation offices. Helpful and always gracious, Simon once had to interrupt a meeting to take a call from the shipyard in

Italy that was building his new yacht. After he told me I did not have to leave the room for the call, he spent the next few minutes discussing various weaponry he wanted built into the ship for his security needs. It sounded like a very special vessel being built for the safety and protection of the former United States treasury secretary.

Jack Poor was as dry and tight a personality as they came, even tighter with money and especially other people's pay increase requests. After Shakespeare's '81 drop-down into his new vice-chair slot, Poor briefly popped back up to reassume COO duties. That meant I had the opportunity to spend more time with Poor. Not a particularly captivating speaker, he once made a dinner speech that I wrote and against my better judgement persuaded him to deliver.

It was a tense labor situation in Muncie, IN. We were facing a Teamster drive to organize our bottling plant's office workers. The union already represented the plant's 100 or more production line workers and route salesmen. Since it was one of our most difficult union situations, we had no desire to see the office staff also go over to the union. Plant and bottling division management felt a convincing speech the night before the vote from RKO's COO at a dinner we were throwing for the employees could sway the office staff to vote against the union. Knowing Jack as I did, I was not so sure, but the attempt had to be made.

Poor and I flew out there together rehearsing on the plane what he was going to say after dinner. The speech was good but the delivery was typical Poor and not so great. The next day the election took place and when the results were announced, we lost 13 to zero. Poor shortly later retired from the Company. That's when O'Neil would reorganize again—installing DeLynn as the new COO, and making him at the same time another vice-chair. Unlike Shakespeare though, Hubert's vice-chair position would be a working one.

The beauty of RKO was that with its game of musical chairs, I was pretty much left alone to operate my department and manage labor relations as I saw fit. Senior management, whoever they were at any given moment, with RKO's changing executive suite, deferred to my expertise and was pleased with my performance. I was able to engage outside attorneys whenever there was a special need and hire excellent lawyers to work for me inside as I was building the department.

I had begun practicing bargaining pro-activity when it was still a novel concept. Working closely with the general managers and their financial people, we came up with strategies to reduce restrictions and gain efficiencies. When necessary, we never shied away from slugging it out across the table or on the streets if that's what it took to achieve our goals. Our mission, even back then, was to eliminate or better control cumbersome work rules, remove excessive costs, and not agree to over-the-top demands.

Through many fraught negotiations this was accomplished. In doing so, RKO was on the leading edge of both broadcasters and bottlers. When it came to serious medical plan changes, this was one instance where labor pains to achieve our goals at the bargaining table might actually have had something to do with labor pains on the real delivery table.

Resisting union demands and beginning to shift away from the prevailing doctrine of a union's agenda always controlling labor talks had gotten big boost in corporate America after President Reagan took on the Air Traffic Controllers union in '81. Even though it took a few years to settle in, pro-activity had now become fashionable. It was a giant wake-up call for many companies to become more aggressive to reduce costs, eliminate cumbersome work rules, and regain efficiency.

My own pilgrimage down this path began around the same time as the general awakening. Broadcasting though, unlike bottling or automobile manufacturing, was blessed with technical operations that gave us a lot more leverage than a Ford Motor Company or a

US Steel to take and survive a strike. Striking workers on assembly lines could easily shut down production and end sales in many industries once inventories were exhausted. Broadcasters though could always keep operations going, despite striking technicians, when trained management replacements would step in and the on-air product would keep flowing. The unions did not like it, but after Reagan set a new national tone, many long-suffering companies got a booster shot of courage to seek needed changes at the bargaining table.

In five cities we had tough IBEW locals representing our radio and TV technicians and the IA in New York. AFTRA was everywhere and sometimes presented real challenges. As engineering or talent talks frequently came down to the wire, we often just did not know if a deal would be made. So we developed a modus operandi to have trained and prepared, non-union replacements standing by and ready to move into position as the hands moved closer to midnight. Most of the time when the unions knew our capability, acceptable final compromises were normally reached as the clock ticked on and threatened strikes were averted.

With rapidly emerging new technology, one of the biggest things we did was to negotiate out of the IBEW's radio jurisdiction, as we had in New York with the IA. Simple logic dictated there was no reason any longer to have two people in the radio announce studio performing functions when it could easily be managed by one. Why have a technician play records, insert cassettes, and operate switches and controls on the board, and a second person, a disc jockey or host, just sit there and speak into the microphone. AFTRA, the union that represented those with the golden voices and slick witticisms, the DJs, oftentimes with catchy names, won out as IATSE or IBEW radio engineering jobs faded away.

The RKO Radio stations took the nationwide lead among group owners in going "combo." 125 or more no longer necessary radio engineering positions were eliminated in a few short years representing many millions in savings. Generous severance packages were always provided for the downsized workforce that technology had made redundant.

Bottling labor relations, while a lot tougher, were also occasionally a bit more interesting than broadcasting's. While often more challenging, those talks were though never as much fun. Various Teamster locals represented our Pepsi delivery drivers and bottling plant production workers at most of our Pepsi Cola franchised bottling plants. Each plant had a population of between 100 and 150 delivery drivers, called route salesmen, bottling line employees, and warehouse workers. Bargaining was occasionally nasty, and over my dozen RKO Bottling years we had a few, tough strikes.

At one Toledo, OH, negotiations, the plate glass windows along a stretch of one exterior wall were blasted out at night by what we thought were drive-by shotgun shootings. Fortunately no one was hurt. The plant general manager surprised me by refusing to simply plywood up the windows as I suggested, and insisted, as a sign of resistance and strength, to spend the money and replace the expensive glass. Happening at least three times during the strike, the next day the broken glass would be cleaned up and new glass installed. Several nights later, it would happen again.

The Toledo GM prophetized over the phone one day that if a week went by without any broken glass, that would mean the strike was over and the union business agent would soon call. Sure enough, that day arrived when I got a call after about a week of quiet and was told it was time to fly out and make the deal. Never hammering up the plywood was not a lesson I had ever learned in law school or from any other previous bouts in the labor arena.

On another nocturnal adventure, one of our plants in Indiana was nearly hit with a Molotov cocktail tossed by an unhappy striker. There was, however, a strong wind blowing that night that blew the cocktail and flames away from the plant and set the open field from which the cocktail was launched on fire. The thrower, I heard, experienced some burns.

On still another occasion in Muncie, we had a serious situation. One of the union bargainers showed up at the table at the local Holiday Inn conference room where we were meeting. At a tense moment, he pulled back his suit jacket to show our side sitting across from them that he was wearing a shoulder holster and that it contained a gun.

When my negotiator came back to New York a bit nervous and not wanting to return to Muncie, I assured him not to be concerned because we would get him some protection. When the following week our newly engaged bodyguard joined the bargaining table - handsomely dressed in his own business suit and tie to blend in with the rest of our committee—he pulled back his jacket to show we were not intimidated. The Muncie police were called about guns on the hotel premises. However, when they showed up, it was only the RKO Pepsi bottling negotiating team that was thrown out. Someone commented that the local police who tossed us were represented by the same Teamsters local, but I never was convinced.

When Teamster strikes took place, we'd shut down the bottling lines. But we continued to deliver the Pepsi product that had been bottled and stockpiled in our large warehouses in preparation for an extended work stoppage. Having hired a special strike consultant who knew how the game had to be played, we had plenty of extra security. Picketing was raucous on the lines outside our plants but our trucks got through largely unscathed. Our consultant made sure the well- paid replacement drivers we hired to continue delivering Pepsi product had armed escorts in cars both leading and following each truck—just as a precaution. Despite the huge extra costs and logistics, the bottling managers knew, with this consultant's help, how to best protect against the local Coke bottler's incursions into Pepsi's valuable shelf space during these challenging times.

The bright side of Teamster bargaining, however, despite all the turmoil we went through, was that when tough talks ended or the occasional strike was settled, we hardly ever heard from the Teamsters again—until the contract was up for renewal in three years. The employees were happy with the contract results, and so were the union officials. The business agents were mostly interesting individuals but in a completely different way from the ones I was used to in broadcasting. I got to know a few from occasional lunches or drinks and admired the job they did representing their members. It was with a special kind of vigor that I simultaneously both respected and detested. Best of all, hardly a single grievance that I can recall was ever filed by any Teamster local at any of our bottling plants during the term of the contract once we shook hands. That can be chalked up to excellent management as well as superb labor relations—at both ends.

Once when we had a negotiations, or perhaps it was a major meeting, at our Lima, OH, Pepsi facility, the worst storm of the decade hit the Midwest. It was the blizzard of January 1978. Some of us wound up snowbound for nearly a week at the local Ramada Inn. All the interstate highways were closed because of snowdrifts and ice. There was no way to get to the Dayton airport over 70 miles away and fly home to my wife in New York. To make the situation more ominous, the hotel was running out of food to serve the stranded guests.

Our Pepsi plant general manager was busy on his snowmobile rescuing stranded truckers and taking them to his home. He even made a mercy trip in on it to the hotel one night to bring me some needed cold medication. A truck driver, stuck like the rest of us, took over cooking what little food he could find in the hotel's refrigerators and pantries. With the local TV station in Toledo off the air, all we could do was hang out in our rooms, in total boredom, reading the same issue of *Time* magazine over and over and watch the snow banks piling up. I even filed a news report or two about the blizzard on WOR Radio that played on the morning

Rambling with Gambling show—"The snow is up to my second story windows, John, and climbing fast," I reported.

My administrative assistant back in our New York offices tried every day to get me ticketed on the eastbound, mainline Amtrak train from Chicago to New York that stopped in Lima. But each night it was cancelled. Starting out first reserving a regular coach seat, by the time Thursday night rolled around four days later she had been reserving an entire sleeping compartment just to secure a single seat. But it did not matter because the train never left Chicago due to the impassable tracks.

Finally, towards the end of the week, two groups of frustrated businessmen got into rental cars and blasted our way through the snow-bank-plowed-shut entrance to the closed interstate. Carefully driving along the icy, deserted highway at very slow speeds for hours, we finally got to Dayton 75 miles away and caught planes to our home destinations. I was never so glad to see Monica. Winter travel to the Midwest was never any fun, but it had never been like this before.

Several times over the years, usually though not in winter, I arranged to bring a lawyer I had met many years before at John Cuneo's NLRB Christmas parties, Al DeMaria, out to Fort Wayne do some union avoidance training sessions. Al had been doing some other bottling work for me. It became a highlight for many managers of our non-union plants. Seeing Muncie, Toledo, and some of the other Teamster facilities, they were dedicated to keep their plants union free. Al— with his unusual, haunting refrain of "Why do you need them, why do you want them?"—had developed a national reputation and prominence as both an excellent instructor and formidable labor attorney.

10

The "Traveling-Most Man in the Company"

I had once been called that by Tom O'Brien, the president of ABC Radio News, back in my first tour of duty days at ABC around 1970. Tom was probably referring to his occasional difficulty in scheduling meetings because of my frequent travel to the Midwest.

Frequent flying at or around 36,000 feet was routine at ABC and NBC. It would only accelerate after I joined RKO. Before my four decade career would finally end decades later, thousands of hours were logged and a few million miles flown—on many kinds and sizes of aircraft and in vastly different weather conditions. Beginning in the early '80s when airlines started their frequent flying programs, at least those miles would yield some excellent, personal flying advantages for European vacations.

It usually was out to Los Angeles seven or eight times a year on various issues or negotiations with different unions. Once or twice it was even insane, same-day intercontinental round trips. In between was more normalized travel to San Francisco, Chicago, Boston, and Memphis. Occasionally it was Washington, or even Fort Lauderdale. But the trip south to our WAXY property was only made during bitter New York winters. Then there were also the short-haul flights, often with very tight connections, to the Midwest and other Pepsi bottling plant locations.

Every summer during the mid-'80s I'd try to schedule some negotiations or other work for myself in Los Angeles. There was a lot to do out there at our three stations with the IBEW, AFTRA, or our other unions. I'd take along Monica and our young sons, Josh and Alex, and we'd stay for a week, sometimes longer, at the Beverly Wilshire Hotel in Beverly Hills. Since that was my regular hotel on my normal, frequent visits, the front desk manager would normally upgrade us to a two-room suite right on, and with direct access, to the pool. It was great for Monica and the kids hanging out at the pool during the hot Los Angeles summers when I went off to work.

One year on the LA flight, around the time in '83 that the blockbuster *Return of the Jedi* was released, we were sitting in the first class cabin on a Pan Am flight to LA. Josh, aged five, was next to me. Monica and two-year old Alex were in the row behind. Seated across the aisle was a man who looked familiar. A woman who I guessed had to be his wife and their son around Josh's age were behind him. I think it was Monica who first noticed when we boarded the plane that it might be *Star Wars* star, Mark Hamill. Josh and their son, around the same age, soon found each other once the plane took off. The flight attendants just walked around the two little kids playing on the floor.

Hamill's son had a bag of toy figures, which he opened, a large assortment of *Star Wars* characters. I thought Josh and Alex had a giant collection of these figures at home with their beloved *Millennium Falcon*, but there on the floor of the cabin were maybe 15, five-inch tall, plastic characters. It included all of their favorites—Han Solo, Han's wookiee companion Chewbacca, Bubba Fat, Jabba the Hut, Lando Carlissian, and, of course, Luke Skywalker.

The kids were playing nicely when a verbal fight suddenly

erupted. Josh shouted out excitedly as he picked up one figure, "This is Luke Skywalker." Hamill's young son took major issue and yelled back, for surrounding passengers to hear, "No, that's my daddy." So it went back and forth like this for a minute or two until both Hamill and I, laughing, got up from our seats. We separated the boys and told them that they were both right. It was, we explained, both Luke Skywalker and "my daddy." After peace was restored, Mark and I introduced ourselves and we chatted across the aisle. The name RKO resonated with Hamill as I went on to describe my job of negotiating with his unions—absent any lightsaber in my hands.

Later back in New York, I arranged through RKO's theatrical people and Hamill's agent for Josh and Alex to have a meeting backstage with Skywalker. At the time, he was on Broadway playing the role of Mozart in *Amadeus*. We didn't go to the show because the boys were too young but just met backstage after the performance. Hamill had remembered the plane incident when he had been contacted and had agreed to meet and sign for both of them copies of his *Star Wars* book. Both Josh and Alex had built up this meeting with their great hero and while it was brief, the signed books are now among their valuable collectables. The live meeting though with Luke Skywalker for them has long been forgotten.

The coast-to-coast travel of my early RKO years had been mostly on American Airlines. American, like most of its competition on those trans-continental flights, flew the big, comfortable, and fuel-guzzling Boeing 747s. Its first class consisted of six rows downstairs for the non-smokers and upstairs another six rows for the first class smokers. Row 1 downstairs in the narrow nose of the aircraft faced backwards, one seat on each side of the aisle, opposite the duo of seats in row 2, with a small cocktail table in between. Since normally nobody in those days wanted to fly sitting backwards, the single seats on both sides of the aisle in row 1 were most often vacant.

I always preferred to be seated further back in row 5 or 6. There I would spread out my papers and do as much as work as I could on those long flights to prepare for negotiations or the next day's meetings. But I began to notice that the front two rows facing each other often became a little cocktail lounge if those row 1 seats were filled. Natural conversation ensued. Booze was served and kept flowing. Voices were raised as social chatter flew over the cocktail table space. The more that row 1 and 2 people facing each other drank, the louder became the conversation. Since noise always drifts backwards into the rest of an aircraft, it became annoying. It was preventing me and other business people normally populating first class from concentrating on any work we might be doing.

Further, there were more times than not that a smoker was put into that row of backwards facing, row 1 single seats. It was usually done at the last minute before takeoff when there were no more seats available in the first class smoking section in the upper deck. Frequently when it was done, I could see a person lean over from his row 1 seat and ask the person opposite him in row 2 if he could smoke. People in those days were reluctant to say no to such a request. So he, and it was usually only males in those days, would light up, and the smoke, along with the noise of their chit-chat would travel backwards to the rest of the cabin. Stewardesses most of the time did nothing about the smoking violation.

There I was in row 5 or 6 of first class, in the window seat, trying to do my work in relatively quiet and smoke-free air. But the air was filling with noise and often cigarette smoke drifting back from the ersatz cocktail lounge created in the nose of the plane. Finding both the noise and smoke extremely bothersome, I wrote to American Airlines.

I told them that United Airlines in this same 747 configuration had a closet in the front of the first class section in the nose of the plane instead of AA's two single, backwards facing seats. Clearly, with so much less an opportunity for disruptive noise and smoke, it was a much better working environment for business people flying to and from Los Angeles than what American was providing its highest paying customers. Since the cost of these premium seats was high and the competition fierce, I thought there was an outside chance American Airlines might pay some attention to my complaint. Fear of losing valuable, first class, business customers just might motivate them, but I was far from certain I'd get a reply.

A number of weeks went by before much to my amazement, I got a letter back from American. It was signed by Bob Crandall, then its head of marketing and later to become its CEO and legendary leader during its glory days. He thanked me for my note and said that he sent some of his people up in the air to check out what I had said about this bad 747 seating configuration. Going on to say that I had been exactly correct, he notified me that he was issuing orders. From that day on, all the backward facing seats and cocktail tables across the American Airlines fleet were removed and row 1 space in the nose to be converted, like United's, into a closet.

Can anyone imagine an airline today taking out any seats, let alone its highest revenue, first class seats? Crandall listened to customers. That's one reason why Bob Crandall went onto become the most successful CEO of any airline in that era. He was the kind of chief executive all airlines so desperately need today in our troubled times.

After Pan Am was allowed domestic routes following its National Airlines merger in '80 and I had switched to flying Pan Am on my way out to the West Coast, the first class cabin on one flight had two celebrities. One was Frederick "Fritz" Lowe, the acclaimed composer from the famed Broadway musical team of Lerner and Lowe. The other was the prominent television and movie actress, Mary Tyler Moore. I was used to celebrities on transcontinental flights, but this time with two was unusual. It was a Sunday night flying out to Los Angeles on one of their Pan Am 747 *Clippers*.

Being a Sunday night flight, not too many of us were interested in working but rather just relaxing at the end of a weekend.

The Pan Am stewardesses, and they loved being called "stews," were always great. Gorgeous, smart, largely international, highly competent, and gracious, they were the best of any airline—past, present, or future. Somehow, they found out that it was Lowe's birthday. So, they decided to form a small chorus and entertain him at this seat with a surprise medley of his most famous tunes from *My Fair Lady, Gigi, Camelot,* and his other musicals. They asked the first class passengers to join in, individually going from row to row—quietly telling us what they were planning and getting us ready.

There we were, flying at our standard altitude on our way to Los Angeles, well-fed after caviar, scotch smoked salmon, and filet mignon. Refreshed after several glasses of champagne and lovely wines, we joined the full first class cabin in enthusiastically singing along with the stews in a birthday tribute to Lowe. All his great tunes such as "Get Me To the Church On Time," "On the Street Where You Live," "Thank Heaven For Little Girls," "Camelot," and "Gigi" were belted out. It was a rhapsodic, joyful, moment like none other I have ever experienced on any flight—or anywhere.

Except, there was one first class passenger chose not to join in the group sing-along. It was Mary Tyler Moore. Whatever her reason, and maybe it was her deep sense of privacy, the famous actress, who had been so beloved by her television audiences, just couldn't get herself to participate. A few of us who were standing in the aisle near Fritz' seat while serenading him could not help but notice her sitting nearby, silent. It just seemed so very odd.

On another Pan Am *Clipper* out to California, there was Mel Brooks. Brooks had always been a special person for me. I loved him not just from his movies like '67's *The Producers,* but also from his earliest days doing standup comedy. His *2000 Year Old Man* routine was one of my favorites and I had the record at home. On it was the famous skit about Revolutionary War figure Paul Revere being called an "anti-Semite bastard" by Brook's character—the 2000 Year Old Man.

The great actor and film director, Carl Reiner, who died in June of 2020 at the age of 98 around the time the words on this page are being written, played the straight man in those skits. He asks the 2000 Year Old Man why he called Revere this horrible name. Brooks responds with, "Because he rode through the Massachusetts countryside on horseback crying out 'the Yiddish are comIng, the Yiddish are coming.'" In the famous skit Carl Reiner corrects him and says, "No, no, he did not say the 'Yiddish are coming,' he said the 'British are coming, the British are coming.'" The 2000 Year Old Man pauses for a moment and says, "Oh, I'll have to send a note to his mother."

So there's Brooks on the plane. Having to find a way to talk to him, I kept my eye trained and waited for him to get up and go to the toilet. That's where I would be standing outside. It was not exactly stalking but when he emerged I looked at him and said my carefully rehearsed line, "Pardon me Mr. Brooks, but did you ever send that note to Paul Revere's mother?" Looking at me for a moment with that Brooks' twinkle, he responded quickly, "So you know my work!" We exchanged a few words, my telling him how great a fan I was. Quite charming and graciously speaking with a fan, he was unlike so many of the other show business celebrities I met over the years on flights and in restaurants.

On still another flight I had the acclaimed actor, Jason Robards, Jr., as my seat mate. Of course, anyone clever enough to marry Lauren Bacall after Humphrey Bogart's death was high praise indeed. While no Bogie, he was an accomplished actor doing Eugene O'Neil's plays on Broadway and star of many noted Hollywood films. After I introduced myself as the head labor relations guy at RKO and a frequent, friendly adversary of his unions across the bargaining table, that opened up a dialogue.

I knew a consultant from the theatrical production side of the RKO business named Archer King. Archer was a real character in his own right. Before he had joined RKO, he had a long career as a theatrical agent. Recalling that Archer had once told me that he had represented, among other actors, both Gig Young and Jason Robards, I mentioned Archer's name to Robards. In doing so I was taking a chance that Archer, prone to exaggeration, had been telling me the truth. Robards at once lit up and we had a glorious five-hour trip to California exchanging many amusing Archer King stories. When I later related this story to my friend, Archer, back in New York, he could not have more pleased about my conversation with his old client.

Whether it was RKO, ABC, NBC, or Disney—both earlier and later in my career—in chalking up those millions of miles and thousands of hours for meetings, negotiations, events, and even some vacations, there were many interesting moments and not just with the normal run of celebrities.

One of my road warrior experiences was a trip to Memphis. It was in the early '80s and also on American. I was on my way for a few days of negotiations with the IBEW over a new contract at our radio and TV stations in that Mississippi River city. This was when the union negotiator, also a lawyer, had taken serious umbrage with something I had said across the table. Occasionally when I did not want to use the words "fight" or "battle" over some issue, I would substitute the less edgy term "brouhaha"—as in "I do not want to get into a brouhaha with your union over this."

Later that day the station controller pulled me aside. A bit concerned because he himself wasn't familiar with that expression, he related that the IBEW official had told him privately that I was talking down to him. I was using, complained the IBEW-guy, "some Latin term I had learned at my fancy law school." So I called him out into the hall and apologized for my use of not a legal term I had learned at law school but rather a slang expression he apparently had not heard before. It was quickly forgotten, but for this quixotic memory. Maybe it was just not a southern expression, but it told me to be a little more careful in words I chose because one never knew what could set off a brouhaha.

On perhaps that or another trip to Memphis, across the aisle from me in the small first class section, sat a rather diminutive and very proper-looking older women. She was what we used to call a "real lady." Simply but elegantly dressed, she appeared to be in her early 80s. We exchanged smiles when we were first seated and nodded hello but really did not speak. When the plane landed in Memphis and was about to pull up to the gate, the captain got on the horn from the flight deck and asked all passengers to remain seated until a special guest could be escorted off the flight. We knew immediately it had to be a very important person. But I, and I imagine all the others on board, not recognizing anyone famous, had no idea who it might be.

What looked to be the Memphis American Airlines station chief got on when the door opened while we remained seated and he walked up the aisle. He stopped at this lady across from me and said, "Mrs. MacArthur?" It was, "Yes, of course, sir" as she arose and was escorted off the plane. Those of us passengers who heard the exchange sitting nearby were silent, and in awe. It was Jean MacArthur— American royalty—the widow of five-star general and great Second World War hero, Douglas MacArthur, who had died decades earlier. I later learned she was born and raised in Tennessee, and must have been returning to visit relatives or friends still living there. At the end of the jetway as we deplaned was a large and still loud assemblage of American Airlines employees who had gathered there to greet and pay tribute both to her and her dead husband.

Decades later, my wife Monica and I visited Corregidor Island in Manila Bay on a trip to the Philippines. We saw the little cottage and famous tunnels where she had courageously lived with her husband and little boy for all those early 1942 months while the battle raged all around them. They lived under constant Japanese bombardment.

When we arrived on that famous island where so many American boys had lived and were to later perish, the flight to Memphis flowed out of my memory. When we later saw the pier from which the PT boat took them out at the beginning of their long journey to Australia—on orders from FDR himself, against the general's own wishes to stay behind with his soldiers—the memory of Mrs. MacArthur's flight with me to Memphis that day flooded back. John Ford's excellent movie, *They Were Expendable,* starring John Wayne, got it precisely right in depicting their harrowing escape.

How many times does an ordinary person have the occasion in life to say something to a former United States secretary of state? It was Henry Kissinger, and we shared the first class cabin on a flight to somewhere. As we got out of our seats into the aisle ready to deboard, I said to him, standing in front of me, "Mr. Kissinger, you and I both have the honor of having attended the same college." He smiled and responded—"Harvard?" And I said, "No, Lafayette College." We both had a laugh.

It turns out that during the Second World War, the army had set up at the college a special training program for future officers. Kissinger had studied there for the better part of a year before being shipped overseas. Many years later when I again met Kissinger at an event at the Jewish Museum of the Holocaust in New York, I reminded him of the Lafayette connection, and again we both had a good chuckle.

For someone who flies and is allergic to dogs and cats, it's very serious to sit next to someone who has brought a dog or cat onboard. For me, cats are far more dangerous. Normally, cats are carried on board by a passenger in a box or case that fits under the seat of the person in front of them. It's particularly serious on a long flight—where my breathing difficulties and eye and throat itching symptoms begin soon after takeoff and last for the duration. A very uncomfortable medical issue, I never hesitate to speak up when a person appears in a seat near or next to me with a cat or dog.

One day on a trip from Los Angeles back to New York, this attractive woman appears. Wearing large sun glasses, she says, "Pardon me" as she crosses in front of me to take her seat next to the window in the first class cabin. I see right away that she has a cat-carrying box, with a cat inside. As I am turning towards her, while she is getting adjusted in her seat, to tell her that this is impossible and she will have to check the cat and cat box under the plane, she takes off her sunglasses. I recognize immediately that she's the Broadway musical star, Bernadette Peters. It had to be around the time that she was doing *Sunday in* The *Park with George*.

Calling an audible, I said, "Oh Bernadette, so nice to be sitting next to you and I just love your work." She thanked me very graciously and I proceeded to introduce myself and what I did in "show business." We went on to have a lovely five-hour flight back to JFK, talking most of the time about the roles she had played and a bit about her three acting unions—Actors Equity, SAG, and AFTRA. She was very interested in my negotiating stories with her unions. Call me a coward, but I sat there with my eyes increasingly tearing, my voice changing, and my chest wheezing. She didn't notice any of the distress I was experiencing as I covered up my near medical emergency for the entire trip. While every moment of our lovely chit-chat was thoroughly enjoyable, Bernadette never knew her cat almost killed me.

I met and mixed with star performers in other ways than airplanes during my RKO years, and I have to admit I loved every moment of it. AFTRA once called a major conference of its New York members to launch a campaign fighting alcoholism. It was and still is a serious, common affliction among the performing community. One of the guest speakers, talking quite openly about and with great emotion from his own history with the disease, was the stage, screen musical, and TV actor Gordon MacRae. AFTRA had been looking for entertainment companies to help sponsor the conference, and I quickly signed up RKO as one of the major sponsors. At the reception before the conference began, I had the opportunity to chat at some length with the outstanding singing star of such landmark Hollywood musicals as *Carousel* and *Oklahoma*. And oh, what a beautiful morning it was.

From transcontinental wide-bodies to commuter flights, bottling was a different story. It was a lot of US Air flights. Some of the smaller Midwest cities where we had bottling plants were only accessible through those annoying connecting flights and on small aircraft. I once flew from Greensboro, NC, into a flattened-off, mountaintop Mercer County airport runway in West Virginia aboard a local carrier's six-passenger, single engine aircraft in order to visit our Pepsi bottling plant in nearby Bluefield.

The 25-minute flight was a real white-knuckle experience that I made sure would never be repeated. If the flight itself didn't do me in, the landing on that short runway, braking to a stop at the very edge before nearly toppling from the mountain, accomplished the rest. The next time I had to go to this plant I chose to drive the four hours through the Appalachian mountains.

11
CHAPTER

Shocks, Surprises, and Scholarships

Shortly before Bob Glaser was to leave the Company for his new senior position with Viacom, I got a call from a friend in the labor relations department at NBC. He went on to tell me about a group of visiting Japanese labor relations executives who would be traveling to New York the following week. They wanted to see as many different TV broadcasting facilities as they could and meet with senior labor relations executives at a number of American broadcasting companies to discuss our different labor relations rules, customs, and cultures. My friend wanted to know if I was interested, and whether RKO could host a luncheon for this group. Apparently there was going to be around 20 of them and an interpreter. Thinking this would be an interesting experience, I immediately said yes to hosting the group and showing them around the WOR-TV studios on Broadway.

Since I had no budget to host a lunch for a group this size, I went immediately to see Bob Glaser. Bob was and remains a real internationalist. He had recently been to Japan on a trip set up by Frank Shakespeare to visit the American army field commanders with whom Frank had connections through his friends at the Pentagon. It was part of Frank's idea to expand the experiences and minds of his broadcasting heads and GM's by sending them on overseas trips. Bob, with his unlimited entertainment budget, as I was hoping, jumped at the idea to host the luncheon with the visiting Japanese executives.

When the day of the visit arrived, we first met in a conference room on my floor and discussed through the interpreter our different employment cultures. All thin, black-haired and suited, white-shirted, and narrow-tied, the labor relations guys talked about the custom of jobs for life with Japanese companies, and the great difficulty in getting rid of poorly performing workers. In that latter respect, I commented Japan was not that different from us. Then after a few hours I gave them the tour of our studios. Grateful for the time and respect I had given them, they presented me the gift of a pearl tie tack. We walked the few blocks east to one of Bob's favorite restaurants that he had chosen, Christ Cella. Now long gone, it was well-known at the time for its steaks and seafood. Bob probably figured the Japanese, accustomed to their Kobe beef, would love the place.

Once we arrived, the manager directed us upstairs to the private room that Bob had reserved. Glaser and a few other RKO executives he had invited were already inside awaiting our arrival and sipping cocktails. Imagine the reaction from the Japanese when they entered. Staring them in the face were giant wall murals. Depicted from floor to ceiling on the paintings were American Army Air Force, Second World War bombers—flying bombing runs over major foreign cities. All the cities below were aflame. Our room—and I'm pretty sure it was called the "Hap Arnold" room—was named by the restaurant's owner after a legendary Army Air Force general under whom he had served and who had engineered the plans to bomb Japanese and other enemy cities.

While Glaser had thought nothing unusual about the wall decor—probably having been in that room on many occasions—the Japanese and I—certainly did. Instant shock and pain was all over their faces as they were frantically gesturing and commenting to each other in their native tongue. It had to be the equivalent of, "What the fuck is going on here with these American idiots insulting us this way?" After we spent the next few minutes tripping all over ourselves with apologies for the terrible insensitivity just shown and the anguish they were suffering at seeing their cities bombed, our stunned guests settled down. The rest of the luncheon went well, or so it seemed. I'm convinced the Japanese labor relations people never forgot the terrible insult for the rest of their days and are probably relating it in their own memoirs.

EVP Hubert DeLynn had been at RKO since the late '60s. It was Hubert who was in charge of RKO's FCC legal case and working with the Washington law firm handling the matter. A Harvard-trained lawyer, he had the legal department and its general counsel reporting to him. Hired by Tom, he was probably Tom's smartest hire ever. Without any operational experience whatsoever but hugely appreciated for his strong intellect and sound judgment, DeLynn was surprisingly promoted by Tom in '81 to be vice-chair and COO upon Jack Poor's retirement and Shakespeare's sidelining. Tom's son, Shane, would gain his EVP stripes at the same time—a further step in Tom's plan for Shane's one day soon heading the Company.

DeLynn had gotten to know me well during my six years. Interested in my views about RKO more generally, he gradually brought me into his confidences. Not shy in sharing my opinions, particularly when asked, I had told him what I thought about some executive competence, departmental structure, and the need for deep strategic planning. Of course the clock could not be turned back 20 years, but both of us remained optimistic the RKO ship could one day be righted. High among my suggestions had been bringing in major public relations help to rebuild our shattered public image. DeLynn listened and was mostly in complete accord with all my expressed views.

After his elevation to COO in '81, he promoted me to Vice President of Administration. A newly created position, it included oversight of my old labor relations responsibilities plus a myriad of new duties. Personnel, now retitled under my watch the more modern "Human Resources," benefits, equal employment opportunity, security, real estate facilities, as well as some other functions were bundled under "administration" and given to me to watch over. I knew that many of these were foreign areas, but I was to be allowed to bring in real experts reporting to me to run them.

It was an excellent position, directly on DeLynn's staff. And Hubert, respecting my skills and abilities, but mostly my judgment, gave me total independence. Reorganizing and soon hiring some very capable directors in all these functional areas, we were able to upgrade the quality of the departments and contributed to a much stronger RKO organization.

Once promoted into the new job, I would go on to leave direct involvement in labor relations matters and at the bargaining table to my newly hired labor relations director. In a few years that attorney would leave and be replaced by Olivia Cohen-Cutler. Hired from a prominent management-side labor firm the year earlier when the department expanded, Olivia had not only remarkable labor relations skills, she also possessed the vitally important right instincts and best personality traits to make those skills effective. She would go on to be a major part of my career for many years. With my new administrative position requiring so much oversight of my expanded duties, my day-to-day involvement in labor relations ground to a halt. I was kept up to speed and got involved only when required, but someone else was now in charge.

However, RKO's legal problems with the FCC over its alleged '60's sins and those committed by the parent General Tire, continued to threaten our future. Despite the new decade's change to a Republican administration in Washington under Ronald Reagan, RKO's poor treatment by the FCC and the license challenges had not gone away. Consequently, our stations' broadcasting licenses remained in grave jeopardy.

Union leaders who I would still see from time to time were always pushing me to share with them what I could about our FCC legal challenges and what I saw as the Company's future. While their members were usually the most secure in their jobs because of labor contract protection, the unions wanted answers. Like the rest of us, they were keenly aware that the FCC had first in 1975 and then again in '80 placed the RKO stations in extreme danger. A sword like this hanging over the heads of everyone was never a very pleasant topic of discussion but there was nothing more specific I could tell them.

To help counter these threats to our future while there was still some opportunity, Hubert DeLynn embarked upon a program of philanthropic and eleemosynary initiatives to build a new image and perhaps gain public support. One such initiative was a large, announced contribution to rebuild, after a disastrous '82 fire, the popular Wolf Trap Performing Arts Center outside of Washington DC. Performing concerts there every summer, the acclaimed National Symphony orchestra and other artists regularly appeared before audiences including government officials. Among those attending were influential senators, congressmen—and Supreme Court justices.

An effort was designed to tell our side of the story by drawing attention to RKO's charitable acts, like our Wolf Trap beneficence, in full-page ads we placed in major newspapers such as *The New York Times* and *The Washington Post*. Supreme Court justices and major government officials read those pages and would hopefully see those ads promoting our good name.

One assignment Hubert handed me was dealing with an

organization called the National Black Media Coalition. It was headed by an interesting, clever, and persuasive Black entrepreneur named Pluria Marshall. I would go on to become fond of Marshall and admiring of his resourcefulness, methods, and successes. Challenging our FCC licenses in a number of our cities, as it did routinely with other broadcasters, Marshall's group hit on our employment of minorities practices.

Like most broadcasting companies at the time, our numbers were not particularly strong. Since improving minority hiring and equal employment opportunities now fell within my expanded portfolio, I was in charge of devising a plan to deal with Marshall and defuse his complaints. Unlike other broadcasters, however, who could more easily weather his charges, RKO was particularly vulnerable to these efforts because of the serious FCC challenges we were facing.

A major part of the corporate initiative with Pluria was a new scholarship program. Jointly administered by both RKO and the Black Media Coalition, the RKO scholarships were to be given at mutually-selected colleges and universities in each of our eight broadcasting cities. He and I picked the schools as well as the scholarship recipients. Much of that arm-wrestling was worthy of a screenplay.

Our funding every year more than two score of several thousand dollar scholarships achieved both his goal of benefitting the Black community and our's in getting him more favorably inclined to withdraw his license challenges. Many years later, I was to learn from some Black executive friends of mine who had risen to high position in the entertainment industry that they attribute their first jobs and ultimate success to Marshall's Black Media Coalition. However, the names of his many corporate partners who funded his efforts and the scholarship program have long been forgotten.

It was enjoyable working with Pluria in some of his other efforts. RKO volunteered to host a cocktail party and buffet at the group's annual Washington conference that several hundred were to attend. Our buffet was for their Friday night event. Working with the hotel catering manager and planning the menu, we presented to Marshall an elaborate and varied selection including roast beef, ribs, chicken, turkey, ham, and many side dishes. Liking it, he advised me, however, that Capital Cities Communications, doing the Saturday night table, was going for the lobster and shrimp upgrade.

Wanting RKO to do no less, he intoned, "Jeff, "you've got to remember that this is really dinner, so you've got to put out a good spread." After Cap Cities had just set the standard, we of course were pleased to oblige. In later years when I was working at that company and became friends with the person in charge of dealing with Marshall, I never failed to thank him enough for steering us into the lobster and shrimp upgrade.

One time at Marshall's annual New York City hotel dinner for his Black Media Coalition members, Marshall placed me on the dais. I was seated next to the former Manhattan borough president, Percy Sutton. Percy was then heading a small radio company that also happened to be a license challenger of our New York radio stations. All night long while we amicably chatted we managed to skirt the issue. At the end of the dinner, there was a moment to stand, hold hands, and sing "We Shall Overcome." There I was— hand in hand with the person trying to take away our stations. For a while we avoided looking at each other but when we finally gazed into each other's eyes, deep into the "Overcome" chorus, both of us broke out in laughter.

Holding hands with Percy was unexpected. But so was trying to show former New York City mayor, Abe Beame, sitting next to me at our monthly New York Urban League board meetings, exactly what page of the agenda we were on. Serving on the Urban League board for most of my RKO years with Beame and other distinguished individuals, including Mrs. Ted Kheel and Mrs.

Cyrus Vance, and doing many good things, were just about the most rewarding experiences of my broadcasting career.

Another initiative DeLynn devised to help save our WNAC-TV license by promoting RKO's good name was the grant of several hundred thousand dollars to create an RKO scholarship fund at the Boston University College of Communications. Putting me in charge of working with Dean Bernard Redmont and school's administrators in setting up the program, I was frequently in Boston to meet with both the scholarship winners as well as key faculty. Redmont, the former CBS network and Group W news correspondent, regaled me with tales about his black market, food shortage days when years before he was running CBS News' Moscow bureau during the Soviet Union's final years.

12

Hollywood and Reagan

There was a disastrous court of appeals decision that had come down at the end of '81 which stripped RKO of our Boston TV license. That court decision had followed and sustained in part an even worse '80 FCC decision. In that startling decision, the FCC, in a partisan four to three vote, with the four Democrats in the majority, had held that RKO's and General Tire's conduct involving certain business practices were so egregious that RKO had to be not only punished but severely penalized. The capital punishment exacted by the FCC, now modified by the court, had been the loss of three RKO TV stations, including Boston. Those stations had been under license challenge and engaged in these proceedings for 15 years. Their collective market value in '81 approached or even well-exceeded $1 billion.

The painful story is complicated, much too legalistic, and terribly boring for most readers except the most curious or masochistic. Nevertheless, it should be noted the while the appeals court agreed that RKO's actions revealed it lacked the proper "character" to be a licensee of the federal government and Boston should be stripped, it decided that the part of the FCC's ruling that Boston's disqualification would automatically carry with it RKO's losing its two other two stations was unjustified and simply too punitive. The specific challenges involving KHJ-TV in Los Angeles and WOR-TV in New York were sent back to the FCC for another hearing.

The modification of the FCC order was significant and a welcoming sign. While Boston sadly was gone unless reversed on appeal, RKO could live to fight another day before the FCC and in the courts for those two other TV stations and, in effect, for all of its remaining 16 stations. RKO's prior law firm whose own actions in defending RKO had figured so prominently in the confiscatory decision had by now been dismissed by DeLynn. Our new Washington lawyers took an immediate appeal of the court of appeals decision to the United States Supreme Court, but no decision was expected before the spring of 1982.

While that appeal was pending and the cases involving our other two TV stations were sent back to the FCC for further deliberations, hope remained we might still be permitted to retain all of our stations and remain a broadcaster. That meant the Supreme Court would have to be convinced to overrule the court of appeals decision below regarding Boston—a tall order—and the FCC would have to reverse its course, too. But we were getting hammered in the press from the constant barrage of terrible news with no real effort to fight back. The external vibe was bad and the internal atmosphere it was brewing was chilling. Some quick and massive PR efforts had to be undertaken to alleviate the situation to the greatest extent possible—both within the Company and as we related to the outside world.

As late as it was, there was still time to get fully into the game and at least attempt to reverse the field. Up to that point we had been getting beaten up pretty badly in all press accounts and in the public eye but nobody was answering and telling our story in an organized and strategic way. Even at that late date with the barn doors almost completely closed, some of us thought every effort still had to be made to change our pubic image. That perhaps could affect the FCC and final court results.

This was the time when Shane O'Neil started his initiative to bring in professional PR help. Enlisting me to assist in talking to his dad who had to approve the new venture and its expected large expenditure, we met with Tom. This was the only time in my career I was in the CEO's office—two doors down from mine. After we were able to convince the first doubtful Tom, Shane and I interviewed a number of leading firms and settled on nationally-respected Burson Marsteller. It was at this time that Shane asked me to assume oversight of the person who had been nominally responsible for what had passed up to that point as PR at RKO.

Our efforts to change our image and reputation both within Washington circles and the public perception from that point on were intensified to a much higher level. Today it would be called "crisis management." A new plan was put together consisting of two fronts. Shane O'Neil was to lead a major effort on the West Coast involving celebrity movie stars to raise public awareness and DeLynn was to undertake a major rehabilitation effort where it really mattered—with government officials in Washington, DC.

The Hollywood initiative started with an idea that had been kicking around for some time. The original plan was to clean out the old RKO Radio Pictures warehouse on Western Avenue in Los Angeles and dispose of both its valuable contents as well as the real estate we owned, which probably by itself was worth in the millions. Contained in that big, *Raiders of the Lost Ark*-type warehouse, were perhaps a thousand boxes of old RKO Pictures material consisting of movie scripts, letters, memoranda, musical scores, sound recordings, notes, and assorted papers. Perhaps, there were even some old hidden movie reels nobody knew existed. With boxes piled high to the ceiling in many neat rows, legend has it that the famed "Rosebud" sled from Orson Welles' *Citizen Kane* had once been stored there, too.

Managed for the better part of the decade by a young film historian and Hollywood enthusiast, John Hall, he had spent untold hours, weeks, and months going through all of these boxes and had compiled a long inventory. Carefully cataloguing each box, he professed to know pretty much what each contained. Every now and then he'd get a call testing his skills from some film historian writing a book or producer looking for a certain document or musical score.

Flying once to New York over a weekend after I became his boss to brief me at my Long Island home on his job responsibilities, he fascinated me with his deep knowledge of RKO's rich film heritage. The RKO Pictures warehouse, the fate of its contents, and John Hall himself had become my responsibility when DeLynn had added real estate to my portfolio. Now Shane wanted me also to help out on the PR end in figuring out the best disposal.

Our new Burson Marsteller consultants started exploring ideas of what we could do with all this material from the rich Fred and Ginger, *King Kong,* and *Citizen Kane* era. Our plan had been to donate all of these boxes of historic film material for a large tax deduction to the UCLA College of Fine Arts, shut down, and then sell the Western Avenue warehouse. While we were considering that, some combination of Shane and BM came up with a major addition. It was a "let's also throw a big luncheon on the UCLA campus, invite back all the old movie stars and production chiefs still living from RKO Pictures' glory days, and make it into a really big deal." It was a brilliant idea to build up the UCLA gift while creating a lot of favorable press and goodwill. With that, we hoped we might perhaps gain some public awareness, trust, and support. It would be coming just at the right moment to help us keep our three, challenged broadcasting licenses sitting only a few miles away from UCLA—KHJ-TV, KHJ-AM and K-EARTH 101.

There was an additional piece involved of making a significant cash donation to the American Film Institute's film restoration program. Old black and white movies that had been recorded on silver nitrate film were in serious jeopardy. Sitting in boxes in some not very well-protected warehouses or film vaults, they were all not only highly inflammable but also slowly deteriorating. Large rescue grants like RKO's helped to keep many of these hundreds of old and lesser known films alive for new generations to watch and enjoy.

Since I was involved with the RKO Pictures warehouse project wearing both my real estate but more importantly my PR oversight responsibility hats, I would have to be at UCLA. Monica would love to be attending, too, with the other spouses, so we made plans for this June 1982 event and took our young sons, Josh and Alex.

BM went on to design a special, large movie poster for the event consisting of a montage of still shots from the many famous RKO films that had starred our invited guests. Six copies would be printed and each star entering would be directed to sign the posters laid out on a long table near the entrance. Done so with great flourish by all when they arrived, where the posters reside today and what each would be worth, nearly 40 years later, is anyone's guess.

The June event on the UCLA campus was a huge success. Lots of stories were published, including an eye-catching piece in *Time* magazine and nice articles in the LA papers as well as *The New York Times*. All the local television stations were there including our KHJ-TV. Local news broadcasts that night were filled with footage from the UCLA campus. CNN, just two years old, was undoubtedly there covering this important Hollywood entertainment story. There was much kissing and hugging among many old friends from the acting community. Preening before the cameras as they had mastered during their movie-stardom days, and just awaiting recycling, it came back so naturally.

This was undoubtedly the biggest luncheon gathering of

Hollywood stars since the famous 1949 25th anniversary MGM luncheon photo of its stable of leading performers and the immortal line "more stars than there are in heaven." Our group portrait that day of RKO's more than two dozen stars, with the RKO executives, was nearly as stunning. Coincidentally, Fred Astaire, who had left RKO for MGM in the early '40s to make his last musicals with actresses other than his longtime partner, Ginger Rogers, appeared in both the MGM and RKO photos. In 1949 he was seated at the MGM luncheon next to Judy Garland. Now 33 years later in our group shot, he was next to Laraine Day—sitting between him and Ginger.

The full list of former RKO stars who came to the luncheon celebration was spellbinding. Nearly two dozen, they were all in their 60s, 70s, 80s, and even one in his 90s. But they were still gorgeous and glamorous or handsome and debonair, and so gracious. The list reads like a Hollywood Who's Who. We had Ginger Rogers, Fred Astaire, Joan Leslie, Faye Wray, Laraine Day, Janet Leigh, Ralph Bellamy, Jane Russell, Rhonda Fleming, Joel McCrea and his wife Francis Dee, Guy Madison, Dorothy McGuire, Sam Jaffe, Anne Jeffries, Martha Scott, Harriet Hilliard Nelson, Jane Wyatt, Lisbeth Scott, Jane Greer, Susan Strasberg, and Virginia Mayo. Then there was my old pal, Rudy Vallée.

They had all been major Hollywood actors. Some, of course, were really big and more famous than others. Many had starred in some truly great films. They had all aged, some maybe not so well, but each and as a group were just stunning. My God, I murmured to myself, this is Fred Astaire and Ginger Rogers standing a few feet away and talking to me. None had ever been bigger. I simply could not take my eyes off of Rhonda Fleming (who died in 2020 shortly after these pages were being written). As we stood talking, I was imagining her in those great movie roles and fabulous costumes. And when I looked over at Jane Russell, I could not help but think of the special bra that Howard Hughes had designed for her around the time that he sold his RKO Radio Pictures to Tom O'Neil. Thoughts of Howard and Jane together in his bungalow on the grounds of the Beverly Hills Hotel danced in my head.

America's biggest star and former president of the Screen Actors Guild had been invited but he was headlining in Washington and could not attend. Sending his deepest regrets, Ronald Reagan, who had made a few movies for RKO, like the somewhat less than smashing hit *Cattle Queen of Montana,* was too busy playing the starring role of President.

Rudy Vallée's story is very special. Joe Franklin, our legendary New York WOR radio and TV host with whom I had become friendly, once told me that on one of my next trips to Los Angeles I had to meet his friend, the former stage, screen, nightclub, and recording artist. Rudy had been the biggest recording and radio artist of his day until he was replaced as America's number one crooner in the late 1930s by another great singer—Bing Crosby. Joe claimed he had interviewed Rudy on his *Down Memory Lane* television show dozens of times. After I called Rudy, we met for dinner on my next trip to Los Angeles at Rudy's chosen favorite restaurant, Scandia, on Sunset Boulevard.

Rudy brought his wife, Ellie. It was a lovely dinner, punctuated by an occasional display of Rudy's temper. It happened the first time when he told me he had ordered two caesar salads for himself, plus a third for Ellie, to bide the time while awaiting my late arrival. The second mild outburst occurred when he recalled in mock-anger RKO Pictures' having paid him only $28,000 for his first starring role in 1942's screwball comedy, *The Palm Beach Story.*

At about $470,000 in today's dollars, despite the huge escalation in movie star's compensation, that's way below what a star of Rudy's stature would have earned for a movie in 2022. So, maybe Rudy's remembered-beef with RKO Pictures was legitimate. He justified his two salads as a touch of getting even. Later during dessert when he was recounting some decades-earlier romantic encounters with

Ginger Rogers, Ellie leaned over and told him quietly but clearly enough for me to hear, "Oh Rudy, don't be so crude." He responded loudly, "But it's true, Ellie."

That night after the Scandia dinner, Rudy invited me to follow him back to their house in the Hollywood Hills. Living on a secluded street humorously named Rue de Vallée, he first gave me a tour of his legendary, under-the-tennis-court-museum. Filled from floor to ceiling with his show business artifacts and memorabilia, all of it was out on display. He proudly showed off his famous raccoon coats he wore and the megaphones behind which he crooned to his swooning audiences.

Proceeding up to the house, the then nearly 80-year old put on in his living room—just to entertain me—a spectacular, hour-long show of his most famous songs. Included were such tunes as his first hit recording, 1927's "Whiffenpoof Song." While strutting around as if he was on a stage, he then regaled Ellie and myself with my generation's more recognizable tunes. We're talking about songs from his comeback vehicle, the '60s Broadway musical and later film success, *How to Succeed in Business Without Really Trying.*

Rudy shared with me he had been bought the house in 1941 from the RKO Pictures star, Ann Harding, and it seemed not to have changed a wink since. Its dark lighting, old kitchen appliances— including a positively medieval toaster and dated-decor—were like stumbling across a little Norma Desmond time capsule of that era. Right from the set of *Sunset Boulevard,* I fully expected to see Gloria Swanson, William Holden, and Erich von Stroheim emerge from that kitchen at any minute.

That evening with Rudy and Ellie was uniquely a night to remember. He later sent me a Christmas greeting card with a photo of him and Ellie. With the two stretched out on top of their bed and dressed in formal, silk evening sleep wear, Rudy was holding a copy of his autobiography, *Let the Chips Fall,* while they toasted each other with champagne flutes. Once inscribing in my copy of the same book, "Maybe Jeff you and I can do a deal together some day," he and I stayed in touch for the few years he had remaining. Rudy was 81-years old that day we met again on the UCLA campus.

But, as our mutual friend Joe Franklin used to say, Rudy didn't look a day older than 80. Joe would have loved to have been invited to this event since he knew so many of the stars, especially Fred and Ginger, whom he had frequently interviewed countless times. It would have to suffice that he was featured in several movies of his own—including Woody Allen's *Broadway Danny Rose* and *Ghostbusters.* And being portrayed by the actor Billy Crystal in his hilarious skits on *Saturday Night Live.*

When Rudy and Ellie walked into the RKO Pictures luncheon that June morning and Rudy saw me, he shouted out across the room in a loud voice that surely astonished some, "Ruthizer, is that you!" As I write this, I am looking at photos I took of that UCLA day. There's one of Rudy mugging in front of an old movie poster behind him of a much more handsome Rudy from *The Palm Beach Story.* Pointing to his former, youthful self, he's sporting a huge grin.

Returning also that day was Pandro Berman, the legendary RKO production executive who worked with *King Kong's* Faye Wray when she was held in the giant gorilla's outstretched hand. He then went on to be the executive producer of *Gunga Din* as well as Fred and Ginger's great RKO musicals. Scenes with him that day reuniting with both Faye Wray and Fred and Ginger were priceless. The marvelous choreographer, Hermes Pan, who designed many of Fred and Ginger's most famous dance routines for Berman's musical productions, also attended.

It was a glorious day for the stars and their off-screen, production- colleague geniuses. Seeing many of each other for the first time in years, they were thrilled to be there mixing it up with one another and even enjoying their conversations with the "suits." Acting before the camera came back to them like riding a bike.

And dancing. On that day in the spring of '82, Fred and Ginger danced with each other—to much applause and with many cameras rolling. It was their first time taking to the floor together since their musical days on the RKO sound stages four decades earlier. It was another priceless moment.

The several senior RKO executives who flew out for the event besides Shane O'Neil and myself, included our COO DeLynn and TV head Pat Servodidio. Pat, the last GM of our Boston TV station, had by this time taken over from Glaser. After the outdoor ceremony where the thousands of John Hall's meticulously kept documents were virtually turned over the UCLA dean and a few speeches given, we all sat down in the adjacent tent for lunch.

Each senior RKO executive was asked to host a table. Monica and I chose one with two of our most favorite actresses—Janet Leigh and Dorothy McGuire. Dorothy, who had just stood next to me in the group photo, was utterly charming, sweet, and so very nice, just like the many roles she used to play. I kept thinking of her in *Friendly Persuasion* with Gary Cooper. Janet Leigh had earlier kissed me on the cheek, said something endearing, and was equally gracious. As we sat at the table talking, I was imagining her in the famous shower scene in Hitchcock's *Psycho*.

Also sitting with us was Sam Jaffe. Talking with us about his long career, Sam bore little resemblance to his younger self when he played the title role in RKO's 1939 classic *Gunga Din*, starring Cary Grant and Douglas Fairbanks Jr., or Dr. Zorba from ABC's '60's television series, *Ben Casey*. Looking not surprisingly somewhat frail at age 91, the oldest actor present, and more like the role he had played in *Ben-Hur*, he was to pass away just two years later.

Because of Ginger's early and intimate involvement in the event, I had gotten to know her a bit when we arrived in Los Angeles a day or two before it began. After my asking her to serve as kind of the stars' liaison, she very kindly agreed and would go on to do so. Later that day, she graciously accepted my request to sign a 1935

Top Hat publicity photo of her and Astaire dancing together. It still hangs on our wall. When Astaire, at the age of 83, also looking frail, signed the same photo, we were thrilled not only to have chatted with both but also to have gotten their autographs.

Arriving back at the Beverly Wilshire Hotel, we first rescued the babysitter. Then we looked closely at what we thought would be a very valuable, signed photograph. Ginger had dutifully signed it, "Dear Monica and Jeff," but Fred had written—"To Monica and Jack." Addressed to both Jeff and Jack, at least to my mind that makes it even more of a cherished item.

The West Coast event got us a great deal of excellent publicity but it was just a temporary buzz. It did nothing to drive an outpouring of public support for RKO in its legal battles with the FCC. It surely did feel good though to mix with all the stars—our movie heroes while growing up. Monica posed and fell in love with a still very handsome Guy Madison, also known as TV's *Wild Bill Hickok*. And for me, I was very content standing alongside Rhonda Fleming while also admiring Virginia Mayo across the room. I kept thinking back to Virginia's splendid role in and uttering the immortal, title-line from Samuel Goldwyn's and RKO's award-winning *The Best Years of Our Lives*—my personal all-time favorite movie. UCLA that day made for one of the best days of our lives.

Mere weeks before that June event, the Supreme Court had delivered its devastating news that it was refusing to hear RKO's appeal and overturn the loss of our Boston TV station. Depressing to all, as of that moment we were no longer in Boston just a dead man walking. Now we were now an actual corpse—laying on a slab in the FCC morgue. The only good news, if one could call it that, was that so far the rigor mortis had only set in at WNAC-TV. We left Los Angeles praying the FCC ordered proceedings involving our other stations would go better and allow us to keep our valuable KHJ-TV, WOR-TV, and all of our other properties.

After we had received the news but prior to the UCLA event I had been asked by DeLynn to go to Boston and participate in the sale of WNAC-TV's assets. For the five or six of us at that table, it was the sorriest day of our lives. It was not the kind of delivery table to which I was accustomed. Sitting across from us were the victors—a Boston super market magnet and his new partner, the other challenge group. After 15 years of trying, they had joined forces and finally succeeded in wresting ownership away from RKO. Despite our despondency, one of our goals was to make certain they were taking over our IBEW, AFTRA, and DGA contracts in order to best protect our employees after the transfer was complete.

The victors tried to be as affable as they could and not too smug, but it was difficult for them to suppress their glee. The lucky individuals were getting a major-market CBS affiliate which with an FCC license would have cost them north of $200 million. Today in 2022 its worth is probably $1 billion. It was a fire-sale. With no leverage whatsoever, we sold the building, property, equipment, and transmitter for a mere $22 million. With the final offer they presented, they were prepared to walk away if we did not accept. I actually felt as if I was back at the labor table giving one of my take it or leave it speeches, and now I knew how it felt. It was kicking and discomfort at the highest levels possible—but with none of the accompanying final joy.

On the Washington scene, our expected efforts to rehabilitate ourselves couldn't be quite as sociable as it had been on the UCLA campus. It was essential to focus in on influencing the governmental power structure if there was any hope to save our other stations. To do that, our efforts had to be far more serious—and focused.

DeLynn engaged a high-powered, Washington lobbying firm which went on to plan a series of major meetings for us during a week in the fall of 1983 while the FCC's re-determination of the KHJ-TV and WOR-TV license challenges was still pending.

The highlights were going to be a special White House meeting with President Reagan to be followed the next day by a private breakfast with the Senate Majority Leader, Tennessee Republican Senator Howard Baker. Overall, there would be between 30 and 40 senior RKO executives attending, including our remaining TV and radio GMs, news directors, and public affairs directors plus Hubert, Shane O'Neil, and some senior corporate staff such as myself. The not-so-subtle purpose was to get RKO some needed exposure directly with Reagan while ostensibly gaining insight into Washington's workings. If our FCC destiny could be boosted by building up our good name among the right decision makers, perhaps it was not too late. Whatever political influence Reagan himself might bring to the process by the right word spoken here and there, the fate of our remaining stations could be vastly improved.

The White House meeting was set up as first a private briefing by Jim Baker, the President's very powerful chief of staff. Then we'd have Reagan himself addressing us. This was such an important event that even our CEO, Tom O'Neil—who rarely attended these events—flew down to Washington.

Grabbing seats as we first entered the briefing room in the Executive Office Building, I chose one in the first row next to my friend and our TV head, Pat Servodidio. It was rather an intimate setting—with five seats in a row on each side of a center aisle and about ten rows. Pat was seated on the center aisle, almost directly in front of where the President would be standing at the lectern while addressing us. Shane O'Neil, our EVP and presumptive next Company leader, took a front row seat directly across from Servodidio on the other side of the center aisle. The front row was maybe eight feet away from where the President would be speaking to us— standing at ground level.

I'm studying a photo of the seating in that room as I'm writing this passage nearly 30 years later. And I'm still marveling at the events that unfolded.

Reagan would be running late, said Baker, as he started his briefing that ran maybe 15 minutes. The President had not yet arrived so Baker said it was okay to take a short break, leave the room, and enjoy some light refreshments the White House had set up in the reception area off to the back. He told us to hang around in that area but to be alert for the call when the President, walking over from the White House through the tunnel, would be close to arriving. Baker said he would give us about a two-minute warning to get back into our seats.

All of us left the our individual programs on our seats to claim possession and headed for the cookies and cokes in the back where we stood around chatting while waiting for Baker's two-minute warning. When it came a few minutes later, we all hustled back to the same seats we had just vacated. I was back in my front row seat. As we were seated, we heard the familiar—"Ladies and gentlemen, the President of the United States." We stood as Reagan entered from a door opposite us and marched up to the lectern.

That's when I first caught that not everyone had made it back on time. Servodidio's front row seat next to mine on the center aisle remained empty as did Shane's seat directly across from Pat's. Apparently these two had stood around chatting in the refreshments area for too long, or perhaps they had used the toilet facilities. In any event, they both had missed Baker's two-minute warning and were AWOL. While it was unfortunate these two leaders had missed Baker's shout-out, we just assumed as second best they would stand in the back of the room and observe the President's remarks from there.

As was to be expected, the room was ringed with Secret Service agents. One was standing off to the left side in the front of the room, looking out at us, and there was another to Reagan's right, on the opposite side of the room. Baker and Reagan's press secretary, Larry Speakes, stood about five or six feet away from the President to his left—in between the President and the agent on the far left side of the room. These details are important for the reader to understand only because of what next transpired.

Reagan started talking about the recent passing of RKO's veteran White House correspondent and his friend, Cliff Evans. While the President was eulogizing Evans, much to our amazement, in walked Shane. He entered from the rear. As we caught sight of him, he briskly walked down the aisle on the right side of the room, made a left turn at the bottom where the agent stood and continued walking in a path directly in front of the President to get to his seat another ten feet distant. As he passed in front of Reagan's lectern, he was mere feet away. The President casually glanced up as Shane glided by but Reagan continued talking.

As the photograph of that day so well documents, Servodidio's first-row, empty seat remained vacant throughout the White House briefing. When I turned around in my seat, I could see Pat standing at the back of the room and observing the proceedings.

Not exactly White House protocol, it must have to been difficult for Shane O'Neil to make that awkward entrance. But he did so with confidence and class. When he had realized he had missed the two-minute warning and everyone else was seated, instantaneously he must have decided he had to walk in even though the President had already begun speaking. The only path to his front row seat was to walk directly in front of the President of the United States. As the presumptive next president of RKO, he simply had no choice but to make that entrance into an event that might prove to be highly consequential for the Company.

Unlike Pat Servodidio, he could not allow himself to be standing room only in the back of the theater. SRO might be appropriate for Servodidio, with only his divisional responsibilities, but not for the O'Neil who soon would be be heading the entire Company. Looking back, I admired his ability to think quickly and adapt to circumstances in calling that audible even though he must have felt a certain degree of discomfort in doing so.

Towards the end of Reagan's briefing about his upcoming trip to China and other assorted news headlines, my peripheral vision to the left, now unimpeded by anyone sitting next to me because of Servodidio's vacant seat, spotted something going on. I caught Shane take out a piece of note paper and write something on it. Curious at what was happening, I turned my head to observe that he folded it and passed it down his front row.

The note wound up at the end of the row in the hands of Bob Williamson, the relatively new head of Radio. Bob looked over at Shane. O'Neil head and hand-motioned Bob to get out of his seat and walk the note up to the Secret Service agent standing on the left side of the room directly in front of where Bob was seated. It could not have been more than eight to ten feet distant from Bob. The agent himself was maybe 15 feet from where Reagan stood at his lectern in the center of the room, with Baker and Speakes in between.

Williamson looked at Shane and seemed to balk. But Shane motioned him again to get up and deliver the note. Obviously not wanting to get shot as an attempted assassin, as anyone might fear who gets out of his seat and suddenly walks towards a Secret Service agent in a small, safe space where the President is exposed just feet away, Williamson still balked. He was probably very mindful that Reagan had survived an assassination attempt just two years earlier, so the agent might be trigger-happy. But we could then observe him obeying his orders. Hesitantly rising from his seat, seemingly not to alarm the agent, he slow-walked the note in his outstretched arm. "Willy," as he was known, a rather big, well-over six feet and formidable-looking guy, extended his arm to show it was just a piece of paper.

Watching the whole scene play out in just a few seconds, it looked to me that the Secret Service agent appeared taken aback. Anyone's forward motion out of one's seat, to say the least, is highly unorthodox and not the least bit recommended anytime the President is in that protected bubble. As the agent was digesting the sudden movement of a pretty large individual for no apparent reason into secured presidential space, with just a moment or two to decide whether to draw his gun and shoot poor Willy dead, he thankfully made the right call.

Deciding not to kill him, he took the note from Williamson's outstretched arm, looked at it curiously for a split second, and walked it over to his left maybe seven or eight feet to where Baker was standing. Baker, who surely was watching this high drama unfolding directly in front of him, took the note, opened and read it, crumpled it, and put it into his jacket pocket.

At day's end, we were relaxing over drinks at the hotel bar and reviewing events. Someone commented on the drama of Willy's approaching the Secret Service agent and almost getting shot. Maybe it was even Willy. Shane was asked what the handwritten note had been all about. His response as best I can recall was that he was just trying to be polite and find out from chief of staff Baker if proper decorum would allow him to stand up in the room and thank Reagan for taking the time to address the assembled RKO executives. Extremely powerful at the time, Baker, the subject of a recent 2021 biography aptly entitled *The Man Who Ran Washington,* obviously did not think any expression of thanks from Shane was necessary.

The next day, there was a private 8 A.M. breakfast meeting with Senate Majority Leader Howard Baker that Hubert and the Washington lobbying firm had arranged. There were about a dozen of us senior executives, including Shane and Hubert, gathered around a round table in one of the hotel's private dining rooms.

The understanding with the Senator's's office, set up by our lobbyist, was that in return for a $10,000 speaking fee, the Senator would talk to us about the Washington scene, politics, and government in general. But there could be absolutely no discussion of RKO's legal problems then moving their way through the FCC redetermination process and probably back into the courts. Nor could there be any mention of our prior year's Boston loss in the Supreme Court. DeLynn had in advance made sure that each of us attending the breakfast knew the important ground rules.

At one point during the meeting, however, some executive, apparently not understanding this instruction or never having received it, jumped in with a few comments about how unfair the FCC and the courts had been to RKO. It was a consternating moment for the rest of us who just sat there incredulous. Baker chose to ignore it. Later in the day, Hubert shared with me privately that the senator's office had called the lobbyist to inform RKO that the senator was refusing to take the $10,000 or any fee. Clearly an honorable politician—his display of ethics and morality that day was in sharp contrast to what we see constantly unfolding around us in Washington.

At the end of the day, all of the public relations and government relations efforts that were undertaken proved useless. It was as if the Hollywood UCLA celebrity event, the Reagan White House meeting, and the millions of charitable giving had never happened. The United States government would go on not only to deprive RKO of all its radio and television broadcasting licenses but also not allow it to remain a broadcaster. All of the initiatives to rehabilitate our image were brilliantly conceived—but they were about 20 years too late.

The final curtain only happened because some new revelations soon surfaced in early '84. It had to do with a few employees at the RKO Radio Networks engaging in deliberative acts of falsified billings, ratings lies, and phony audience reports. It amounted to about $8 million-worth. At the time it went on the air just a few years earlier and achieved 1500 affiliates, the RKO Radio Network had been America's first, new radio network in over 40 years— and the first to be broadcast by satellite. While its good initial ratings and first years revenues had pointed towards it being a well-managed success, the new allegations were a crushing blow.

After an internal investigation was conducted and the facts confirmed, the new dishonesty hit RKO like a tsunami. The disaster on the horizon was clear for all to see. Again, it was another forceful demonstration of RKO somehow lacking sufficient legal and financial controls to prevent internal governance calamities. We couldn't blame this deliberate scheme to cheat on any act by General Tire. With this new stain on its already tarnished character, any hopes we still might have harbored that the FCC and the courts would allow RKO to remain a licensed broadcaster were fully and finally dashed on the rocks.

When the scope of the disaster became clear, General Tire, now known as GenCorp and operating under a new president and COO, after Jerry O'Neil had been removed, took major action. Three of RKO's most senior executives—its radio head Williamson, its CFO, and its general counsel—the ones deemed most responsible for the Radio Network debacle, were given their immediate exit visas. As the entertainment industry newspaper, *Variety,* called it at the time, it was a "Saturday night massacre."

The next day's edition of *The New York Times* reported the story of their sudden resignations for "personal reasons." The *Times* article went on to state that CEO Tom O'Neil and COO Hubert DeLynn were considering their own resignations and that vice-chair Frank Shakespeare already had submitted his. None of that, at least at that moment in time, was true. Our crisis management PR people were trying to manage this as best they could, but the news was overwhelmingly bad and getting progressively worse.

Immediately, GenCorp's COO, Bill Reynolds, sent in its own auditors, a temporary CFO, and an acting general counsel. At radio, Jerry Lyman, the squeaky-clean GM of our Washington classical music station, WGMS, was brought up to New York and promoted to division president. Shakespeare soon left the Company while O'Neil and DeLynn remained. It was clear, however, as the full consequences of this disaster were beginning to be understood—that it was only a matter of time before other major internal structural actions would need to be taken.

RKO's final days as a broadcaster were fast approaching. The discovery of the massive dishonesty at the RKO Radio Network had happened on DeLynn's watch although it had begun years before when others were in overall charge. It would go on to destroy everything that he had been working to salvage. Although not responsible for—or even an executive—during those original '60's actions onto which the license challengers had thrown their hungry grappling hooks, DeLynn took the hit.

It must have been decided by some wise men masterminding the entire situation from the Akron rubber capital of the world, in conjunction with a few Washington lawyers. Any chance of saving RKO, in any new recast business model, meant Hubert DeLynn had to go.

13

A Special Birthday Gift

Despite numerous threats and many close calls, there was only one actual broadcasting strike in my dozen RKO years. And it was a beaut. It was to happen in 1984 after NABET succeeded in challenging and finally ousting rival union IATSE at our New York broadcasting operations. WOR-TV, WOR-AM, WRKS-FM, and the then five-year old RKO Radio Network employed perhaps 225 or more engineering technicians. But the vast preponderance was on the TV side.

IATSE had represented these employees for decades. There had been one negotiations soon after I joined the Company in '75—when Shakespeare had so enthusiastically pranced around his office offering champagne to the victors. Another set of IA talks followed three years later without too much stress or histrionics. The union's regular lawyer, Harold Spivak—spoken about with reverence earlier in these pages—handled the legal and some of the negotiating work. By now, his son, Steve, recently out of law school, had joined the law firm. We had worked well together representing our respective clients to fashion reasonable and peaceful deals.

The IA's bargaining representative who handled the WOR group was not out of IATSE's New York's headquarters or from a New York local. For some reason lost to history, the way the IA had organized it internally decades before was that the work for the WOR engineering group was done by a union representative who lived in the middle of Pennsylvania. Traveling wherever he needed to be sent, he came from a division that I believe was called at the time their "R and T" (Radio and Television) department. The IA official was competent, nice, and got the job done representing his members. But he was not a New York-style bulldozer the way some in the unit apparently wanted.

At some point, a few television engineers decided they needed a change in representation. Somehow, the NBC NABET leaders were brought in. The word was that one of our employees had a father high up in the NBC NABET ranks. As they talked up the benefits of what NABET could provide from its ABC and NBC contracts, more than a few of the IA-represented WOR-TV technicians became interested. Once the top NBC NABET officials involved heard my name, I'm certain this got their juices really flowing.

Poaching another union's turf was and remains highly unusual in any industry. Broadcasting's three different engineering unions—IATSE, IBEW, and NABET—had in the past always respected each other's jurisdiction and established contracts. For some reason at that time, NBC NABET no longer felt it had to abide by the rules of the game.

WOR-TV was one of New York's three commercial, independent television stations. Its contract pretty much matched the basic terms and conditions of the other two commercial independents—WNEW-TV owned by Metromedia and the Daily News' WPIX-TV. While the pay scales and general provisions were roughly the same among the three indies, all three contracts were far less complex, expensive, and restrictive than the three other network-owned local commercial stations—NABET's WABC-TV and WNBC-TV, and the IBEW's WCBS-TV.

NABET's NBC local began organizing. It did so very quietly over many weeks before word leaked out. Promising it was going to be a new day, they assured those listening they were going to get them many of the same work rules, money improvements, and tight jurisdictional restrictions the union had beaten out of ABC and NBC. But first, they would have to get enough signed authorization cards to file for an NLRB election. If they succeeded in tantalizing enough employees and went on to win the vote, IATSE would be kicked out.

What ensued for a few months in early '84 was first an organizational campaign and then a jurisdictional battle. The two international unions competed for the hearts, minds, and wallets of the voters as the IATSE contract's expiration date was approaching. The big "WOR" shop represented a lot of dues money and initiation fees to any union. One union did not want to lose those finances while the other was eager for a new stream of income. Despite the fact that the umbrella organization of all American labor unions, the AFL-CIO, had rules against raiding by one member union of another's jurisdiction, a charge claiming NABET was violating its rules was filed but proved unsuccessful.

Off watching on the sidelines and waiting to join the fray, if it could figure out how, was an IA local. Local 771 had a clever business agent from a Teamster background who already represented a small number of Channel 9's news and feature film editors. Seeing an opportunity to keep the stations' engineers under the IA umbrella, he also saw a chance to enrich his own local's finances. Attempting to intervene to get on the ballot and promising the group a reinvigorated IATSE-representation, he needed to come up with a more inclusive name for his "film editors" local.

With my providing some suggestions, he figured out a new name of more general appeal when he added the words "video employees" to the "film editors" title. While the new "video employees and film editors" Local 771 was successful at getting on the ballot, NABET won the NLRB election pretty much hands down after convincing the engineers it could better represent them than either the old IA or Local 771.

The WOR stations' management had never suffered a work stoppage in its long relationship with the IA. But they were painfully aware of NABET's long history of frequent network strikes. When NABET won the election, that reality set in and a new strategy was necessary.

Frankly, I had not missed this union's presence in the near decade I was with RKO. In my new promoted position as vice president of administration and many other assorted things, I had little time since '81 to deal directly with most labor relations matters. But this one got my attention. Olivia Cohen-Cutler had joined my staff the year before and had by this date been promoted to director of labor relations. I reluctantly reached the conclusion, and she readily agreed, that she did not know NABET well-enough and was not yet ready to handle the upcoming negotiations. But I had no time to jump in and do it myself.

My old boss, Dick Goldstein had left NBC. It was after the fiasco of NBC's agreeing in 1976, once I was gone, to a new contract with NABET that turned out to be expiring a few months before its next summer Olympics in Moscow in 1980. That poorly-chosen expiration date would go on to provide NABET with tremendous leverage. While the Moscow games ultimately never materialized because of the boycott following the Soviet Union's invasion of Afghanistan, NABET took advantage of the situation when everyone was still of the belief the games would go on as scheduled. It was able to extract from a very nervous NBC a huge and what most observers saw as a totally undeserved payday. Goldstein, blindsided in '76 by his RCA bosses about their plans for the '80 games, left the company and went into private practice. I had the brainstorm one day while shaving to hire him to negotiate with NABET. Cohen-Cutler would be his second chair.

No one knew the NABET contract better than Goldstein. Partially responsible himself for some of its worst provisions in the days when NBC and ABC were always giving, it was now post-Reagan Air Traffic controllers time and he was re-oriented. Sitting him down in my office one day with Cohen-Cutler, I emphasized that under no circumstances could RKO wind up with anything remotely approaching the terrible network agreement. Making it clear a strike would not be unwelcome if that was the only alternative, I instructed Dick how we wanted it handled and Goldstein readily agreed. All of us were in sync that our game plan was to work within the existing IA contract's framework and make some modest adjustments, as necessary. The very next thing we did was to seek management volunteers and organize strike training school.

NABET entered into talks with us in the spring shortly after it won the NLRB vote. As we suspected, the union's strategy was to replicate much of the framework from its ABC and NBC contracts. Surely, they were surprised to see their old foe Goldstein sitting across from them that first day when I also joined them at the table. Perhaps they were thinking that RKO would be a real pushover.

With me keeping a sharp eye on these talks, and Cohen-Cutler involved assisting and gaining NABET experience, the talks dragged on for months as Goldstein, representing his client's wishes, resisted the union's demands. All the time we were preparing for the strike, the union undoubtedly was planning to inflict pain upon us at a time of its own choosing. Getting more tense at the table each time we met with no progress, it was looking like only a matter of time before their frustrations would explode.

It came on August 22, 1984. Cohen-Cutler and I were out on the West Coast. It was my birthday—my 43rd—and NABET knew it, so they presented me with this special gift. Insisting as I had from the very beginning of talks that RKO spend a lot of time, money, and effort to prepare for a strike and train necessary management replacements, we were entirely ready for their birthday present when the strike news reached us.

Cohen-Cutler and I were that day in San Diego at a special meeting with the IBEW's LA local business manager, Andy Draghi, when I got the call. Lou Shore, my good friend for many decades, first in his IBEW, later CBS labor relations, and finally in our Florida retirement days, was with us that day in his capacity as Draghi's assistant business rep. Draghi was another of those real IBEW characters. He and I had over the years gone through a few tough rounds at our KHJ negotiations but had a decent relationship. Cutting the session short as we raced out the door, Cohen-Cutler and I flew back to New York on that night's redeye to deal with the strike.

The evening after we had landed back in New York, WOR-TV had its first broadcast of a Mets baseball game from Shea Stadium against the San Francisco Giants. We had done a dry run of a high school game a week or two earlier to give the replacement crew a little experience, and it had gone well. The Shea game though would be the real test whether we could survive. With the replacement crew that night consisting mostly of our TV salesmen operating the normal five or six cameras, not only was it a perfect broadcast, the sales guys had a hoot doing it and were hungry for more.

The broadcast was so stellar that TV group president, Pat Servodidio, watching the game from his home, as I was watching it from mine, soon called. It was an ecstatic, "Jeff, tonight we just won. It'll take them some time to come around, but we will prevail." Going on to thank me for pushing him into the costly but comprehensive strike training program, he was proud of what his sales guy had just accomplished. Pat, a good friend who died in 2011, way too young and after a stellar post-RKO broadcasting career, loved those sales guys because he had once been one of them.

Loud and raucous picket lines were set up at both our 1440 Broadway headquarters where our two radio stations and the radio network had their operations as well as across Broadway where WOR-TV had its offices and studios.

Most of the more technical studio and transmitter work was being done by professionally trained, chief engineers, and engineering supervisors from whom we had brought in for the strike and local engineering management. We supplemented with other replacement personnel from the regular stations' staffs we had trained to take over the other engineering positions. On-air AFTRA talent working with the replacements in the studios didn't care. Nor did the WGA and DGA members. Replacement people working both strike duty and also their regular jobs got healthy strike bonuses on top of their regular pay. Something I had picked up from my previous network experience, it proved to be a great motivator.

NABET had been IATSE's historic rival for years. But now bad feelings were intensified after it had been booted out by NABET from representing these very same striking employees. IA film crews under our other WOR contracts enthusiastically worked the streets gathering news. Attributable to old relationships paying off, IA officials did whatever it could to lawfully assist us. All our other unions with no-strike clauses assured us they had no issues with their members crossing the NABET picket lines and reporting for work to perform their normal duties. Getting calls late at night from helpful IA officials who were my friends and wanted to see NABET beaten, they offered advice and assistance. My life and RKO's collective lives, even though hassled and highly stressed, essentially carried on.

About ten weeks into this very visible strike, we were still operating almost entirely without any glitches. We had no lost advertisers and suffered few blown commercials. News, Joe Franklin's *Down Memory Lane* and all our other shows were being expertly handled. TV and radio ratings were unaffected. Mets games from Shea had continued through the end of the baseball season—with the Channel 9 sales guys still having a blast. Studio replacement crews were getting better as each day passed. The two radio stations and the radio network had it much easier because operational jurisdiction had been negotiated out of the IA contract a half decade earlier. Even with the costs of beefed up security and strike bonuses, we were saving, with the engineering payrolls suspended, a real bundle.

The strike though was beginning to become psychologically wearing on our replacement workers and operating management since many had to work both regular jobs and also do strike duty. Days were long. Crossing the loud and abusive picket lines was difficult and tiresome. Yet we managed on. Many of the strikers though had to be in deep financial distress. Despite the financial pain their members were suffering—thousands of dollars per person—and our managing so well without them, the union showed no signs of wavering in their effort to wear us down.

Even though everything was going relatively smoothly for us, we decided one day to end it. I notified NABET that we were going to replace all of the striking NABET workers unless they accepted our final offer within 48 hours. Under law we could do this, as our outside lawyer, Bob Batterman, from the Proskauer firm, had so meticulously researched and advised. Not a typical move in most bargaining situations, very few companies in any industry ever took this step to permanently get rid of an entire workforce. But we had had enough.

It was a gutsy move that no network and few others would ever have implemented let alone even considered. We had actually prepared, or perhaps even placed, some big advertisements in New York's tabloids looking for new workers to replace the strikers in these high paid jobs. Thousands of applications from qualified individuals did or would have swarmed in, and we were prepared to carry out this plan.

Not surprisingly, we were attacked by the union for taking this extreme position. But our announcement to eliminate jobs quickly brought NABET back to the table. And this time, believing we meant what we said, they came in with a much more reasonable attitude. What the union could not risk was our actually replacing over 170 striking employees and its potentially losing a shop of that size—with all the dues and initiation fee money this shop represented.

When their International president, Ed Lynch flew up from Washington at the last moment to take over the the talks and try to save his members' jobs, I joined Goldstein and Cohen-Cutler at the table. It was my first time there since the opening day. Lynch pushed back for a while but recognizing the game was over, he quickly withdrew their principle demands. Gone were the gaggle of proposals to replicate the much detested and very badly flawed ABC and NBC network contracts. When he reluctantly accepted our final offer with only a few slight modifications, the deal was quickly made and the strike ended on our terms—a total win for the Company. The employees, although feeling disillusioned by NABET's empty promises that had cost each of them several thousand dollars, were happy to be finally back at work. Their feeling of disappointment and probable regret hung around for some time.

When the deal was made, the station was still called WOR-TV. It would not change its call letters to WWOR-TV until its 1986 move to New Jersey. Adding that "W" had been my idea. Like just about everything with RKO, it had its origins with our FCC license challenges.

A year or two before the '84 NABET strike, I was at a COO DeLynn staff meeting. We were deep in our planning, after some rough FCC and court developments, to move WOR-TV across the river to New Jersey to have a better shot at saving its license. DeLynn had gone around the room looking for suggestions about how we might be able to keep our station's close viewer recognition and loyalty once we moved to New Jersey if we could no longer utilize our easily identifiable, highly unusual, three letter call sign "WOR." Since RKO would be selling our WOR-AM Radio station and call sign, we were barred from any longer using the famous, three letter, WOR name for the new TV station to be built in New Jersey. All kinds of suggestions were tossed on the table.

I threw out a simple solution that just popped into my head. Why not, I said, just add another "W" up front and make it a four letter call sign. Since this was permissible under FCC rules, and DeLynn and everyone liked it, once the FCC approved, it would become WWOR-TV forevermore. The station, after more bad news and RKO was barred by the FCC from further ownership, would be sold in a few years to MCA after we had operated it in its new Secaucus building for some time as WWOR. We thought the move to New Jersey would salvage the license, but nothing could save the sinking ship.

14
CHAPTER

The RKO Story Continues to Final Credits

Even though DeLynn was gone by the end of '84, the all-enveloping FCC crisis that began in the early '60s was continuing to its final, almost predestined, climax. It would go on over the next few years to consume not just the rest of RKO's days as a broadcaster but also snuff out the Company's very life itself when the entire organization would finally implode.

Our ultimate fate, as later re-determined by the FCC after the RKO Radio Network disaster, after all appeals were exhausted, would be that RKO could not continue to hold any of its remaining radio and TV licenses granted by the federal government. And it would never again be permitted to have a broadcasting license. Unlike Boston where we had been stripped of our $200 million license and had to sell our property for pennies on the dollar, the new FCC decision at least permitted RKO to retain temporarily its other licenses but ordered that each station had to be sold on the open market to the highest bidder.

When sold, however, as much as one-third of the negotiated sales price of each station would be required under the FCC order to go as a payoff to the local challenge groups who had been insightful years before to attack a vulnerable RKO. Our staggering financial fine would be the challengers' stupendous economic windfall.

For example, when KHJ-TV in Los Angeles would be sold in 1986 to the Walt Disney Company for $324 million and become KCAL-TV, RKO and its GenCorp parent were permitted to keep only $218 million. The remaining $106 million paid by Disney for this prime piece of broadcasting real estate went to the 23-year-long license challenger, the extraordinarily lucky Fidelity Television. WOR-TV's ultimate $400 million sales price, and that of all our other stations, would suffer the same financial fate when nearly a third of their sales prices would also be taken away from RKO and delivered instead to the lucky challengers as a reward for their so-called public service but really their economic greed. As the result, RKO was deprived at the time of hundreds of millions of dollars of asset value as well as an untold further sum of future annual operating profit that easily over a 35 year span amounted to many hundreds of millions more. Possibly it would be billions.

It was the most shameful and overly severe punishment of a broadcaster in the entire history of broadcasting regulation. The FCC decision was a shock to all within the industry that a major group owner— in fact a broadcast pioneer—could lose all of its broadcasting licenses, face fines of this magnitude, and be forced to exit the broadcasting business. Certain of those TV stations it had to surrender in the 1980s, today in 2022 would be worth quite possibly $1 billion or more each. It was startling to a great many that a broadcaster of such preeminence could be forced not only to sell stations but also never be allowed to be in the broadcasting business again. Yes, wrongs had been committed, but did the punishment fit the crime?

Like General Electric, NBC's parent in later years, contaminating for decades New York's Hudson River with deadly substances. General Electric paid a heavy price approaching $1 billion or more to clean up the hazardous Hudson River waste it had over decades secretively deposited. But it never was punished with the taking away of NBC's valuable broadcasting licenses. Nor was GE or NBC barred from ever being a broadcaster.

Despite the fact that the late-in-the-game disclosures of financial irregularity at the new RKO Radio Networks torpedoed an unsteady but still floating ship, a real question remains whether RKO's most severe capital punishment was deserved. RKO's news and public affairs programming on its 17 stations for many millions of listeners and watchers had for decades unquestionably served the public interest. The Company undisputedly did many good things. Its stations had carried on with many initiatives and won many awards. It and its employees did not deserve this fate, particularly one initially set into motion by a 4-3 partisan FCC vote along strict political lines.

The human toll on 2500 or so radio and TV employees at our 17 stations, hundreds more on the headquarters staff, and thousands of family members, would be enormous. Many of the employees, all good, decent, and hard working, had been employed for RKO for decades. Most of the non-union people at the stations feared that they would lose their jobs when the new owners forced on them by the FCC took over on that day of reckoning fast approaching. Indeed, many if not most of the high and middle ranking management people later did lose their jobs. Part of the job I was responsible for was to keep the stations' key personnel motivated and the stations functioning during the many months of uncertainty while the sales to challenge groups were going forward.

The union people, on the other hand, whether performers, directors, writers, news crews, or engineers, were protected by their labor contracts and mostly secure in their jobs with any new owner. Their unions gave us the usual expressions of regret that RKO would be exiting the scene, but their show largely would go on—just with new bosses.

As the FCC situation had been deteriorating and our fate becoming more clear, I had considered leaving. Seeing it accelerate after the Boston debacle, I did not want to be around when the tsunami on the horizon actually hit. Yet I could not reveal in any way to my colleagues, and especially my staff, that I was that pessimistic. With morale probably suffering even more badly if I had, my search had to be in the "run silent and run deep" mode. I kept moving along, like a submarine, quietly navigating very deep and cold, uncharted waters, looking for that escape corridor.

As the radio and TV properties began to be dismantled, I had in 1984 some discussions with Paramount for the senior labor job on the West Coast. The following year as degradation continued, I was in California again. This time it was with the major toy manufacturer, Mattel Toys, for a position as its worldwide senior human resource vice president. At the wire, however, it did not materialize even though Monica and I had flown out to look at houses in Palos Verdes— allegedly just down from the actor Chuck Norris. Bill Simon, through the Frank Shakespeare connection, continued to be helpful. But a senior labor relations and human resources position like mine was not easy to find in any industry, particularly in entertainment. And RKO's reputation was not exactly boosting my job search possibilities.

In 1984, General Tire had gone through some major organizational changes of its own. The board, finally facing up to the losses of RKO's broadcasting properties that certainly pointed some fingers of responsibility at the O'Neil family management, had finally mustered up enough strength and ousted Jerry O'Neil as the company's chief executive and operating head. Bill Reynolds had been brought in from TRW at the same time and the corporate name was changed to GenCorp. One of the first things he did was hire a corporate HR chief to coordinate the HR and LR activities of all four subsidiaries—an idea long overdue. So the four of us in charge, with the new GenCorp HR leader, became closely inter-involved.

Bill began to run GenCorp as any president/COO would. He started to manage his troubled RKO subsidiary with the true oversight it had never experienced before. That was around the time that RKO's "Saturday night massacre" of its three senior executives took place when the radio network's dishonesty had been exposed. Unshackled from any overriding O'Neil family control and influence, particularly after Tom O'Neil retired as RKO's CEO the following year, in 1985, Reynolds began to focus in on RKO like a laser. '85 is also the year that he would add CEO to his GenCorp title and really take command.

Shane O'Neil was heading up RKO after DeLynn's '84 departure. Within a year, he reported, in every sense of the term, to Bill Reynolds in Akron. This was a first time in four decades for any RKO-O'Neil to be reporting to someone outside of the family—not a father, brother or uncle anymore. Reynolds and the GenCorp board had to be sorting out what they would do with its RKO subsidiary—and its leadership—once RKO's exit from broadcasting was complete.

Shane O'Neil, having gotten to know me well and seeing what I had accomplished, liked my work and continued my broadly expanded duties that DeLynn had first promoted me into. I liked Shane and he appreciated my advice. I tried to develop in him, along with the efforts of others on his senior staff, the skill set we thought he needed to succeed in the new, non-broadcasting world into which RKO had been thrust. His success, we all appreciated, would be our's.

O'Neil's excellent public relations gene had sprung into action a year earlier when he brought on a new PR head, Steve Ellis. Steve had come from the Burson Marsteller firm where he had been involved early-on when we first engaged that firm for the UCLA venture. He now ran a new department that Shane was keen on establishing to help build RKO's different future. While it was 20 years too late to save RKO as a broadcaster, Shane was intent on building a new company and Ellis would play a major role in accomplishing that goal. Managing PR as well as he did, he would be later snapped up by Reynolds and moved to Akron to run GenCorp's own sagging public relations fortunes.

Shane O'Neil's strategic game plan for RKO's new future was to return to its roots—movies. He had tried a bit of video, cable, and Broadway stage co-production, plus hotel development, but none of that went very far. If broadcasting could no longer be our major business, why not return to the old days when RKO was a major Hollywood film producer. Because we were now back in heavy union territory with the Hollywood unions, labor relations would be getting much more deeply involved.

It was to be either original productions or co-ventures with established Hollywood movie companies. Believing he could save RKO by making money in the after markets to pay off the movie production costs, he heavily ramped up this new part of the organization. He began his efforts to convince Reynolds that not only could he run it but that it could pay off handsomely for the reimagined RKO, and for its GenCorp parent.

Shane hired an experienced hand to run the new movie division and he in turn brought on others quite knowledgeable and creative. Lots of new employees, many very capable, were soon coming on board. He started a London-based production subsidiary that included one of the famous Korda family. London was soon ramped up and required my travel several times over the pond to help finalize both its real estate and specialized UK pension plans needs.

Seeing himself as a kind of studio head from the old Hollywood and RKO movie productions days, Shane loved this end of the business. Indeed, his personality and drive were well-suited for that. I'm convinced in a perfect world and at different time he could have been one of the greats. Commitments were made, deals cut, and films produced. A few were pretty good, like towards the end of its days the acclaimed '87 Vietnam War drama, *Hamburger Hill.* Most, however, were average at best and turned little if any profit.

Reynolds was watching closely. Trying to give Shane O'Neil as much respect, leeway, and time as he could to turn around the faltering Company, he became increasingly skeptical about RKO's future in the film business. Reynolds was an industrialist—not a movie maker. His imagination went as far as tires, rockets, and plastics—not to dreams and fantasies. When he would in short-time scuttle the entire film venture, with every broadcasting station either gone or on its way out the door, and RKO's very substantial Pepsi Cola bottling business on the blocks to be sold—it would take down with it the entire RKO ship.

It was around this time that RKO decided in order to keep itself afloat to invest in a ship of its own. It was a yacht. And one of considerable size. Designed as many were, it was to allow the new RKO movie company to wine and dine celebrities and entertainment executives attending the annual Cannes and other south of France film and television festivals. What better way could there be—using the extravagant method Hollywood knew best—to introduce the world to the emerging film power, the reimagined RKO Pictures. The unconfirmed rumor at the time, as word of this purchase spread throughout the senior executive ranks, was that it was a $1 million leased or bought boat. Akron, however, not on any body of water large enough to sail this or any other sea-going vessel, stepped in and put the ship into permanent dry dock.

In late '85, it had been announced that Tom Murphy's little Capital Cities Communications, with its broadcasting, cable, and publishing operations, surprised the business world by making a successful $3.5 billion bid for Leonard Goldenson's huge ABC. The deal had been put together with Berkshire Hathaway's Warren Buffett providing substantial financial backing. Buffet would go on to serve on its board. As *Variety* newspaper reported at the time, "the minnow has swallowed the whale." Ironically, its cable operations, which it now would be required under FCC rules to sell, had been acquired just a few years earlier from RKO when it had been our Cablecom General.

With RKO in its death dance, I saw this as the perfect opportunity and began to energize how I could find a path back to ABC to work for the legendary duo of Murphy and COO Dan Burke. The Cap Cities and ABC merger was very complicated. It would take a long time to work its way though the needed Washington regulatory clearances. Rumor had it that it would not be completed until sometime in mid-1986.

I later learned sometime in '86 from some of my old colleagues still at ABC that the new company was looking for a person to replace its soon-to-be-retiring head of labor relations, Dick Freund. What a perfect opportunity this presented. Dick was the longtime labor relations chief who had hired me in '68 when my broadcasting career first began. Staying close to him over the years, I took him to lunch one day where he confirmed that he was planning on retiring in early '87. Dick said he thought I would be perfect for the job and would be very happy to recommend me, but the call was clearly the new Company's.

This job had my name written all over it. In capital letters. It was a marvelous chance to return to my roots. I could put all those administration matters like security, real estate, benefits, and HR behind me and get back full time to my true expertise and real love. Some of those labor pains I so craved had not been coming quite as regularly when my job had widened in 1981 to include all the other functions. In dealing with unions again, and its associated kicking and discomfort, I hoped those pains, in acceptable doses, and the ultimate joys, would soon return.

After the US government had cleared the ABC and Cap Cities merger in 1986, I sent a letter to Steve Weiswasser, the new company's general counsel, to whom this position reported. Responding quickly and apparently impressed with my credentials, we met, he checked me out and concluded that with my strong labor relations skills and background, plus most importantly my prior ABC labor relations experience, I was a perfect fit for the job.

Some further interviews followed and in early 1987 CapitalCities/ ABC made the decision to offer me the position of corporate Vice President of Labor Relations when Freund stepped down. It would prove to be a splendid job with 14 lawyers on both coasts reporting to me. I'd have responsibility for the Company's labor relations with many unions and over 100 contracts covering many thousands of employees.

Weiswasser arranged a meeting for us with CEO Tom Murphy and his COO partner, Dan Burke, at the old Cap Cities offices on Madison Avenue. It went extremely well. Of critical importance, they assured me that I would always be directly included in any business matters with serious labor relations implications. Direct access, not filtered through my boss Steve Weiswasser, as I wanted and was accustomed to, was critical for me and vital for any success I might realize for the Company. It was also important for Weiswasser and his bosses.

Sharing with me that they had considered not buying ABC because of labor contract restrictions they were not accustomed to in their broadcasting operations, particularly NABET's, they saw me as the instrument to fix that problem. With their promise of direct access, total support, and independent authority, I could not be happier.

Totally trusting that they would be true to their word, I gave my notice to Shane O'Neil and then informed my staff. Unions, my colleagues, many friends throughout the Company, and my staff were surprised at my announcement. The first of Shane's senior staff to leave, my exodus would soon be followed by others as the implosion accelerated.

Shane O'Neil was disappointed to see me go, but understood the reasons and major leadership position I was accepting at CapitalCities/ABC. Graciously, in typical Shane style, he hosted a going away dinner in a private room at one of his favorite New York restaurants, Colombe D'Or. Inviting the corporate staff, my direct reports, and closest associates, of course with spouses, we probably numbered 25 to 30. A few of the radio GMs with whom I had become closest, especially my good friend, WOR-AM's Lee Simonson, joined us. Monica was pleased to be there to hear the many speeches extolling her husband's achievements and testaments to his high character.

Best remembered of all the praise that was showered on me that evening was the comment from John Cahill. John, another vice president on Shane's corporate staff, included in his remarks that "Jeff Ruthizer is the most contentious person I have ever known." A bit astonished to hear the exact phrasing of this particular adulation, I nevertheless took it, as I am sure it was intended, as very high praise indeed. I knew John to be an extremely smart individual and fully expected he would go on to have an illustrious business career. Proving my instincts right, Cahill went on to run Pepsi Cola as well as Kraft and later served as a board member of American Airlines.

With a case of 1983 Chateau Margaux as a parting gift from Shane O'Neil to help ease the discomfort of my expected new labor pains, I was gone to the next chapter in my 40-year broadcasting career with Tom Murphy and Dan Burke. Within another year or two, RKO General would be in the dustbin of history. Every broadcasting property meticulously put together by Tom O'Neil many decades earlier would be sold to new owners—under the severe FCC constraints. All Pepsi bottling plants changed hands. No more movies were made. RKO's senior management and staff disappeared into other jobs if they could manage it or simply retired.

GenCorp itself was substantially restructured into a much smaller company after RKO vanished, the O'Neils exited, and the General Tire division was shortly later sold to Germany's Continental Tire.

The last bottle of that pretty good '83 vintage was consumed just a few years ago.

15

Beginning My Second Tour of ABC Duty—
What It Was Like to Work for Tom and Dan

The American Broadcasting Company that I returned to in the spring of 1987 was a far different place from the ABC I had left in '72 when my first tour of duty ended. For a long time, it had not been considered any longer the "half" a network, or the "Almost Broadcasting Company" that it had been called when I first joined in '68. By the time Capital Cities Communications had decided to acquire the Company in 1985, ABC's growth was dramatic, sustained, and had changed the three-network competitive landscape significantly.

During that period, ABC had become a thriving organization under Leonard Goldenson's leadership. While still generally ranking a strong third but sometimes even a second in the primetime TV ratings, it had grown considerably after Goldenson in '72, the year I left, had made Elton Rule its COO and president. Elton in turn had brought in Fred Silverman in '75 to be in charge of ABC Entertainment. Under these two, ABC's ratings lunged forward to become very competitive with both CBS and NBC.

The success continued into '85 when Tom and Dan bought the Company.

Under the new CEO Tom Murphy and COO Dan Burke leadership that took over in '86 after the merger was approved, the American Broadcasting Company, or ABC, was reborn as the broadcasting group under the new parent, CapitalCities/ABC, Inc. The old company was considerably reorganized as many senior executives running its various business units and departments went into retirement or otherwise departed. Thus I came aboard to bring new life and order to the Company's labor relations efforts in my new corporate position.

It was notable that when I started that April day that I had to walk though a union picket line to get into the ABC building on broadcasting row. It was both another omen of things to come as well as a throwback to the past. A WGA news writer strike involving about 200 employees in New York and Washington had erupted a week or two before and was still in full swing. While lasting for only a few more days until I stepped in to settle it, it threw me into immediate contact with a number of ABC's key news executives with whom I would be spending a great deal of time in the years to come. It was extraordinarily reminiscent of my first day on the job at the old ABC 19 years earlier when I had walked through an AFM picket line right behind Howard Cosell.

The new ABC broadcasting entity consisted basically of four groups—the TV Network, the Owned TV stations, the Radio Network, and the Owned Radio stations. My staff and I would be responsible for all of their labor relations activities wherever there was union representation or its potential.

The other group of the new parent company, where I would not be involved, was publishing. Consisting of prominent daily newspapers in several major cities such as Kansas City and Fort Worth, and weekly newspapers and shopping guides throughout the country, it also published a number of magazines and owned

Fairchild Publications. Fairchild published *Women's Wear Daily*. The entire publishing group, headed by Phil Meek, was generally to remain in the hands of its longtime, outside labor counsel, Bob Ballow, and his law firm. Every now and then though I would gently look over Bob's shoulder.

The Company also had substantial cable network interests that came with the ABC acquisition as represented by its ownership share of ESPN, Lifetime, A&E, and the History Channel.

ABC's TV Network, often just referred to as the "Network," was led by broadcasting and Cap Cities veteran John Sias. Its population was several thousand organized into nearly a half-dozen different business units. The operational groups that reported to Sias consisted of ABC News, ABC Sports, ABC Entertainment, ABC Daytime, and *Good Morning America*. It was headquartered in New York but also had major offices in Los Angeles that mostly supported LA-based ABC Entertainment. Its departments included programming, sales, finance, research, affiliate relations, and administrative support people. BOE remained the Network's technical facilities and operational arm assigned to manage its approximate, 1200 strong, NABET-represented, engineering workforce in New York, Los Angeles, and Washington.

ABC News, led by Roone Arledge, was based in New York but had bureaus around the world including Paris, London, and the Far East. In the US, it had a large physical presence in our Washington bureau across from the Mayflower Hotel, but it also had domestic news bureaus in Atlanta, Los Angeles, Miami, and Chicago. Its major anchor had long been Peter Jennings. With a bench of other strong anchors and correspondents, News had a substantial viewing audience and a worldwide reputation for scope and depth in news coverage. Because of its considerable radio news network reach, it was able to boast that more people watched or listened to ABC News than any other news organization in the world.

Roone had dramatically re-engineered ABC News upon taking

it over in 1977. From that time until Murphy and Burke's arrival, he had served as president of both ABC News and ABC Sports. By the late '80s when I joined, under his direction it had grown into a very worthy competitor of both NBC and CBS News. Roone had his Mount Rushmore—with Peter Jennings its undisputed star and *World News Tonight* our leading news product. But there was also the enormous talent of Barbara Walters, Cokie Roberts, David Brinkley, Ted Koppel, Diane Sawyer, Hugh Downs, Charlie Gibson, Sam Donaldson, and a host of other anchors and correspondents.

With Tom and Dan's deciding to end Roone's dual running of both News and Sports, Roone chose News. ABC Sports was now led by Dennis Swanson. ABC Sports remained the nation's preeminent television sports broadcaster. Having dominated the Olympics for the previous two decades, it was then preparing for its February '88 *Calgary Olympics* games coverage. Its regular sports productions included *Monday Night Football,* college football, NBA and college basketball, golf, bowling, auto and horse racing, skiing, and gymnastics. Every Saturday afternoon across America viewers would tune in to see Jim McKay's *Wide World of Sports.* Normally broadcasting more traditional athletic but less popular competitions such as track, skiing, and gymnastics, *Wide World* would also venture into some of the more fanciful "sports"—like arm wrestling, log rolling, high diving, lumberjacking, and even barrel jumping.

ABC Entertainment in Los Angeles was responsible for the Network's vitally-important, prime time entertainment schedule. Brandon Stoddard ran it when I joined the Company. But shortly after the following year's Calgary Winter Olympics Games, its new head would be Bob Iger.

The Network's Daytime group run by Josie Emmerich produced soap operas for television's hugely popular afternoon viewing audience. We then had five. Widely successful as a genre, most significant were its three, one hour hits—*One Life to Live, All my*

Children, and *General Hospital.* The first two were produced in our New York studios while *General Hospital* came out of our LA Prospect Street studio lot. I would go on to become a good and decades-long friend of Paul Rauch—*One Life's* superb executive producer.

Our *Good Morning America* was headed up by Cap Cities-veteran broadcaster, Phil Beuth—called by all who knew him well as "Philly." The two-hour morning entertainment program had been previously produced by ABC News but Murphy and Burke decided it would do better outside of News' realm. Then starring co-hosts Joan Lunden and Charlie Gibson, it had been moved into Philly's capable hands. It was well known within the upper reaches of the Company that Philly was the first employee Tom Murphy had ever hired when he began managing the initial Capital Cities station in Albany, NY, decades earlier. Rumor had it that Philly probably owned more Cap Cities stock at a lower average share price than just about anyone else in the Company other than Tom himself.

Responsible for the 18 owned AM and FM radio stations around the country as well as the ABC Radio Network, Jim Arcara was another Cap Cities- veteran. Organized into two groups, many of the radio properties were the legacy stations that had come with the merger. Cap Cities, however, had added several of its own into the mix in such cities as Detroit, Atlanta and Houston. Mostly top rated music or talk stations in their respective markets, they were mainly strong and profitable. The ABC Radio Network carried on as it had for decades as news and commercial delivery services to its many hundreds of radio affiliates across the nation through its four, distinct programming arms—also called "networks."

The TV Station group was spilt into two with each led by a veteran-Cap Cities operator. Ken Johnson ran the Western group of four stations in Los Angeles, San Francisco, Fresno, and Houston. Larry Pollock ran his Eastern group of four in New York,

Philadelphia, Chicago, and Raleigh- Durham. All of the ABC stations were extremely successful at either number one or two in their respective markets. With dominating early and late news programs the group probably enjoyed the highest profits and profit margins in the broadcasting industry. Within a year or two, the groups would be consolidated under Pollock's leadership.

In New York, WABC-TV's star anchor for many years had been Roger Grimsby. I had gotten to know Roger a bit during my first tour of duty. Let go shortly before my return, his memory lingered. Known for his acerbic wit and zinging one liners, he had once said before cutting to a commercial—"If no news is good news, Eyewitness News has the best news." I remember watching it from home and cringing at his bad judgment and poor attempt at humor. Not thrilled either with that shocking comment and other unpredictable outbursts, his bosses finally axed him when his ratings slipped. But Channel 7 in New York had come roaring back stronger than ever with his former partner, Bill Beutel, teaming up with new anchors.

The other ABC television stations that Tom and Dan had acquired as part of the deal were WLS-TV in Chicago, KABC-TV in Los Angeles, and KGO-TV In San Francisco. Each was top performing in its market. They were now joined by another hugely successful station, WPVI-TV in Philadelphia, where Jim Gardner famously sat alone in the anchor chair and established all sorts of ratings records. Cap Cities had also brought into the mix its KTRK-TV in Houston and two other stations in the smaller markets of Fresno and Raleigh-Durham. ABC's former station in Detroit, WXYZ-TV, the site of my 1971 run-in with the Teamsters, along with its radio sisters, had to be jettisoned as part of the acquisition.

When it came to profit, the ABC Network, normally still in third place in the prime time ratings, was at the opposite end of the spectrum from the TV station group. While the quality of its entertainment prime time programming had dramatically improved and its advertising revenues had grown substantially, its profit had not. Largely due to staggering development and production costs and far too-few hits, prime time profits were usually more imaginary than real. Most often, any operating profit the Network might generate in any given year would come from its hugely successful, hundreds of million dollars-profit, Daytime schedule of popular soap operas. Tom Murphy and Dan Burke intended to turn the Network's dismal prime time profit picture around. John Sias was the executive they chose to lead the effort.

Sias came from the publishing side of the Cap Cities enterprise although he had TV experience from his earlier Metromedia sales days. Directed to reorganize and reinvigorate the Network, his mission was to make it more efficient, reduce staff, improve its product, gain prime time audience ratings, increase sales, and, for a refreshing change, make some real, prime time money.

Everyone in the business who knew Sias has a great story or two. A real character, he was different from most everyone at ABC or any other organization where I ever worked. I got to know John over the years and liked him a great deal. Finding out—because I think he told me—that he had attended law school for a short period before dropping out, he saw himself knowledgeable and wise to "lawyer tricks," as he called them. "Be on your guard, Ruthizer," he might have said, and I constantly was.

A paratrooper in the Second World War, his hitting the silk in combat told me that he had to be considered one tough dude. Enjoying a reputation as a practical jokester, which I didn't know about at the time we first met, he must have had an entire closet overflowing with whoopi cushions, wigs, hats, horns, and whistles. Famous for doing phony impersonation telephone calls and loud, embarrassing shout-outs in restaurants or elevators, his repertoire was strange and ample.

It was my first week on the job in the old ABC building that April when he dropped by to see me, unannounced. I was later to find out that it was part of John's management style to stop by unexpectedly to see people in their own safe office spaces.

John must have learned of my hiring from the normal internal PR releases even though it's quite probable that Murphy and Burke, who were very close with him, had already filled him in. John felt so attached to them that he had hanging in his office a large, oil painting of *The Three Musketeers* that he had commissioned some artist to paint. In their 17th century French attire, it was complete with feathered, broad brimmed hats and dangling swords. The faces of Tom, Dan, and John were painted in as the famous Alexandre Dumas sword fighting trio of Porthos, Aramis, and Athos. So when John might say, "Be on your guard Ruthizer," he meant it.

Undoubtedly John had stopped by that morning in that surprise manner to get the cut of my jib. I'm fairly certain he succeeded. The Network was a very big client and had many union problems that needed solving, mostly stemming from NABET. John, as I was to learn beginning that morning, was not very fond of unions. I later learned about his unorthodox conduct that caused quite a stir at publishing's Wilkes Barre, PA., daily newspaper. Unions never forgot he had brought German shepherds into the unionized newsroom to sniff around for drugs.

Murphy and Burke sold the old headquarters building on Avenue of the Americas to a Japanese consortium for a rumored $75 million and erected a new headquarters building adjacent to our television studios on West 66 Street. It made much sense to Tom and Dan to leave broadcasting row behind and put headquarters and operations together on Manhattan's Upper West Side even though many employees preferred the old, much more convenient midtown location. The new building though would not be ready for another year and maybe closer to two.

Tom and Dan introduced the management committee concept as a part of their information sharing culture that they were constantly encouraging. Consisting of about 25 or 30 business unit leaders from broadcasting and publishing, plus corporate staff, the group met monthly. Business initiatives, announcements, and major developments everywhere were to shared. Occasionally, there were guest speakers. One such time Murphy brought in Ed Rollins, the political guru, to give the group his reading of that year's upcoming elections. All the key players were expected to regularly attend and address what of note was happening in their particular businesses.

Since I was a corporate vice president, I was a regular. Shortly after I started there was a meeting where I was introduced as the new head of labor relations by either Tom or Dan and got a warm welcome from what I soon learned would be a collegial group of the Company's leaders. The chair was rotating, and I had a few shots at it over the years preparing the agendas and running the meetings.

One of the best exchanges was highly revealing about the Company and the times. It was the late '80s when Alan Wurtzel, the head of Network research, was delivering his normal three-network, prime time ratings report. Roone Arledge jumped in and said—"Hey guys, isn't it about time that we called it the four-network ratings by including Fox?" "Good point," responded the head of research. Because the Fox network by that time had become a real competitor, there could be no more denial, particularly after Tom and Dan agreed with Roone's suggestion. Forevermore, it was to be Wurtzel's four-network ratings report.

At one management committee meeting when I was delivering my labor report, I thought I would spice it up a bit. I went on to describe a scene at a recent negotiations where there had been some near physical blows. I think I said something about fists nearly flying and kneecaps almost being broken. There were some murmurs and a comments like, "Jeez, Jeff, how could it get so rough with the union?" Then I smiled and added that the near altercation was just a meeting of our side, at a company caucus, with executives heatedly fighting among ourselves over some key issues. It got a medium size laugh from most in the room. But when at times I was to deliver the real NABET report on negotiations or strike preparations, or a talk on the WGA's most recent walk out in Hollywood, I had the room's rapt attention.

Once the new building opened, we'd meet in the big board room on the 22nd floor. At the other end of the floor was the executive dining room, with its expansive views over the city. Open to anyone of vice presidential rank and above, its overall concept had been designed by Tom and Dan. No more would it be like the old ABC executive dining room—with its limited number of waiter serviced, private small rooms. Since that space had not been big enough for all the vice presidents, it had been restricted to only the most senior executives. Only they could reserve those rooms for small group luncheons. The old ABC space just did not sit well with the new bosses.They wanted their new luncheon space to be open, large, egalitarian, and communal.

Lined up in a long room side by side were perhaps a dozen oblong tables of maybe ten feet in length that each sat eight or ten. My best guess was that the room had a capacity of about 120. It was self-service only, a large daily spread of mostly cold dishes with a few hot specials set up on one one side of the room. We each got on the buffet line, served ourself, and then found an open chair at any table. The whole operation was run by the head waiter and a few assistants with food that was prepared off campus and brought in fresh daily. Unlike, however, RKO's unique executive dining room environment I had just left, there was thankfully, as was the norm in corporate America, absolutely no alcohol offered.

It was in concept much like my army mess days at Fort Ord, but in the CapitalCities/ABC world, the commanding generals ate with the rest of the officers. Our two generals joined us frequently, enjoying the experience of sitting down randomly where there were open seats and talking to whomever was sitting at that table.

Murphy and Burke learned a lot from us about what was going on in our areas, and we learned from them as well as from each other.

Information and mostly good cheer flowed back and forth. Sports people sat and talked with sales or programming executives or financial people. Lawyers sat with PR people or news executives. Maybe auditors were at tables with HR people and station managers. It was just normal lunchtime conversations among colleagues. What made it even better in its early days was that it was an executive perk.

Tom and Dan would ask friendly questions about what was happening in a way that elicited responses they seldom would get from routine office meetings. No one felt any pressure to perform. Tales of that was going on in my various labor talks or what the unions were up to generally always seemed to catch a lot of interest. It wasn't all business though as subjects as varied as the Knicks to New York's Mayor Giuliani to the latest films or the world's best golfer often dominated the conversations. Collegiality and esprit de corps reigned. For those executives who needed a private room to discuss business matters or hold staff luncheons, there were four or five of those down the hall that each sat up a dozen or so and were also self-service.

In short order, both of them, but more so Burke, came to understand that the TV Network and the acquired ABC TV stations were vastly overpopulated. It was far too many employees, both union and non-union—representing excessive cost. I soon learned that one of Tom Murphy's favorite expressions was "you don't need more people than you need." It was so powerful in its simplicity and a counterpoint to the former ABC culture. ABC's bottom line profit had grown significantly over the preceding decade as the result of better programming, improved ratings, and increased advertising revenues. As in all businesses, a successful company always feels the pressure to add more people. Although many new positions would normally have been required as the old Network and stations grew and technology changed, many of us, and particularly Dan, had the impression few requests to add bodies in the prior company had ever been denied.

Capital Cities Communications, on the other hand, had become successful and predominant as a broadcaster by intentionally keeping its the head count as low as possible. As a model for its lean philosophy that minimized costs to maximize profits, its New York City corporate headquarters' staff had consisted of no more than about 35 people, and that included Tom and Dan. That low headcount had become a legend in the industry.

Downsizing was to become one of Dan Burke's earliest and most resolute missions. On the union side of the equation, I was to be his partner. At various times and on multiple occasions we'd talk about the challenges of our serious overstaffing. We were once both in New Orleans during the 1988 Republican National convention. During some down time one afternoon walking the floor, we happened to run into each other. The subject popped up about the dozens of ABC engineers all around us Dan saw setting up for that night's convention coverage. It always seemed too many for Dan. He knew I was getting ready for the next year's NABET negotiations and it prompted him to comment about the staffing problem and contract issues we'd have to tackle in those talks.

Appreciating that flexible contract terms and relaxed work rules were the key to staff reductions, Burke was very proud of what he had himself accomplished. Through his own involvement years before in negotiations at the Cap Cities'-owned *Women's Wear Daily* apparel industry newspaper, he had managed major downsizing through healthy severance payouts. That peaceful deal was made at the same time major New York City newspaper publishers were in the midst of painful strikes with the same union over their own desired staff reductions. Burke would always be willing to agree to generous severance packages if it meant he could peacefully get the staff reductions his businesses needed. Buyouts were paid once, but, as Burke reminded everyone, paybacks affecting the permanent bottom line lasted forever.

Spending a fair amount of time in those early days with my boss, Steve Weiswasser, he was always very interested in my progress with the various unions and my staff. Normally accessible but sometimes too busy to meet during the day, he'd often, and for a while weekly, take me to dinner at one of his favorite nearby restaurants. Sitting comfortably and more relaxed, we'd review a whole list of items on which I was working.

My team of eight lawyers in New York with another six in LA had nearly doubled in size since I had left a decade and a half earlier. It operated, I imagined, much the same as any other labor relations department at a major American cooperation in handling everything labor—contract matters and NLRB activities. Taking a deep dive, I set out to learn about the work we did and the lawyers doing it. Just as important was learning who our clients were, what they thought about the job my lawyers were doing, and what they expected from us.

It was basically the same group of over 100 union contracts we had during my first tour of duty but now renegotiated several times over. A large exception, however, was that with the major shift in news camera technology, all news gathering work had shifted a decade earlier, when news film died, from IATSE to NABET. No longer were IA camera, sound and lighting, and film editing locals representing workers in these jobs. In New York alone, more than 200 jobs had moved over into NABET's jurisdiction.

In Washington and New York, the WGA had several hundred staff news writers in one contract and many dozens of freelance soap opera and other entertainment show writers in another. We had the same mix of staff and freelance contracts with the DGA. IA locals were still many but just not working any longer in the gathering and editing of news. We had IA stagehands, graphic artists, hair and makeup artists, feature film editors, and wardrobe attendants. There was a group of AFTRA contracts at TV and Radio networks and local stations covering our many hundreds of radio DJs and hosts, announcers, TV anchors and journalists, as well as the additional hundreds of TV freelance performers.

Scenic artists who designed and painted our serial sets were in a United Scenic Artists local. We even had a few IA projectionists and some scattered other unions around such as the house IBEW electricians. Multiply that number and variety by Washington, Chicago, Los Angeles, and San Francisco to see the full load of our union-represented workplace. My West Coast group had even more IATSE contracts, Teamsters, and the host of freelance WGA, DGA, AFM, and SAG agreements that centered on prime time entertainment production, which brought in the AMPTP.

While the old pre-merger ABC was highly union-organized at the local station level—on both sides of the camera or mic— Capital Cities Communications' stations weren't. Some of the TV and radio stations it brought into the new corporate mix—from Detroit, Atlanta, Houston, Philadelphia, Dallas, and Raleigh-Durham—were either in part or entirely non-union when it came to performers, news camera operators, or technicians. Smart management, with some help from ABC's labor relations, would manage to keep our non-union facilities that way.

One of the first things I discovered was that we were living in the same kind of NABET grievance hell that I had first experienced during my first tour of duty nearly 20 years earlier. If anything, matters had gotten much worse. We had more grievances, and consequential ones, leading to arbitrations. Relations with the NABET leaders in a few of our five cities were unreasonably adversarial. One or two were on the verge of explosion.

What got my attention was that far too large a percentage of the hours spent weekly by nearly all of my lawyers was devoted to issues pertaining to this one union. NABET's major thrust was our engineers, but there were 18 other NABET units in four of our five cities, albeit small ones. Jobs ranged from plumbers in LA to publicists and motorcycle couriers in New York. The largest non-engineering groups were the three news writer contracts in Los Angeles, San Francisco, and Chicago—with maybe 30 employees each.

Lawyers were constantly handling NABET contract questions from operators, planning strategies, meeting with union officials, arguing over grievances, investigating grievances, conducting grievance meetings, and helping to decide proper discipline. They were also fighting off the usual NABET attempts to organize other groups of ABC's non-union employees. When it came to NABET arbitrations, the lawyers spent a great deal of time preparing their cases, presenting at the hearings, and writing post-hearing briefs. In addition, there was the huge amount of time that would be taken up by the three or four of us dedicated to prepare for and negotiate our next NABET contract.

It was my guess that a good 40% to 50% of the department's overall time on both coasts was NABET-oriented. This one union was the main reason the department had grown in size from eight or nine lawyers in 1972 when I left to the 14 when I returned.

My 12 years at RKO, in retrospect a very welcomed holiday, seemed so foreign and removed. Even when NABET had popped up in 1984 and brought with it the WOR strike, its presence there did not represent this level of churn and contentiousness. Averaging now upwards of 100 new grievances every year at each of our five cities, many took on a life of their own. Just for comparison, ABC hardly ever had a grievance with any of our other dozens of unions and even less frequently did we experience an arbitration. In my dozen years with RKO, I could recall only a small number of grievances from all of our unions and maybe a handful of arbitrations.

With dozens of NABET arbitration dates scheduled and a huge backlog of unsettled grievances, the entire cottage industry created years before was still going strong. It reminded me of the line from *Guys and Dolls*. We had "the oldest, established, permanent, floating crap game in New York." Many hundreds of hours of our managers' time—torn away from their normal operational duties—were involved in contractual disputes in all our NABET cities. It was our job as lawyers, but it had become demoralizing to both lawyer and operator alike. However, as long as the NABET contract remained a morass of endless rules that many viewed as gopher holes, sand traps, spite walls, and money machines, nothing could be done to bring relief. This was to become my focus over the ensuing 20 years. But first, my focus would be the 1989 contract talks.

Our contract designated or American Arbitration Association appointed arbitrators were nationally known and widely respected. Mostly lawyers, they were a group of highly intelligent, labor relations-knowledgeable professionals experienced in listening to arguments and deciding winners or losers. If they found too often in favor of the Company, they risked dismissal by the union. While the majority of the cases submitted to arbitration were won by the Company, the occasional loss in operational matters could be consequential.

Many bad decisions ruling our lives sat in dozens of black binders lining our shelves that I had to walk past every day just as a reminder. Arbitrations were becoming increasingly expensive as hearings frequently dragged on for several days. In short, our grievance and arbitration culture was a major problem crying out for a solution.

There were many wacky decisions filling those books. Or almost making their way in. Like the real one requiring that a small camera lens on its way to a sports remote could not be carried in the pocket of a producer on his way to the event but only by an engineer. It seems small, but not so. Suddenly, the union was given jurisdiction by an arbitrator over the transportation of technical equipment and no longer just its operation. How about ABC being told it had to pay double-time to its engineering crew aboard a US navy carrier on a day off at sea during a week it was awaiting an astronaut capsule splash-down. Because—the union claimed—there were no shops or other amusements aboard to enjoy proper day off at sea on their regular day off, so the "golden time" penalty had to be applied. Or the claim, if the Company had not prevailed, that only a NABET-represented technician could drive a motorcycle that carried on its back a NABET cameraman shooting the New York City Marathon—in a grab for driving jurisdiction, too.

As I got to know my staffs on both coasts, it became clear I had mix of talent. Some I knew from my first tour of duty. On the West Coast, the vice president heading up the labor relations unit was Irv Novick. Once my boss, he and I had worked together 16 years earlier during the 1971 AFTRA strike in Detroit. A good negotiator, he had taught me much during those four years. Having forgiven him long before for going off to Europe and leaving me to deal with Chuckie O'Brien and the Teamsters, we both knew our personal dynamics would be a bit of a challenge now that our positions were reversed.

One lawyer still there on my New York staff from my first tour of duty, whose job was essentially our NABET grievance ringmaster, would leave the Company within a few years for a new job. After getting over the initial shock of his going to work for NABET, I called Walter Liss, the WABC-TV president and general manager to give him the news. Liss, who had had experienced his own issues with this individual over differing approaches to labor relations matters, replied with an immortal line, "So Jeff, what else is new?"

Concluding that I needed to import some new talent into the department, within a few months I brought over from an imploding RKO, Olivia Cohen-Cutler. Dynamic, sociable, and smart, she had developed considerably since I first hired her in 1983. A certain sense of strength, confidence, and power exuded from her. Most importantly, her underlying labor relations philosophy, skills, and style were very much aligned with mine. A fast learner and extremely dependable, she was to become my chief assistant and confidante.

Soon flying out to the West Coast and visiting San Francisco and Los Angeles, I met with Network and station managers as well as my Los Angeles labor relations team. That trip was to be the first of many dozen over the following two decades. The visit opened my eyes to the fact that our Los Angeles and San Francisco operations were mired in their own NABET morass. The union leaders in those two cities were difficult and often far too adversarial. My people felt it was excessive and I soon agreed. It was a demoralizing situation for them as well as the operators they represented. Isolated on the coast, they said they had not felt the love of New York for quite some time. What I promised them was that in fighting hard for our clients, they would always have my as well as Tom Murphy's and Dan Burke's unbreakable support. It was to be a new day.

16
CHAPTER

Preparing for the War We Hoped Would Never Come

Julie Barnathan was still BOE's president. I had gotten to know Julie fairly well from our time together during my first tour of duty. Not having seen nor spoken to him for close to 14 years since our last time together at the combined ABC-NBC '73 NABET talks, I went over to his office for a visit. A great deal had changed within me during those years but a decade and a half later, it was the same down-to-earth Barnathan who welcomed me back with one of his big bear-hugs.

Among the first senior executives I went to visit was ABC News president Roone Arledge. Roone professed to have remembered me from my first tour duty when he ran ABC Sports but I was sure he did not have the faintest recollection. Operating at the level to which he was accustomed, I felt he was largely unaware and basically unconcerned about the underlying NABET contract problems that I had been hired to address. For the rest of the time I would work with ABC News while he headed it, this feeling never changed. I never had the sense that he recognized or cared much about the costs and the below the surface inefficiencies. From where he sat running his worldwide news empire, he just wanted the best possible productions and wasn't concerned—like his bosses Tom and Dan, or John Sias—about how costly and inefficient that might be.

I sensed from the outset that ABC Sports was going to be my favorite client. SVP Steve Solomon, who I knew well from my previous ABC tour of duty and had himself once been an ABC labor lawyer, was very welcoming. In fact, Steve had taken my place when I left the Company in '72 to join NBC before he shifted into HR and then Sports management. Steve was the person who had initially introduced me to Weiswasser, so I was especially indebted to him.

Traveling to any number of ABC Sports remotes in those first few months, I was learning its different operations from the ground up. If I was going to assist in addressing Sports' problems, I had to become knowledgeable. It took a while before I would get out to the Indy 500, but I went to many other events. I soon got to know another key Sports executive, SVP Bob Apter. Later with me at the '89 negotiating table, Bob proved to be an invaluable asset and good friend for years—up to today. Sports' issues, as I was discovering, cut across a wide swath of the NABET agreement. Very worthy of relief, they got my rapt attention for years to come.

Visiting with Sports chief Dennis Swanson, he related with relish a particular story about his own frustrations with the NABET contract. In his former Chicago WLS-TV station management days, he had come across one of those seemingly insurmountable problems. The NABET contract permitted as discipline only the discharge of an employee for just cause. He felt it defied common sense that any company could not suspend an employee for an infraction but could only seek a discharge, regardless of the nature of the offense. In essence, we had been limited under the contract to capital punishment, as some arbitrators sometimes called it, or no punishment at all. Swanson strongly felt, as did others, a suspension had to be part of management's nuanced options. Later in that negotiations, after Swanson's push for it, that negotiated change was accomplished.

I took away from his story that I would have in Dennis a great ally in seeking major contract reform. It was in my early visits with Swanson, Apter, and other Sports executives that I first met Bob Iger. Bob was then involved in planning for 1988's Calgary Olympics. After Calgary, he was soon to become the new head of ABC Entertainment—the prelude to his rise to the top of ABC and finally Disney management.

Good Morning America's Phil Beuth was concerned about programming restrictions hurting his morning show. With vast technology changes including satellite delivery, only some of which *GMA* could take advantage of under the strict jurisdictional rules of the contract, his programming options were limited. Then in fierce audience competition with NBC's *Today Show,* Beuth was convinced the rules affected his program content and ratings. He needed flexibility. As the result, he, too, was full of energy for significant contract reform.

I spent some time those first few months with the overall Radio president, Jim Arcara, his two station group presidents, and his ABC radio network chief. All four were anxious for fixes in the many ways they saw necessary from their previous Cap Cities experiences or competitive conditions. Both the radio stations and the network were particularly stymied by too many engineers and the overwhelming cost that represented because they had no ability, like other broadcasters, to go "combo."

Larry Pollock ran the East Coast group of TV stations and Ken Johnson headed up the West Coast group. As experienced, hands-on Cap Cities general managers, used to dealing with common sense, low headcount, and basic efficiencies, Larry and Ken were enthusiastic about my hiring. They looked forward to working closely with me to achieve major changes in a NABET book they found bewildering. It was immediately clear that the Owned TV Station group would be leading the charge for significant reform, if not outright revolution.

After about my first three months in the job, Steve Weiswasser called to say I should get ready to travel to Chicago for an important operational meeting with WLS-TV station management. It was to be Larry Pollock's meeting and he wanted me there.

Larry Pollock was one of the most interesting people I ever met in my career. Coming from a research background before moving into operational positions, that research mind allowed him to zero in on just about any subject before him, like a Norden bombsight. Smart, inspirational at critical moments, and sharp-tongued when he felt the need, Larry could also be kind, funny, and gracious. Having managed Buffalo, Philadelphia, and some of the other Cap Cities TV properties under far less restrictive union contracts, he was a fierce proponent of operating flexibilities as the key to head count reduction and cost control.

Joe Ahern was the Chicago TV GM and an ABC holdover from the pre-merger days. He ran a successful operation consistently producing the highest news ratings in town and excellent profits, but Larry wanted them higher. In the Cap Cities world, that was substantially accomplished through careful cost control. Pollock brought with him that day his group engineering vice president, Bob Niles. Ahern had with him his chief engineer, news director, controller, and other senior staff. Larry's boss, EVP Mike Mallardi, another ABC holdover, was there too. Weiswasser and I completed the group of about ten.

Pollock's plan was to review the union headcount and get Ahern to justify each position. It was intended to be an operational review of all union jobs and costs—not just NABET's, even though that union would predominate the discussion. With somewhere north of 400 employees on staff, half of them easily were NABET-represented technicians, news writers, camera crews, and news editors.

Larry wanted to know why the overall station headcount was so high, and particularly in comparison with WPVI-TV in Philadelphia that he had managed before the acquisition and knew so well. Dominating the Philadelphia local market, its audience ratings at the time were huge—equal to the combined ratings of the competing CBS and NBC stations. Its profits were off the charts, reportedly at or over 55 or 60 cents on each dollar of revenue. The station had a contract with an IA local that represented its in-studio technicians but one where the word grievance was a foreign language and an arbitration would be from Mars.

Asking questions such as, "Joe, how many cameras do you have on your 5 and 6 P.M. news," Pollock sought answers. In those days before robotic cameras, each camera had a cameraperson and so the number of cameras would signify the number of technicians assigned. Joe looked down at the report in front of him and responded, with not the slightest clue of what was about to hit him—"That would be seven, Larry. Five for the show and two for graphics." Joe was obviously proud of his number-one rated shows in the very competitive Chicago market. He saw nothing remotely wrong with seven cameras, with their assortment of shots and camera angles, helping to achieve those results.

Larry expressed surprise and asked Bob Niles the same question about the Philadelphia station. Bob looked at his papers and answered, "two, Larry." Surely knowing the answer in advance since he had been the GM there for years, Larry turned to Ahern and said, "Hey Joe, let's get it down to two." Then came Joe's blunder. Responding reflexively and not choosing his words wisely, he uttered—"But Larry, that's Philadelphia."

It was a very big mistake. Witnessing this on several other occasions, nothing got Larry Pollock more mental than someone using the "that's Philadelphia" line. We were talking at the time, and perhaps still today in 2022, about one of most profitable stations and highest-rated news shows across the entire United

States. Philadelphia's market size was ranked fourth, just a slight step behind Chicago's third place, so the two cities were almost equal in audience size. WPVI-TV's production values were also high—just different. Audiences as sophisticated as Chicago's loved Jim Gardner's solo anchoring and the station's other, two-camera shows. To cast off two cameras as just a "that's Philadelphia" phenomenon was like slapping Larry hard across the face.

After absorbing the blow, Larry looked at Joe sternly for a moment and said in a slow, tight voice, "Joe, just get it done. Maybe we'll go for three cameras at most, with the third for graphics. And you don't have to get there all at once." For Larry, that reduction would result in the elimination of three or possibly four NABET jobs and was the start of big money he could cut out of his Chicago operation to build up its bottom line.

Joe and his staff were squirming to find another reason to justify what Larry had just concluded was heavy overstaffing. But it was a staffing Joe and his staff believed was necessary to maintain their Chicago dominance. Seven cameras to two, or maybe three, made no sense to them. The thought had to be racing through their minds of how the productions could survive as the top-rated news programs in town if they had to cut cameras back so drastically. Someone next reflexively blurted out— "But Larry, it's required by the NABET contract."

At that point all conversation stopped and all eyes looked to me. Of course most in that room knew that the NABET contract was bad. Perhaps though one of its few decent features was that it had no manning requirements whatsoever. In an odd way, it was now my moment to stand up for that contract. Brought to Chicago as the NABET expert just for that reason, I answered that this was not so and explained why. Pollock nodded, showing his appreciation for my comments. The meeting continued with this kind of responses the rest of the day of why this, or why that. Each time a staff position or two was blamed in whole or in part on the

NABET contract, all heads in the room would again turn to me. Most of the time I came back with that it was simply not true.

Very little answered that day about the contract's mandates was accurate. There were seven cameras and other overstaffing because that's how the station wanted to manage. It had probably been a succession of news directors over the years that built up to seven cameras, and that number had been producing top ratings for a long time. News directors wanted, Joe agreed, and they had gotten used to seven. They couldn't imagine maintaining their number one ratings by producing it like Philadelphia's Jim Gardner with only two or three cameras—with their limiting shots and angles.

That's why Weiswasser and Pollock had wanted me there. Glancing over at Mike Mallardi and Pollock, Steve had a smile on his face each time I, the new kid on the block, responded displaying knowledge of the contract that I had acquired from my past. With each answer, it validated his choice of me to head Labor Relations. Later that night over a dinner with the whole group at the local restaurant, we were all in a relaxed and celebratory mood. The Chicago meeting was the beginning of much to come.

The headcount at WLS-TV over the years, but beginning that day, was dramatically cut. A big chunk of it—the union part that needed negotiating to accomplish needed operational changes— would later be on my shoulders. Perhaps the reduction over time was as many as 200 union and non-union jobs. It would happen at every one of our four NABET TV stations. Tom's business philosophy of "not needing more people than you need" was being heard loud and clear. Understanding better each day that my expected job was to change the NABET contract to reflect the operational flexibilities management truly needed to get that engineering headcount as low as possible and achieve a firm handle on costs, I was already forming plans in the back of my mind.

Over at the Network, engineering jobs were under Julie Barnathan's BOE's control. Up until the time of the acquisition, however, Barnathan had also been in charge of engineering jobs at the television and radio stations as well as the radio network. While it had caused some internal organizational conflict, no one at the top of the old ABC really understood that each broadcasting property needed to have full control over its own engineering workforce. But Tom and Dan, with their deep station management background, put an end to that right away. Despite the fact that 800 to 1000 jobs were thus clawed back into the separate TV and radio stations, Barnathan's control over about 1200 remaining Network engineering positions still kept him, and BOE, very formidable.

Julie Barnathan had been involved in every NABET for decades. Soon after I came back on board, he told me he had every expectation to be similarly involved in the '88 preparations and to sit next to me at the '89 table. Normally, that would have been expected of any BOE leader—and very welcomed by any chief negotiator. But I soon learned that his view of the contract was markedly different from my own. Moreover, it was at odds with the opinion of just about everyone else in senior management, including Tom, Dan, and Network head Sias. While he might be willing to fight hard against any more "gives" to NABET, Julie's view could best be described that the contract needed from us only perhaps some fine-tuning. That was a far cry from the major overhaul of its deep flaws that everyone else was wishing for and I had been hired to achieve. Julie also shared a close relationship with the NABET leader, Jim Nolan. That, too, made some management people very nervous.

Curiously though, I was soon to find out that his fine-tuning assessment was not shared by his own BOE chief lieutenants in New York, Los Angeles, and Washington. Over the years, these veeps had become increasingly disillusioned themselves with just how tied their hands had become in managing their workforce and running their operations. They had come to believe they were drowning in too many rules and restrictions. The flood of grievances and the frequency of endless grievance meetings were driving them to near madness. Arbitrations were far too often and a terrible distraction from their regular duties.

The four vice presidents working for Julie in these three cities had become convinced major changes in the underlying contract were warranted. But they felt uncomfortable openly challenging their boss' markedly different views. The group also shared the discomfort of others that their boss was a little too tight with NABET's Jim Nolan. Whatever their misgivings had grown into, Tom and Dan's arrival, and the dawn of a new reality in my now occupying the chief labor relations chair, gave them great hope.

All of these circumstances brought me to a new realization. If the Company was going to head into the next set of talks in 1989 with NABET unified across the board and committed to achieve real change, Julie's involvement, as he was expecting, would present an unimaginable challenge. Fine-tuning was no solution to our deep-rooted problems, and only Barnathan was still believing that.

The conflict came to a head at the following year's annual Phoenix meeting for the Company's senior business leaders and corporate staff at the Arizona Biltmore hotel. My boss, Steve Weiswasser introduced me from the podium to the approximate 125 senior executives from all broadcasting and publishing business units as part of his general counsel report. "Get to meet our new vice president of labor relations, Jeff Ruthizer," said Weiswasser, with Murphy and Burke sitting beside him and probably nodding. "Jeff is going to lead the Company-wide effort next year to achieve major reform in the NABET contract by fixing its many serious problems."

Barnathan would go on to display sharp differences with Steve's assessment about my designated mission. When he made his displeasure and disagreement known, it became even clearer that if our planning had any chance of success, Julie would have to be removed from any involvement. Talking that over with Weiswasser after we returned from Phoenix, he was completely in accord. He'd go on to set up a meeting with Tom and Dan after they returned from Calgary where ABC Sports was producing the *XV Olympic Winter Games.*

Calgary, taking up the middle three weeks of February, had famously little snow. It was to be ABC's last Olympics although no one at the time knew it. BOE and ABC Sports management were heavily involved. Busy planning this for years, Barnathan was on site and deeply engaged. Roone Arledge, ever the showman and now running only ABC News, had been invited back to be the executive producer once again, as he had in all previous Olympics. Murphy and Burke were there throughout the three weeks of broadcasts. A charter flight flew scores of company executives including myself up to Calgary for a week as guests of the Network. Although most had accompanying spouses, unfortunately Monica had to stay home to watch over our school-age sons, Josh and Alex.

Much of my week in Calgary when not going to the athletic competitions was spent visiting the various venues with my labor lawyer assigned to the games where hundreds of NABET engineers were working. The week away with my colleagues was a nice break from what was going on in the office. All the time there I knew we had to deal with the unpleasant BOE situation once we returned to New York.

Murphy and Burke never shied away from tough calls. While clearly a highly sensitive subject, when we met upon their return from Calgary they saw at once the necessity of ordering Barnathan to stand down. This meant that going forward, the BOE chief would have to be cut out of every aspect of our planning for the talks and actual participation at the table. It would be an extraordinary new dynamic. Tom turned to Mike Mallardi—Barnathan's boss—and in a solemn voice said, "Mike, you call Julie in and tell him what I have decided." I did not envy Mike, but he proceeded to have his conversation delivering Murphy's message and a few days later called me. I was then free to proceed with a highly confidential, key-player planning conference.

Looking back 34 years, despite hurt feeling and damaged sensitivities, it was the only course responsible leaders could have followed. Once an organization has adopted a strategic vision, everybody in senior management not only has to get behind that decision, they have to embrace it. Anyone who is going to be on the actual bargaining team in any upcoming labor negotiations, let alone be a major player, has to be 100% committed to the organization's objectives and believe in its cause. Or else be removed.

It was particularly challenging because Barnathan's four chief lieutenants would be invited to participate at our upcoming spring planning conference. But the four were barred, despite any pressure they might encounter, from revealing to their boss anything that was discussed. Julie was the head of the 2000-strong BOE organization, 1200 of which were NABET represented employees. Yet he was to be totally embargoed. His being kept in the dark for what turned out to be more than a year was one of the most bizarre management circumstances I had ever experienced in my four-decade broadcasting career. But it was also the most necessary.

Shortly after Mallardi delivered Tom's stern message, I met with the four lieutenants. One of them, a former NABET engineer himself, Preston Davis, would rise in a few short years to take over as BOE president. To a person, they were relieved Murphy and Burke had made the call to remove their boss from any knowledge and involvement. As they saw it, it had to be done—not only for the good of the Company but also to protect the integrity and future of BOE. Understanding that their new roles would be strange and their relationship with their boss extremely uncomfortable, they knew they would have to keep their lips tightly sealed. Taking this "Chinese wall" extremely seriously, the group of BOE vice presidents stayed true to this arrangement for the entire course of the '88 planning stages and the subsequent '89 talks.

NABET's president Jim Nolan, had been lukewarm to me upon my return to the Company in 1987. I didn't think he liked me very much, probably remembering me as the young ABC lawyer who had beaten NABET in several arbitration decisions in the early '70s. Certainly he also recalled our Felt Forum confrontation at the *Grammy Awards* a decade and a half earlier when he had threatened to take the show down over the mic issue. He undoubtedly liked me even less when he learned the news, probably from Barnathan himself, that BOE's president had been cut out of the NABET process and would not be coming to the upcoming talks. Nolan surely had expected Julie's presence in the planning stages and at the negotiating table to have been a moderating influence on the Company's strategy and a brake on me. Nolan had to rearrange his thinking for what was coming next in his and the union's relationship with the re-energized Company.

Thankfully, being a corporate vice president brought with it some associated perks that took me away for brief respites from some of the discomforting labor pains. One of the best of these was to be invited with spouses to gala dinners at hotels like the Waldorf and to movie or show openings when the Company bought tables or tickets. The people in charge of deciding which causes and dinners were worthy of CapitalCities/ABC's money and who among the senior executives should be invited had me high on their list.

As '88 was coming to an end, I was invited to join some senior corporate staff along with spouses in attending the 25th anniversary restoration showing of '63's Oscar-winning *Lawrence of Arabia*. There would be a private dinner afterwards. The guest list for the dinner included the film's principal actors and directing team, the press, film industry notables, and other invited entertainment guests like us. After a quarter-century, the Columbia studio had decided the film was a little tired and needed some sprucing up and restoration work. Jim Painten, later to work for ABC Entertainment where I got to know him, was the co-producer in charge of the restoration cut. Jim, who worked alongside David Lean, the original film's famed British director, in structuring the restoration, gets star billing today when that movie is shown on TMC.

It was one of those glamorous and glitzy, black tie, Hollywood-type premieres—the kind with revolving searchlights—at Manhattan's Ziegfeld Theater. It was a short walk and literally around the corner from the old ABC building. After the nearly four-hour and totally enjoyable showing, we took cars over to the Pierre Hotel for the dinner. Monica, of course, was thrilled to join me with other spouses at our corporate table.

Sitting at the table next to us in the small room were some of the film's stars, including Peter O'Toole and Omar Sharif, as well as its director Lean. Most probably Alec Guinness was also there, but of that I cannot be certain. O'Toole was one of Monica's and my favorite actors, not just from *Lawrence of Arabia* but also from his jewel a few years earlier—*My Favorite Year,* a comedy which gloriously depicted the early days of live television. I particularly enjoyed the movie because it poked fun in a hysterical scene at my IATSE friends, the Local 1 stagehands. It also showed some hilarious NABET control room moments in an old NBC 30 Rock studio.

As the very long night was winding down, well after midnight, Monica gathered up enough courage and led me over to O'Toole's table to ask for his autograph. She carried our two evening programs—one for each of our young sons, Josh and Alex, back at home. Both had practically memorized all of *My Favorite Year's* best lines. In fact, O'Toole's Alan Swan was easily in those days their favorite movie character. I followed Monica as she approached the seated O'Toole. Employing some clever introductory line she recalled from *My Favorite Year,* she got Peter's immediate attention. Turning sideways towards her, he chatted with us for what seemed like an eternity and with great charm graciously signed both programs. Call it "My... no,... Our Favorite Evening."

17
CHAPTER

The Jacket Goes Around My Shoulders

The Rainbow Room atop 30 Rock was never nicer. Tom Murphy and Dan Burke were so pleased with the results of the first '89 NABET negotiations after acquiring ABC that they wanted to celebrate in a big way.

"Bring the whole bargaining team from around the country and their spouses," I'll never forget Dan saying, "and make sure you invite the administrative assistants and their spouses, too." It was so typical of Dan Burke's thoughtfulness and generosity. Everyone from out of town was to be flown into New York. Nothing like this had even been done before. About 20 operators, lawyers, and administrative assistants—my regular team—was reassembled one last time. Dan and Murphy would make sure to invite the division presidents from all broadcasting groups, plus the senior corporate staff. As usual for these events, everyone was expected to bring spouses. I made sure our valuable outside labor counsel, Jerry Kauff, was invited. And another incredibly important person would be there, too. More about Marv Bader in subsequent pages.

This was, as I discovered, the "Cap Cities" way. So the invitations went out to honor the Company's labor achievements. Close to 100 people gathered that cool autumn night for cocktails and dinner. It was on the top floor of 30 Rockefeller Plaza in New York's most glamorous nightclub that we had taken over for the evening. The views of the city—stretching out in all directions beneath us—were just breathtaking.

Ecstatic to be joining Tom and Dan to honor the Company-wide effort that night were their division chiefs. The TV Network's John Sias, Sports' Dennis Swanson, News' Roone Arledge, TV Stations' Larry Pollock, GMA's Phil Beuth, and Radio's Jim Arcara would have been there. If Bob Iger, by now the head of ABC Entertainment, was in New York on one of his frequent visits and not in Los Angeles where he was based, he surely would have been there, too.

Dan had asked public relations head, Patti Matson, to organize the entire evening and she did one of her normally excellent jobs. After dinner, Tom and Dan spoke, thanking us all and noting how significant this negotiations had been. Steve Weiswasser made some remarks, too. Singled out by each for some kind words about my leadership, I followed with comments of my own. First thanking my team for their efforts during this grueling two-year period and particularly their time away from home in San Diego, I expressed my deep appreciation to the Company leaders for their unqualified support. It was a glorious evening celebrating the Company victory, as Tom and Dan were proud to proclaim.

Patti Matson had earlier that year demonstrated her resourcefulness in other ways. At Dan's suggestion to help keep the home fires burning while the boys (mostly) were away fighting the war for five weeks in San Diego, Patti did some shopping on Fifth Avenue. She had chosen gorgeous, Hermes scarves for the wives of the men on the bargaining team and an equally stunning Hermes tie for the sole, male spouse. It was another typical example of Dan's thoughtfulness and generosity, helped along by Patti's excellent taste.

Murphy and Burke had shared with me when I was hired in '87 that they almost didn't buy the Company because of the NABET contract. They were comfortable with unions in general and had union contracts at many of their broadcasting and publishing properties. But as experienced broadcasters and careful businessmen, they were unaccustomed to the overstaffing, inefficiencies, and excessive cost they strongly suspected, and had heard from initial reports, this particular agreement represented.

I was there to identify and fix the problems. To help me, Dan Burke told me one day soon after coming on board that he was going to place his jacket over my shoulders. What an empowering expression that was as I was about to enter this dangerous arena. Dan had a bunch of these very apt expressions, like "jacket," that most of us had never heard before. His jacket got a little worn around the edges as the years went by, but it was always very welcomed.

The strategic plan we needed for our '89 talks began its gestation during our '88 planning year. My senior staff and I ran a week long conference off-campus at Westchester's Arrowwood conference center to begin our preparations. Attending were the senior executives from each group covered by the NABET contract. The individuals most responsible for administering the agreement and managing the workforce, together they employed nearly all of Company's 2300 NABET employees in our five cities.

BOE's four veeps under Barnathan, with their lips now tightly sealed, from its New York, Los Angeles, and Washington operations were in attendance. So were senior leaders from the Network's ABC Sports, ABC News, ABC Daytime, and *GMA*. And one or two from corporate finance. Top executives from the TV Station group, the Radio Station group, and the Radio Network filled out the field. Maybe there were about 30 of us—including my labor relations team of four or five.

The lawyers and I had been busy for weeks researching and preparing materials. During that Westchester conference week, the union contract was ripped apart from stem to stern. Every major nook and cranny of the inch-thick, several hundred page book was explored. From far too many experiences, most of the people gathered in the room knew how deeply their operations were handicapped. Restrictions, costs, and inefficiencies abounded that had built up over decades of bargaining.

My job was to focus the group on the worst of the identified problems, examine options, and prioritize objectives. The biopsied provisions were evaluated against emerging technologies, competitive labor agreements at CBS and NBC, business needs, and just common sense. When the conference ended, a few called it the best planning meeting they had ever attended.

Surprising to some, we took the unusual step to invite a few high NABET officials, including its president, Jim Nolan, to join Tom and Dan and a few of us at a private dinner the evening the conference ended. There were two purposes. The first was to let the NABET's leaders know that we, just as they had been preparing, had been busy planning for our upcoming battle. Its other purpose was to socialize in an informal setting to gain the benefits that leaders knowing each other as individuals might bring at some point down the road if a crisis or special circumstance developed.

It was not the first time Murphy and Burke had met Nolan. Earlier that winter, I had come up with a plan to introduce the NABET leaders, Jim Nolan and Tom Kennedy, to Tom and Dan. A meeting had been set in Tom's temporary offices in the old ABC building with Weiswasser and myself attending. I felt, and Steve agreed, that it was important for Tom to deliver a message that this was now a new ABC. No longer would the Company that Tom had just bought be willing to accept drawn-out contract talks, grant retroactivity, and accept meager results. They had to understand and hear it directly from Tom that this was a complete break from

ABC's past. The second intended purpose was to make it clear that Jeff Ruthizer was in charge, would always be speaking for them, and had their total support.

Putting four Irishmen together like this is always an interesting experience. It's especially the case in an introductory meeting intended to build trust and respect. Nolan and Kennedy started the meeting in a friendly manner when they congratulated Murphy on buying the Company. Tom thanked them and went on to deliver the intended dual messages in his usual cordial but firm manner. It was to be, he said, a new bargaining day for CapitalCities/ABC—no longer the old ABC way of doing business with long talks and constantly-granted wage retroactivity. He then added, "Jeff Ruthizer is totally in charge of the upcoming talks." Tom emphasized that I would always be speaking for him and Dan and had their complete support.

With this, Nolan interrupted. Looking over at me for a moment, he said, "Excuse me Mr. Murphy," to which Tom responded, "Call me Tom." Nolan went on with, "Okay Tom, but I've heard that Bob Ballow is going to be in charge and that Jeff is just going be his mouthpiece."

For some background, Bob Ballow was the lead partner in the law firm that had represented Capital Cities Communications in a number of its labor talks prior to its ABC acquisition and was still doing the Company's publishing work. Ballow was known as an extremely tough negotiator and was universally hated by the unions. But he had absolutely nothing to do with broadcasting labor relations and was not involved in any aspect of the upcoming NABET talks.

Without missing a beat, Dan Burke, with a completely straight face, jumped in with, "Jim you are absolutely right, and Bob Ballow is hiding in the closet right behind you." There was an immediate, couple of seconds pause as Nolan stared at Dan while digesting the remark, exchanged glances with Kennedy, and then went on with the rest of his comments as if none of this had ever happened. The maybe half-hour meeting soon ended with everyone shaking hands and wishing one another good luck.

But the central messages had been delivered loud and clear. It was a magnificent moment—vintage Dan Burke, as I would learn. With that brief meeting and Dan's telling comment, Burke and Murphy had established in no uncertain terms that there was a new sheriff in town. The team of Tom Murphy and Dan Burke had taken over. The old sheriff, Leonard Goldenson, was gone. Jeff Ruthizer was their deputy. I'd fasten the deputy badge to Dan's jacket and go on to wear it proudly for the entire time Tom and Dan ran the Company.

Following the planning conference, my team and I spent many days that summer synthesizing the results and developing our negotiating roadmap. After traveling the country, meeting with managers, and doing some deeper diving into the businesses' many needs, I completed my plan and presented it to Murphy, Burke, Weiswasser, and key group presidents.

After a few meetings so they could digest it better, Tom and Dan gave it their approval. It boiled down to one thing—the contract was full of restrictions, limitations, inefficiencies, and economic waste in a myriad of areas. Their business instincts and initial reports had told them much of that when they had bought the Company. Now they had their evidence from the deep analysis and game plan for change. Charged by them to fix it, I needed nothing more. Tom at that point turned tactical command over to Dan.

All of us were hoping for a peaceful process. But considering the union's history of striking ABC about every ten years, many of us felt we were due. And they had struck NBC just the year before. Faced with the possibility of another real and very hot shooting war, Burke agreed with me just how important it was to prepare our defenses.

Prevailing in a possible long and bitter strike became a critical objective. As we talked it through, it became clear we needed a nationwide strike preparation "czar." Dan asked me to look around and recommend someone who I felt would be the right person. After some discussion as to whom the czar should report—possibly even to me—Burke decided quite correctly that this position should report to him, with a dotted line to me. I'm not sure why Dan entrusted me with the recruitment mission. But he must have felt that any czar running the home front had to be someone who had not just the confidence of him and Tom, the commanders-in-chief, but also myself, the battlefield commander. At the time he asked me to undertake this search mission, I had absolutely no idea who might fill this vital role.

Later that year at the annual National Association of Broadcasters conference in Las Vegas I shared a bus ride with Marv Bader. Marv was a senior ABC Sports executive who like me was attending the NAB. He had just wrapped up some critical work at ABC's coverage of the Calgary Olympic Games and had been in charge of the vast logistics at many previous ABC Olympics. It was a chance meeting, not knowing each other before, and we hit it off as soon as we sat down next to each other for the half-hour ride to the convention center.

Just from chatting and getting a glimpse into his background, logistical mind, and personality, I immediately sensed Bader was the right person to be our czar. Intrigued by my offer over drinks that night, and looking for something significant to do now that there was no new Olympics on ABC's horizon, Marv was fine with my presenting his name to Dan. After they met, Dan wholeheartedly agreed with my choice. We had our czar.

Burke gave Bader wide spending discretion to get the Company ready for the war that might be coming. The final number probably turned out to be several million dollars. Bader put together a top-notch team that set up comprehensive training programs for all of ABC's radio and TV network and station facilities nationwide.

Relying mostly on major vendors and their facilities or leased studios as training sites, he recruited a large group of management volunteers.

Scores of executives and other non-union management employees at all properties were sent to Marv-school to learn how to operate the vast range of equipment. It had to be hundreds of bodies who needed to be trained not just for our television and radio studios but also for remote news and sports assignments. Many news gathering ENG crews would have to be sent out at all properties. *MNF,* NBA, golf, and college football games— everything, all domestic sports broadcasts—would have to be managed with replacement crews. It was a tall order to effectuate a master plan for all necessary coverages at both the Network and station level.

Bader worked with HR and myself to devise a suitable bonus pay program for replacements who would be trained and called for active duty should a strike take place. Many of those management volunteers remembered with fondness the swimming pools they had installed and new cars they bought from their '77 strike bonuses.

When we were strong, ready, and up to Bader's Olympics standards, Burke and the entire company could rest more easily at night. The strength would carry over to my command module at the bargaining table by giving me the supreme confidence we would be ready for any eventuality. More importantly, NABET would also sense our strength and act cautiously, we hoped, when it faced the decision whether to strike.

When the contract along with its no-strike clause expired at midnight that last day of March 1989, the entire Company in all five of our cities had to be ready for an immediate walkout. But even more important was that every location had to remain in a state of preparedness thereafter until a new agreement was signed because a strike was possible at any time. Czar Bader was also planning an ongoing readiness program where there would always be enough management people standing by, corralled in safe areas, or easily summonable, to be able to move in at all locations nationwide quickly to take over in case of a sudden NABET walkout. His Olympic credentials would make sure ABC would be kept on the air—and in perfect order.

Rule Number One for any union contemplating a strike is never to do so unless it is absolutely certain it can beat the employer and win. Rule Number Two is never forget the importance of the first rule. The intended consequence of our openly-advertised strike preparation program was to make sure NABET would know, and long remember, the solid teaching of both rules.

However, despite what NABET might be thinking or planning at any given moment, I had my own Number One Rule. It came from years of dealing with NABET and other unions and governed my own strategic thinking. It was a simple teaching to always expect the unexpected.

So, just as the union was doing, ABC went on a war footing. Part of that planning, like any company entering into major labor talks, was to face up to the dangers of information leaks through both "loose lips" and industrial espionage. It was all wrapped up in our contingency planning for the unexpected. Vitally important was that our negotiations strategy and highly confidential war plans had to remain secure.

Loose lips could be dealt with only partially by a flood of constant admonitions to our tight circle involved in our planning. It was also managed by keeping the tight circle as small as possible. More importantly, when the stakes were as high as ours, we had to be certain there could be no infiltration or Watergate-type break-ins. Our offices had to be safe from clandestine, late night rummaging through waste paper baskets, searching desks for valuable information, or electronic listening.

Even though desk top computerization had taken over by '89, I was still a big fan of paper. The problem with paper was that it could be easily read, lifted, or photographed. Planning books I distributed to a few key senior managers were numbered and had to be signed for. I sent my administrative assistant around to collect them once read because comprising our strategies and chances for success through mishandling could not be risked.

Moreover, I had to have the surety of knowing that our labor relations offices and telephones were secure from electronic surveillance devices. Constantly reminding myself and others that we were dealing with a union largely of audio and video electronics experts, we had to know to a virtual certainty that we could speak freely, keep our documents safe, and remain secure in our own offices. Non-digital in those days, we tried to avoid using cellphones outside of the office for fear of their being easily tapped.

Would the union leaders or its members actually engage in, encourage, or tolerate acts of industrial espionage? Would they bug our offices or our phones or plant sophisticated listening devices with long range capabilities in a space they might rent across 66 Street? Would they perform or sanction late night surreptitious visits to seek documents from our waste bins or desk tops?

We didn't think any of this was probable. But we had heard of instances elsewhere and could take no chances of everyone playing by the same rules we were ourselves following. Since the stakes were extremely high and such times can sometimes lead people to take desperate measures, we wanted to expect the most noble, exemplary conduct but we had to prepare for the worst. Needing a sophisticated security plan to protect against any possible espionage and leaks, I turned to the Company's security experts.

ABC's security chief, a former DEA official, was brought in and developed a rigorous plan involving outside security specialists. As the result, our offices and phones were periodically swept during the several months leading up to our talks for electronic listening devices. Tom and Dan's, too. Many other surveillance and electronic steps were taken. Cameras were installed. Special locks were put on doors to make certain offices of key executives were inaccessible at night to the normal cleaning crews where espionage could easily be accomplished. High speed, bulk shredders were installed. The security precautions were also meant to carry over to our negotiations venue the following year.

Our inner circle was constantly reminded to keep confidential papers in locked desk drawers and lips tightly sealed. I was always raising awareness about our normally assumed safe spaces—like elevators, subway platforms, railroad cars, and local area restaurants and bars where our natural defenses would be down. One never knew when the wrong ears might be listening.

While rare, industrial espionage certainly had happened before in some major union negotiations where the stakes like ours were extremely high. This was particularly true as sophisticated electronic spying devices were becoming considerably more affordable. Every possible measure was taken to make sure there would be no security breaches on my watch that could undermine our efforts.

San Diego had a mystical, near reverential, connection over the years to both parties as a bargaining site. The magnetic pull was just too great so we returned there again in February of '89 for a five-week stay intended through the contract's March 31 expiration date. Close to 18 strong, my team consisted of senior operating executives from our television and radio operating areas plus four of my lawyers and myself. It was basically a smaller version of the group who had attended the previous year's spring conference, plus two administrative assistants, including mine from New York.

We stayed at the downtown Marriott hotel and the union team of eight to ten were at a nearby Shelter Island hotel an easy 15 or 20 minute drive away where the talks would take place. Heading over and back in a caravan, it was often several times a day, including most weekends.

With over an inch-thick, set of proposals containing perhaps

100 or more items that we had fine-tuned during the previous months, we intended it for the first time to be our agenda that governed. Still sailing in the wake of Reagan's nearly a decade earlier taking on of the Air Traffic Controllers union and the lessons it had taught American industry, we were constantly stressing our main reform theme.

No longer, I was constantly reiterating, could we have the worst contract in the industry. Starting that opening day, we hammered away that the contract was inefficient, non-competitive, too costly, and far too restrictive. Not embarrassed to boldly seek change in so many areas, we repeated this central theme so often that not only did the union committee get tired hearing it, which they were not shy about telling me, I got tired of saying it.

The union had the year before gone to the mat with NBC in a long and bitter strike over many of these same proposals. Its chief bargainer, Tom Kennedy, frequently made clear it would not hesitate to strike us if we persisted with our sought-after reforms. Over the course of the next five weeks, the union, still believing it was the old days when their agenda would govern, offered up their own inch-thick set of proposals and would go on to resist our's at every turn. Telling them that "this was no longer your father's Oldsmobile," as the television commercial of the time went, it made little difference on the surface in getting them to acknowledge we were serious. What they were thinking about and worrying over internally, however, was probably very different. We just had no way of knowing.

Dan Burke could never understand why these talks had to be held 2500 miles away, for so long, in mild temperatures, and particularly in a resort city. Why San Diego and not Anchorage he would muse in what I took as only half in jest. "Alaska would get the talks over fast."

Nevertheless, he and Weiswasser flew out on the Company plane for the opening session. Never failing to kid me for years afterwards about the giant box of Winchell's donuts sitting on the side table that both committees but particularly the union's voraciously consumed, he had come out to set the tone. With our COO's unexpected and unprecedented presence that morning, it was again designed to deliver a message. His comments underscoring our broad goals to reform the contract reinforced my own that we had an entirely new model Oldsmobile sitting in the garage.

We ran through our demands first that initial week with ample explanations. And presented experts, such as our head of research, to document poor ratings and unfavorable competitive positions that we argued warranted our sought-after, cost-reducing contract changes. I even arranged for our Entertainment head, Bob Iger, to fly down from LA and give their committee a presentation about the Network's upcoming prime time program schedule. The union, however, showed no interest in anything we said. It would go on to wear its blindfold for weeks while Nolan, Kennedy and the committee tested our determination.

Going through their own proposals the following week, the union pursued what might be called a grab bag approach. It was more of this and more of that and an improvement here and an improvement there. It was always something more, better or an item that would tie us up even greater than we were already suffering. Our basis for selection was simple—the only items we were prepared to consider were those that wouldn't make the contract more restrictive or add unreasonable cost.

When St. Patrick's Day rolled around towards the halfway point of our talks, I had a surprise waiting. I had remembered from my 1971 and '73 negotiation experiences with these Irishmen that they took this special day very seriously. Stopping the morning bargaining session soon after it began, I climbed into the middle of the hollow rectangle tables around which we had been sitting. It was something no one— on either side—had expected. Having found a shop in town that specialized in heraldic crests, I had ordered framed parchment, heraldic family crests for their three Irishmen—Nolan, Kennedy, and Chicago's Dan Delaney.

I had made sure my entire team that morning was wearing our green, ABC Sports logo'ed sports shirts, compliments of Bob Apter. Kennedy, ever the proud Irishman, soon happily joined me in the middle. Sporting that day, with particular relish, a Kelly green Irish cap worn at a rakish angle, he was attired in his own Kelly green sport shirt. Soon laughing and shaking hands as some on both sides snapped away, I presented the parchment crests. That morning's brief festivities were a welcomed respite from the drone of constant rejection and tension. But that moment's levity wouldn't last for long.

The negotiations was a milestone in my career. It was the biggest, highest stakes, and by far the most complicated talks that I had yet conducted. While I had been working in labor relations for 23 years and this was my third NABET network negotiations, nothing previous at ABC, NBC, or RKO had remotely approached the vastness, complexity, and huge number of moving parts that these talks represented.

Steve Weiswasser knew that when he hired me. But he had expressed great confidence then and during the weeks leading up to my departure for San Diego as he saw more of the rollout of our plans and strategy. So had Murphy and Burke. Of course, none of them had seen me in action across the bargaining table, or really understood my capabilities. They surely checked me out when they hired me and perhaps knew a little of my NBC and RKO backgrounds. They might have even heard a few good things from ABC executives still there from my first tour of duty about my skills and performance as a young lawyer nearly 20 years earlier. But that rookie who went to the '71 NABET table with Freund and Barnathan was now a much different person. Those midshipman days were long behind me.

Surely, while Murphy and Burke's business instincts and best judgments about people told them something yet unproven was there within me, they had to be wondering. And probably talking to each other continually as the storm clouds were gathering. It would have been entirely natural for all bosses at any company in America, let alone these close partners. They were undoubtedly asking themselves, and each other as well as Weiswasser, whether labor chief Ruthizer had the right stuff. Was I smart, clever, realistic, and tough enough. Did I have the right leadership skills, legal creativity, and negotiating abilities to lead the team and deal with the union's demands, maneuvers, and strategies. Was I listening properly for hidden messages and possible compromises—could I smell a deal, or detect a trap and upcoming attack?

A great deal was at stake. It was a major, Company-wide undertaking and failure was not an option. Not just was the Company's future relationship with NABET on the line but also my own future. If war actually broke out, a strike could be devastating in its impact on the Company's operations, ratings, and finances. But there could be, as had happened in other major labor disputes, certain war casualties.

Despite our investment of so much time, money, and effort in our common venture, there were no guarantees that Murphy and Burke's broad hopes, and my plan to achieve those aspirations, would succeed. Nor were there assurances that Bader's strike preparations would be successful. Companies in serious labor talks also have their own Rule Number One—it's not to take a strike unless it is absolutely certain it can prevail. Bader had told us we were well-ready for a strike, but that did not guarantee we would prevail. All of us relied on that assurance of strength. We thought we could, but what if we were wrong?

I had studied their chief players and our bargaining opponent in great depth and detail. But this was far from a science. Always expecting the unexpected, I had only my own skills, knowledge, abilities, and instincts on which to rely. And, of course, those of my closest labor relations advisors and outside counsel. The labor law part was relatively easy. It was the labor relations part that was damn hard.

What if we had underestimated the situation or the capabilities of our adversaries in this, a you-can't-make-any-mistakes-arena where no do-overs are ever possible? Had I accounted for enough of the unexpected that might be thrown at us? There was always one more thing to consider in our preparations, but had we done so adequately?

With so much weight on my shoulders, I often felt like the Greek mythological figure Atlas. Every phrase I uttered across the table was measurable and potentially consequential—every intonation and even each eyebrow I might raise. With many sleepless nights stressing out about what could or did go wrong, I also had many long talks with myself. However, most of the time I felt confident that with the unqualified support from the top of the Company my team and I were receiving, we would succeed. That, plus a little bit of luck.

Leading this large and diverse team of senior operational executives —mostly presidents and vice presidents of their units— with differing agendas and favorite issues, strong opinions, and forceful personalities—was an enormous challenge. I wore many hats. I was, however, as the Company's senior labor relations officer and chief negotiator—by virtue of the authority given to me by Tom and Dan—the commanding general of an army in the field. What I said in the battle theatre, after robust debate and discussion—even with these presidents —had to be accepted. It was that way at every major company in America involved in serious labor talks and it would be no different with us. Those were the rules of engagement.

While I had developed a vision and strategic plan for dramatic changes in ABC's relationship with NABET, the union had a history of dealing with companies it viewed as no friend. And attempting to destroy chief negotiators whose strategic views differed dramatically from their own. NABET had gone to the mat five times with both ABC and NBC in less than three decades over serious issues and threats to its future. ABC had experienced long strikes in '67 and '77. NBC had its own work stoppages in '59, '76, and the most recent, long one in '87. Oftentimes, as in all labor talks where stakes are high, it becomes very personal. Leaders on both sides get vilified. Some don't make it back.

18
CHAPTER

The Importance of Being Credible

As the weeks went by in San Diego with no progress, the NABET leaders did not know exactly what to make of the situation. For one thing, while forewarned in Murphy's office that day, they were not used to an early announcement on or near the first day of talks that there would be no contract extension nor grant of retroactivity. Five weeks—I had told them—were enough to make a deal. They had to be painfully aware though of two other things that most often allowed me to sleep better at night. While the first was that I had the total backing of Murphy and Burke, perhaps the second was even more consequential—the depth, scope, and magnificence of Bader's strike-preparation team. Bader and I would make sure to talk every few days.

Dan Burke had thoughtfully arranged for our spouses and children back home in our respective cities to be flown out to San Diego for a visit with us about halfway through the talks. Tom Kennedy, when we announced why we could not meet that weekend because our spouses were flying in, would then and forevermore refer to this as our "conjubial visit." This was a classic

Kennedy remark—as it was a classic Dan Burke act of generosity. Spouses, almost entirely wives, came out with our kids. ABC News arranged through its Pentagon contacts for a special family tour of the aircraft carrier, the USS *Constellation*, docked in port for some refitting. Josh and Alex loved it.

Constantly was I stressing within our own meeting rooms the necessity of operators jumping in on the technical details and explaining the business necessities for the proposed changes. They all strongly believed in our pursuits, but they had to say it. The union had to hear it from the actual bosses of their represented employees and not just from us, their lawyers. The strongest operators among the group, such as BOE's Preston Davis and Sports' Bob Apter, rose to the occasion, as did the TV Station group's representative most often there, Walter Liss. Walter, the president and GM of New York's WABC-TV and an old Cap Cities hand with a strong point of view, would go on a decade later to lead the TV Station group.

I wanted my lawyers to jump in, too, when they thought it would be helpful and not leave every word or discussion point to me. Often, especially those who'd been at the NABET table in San Diego before, had points to make and arguments to answer better than mine.

The dynamics of running a large bargaining team approaching at times 20 people, most of strong personality, over a five-week period away from home and family, presented many challenges. I had to keep the group interested, motivated, and participating actively with me daily at our long sessions. While each day most were doing just that, they also had to take time out to look after their normal operating duties back at their home bases. 1989 was before mobile phones, except those the size of a walking boot, which Walter Liss alone had. So necessary contact with home, office, and subordinates was limited to room telephones before or after our negotiating sessions and the few pay phones in the NABET hotel lobby.

It fell on me to integrate the group, socialize the group, and galvanize the group. Many had not known each other well, or even at all, before arrival. Radio hardly ever associated with TV and television station people did not normally hang out with Network types. Socialization was a critical element to maintain our sanity and perspective. A meeting back in our conference room each day after our bargaining ended was essential to get feedback and build team spirit. Cocktail time each evening to critique the day's events under more sociable circumstances was de rigeur.

Group dinners with our temporary family at local restaurants a few times a week became important parts of our game plan to keep morale up and spirits high. After all, we weren't getting a lot of love at the bargaining table each day. The logistics of finding places with private rooms for 20, including always our valuable administrative assistants, were not always easy. Fortunately we had with us our Laundry and Morale Officer, Bob Apter. Bob often performed magic.

One night Bob and I crossed over the railroad tracks a block behind the Marriott in the old harbor district and headed to the Kansas City Barbeque. I think it was Bob who found the place and insisted I join him. The restaurant had gotten its fame just a few years earlier in '86 when some major *Top Gun* scenes were so brilliantly shot inside. Up against the wall was the famous upright piano where Goose and Maverick had belted out "Great Balls of Fire." In the back room was the juke box where Kelly McGillis had quietly slipped in her quarter. Probably having a burger and beer or two while sitting at that same bar as Tom Cruise's Lt. Pete Mitchell, I'm sure the evening was designed by the ever-thoughtful Bob Apter as a little R&R from our usual tiring and tension filled days at the table.

Dan Burke flew out once during the time we were there to show the flag. Going on to become a custom, it was a great feeling to know that the COO cared enough to fly cross country to meet with his team at a distant outpost, get a progress report, give a pep talk, and fly back.

The team I had brought to San Diego was almost entirely operators or lawyers. The one exception was David Loewith. A corporate financial vice president from the Cap Cities side of the pre-merger enterprise, David had no NABET knowledge, experience, or responsibility whatsoever. But he had a focus, and a feisty, outspoken business sense that I liked when it came to unions that I had observed from other labor matters where we had been involved. Smart and with great analytical skills, he spoke the very welcome Cap Cities language of "We don't need more people than we need," or "we don't need to spend more than we need to spend." Deciding what I needed was David on my team, I invited him to join us and he jumped at the opportunity. His presence was of enormous assistance—both in our own room and across the table.

My legal team of five who had been working on the NABET project for the past 18 months was a combination of the old and the new. A few of these very smart lawyers had been the draftsmen responsible over the prior negotiations for some of the very contract language that the new CapitalCities/ABC business reality now found objectionable. While first there was a bit of authorship pride that had to be overcome, and some necessary reorientation required, it all got managed.

Clever enough to have drafted the language initially, they found the way of putting some of the toothpaste back in the tube. With their wealth of accumulated ABC bargaining experience and NABET knowledge, they were constantly transmitting that information into my brain. Holdovers from Dick Freund's team—Bill Gennerich, Mike Lang, and Bob Key—were of enormous help in not only keeping our San Diego ship afloat but also sailing at full speed ahead. And in the right direction. My newest lawyer, Olivia Cohen-Cutler, joined us in San Diego despite her lack of any deep, network NABET knowledge and was a valuable addition.

Smart, personable, and largely reflecting my own labor relations philosophy, she had gained my complete confidence from our six years together.

In constructing the San Diego team and engaging for the upcoming battle, my boss Steve Weiswasser had been tremendously helpful. When I had earlier gone to him to discuss internal resources and the need for support, he said, "Jeff I will be your support." The enormously busy Company's general counsel constantly made himself available. When we needed time with Murphy or Burke, Steve was always there to make the arrangements and participate. When we needed to get the attention of a sometimes pre-occupied senior executive—like News' Roone Arledge—Steve always succeeded.

Weiswasser and I talked on a regular basis as the talks progressed. He would come out and stay near San Diego for a week towards the March 31 expiration date to assist in any way possible. Never trying to interfere with my running the negotiations, he stayed far away from the table or our bargaining team meetings. Steve helped me sort through our most critical proposals as we were forming our final offer and was tremendously supportive as the situation was moving towards its conclusion.

When a deal is the goal and an absolute stalemate the reality, a negotiator sometimes has to consider a different path forward. Call it a Plan B. So about a week before the contract was due to expire I came up with two powerful incentives to grab the union's attention. After getting Weiswasser involved, and ultimately receiving Tom and Dan's approval, the Company made what we believed would be two game changing proposals. Neither of such a magnitude had ever been offered before in any broadcasting negotiation.

The first blockbuster was a guarantee that virtually protected all of the approximate 2000 staff engineering employees, except those in radio, against being laid off for the first three years of the proposed four year contract. Our thinking was simple and we thought persuasive. Since we had so many major proposals on the table that the union said threatened TV engineering jobs in multiple ways, we were prepared to show our good faith that our changes were not threatening. If they really had these fears about what our proposals would bring, this made clear they would not result in any layoff.

In a conversation with Tom Murphy after we had decided to make this "no layoff" guarantee, Tom asked if I thought he might help sell the package in a private meeting with Nolan. After I agreed, Tom flew out on the Company plane. We met one afternoon secretly with Jim Nolan for over an hour a few days before the contract was due to expire. Trying as hard as we could to convince Jim to take the deal and recommend it to his membership, Nolan would not do so unless we made serious revisions. Since this was not possible, Tom's initiative went nowhere and he flew home disappointed.

The proposal was startling in its design and potential impact by virtually assuring complete job security. We thought it would get a big reception. No other broadcasting company had ever before offered such a guarantee. But the no layoff guarantee, much to our surprise, didn't move the needle. Because it was a pledge for only the first three years, some concluded that the last year would result in massive terminations. We felt that deep down even the union leaders knew that this was not going to happen, but it was impossible to convince them of that sufficiently. Curiously, the union never counter proposed to make it a four year pledge.

Our second mega-proposal was an unprecedentedly large ratification bonus. The industry at the time—and we concurred, had developed a new approach of giving technicians a first year ratification bonus instead of the normal wage increase. Weekly salaries had gotten very high, and this was a way designed to make a one time payment but keep wage rates frozen. We had already offered a very significant 5%, bonus—now we doubled it to a startling 10%. But it was tied to, and only payable if and when there was a ratification.

Like any deal, we were trying to buy what we needed. Nobody was offering big money like this at that time, or ever. If anything could, we thought, this 10% would get their attention and open them up to wide agreement on the many points we were proposing. Asking for a lot, we were prepared to pay a lot. We tried to sell it as a major breakthrough for any union. Representing many thousands of dollars per person, it though could not get the NABET engine off of idle.

Of course the full 10% bonus, as had the earlier 5% proposal, was tied to acceptance of our final proposal at contract expiration time. Emphasizing it again, we made clear that for every week that went by after the March 31 expiration without a deal, a week's worth of the potential 10% bonus would fall off the table. But that self-reducing nature of the bonus if time dragged on did not seem to have any impact either.

Even with these giant proposals that we thought would break the stalemate, they continued to reject or ignore everything placed before them. As the days of bargaining rolled by bringing us closer to the March 31 contract expiration, nothing was happening. In constant touch with Marv Bader, I was assured, as was Burke, that he and his team, and consequently the Company, were prepared for a strike when the contract was due to expire at midnight. Bader had done the Olympics many times over, so we had perfect confidence that this would be another gold medal performance.

Two nights before the contract's March 31 expiration was the *61st Annual Academy Awards* show from Hollywood. It was ABC's biggest entertainment show of the year that just happened to be also the largest NABET production. Involving millions in advertising revenues and several score of LA based engineers, ABC would once again be broadcasting the show to the nation and world. For years, it had been a source of pride for the Company, the union, and the many NABET-represented employees who regularly worked on the crew.

It was usually broadcast in late March but occasionally in early April. When every fourth year there was a March 31 NABET expiration date, our Network programming people in consultation with labor relations made certain to arrange with the Academy that ABC produce the program before the contract's expiration. No way were we going to endanger the show in the event of a strike or have it used as leverage against us.

Late that afternoon after the daily talks had ended, the whole bargaining team settled into comfortable couches in our large Marriott suite. Enjoying a lavish room service order for 20, we watched *Rain Man* and *Mississippi Burning* slug it out for top honors. Bob Murphy, a veep from ABC News who would periodically pop in, was there. Usually in San Diego to weigh in on significant news issues, he brought with him that night a huge, maybe 20 gallon, container of ice cream. There may have even been some chocolate topping. It was a gigantic and highly caloric tub surely intended by Bob to keep us not just fattened up but also even more deeply committed—in News' overindulgent but very welcoming ways—to their pressing issues.

The rest of the Company's labor relations activities did not stop just because I and four of my lawyers were away in San Diego for a month. I had to keep a distant eye on those, too. NABET grievance meetings continued although arbitrations were suspended. Other contract talks might also be going on. It was never quiet with AFTRA, AFM, IATSE, WGA, SAG, the DGA, or any of our other unions. Sometimes those matters—and even negotiations—also required my attention. Our remaining lawyers on both coasts not involved in San Diego had their hands full with most of this other activity and would get me involved when necessary.

As the end of March came closer, it was just too hard a pull to bring NABET into the new order. It was still the game of denial and avoidance. In fact, as the last days in San Diego approached they had still not agreed to a major item we had proposed. The two new huge incentives made little difference. The only exceptions were some minor proposals mostly benefitting the union. Negotiating with ourselves over our own proposals to reduce or modify the package in size and impact, while they sat back doing nothing, that became an internal flashpoint that had to be calmed.

Our final offer that we were preparing incorporated the self-reducing feature of the potential 10% bonus. We gave them until six weeks— out to May 15—to ratify or else the retroactivity reduction would go back to March 31. If it took a year of talks and stalls for them to agree, it would be 52 weeks of loss. And that meant a zero dollar bonus. Of course, a strike would kill hope of any retroactivity. Since ABC had never gone this non-retroactivity route before, NABET's bargaining team, although they were not raising it, was most probably not believing it. Tom Murphy's earlier warning and my earlier cautions across the table that this "was no longer your father's Oldsmobile" did not seem to have gained any traction.

The process of selectively jettisoning our less important proposals resulted in a package of perhaps 75 items. All of them were designed for reform in varying degrees. We estimated among ourselves that upwards of $60 million of operational savings would result over the term of that four year contract once the changes were effectuated. What we had constantly referred to as the most restrictive, inefficient, and limiting contract in the American broadcasting industry would be dramatically altered.

Many restrictions and limitations were outright removed while others were substantially modified. Uniform and restrictive seniority rules that previously tied together into a single group both radio and TV engineers in each city were altered to provide for separate seniority groupings. The ability to hire employees by the day instead of a regular, 52-week a year staff basis was added, but in limited numbers. New programming origination rules were introduced opening up possibilities of programs from outside producers without the necessity to use NABET technicians. Many hampering work rules and several grievance settlements were substantially changed or eliminated. In an area never before attempted in any ABC negotiation and hardy ever proposed in any other labor talks, even a few harmful arbitration decisions would be nullified. Cumbersome, costly, and restrictive health care plan rules were modified.

One of our most important proposed changes would eliminate NABET from operational duties at our radio network and eight of our owned, NABET-represented radio stations. Achieving this change would eliminate perhaps as many as 150 radio jobs. Where we had, for example, nearly 36 engineers just at our two New York AM and FM stations, it would be reduced by more than two-thirds. Severed engineers would receive an unprecedented, generous buyout of up to four weeks pay for every year of service. ABC's Radio stations and network were perhaps the last major radio groups in the nation to remove engineers from the announce booth and launch into what was called "combo." From that point on, ABC Radio would require its DJ's, newspeople, and program hosts to run their own technologically simplified boards or play their own music. And the union's radio jurisdiction would be limited to maintenance.

AFTRA, as it had done all over the country, would be taking on this additional work as a natural extension of the announcer's voice and at our music stations, part of the DJ's job. In comparison, I had accomplished this combo change at RKO's radio stations well over a decade earlier. NABET was firmly opposed and fought us every step of the way. They argued, and not without ample reason, that if we were permitted to do this in radio, the next step would be ABC's demanding major operational changes in TV.

There was one feature in our package that was particularly

satisfying to Burke. During an early point in our planning, Dan had learned that ABC Sports' technicians at football games and other remote broadcasts made a lot of money from one specific work rule penalty relating to lunches. Sports technicians enjoyed their jobs and were richly rewarded for their efforts under the contract's normal pay provisions, but the application of this penalty was just too much for him.

The work rule had been agreed to years before by the Company to solve what it had become convinced was a legitimate meal and meal break problem. The rule stretched out the meal corridor, with the technician's approval, in return for paying an hourly penalty of overtime compensation. Over the years it became abused and manipulated. Clever employees had figured out how they could earn the penalty's extra pay formula for many hours whenever the penalty was triggered. It could amount to as much as an additional $100, $150 or $200 per day per person.

Multiply this for a crew of maybe 50 or more engineers and multiply that many times for all the remotes ABC Sports and ABC News had each year. It added up annually to several hundreds of thousands of dollars. It was huge chunk of money being spent unnecessarily even though the employees always had ample free food and the opportunity to eat. As one of the vice presidents on my staff was fond of saying, "It had absolutely nothing to do with nutrition."

What had been granted with the best of intentions had morphed over time into another example of human greed. Not getting the meal on time was one thing, but becoming the beneficiary of this exorbitantly rich, windfall that would become known as the "blown lunch" penalty, was quite another.

One sports technician famously made so much money over the years from the penalty that he bought a boat and named it the "Blown Lunch." To Burke when told this story it was like a stick in his eye. The penalty's having become so distorted struck Burke as the height of inefficiency and wasteful spending—something he had opposed his entire broadcasting career. "Jeff," he said to me on this one occasion—"this is my new number one proposal. Get rid of it and tell them it's coming directly from me."

But NABET during the final days in San Diego had not agreed to eliminate the "blown lunch." Nor had it agreed to any other proposal, except the few we had offered benefitting them. Despite our urging to stop their constant denial and get to "yes" at least on some things, they continued with their playbook and refused to recognize the new day.

We just had to find a way to get to "yes" without a strike. It was my belief that Nolan, coming off his long and unhappy NBC strike the year before, did not want it either. Having thought that with the two huge sweeteners, the "no layoff" guarantee and doubling the bonus to 10%, we had found the key to motivate the union committee to start bargaining and make a negotiated deal, we had been mistaken.

The Company delivered our final proposal and was fully prepared for a nationwide strike the night the contract expired on March 31st. Marv Bader's many dozens of fully-trained, ready-to-move-in-and-take-over, management people were about to be called in. As soon as they were, they'd be stashed away in secret, safe offices and conference rooms at our facilities in our five NABET cities nationwide. Standing by, they were prepared to step into operating slots at the precise moment the union walked.

We were readying copies of our final proposal for delivery when Nolan called on that last day just as both teams were scheduled to break off talks and head home. An unexpected development that frankly I had not anticipated, his message was that his bargaining committee had decided not to strike at midnight. Instead, said Nolan, they would take the Company's final package back to the membership for a vote. Refusing my urging them to remain neutral, he advised they would unanimously recommend against approval— even with the two eye-popping, unprecedented sweeteners we had added.

Immediately, I relayed this news to my San Diego team, with bags packed and itching to leave town, and to Bader and Weiswasser back in New York. Since there wouldn't be any midnight strike, we were probably safe until their normal six week voting process was completed on May 15.

Without the protection of an extension agreement guaranteeing both wage retroactivity and no-strike protection after the contract's expiration, we were vulnerable to a job action at any time. While we took Nolan at his implied word there wouldn't be a strike pending the vote, we couldn't be certain something unexpected might not develop. Since these were entirely new waters in which we were treading, Bader was taking no chances. In his best Olympics tradition, he was making sure with an around the clock skeletal force to keep our broadcast product fully protected. The flame would continue to burn brightly.

On our way to the airport that night, we dropped off perhaps a dozen copies of our inch-thick, official final package at the union offices. On the plane that evening back to JFK, Bob Apter, Preston Davis, and I toasted each other simply over the fact that the union had not struck at midnight but was actually going to take the offer back for a vote. Even with a negative recommendation, it was a first for NABET in any ABC negotiations. And that we all saw as a good sign.

Shortly after our return from San Diego and while their voting process was ramping up, Tom Murphy took to the internal, closed-circuit airwaves to help sell the deal. He and Burke were famous within the Company for these candid and unscripted video sessions in which they talked directly to employees. Addressing the entire company but specifically directed to the NABET technicians, Murphy related the history of the negotiations and emphasized the Company's seriousness in standing behind its final offer.

Stressing our unprecedented 10% bonus and three year guarantee against layoff offer, it was one of those "I mean what I say" Tom moments for which he was famous. In retrospect, considering that the employees were to go on to lose nearly a third of their 10% ratification bonus, which amounted to several thousand dollars a person, I'm certain many regretted that they had not heeded Murphy's words.

With the union committee's unanimous recommendation against accepting the Company's final proposal, not surprisingly it failed. The vote was overwhelmingly against the deal in all 19 separate units when the 2300 votes were counted six weeks later in mid-May. So now a real loss of retroactivity back to March 31 was starting to build.

After the turndown, talks resumed early that summer for about a week in the brutal heat of Washington. Some minor changes were made in our final offer but our major proposals NABET was so opposed to remained unchanged. Talks again broke off. A short time later there followed an additional week of negotiations in Washington where we called in the federal mediators for their assistance.

But again, nothing much changed in any of our key proposals and the union continued to reject or ignore everything in our package. With some final touches, I labelled it our "last, best, and final"—so NABET knew it was real. Yet when that round broke off, Nolan still had not taken a strike vote, which some of us believed was probably for fear of a positive tally and the folly of a strike.

As the summer dragged on, Nolan and I one day had a serious conversation. The Company, after consultations with our outside attorney, Jerry Kauff, had made a major tactical decision. I informed Nolan that since we were at a complete stalemate after five months of fruitless talks, we had no choice but declare an impasse. Under prevailing federal labor law, as Nolan well-knew, declaring an impasse would allow the Company to implement our final offer. I did not give him a date on which we would be implementing but wanted to use this head's up as an inducement for him to finally accept the offer.

Nolan understood that the Company intended to put into effect everything favorable to it but not the elements good for the employees. Paramount among the items not to be implemented was the still- remaining big chunk of the once 10% bonus. Although now reduced by a percentage point or two, it was still worth thousands of dollars per person.

More importantly, the practical consequences of our implementation would also have meant that the negotiations would be over. When at the same time it became clear to us that our "no layoff" guarantee was not creating the positive reaction we had expected, we withdrew it. As we did that, the clock was still ticking away on the self reducing, 10% ratification bonus.

After the second round of fruitless talks failed, we thought at least we might have come closer to a settlement even though they were still rejecting the last, best, and final package and bad mouthing it publicly to their members as well as in the press. Getting their attention with our threat to implement, their choices were severely limited and getting worse daily. In desperation, the union filed some unfair labor practice charges against us with the NLRB in New York.

Nolan, ever the pragmatist, called Dan Burke for a private meeting. Having introduced the two a year earlier for exactly this possible opportunity, I was not surprised he reached out. Meeting over breakfast one day, nothing better emerged for Nolan as Burke just sat and listened patiently to his list of unsatisfactory items.

Walking away even more frustrated, Nolan decided to play his truly last card—the Tom Murphy card. He telephoned Murphy and made his plea. Tom listened and told him he would get back. Calling a meeting in his office, Tom invited Burke, Mallardi, Weiswasser, and myself.

Tom related what Nolan had said—he and the union committee were finally agreeable to everything we had in our final offer, including the massive radio reductions. We all knew this really meant that Nolan was agreeable. But, said Nolan, he needed just one thing to close the deal—the full 10% ratification bonus and not the approximate 7% retroactivity to which it had been reduced.

Murphy wanted to know what each of us thought. Proceeding to go around the room, I was the last to speak. All the others before me pretty much said the same thing—Nolan's call was a welcome opportunity, signaling a Company victory and while it was distasteful, and they hated doing it, they would agree to the full 10% retroactivity. It was time, they said, to end this five-month, drawn-out ordeal, grab the win, get the Company back to normal, and not stand on principle.

Then came my turn. It's never easy to speak in opposition to something of this magnitude that your direct boss the GC, the COO, and other senior management in the room are willing to accept. But I just could not go along. It was the opposite of everything for which we had been striving. I took a deep breath and spoke the truth as I saw it and believed Murphy, Burke, and everybody else in the room would want to hear. They had hired me for my expertise and best judgment, and that was what I was going to give them. I launched into:

> "No, we can't do this. It's a throwback to old ABC. We can't reward them for dragging out this negotiations after we had continually warned them for five months they would not get full retroactivity if they stalled. CapitalCities/ABC has a one time chance to break from the bad ABC ways of granting retroactivity. And 7% is still great and lot better than zero if they keep stalling. Nolan knows that. This is more than just principle. Our word has to mean something in order to be believed in the future."

I went on to add that I was fairly certain Nolan was staring down our threatened implementation, desperate for a deal, just testing the waters, and would take our offer without the full 10%.

Tom Murphy thought for only a brief moment but knew I was completely right. He said—"I agree with Jeff. NABET needs a haircut. Call Nolan."

When I made the call a few minutes later, Nolan acted as if he had been expecting this response all along. He congratulated me and told me to start preparing the papers that he'd be over to sign the next day. The next morning we made a few technical corrections and signed the documents. The ratification bonus was frozen at roughly 7% while the union's normal six-week voting process unfolded. If it was ratified, they would get the approximate 7%. Rejection would mean at least an additional six weeks of lost bonus pay.

Nolan and his bargaining committee this time took a neutral stance despite our urging them to endorse the package. Many of us saw neutrality as a sign that the deal would pass since the employees would view it as a silent endorsement of the best deal possible under the circumstances. Anyone voting against it had to know they were not sanctioning a strike but rather just seeking prolonged and fruitless talks where the bonus would be even further reduced.

As it turned out, neutrality was a good thing for a peaceful outcome. Tom Kennedy called me in an exhilarated mood six weeks later when the votes were counted to tell me the deal passed. Surprisingly, it was by a razor-thin margin of only 20 votes in the critically important, 2000-person engineering group. Many people who voted against the deal had to be upset the union cost them a third of their potential bonus amounting to thousands of dollars. Yet that healthy, near 7% bonus check, larger by far than anything other broadcasting companies were offering, or ABC NABETs had ever seen before, was hardly sneered at when cashed the following week.

As we were later to hear, there were some voters who thought the withdrawn "no layoff" guarantee would have been a good thing. Others who voted against the package were still clamoring for a strike even though that option was purposely kept off the ballot by a wise Nolan and Kennedy. Thinly sliced, we still had our deal. Our strategy had been proven correct and our credibility was intact, waiting to fight honorably another day. Many press accounts were written about the settlement including one in *The New York Times* where I was quoted.

The Rainbow Room celebratory dinner for the 100 that glorious September night soon followed.

For the next CapitalCities/ABC board of directors meeting in the 22nd floor boardroom, I was asked by Tom Murphy to make a presentation on the results and significance of the NABET deal. Introduced by Murphy after some kind words, I gave my report to the interested and appreciative group. Some questions followed from a few of the more curious. Surely one must have come from board member Warren Buffett.

At the following year's Annual Phoenix meeting at the Arizona Biltmore in February of 1990, which Buffett, as was his custom, again attended, Tom Murphy singled me out for praise during his opening remarks. He commended my "tenacity" at the bargaining table and thanked me for the great results that I had produced in restructuring the NABET agreement. It was nearly two years to the day since Steve Weiswasser had introduced me from that same rostrum as the new head of labor relations who would fix the contract's many problems.

Murphy got a few questions to further explain its significance and I got a nice round of applause. It might even have been a "standing O." It was a good feeling—in fact a great feeling. Immediately after the meeting, and pats on the back outside the room from my colleagues and friends, a number of them equally happy members of my San Diego team, I called Monica back in New York.

19
CHAPTER

The '90s Begin

As we were entering the 1990s, we were coming out of a decade where there had been three Writers Guild strikes affecting Hollywood movie and television production. Two of them, in 1981 and '88, had been long—three months and five months. The third in '85 had miraculously lasted just two weeks. After the Fox network had arrived on the scene in '86, it was now in '88 four TV networks whose prime time entertainment product was summarily cut off.

When writers vote to strike and set up picket lines, tens of thousands of other entertainment industry workers, mostly in Los Angeles, but some in New York and elsewhere, also lose their pay checks. Not only does all new AMPTP produced prime time television and film production grind to a halt, but also the economy of the entire Hollywood community is badly hurt when ancillary businesses—such as restaurants and catering companies—are impacted.

Actors stop acting, directors can't direct, and teamsters stop driving production vehicles wherever movies are shot or television productions are made. IA workers don't perform any of their million different duties. There's no more camera, lighting, editing, wardrobe, set design, makeup or hair—no anything they normally do. Every trade and craft comes to a crashing halt until the writers decide to return to work. A number of filmed or taped television episodes had been shot in advance of the strike, so there were programs already in the can awaiting broadcast. However, when that small inventory ran out, the networks with no new product would be in deep trouble.

There just didn't seem to be any solution to the frequent economic woes the WGA was inflicting on the TV and film industries while its discontented members were noisily walking the pavement in pursuit of their own interests. Network prime time ratings, linked to our revenues and profitability, plummeted when viewers could no longer watch new episodes of their favorite programs. Doubling down with more re-runs was hardly a solution. With nothing new entering the pipeline, the four networks' fall prime time seasons were all delayed.

Other parts of the network viewing schedule besides prime time were similarly affected. Daytime, which had been ABC's rich source of network profitability, got hit hard. Its head—needing to fill four hours of ABC's afternoon drama air-time of five soaps—initially tried to carry on with replacement writers. But what she got was script writing not up to the normal high standards her soap fans were used to and demanded. It was soon discontinued and Daytime also reverted to reruns. My wife, Monica, with her writer's background, had tried her hand in writing for one of our struck Daytime dramas. But because she was never a real fan and not familiar with the complicated story lines of *One Life to Live,* produced by my good friend, Paul Rauch, it was a lost cause before she even started.

Late night entertainment programs such as NBC's Johnny Carson's *Tonight Show* were also impacted. When his writers took a walk and Carson along with other network late night hosts stood in sympathy by refusing to go on camera, those shows also shut down and went into re-runs. With *The Jimmy Kimmel Show* still a dream and decade away, ABC's late night, then featuring Ted Koppel's news program *Nightline*—like all other news programs—was unaffected.

Clearly though the major impact of the long strikes was on the networks' bread and butter—our prime time schedules. Replacement writing was not even remotely possible. A number of ABC's major programs when they returned in '88 after 150 days out had seriously damaged ratings. Some, like *Moonlighting,* which ABC itself was producing, were on their near-last legs anyway. Costing over $3 million an episode, it was the most expensive hour on the ABC schedule and perhaps in all of television. After four years, Maddie and David's sexy standoffs were never to be seen again once the hiatus killed what little life was left in the show.

The '88 WGA strike, caused by producer demands for residual reforms and writers' demands on creative rights issues, had lasted a lot longer than most had thought possible. At the time the strike began, ABC's head of Entertainment had been Brandon Stoddard but had been replaced some time into the strike by Bob Iger. Both Stoddard and Iger, as well as their bosses, Tom, Dan, and John Sias, had taken some comfort in knowing that while it was bad for ABC, all four networks' prime time schedules were equally suffering.

Desperate for new production sources to fill those prime time hours as the strike went on, each network experimented with different forms and combinations of replacement programming. Some of those jerry-rigged approaches involved new reality shows, increased sports programming, and English-speaking, foreign productions from Australia and other countries.

I didn't have much to do with the dynamics of the negotiations that led to the strike other than my normal oversight of our West Coast negotiators sitting in with the producers and wrestling over the issues. Since Hollywood was where the talks were held, my

West Coast people were the Company's experts who knew those writers contracts and major players best. It made the most sense to defer to their expertise and judgment and not get directly involved at the table.

Early on as we were getting ready for the strike, we had a preliminary, high level meeting with Nick Counter, the head of the Alliance of Motion Picture and Television Producers. Known as the AMPTP, this was the Hollywood producers' negotiating arm. Nick had called me to set up the meeting. He wanted to fly into New York to sit down with Murphy, Burke, Sias, and myself to brief us on both the probability of a strike and its being a long one—as in '81.

In a pitch that always resonated with Tom and Dan, he wanted to make sure they understood the critical cost control issues underlying the AMPTP's key demands. ABC was well aware of over-the-top Hollywood production costs—perhaps in the extreme—from our nose-bleed *Moonlighting* producing experiences. Underscoring the need for the ABC Network to line up multiple sources of replacement product, Counter emphasized it had to be done quickly—just as our competitors were doing—before the limited sources ran dry.

When I had returned to ABC in '87, I had pretty much made a decision to distance myself from direct involvement in our West Coast talks as much as possible. I just could not be at that table full time that being our head negotiator in those talks would have required. Not only did it demand a super human amount of air travel, it also would mean huge time spent on the ground in Los Angeles for extensive periods. With my East Coast department to manage and its many clients and issues stretching out from New York in all directions, that would not have been even remotely possible.

Particularly high on my agenda and already taking an enormous amount of time and energy was getting the Company ready for our expected '89 NABET talks. Perhaps most importantly, I had a family with a wife and young kids at home. Nor did it make any sense for me to fly out and drop-in across the table every now and then just to show my admiral's flag as ABC's labor chief. In fact, drop-in visits to satisfy my ego would have been entirely counterproductive and marginalizing to my West Coast people charged by me to handle the talks.

In addition, I never had much interest to participate directly at the table in the West Coast industry-wide talks. Those unions were essentially the WGA, DGA, AFM, SAG, and IATSE. Conducted under the umbrella leadership of the AMPTP, 10 or more vice presidents of labor relations, all first-rate minds and many of them friends, would be in the room at any given moment. Arm-wrestling with each other in the preparatory rounds, they were getting ready for the featured bout. Accompanying them would normally be their second and third tier vice presidents and lawyers, plus each company's senior production executives. It could easily total 40, 50, or more people just on our side. I just couldn't see myself participating on a regular basis in that group process.

Several if not all Hollywood labor relations chiefs who were regular players in this negotiating process had huge personalities and large egos. They all had something to say. And often it was at the same time. In those days the major AMPTP companies meant Columbia (not yet Sony), Paramount, 20th Century Fox, Universal, Disney, United Artists, MGM, and Warner Brothers. Usually seated with them but not yet as members were the networks. But in those days—before the FCC production rules changed—we were not there like the AMPTP companies with their big prime time production schedules for their network customers. With severe regulatory limitations still in place, ABC was only allowed by the rules to produce a single program, and that was *Moonlighting*. We were, however, along with the other networks, deeply involved at the table as Daytime serial producers for our own air. ABC was the biggest soap opera producer of all.

When it came though to industry-wide talks with AFTRA, I

viewed those differently. Here it wasn't the gaggle but rather just the three networks at the table. As still the major producers of AFTRA-covered acting product, the networks had retained control of the bargaining process. At the time I returned in 1987, ABC, with its vast schedule of daytime soap operas, as many as five, was the largest producer and employer of AFTRA talent in the country.

I had always felt that a company at the bargaining table must be in command of its own destiny to the maximum extent possible. I never felt the system of jointly bargaining with competing companies for a common contract fully permitted that. In some instances though there are benefits when joint bargaining gives companies more protection against strikes targeting any single company. It also provides some greater degree of leverage if the union has to call an industry-wide strike rather than just targeting one company as it might prefer.

Decisions in industry-wide talks often were based on what the overall group settled on. Independent beliefs and priorities that each company might have had going in to the talks could too easily get subjugated to the will of the majority on each issue and proposal—both managements' and the union's.

Good ideas any individual company might have going into the talks could be embraced by the group. Just as often, however, they could be watered down or disregarded. Strong feelings one or more might have in support of or in opposition to union ideas could be marginalized. Stampeding into errors of judgment, when the "herd effect" took over, was all the more possible. Perhaps, with its established, decades-long history of doing business with Hollywood unions through industry-wide contracts, there was no other way. And sometimes the "herd effect" drove the right decisions, because it often takes a herd to build a village. But I decided it was just not worth it for me to sit there for these elongated periods and be part of the group bargaining process. Moreover, I felt I could not control anybody else's bad arguments, foolish comments, or wrong remarks made across the table or even in sidebars since I had enough difficulty controlling and monitoring my own.

Leaving the nuts and bolts of these significant West Coast talks and ABC's presence at the table to my capable labor relations team out there, notably in those early days it was either LA chief Irv Novick or his chief lieutenant, Bob Key. As the Company's overall chief negotiator, I preferred to concentrate my efforts and firepower elsewhere. My focus was on where I knew I would make a sizable difference and have the most control over our own destiny.

So that meant staying in New York and directing my attention to the wide variety of other negotiations and labor matters for which I and my labor lawyers were responsible. Devoting a great deal of my time to what was to become our quadrennial massive effort, that most important undertaking was NABET.

When Bob Iger at a meeting once called this every four-year venture my Olympics, I took this coming from Bob, after his successful involvement at the Calgary Games and working on so many others, as quite a compliment. My Olympics involved, of course in a much smaller way and different variety, the same kind of intense training, advance planning, preparedness, and high degree of difficulty that producing the real Olympics every four years required.

It wasn't too long after Tom and Dan's '89 Rainbow Room festivities celebrating our victory that I started thinking about our next Olympiad in '93. Suspecting that NABET would no longer remain an independent union and would need a big brother's protection, I would not be surprised to learn some time later that it was merging into a much larger union.

In the meantime, we began yielding the operating dividends from our '89 bargaining gains. For example, we now had a much improved ability to hire workers for the day—when and where we needed them, and not on just a guaranteed weekly, annual staff basis. Even though it was in limited numbers, it was a huge breakthrough. In time it would only grow. This change alone gained major efficiencies in managing our Sports and news production costs. We could now take in outside produced live programs, not just those on tape, so our future programming landscape was now much expanded. We also had ended NABET's ability to block needed company-wide medical plan changes. That item alone would prove to be worth more than $100 million over the coming decade as across-the-board medical plan changes to reduce the Company's burgeoning medical insurance costs became the norm. Just as was applicable to management, subsidized retiree medical benefits were grandfathered.

Dozens of restrictions had been lifted and flexibilities gained. In fact so many operational easements and work rule changes had been achieved that Dan Burke several times expressed his concern that front line supervisors and managers would not know how to manage properly their workforces. After all, he said, "It's not that book any longer telling them what they can and cannot do. They might actually have to use their brains." Burke was not far off from the truth now that so many shackles had been removed.

It was such a worry that Dan and I had some serious talks with HR about setting up a management training program to re-introduce managers and supervisors into the basics of how to supervise employees. But yet with all we had accomplished, what was churning inside of me was that there was still much to get done in the next contract negotiations.

An unexpected dividend was that my reputation within the Company had risen considerably. Tom Murphy had contributed to that in a major way with his shoutout at the '90 Phoenix meeting and the reception from others that his high praise had achieved. As my stock rose, so did that of my labor relations department.

Having been a relatively unknown commodity within the Company when Weiswasser hired me, senior management liked the process and appreciated the results. It was not just my novel approach to planning, it was also my leadership and "tenacity," as Tom had called it from the '90 Phoenix stage at the Arizona Biltmore. Thinking like a Cap Cities guy, and having produced Cap Cities-like results, I enjoyed my two minutes of fame. Weiswasser had placed a bet on me that management had cashed in on.

Shortly after the Rainbow Room victory celebration, there was another industry dinner at the Waldorf Astoria. Patti Matson made sure at Tom and Dan's request that my wife, Monica, and I sat at their table with other senior corporate officials. When we did, Dan Burke insisted he sit next to Monica for a few courses, engaging her in a lively conversation, and then switched with Tom Murphy sitting next to me. It was an enjoyable evening and probably another part of my reward. Enthusiastic about the results, they wanted to get to know this guy Ruthizer a lot better in more of a social setting. And it worked the other way, too. It was another of those special, Cap Cities experiences.

The summer of '90 was ABC Sports' first broadcast of the *Tour de France*. The marathon bicycle race was to be a large production effort over three weeks for a mostly French crew of about 100 technicians and other personnel. With our sons off in summer camp, Monica and I had been planning on being in France that July for a two week vacation. When I realized our holiday and its specific region coincided with part of the race's itinerary that year, I thought it would be great to be "closeup and personal" for a few days with the ABC Sports production team.

For the first time, an American, Greg LeMond, had won the 1986 race, and then had a repeat in '89. So with LeMond returning as defending champion, hope for another American victory was again in the air. That made it even more compelling for us to be there. After I spoke with Sports' president, Dennis Swanson, he graciously extended an invitation to join his production team.

We showed up at Futuroscope Park in western France where the race was to begin. Picking up my official ABC press credentials, I would be joining the throng of press and racers at the start point. My brand new, consumer Sony video camera would go on to give me some amazing footage. LeMond started off where he had left when he got that first day's day's yellow jersey. Traveling up the French Atlantic coast for the next few stages with the ABC Sports team, we were always in the midst of the racers and the huge support entourage.

Tens of thousands of cheering French race-enthusiasts lined the roads daily as we swept by in our press cars normally following the peloton. With credentials and camera, I was in the scrum at various places, often in the first row of the medal award ceremonies. Or I'd position myself with my little Sony at the finish line as the winner came gliding past.

One day Geoff Mason, ABC Sports' producer in charge, invited us to travel with him in his command car. We were following the peloton when French sheep farmers decided to hold a demonstration. French farmers were always protesting over one issue or another. And this day was no different when they decided to cut down some trees to impede passage on the main road the racers would be using. As everyone slowed, the farmers threw handfuls of wet wool at the passing vehicles. Busy shooting the demonstrating farmers with my camera from the open window of Mason's rear seat, I got hit with a large and wet handful. It landed directly on my Sony lens and smack into my face.

Apparently, I was the only camera operator who got a literal head shot of the flying and very wet wool. So when the show director, Larry Kamm, asked over the earpieces if anyone had gotten a shot of the farmers throwing wool, I quickly responded that I had the footage he was seeking, plus a stinky, wet face to prove it. As far as I know the Ruthizer footage was never used. It was my only shot ever at being an ABC Sports cameraman and I blew it.

It was an exciting experience to spend time with ABC Sports' production managers and our on-air announcing talent. Warmly treated by all as members of the ABC Sports entourage, one night we had dinner with the announcing team—now joined by Pierre Salinger. At the time no longer a US senator representing the state of California, Salinger was the head of ABC's Paris news bureau. Pierre had come down from Paris to see part of the race and do a story.

At dinner that night over many bottles of wine, he regaled us with tales of the Kennedy White House when he was JFK's press secretary. Much was revealed about JFK's well-known sexual escapades that challenged even his Secret Service protection. Monica has always, and to this day, hated tobacco smoke. She was never before shy about saying something to anyone about errant smoke, and particularly cigar smoke. But not that night. We were all in such rapt attention listening to Pierre's stories that she never uttered a word of even mild protest as he smoked away throughout dinner.

Another evening we had dinner at a good local restaurant where we had dined a few years earlier on a previous trip to France. I invited the production's director, Larry Kamm, and our expert on-air racing commentator, Sam Posey, to join us. Knowing a great deal more than either of us two novices about bicycle racing, Sam seconded Monica's strong feeling that LeMond would take it all.

Much as my wife had predicted, the overall race a few weeks and 2000 kilometers later, long after we were gone, was again won by the LeMond and his racing team. It made it all the more exciting for us to have been there at the start, captured by me close up and personal— with great stills and video to prove it.

Taking our two young sons, Josh and Alex, to many ABC Sports events while they were growing up was one of the great perks that accompanied my senior executive status. They had gone to some NHL, NBA, and MLB events when I had worked for RKO, thanks to WOR-TV and WOR-AM, and enjoyed the Knicks and Rangers from the Madison Square Garden skybox, but this was at a whole new level. It was through my friends at Sports and particularly Bob Apter. Whether it was *MNF* or college football, MLB, World Cup, college football championship games, the Orange, Citrus, and Sugar bowls, NHL, or college and NBA basketball, we'd get tickets and normally good seats usually whenever I asked. Chris Schenkel's PBA bowling tour held no appeal.

As we were relaxing a bit from NABET and moving into our preparation phases for the next talks, we had in late '91 a major three-network "Code" negotiations with AFTRA. The AMPTP, now more involved in producing some AFTRA-covered product, was going to be participating with us for the first time.

It was a few months before the AFTRA talks had opened that David Westin became my new boss. Coming from the same Washington law firm as had Weiswasser five years earlier, Cap Cities' outside counsel, he took Steve's place as GC. At the same time Weiswasser moved over to ABC News as its new EVP under Roone Arledge. Engineered by Murphy and Burke as part of their broader succession planning, the move was widely read within the Company that Steve would be Roone's successor when Roone stepped down in a few years.

Word coming from friends at News was that Roone, now unhappily sharing his private conference room with Weiswasser, was not thrilled with Steve's elevation. Because of his total lack of any news experience, many News executives who were now reporting to him were not happy about it either. They would have preferred one of their own—an established news executive, and certainly not a lawyer.

Nevertheless, my own view at the time, reinforced many times since, was that this was a great move for the Company. Steve, with his excellent instincts and solid judgment, was a lot more than just a very good lawyer. I think he would have been a brilliant ABC News president and a very worthy successor to Roone. I had always felt when I was working for him that he had more than a little operator's blood running deep in his veins and was just waiting for an opportunity like this.

I was sorry to lose Steve as my boss but Westin was personable and bright. Having clerked for a US Supreme Court justice after his Michigan Law School days, he would go on to be an equally supportive boss. When we got into the details of any labor talks or issue where he and I had a rare disagreement on tactics or strategy, David carried on in the old Weiswasser tradition. Like Steve before him, David would say—"Jeff, you're the doctor on all things labor, but on this I disagree strongly, so let's go see Dan for his view."

Westin and I would go to see Dan and he'd ask, "What's up fellas." I usually set the landscape and David normally would first present his view. Dan would then ask my opinion. Most of the time on the handful of occasions that we'd see him like this, Dan would go with my view.

We'd leave Dan's office and David was always so gracious. Another member of the Tom Murphy famous "never look back" school, he'd grab my hand for a shake or pat me on the back and say, "Way to go Jeff." That was it, and he really meant it. Game over. It was the perfect process for the best management possible. That was CapitalCities/ABC under Tom Murphy and Dan Burke. Every executive I knew was proud to work there.

20

The Supreme Court Bench Meets Denny's Bench

By '91's early fall, the network talks with AFTRA had gotten a little off the rails. I had kept Westin up to speed as matters deteriorated. Together, ABC, NBC, and CBS had our position on a few major issues and the AMPTP companies, including Fox, had their's. One issue of great importance developed into a major standoff between us and the AMPTP negotiators. So the three network labor heads decided we needed to have a three-network CEO meeting to get their combined support and use it as a show of strength in our AMPTP arm-wrestling. Such a summit was rare and while I had heard of them, this was the only one during my 20-plus leadership years.

NBC's labor chief, Day Krolik, offered to set up the meeting in his chairman, Bob Wright's, office. A few days later Dan Burke and I taxied over to 30 Rock together and David Westin joined us. CBS' CEO, Larry Tisch, arrived and was accompanied by his labor head, the acknowledged industry labor relations "dean," Jim Sirmons. Jim had been around running CBS labor relations seemingly forever. NBC's Krolik, who I had hired 20 years earlier at NBC was there with Wright. As the meeting was about to get underway that September morning, Wright said, "Hey guys, Anita Hill is about to testify, so do any of you mind if we catch just a few minutes before we start?" It was the Clarence Thomas confirmation hearings before the US senate judiciary committee for his seat on the United States Supreme Court.

Of course we all said "yes," so Bob turned on the set in his office and we proceeded to get into the high drama unfolding before us. Three hours later, after a constant replenishment of danish, coffee, and cokes, we were still sitting on those couches in Bob's office totally mesmerized. As the judiciary committee was breaking for lunch, someone said laughingly, and I'm pretty sure it was Wright himself, "We really solved that problem, didn't we fellas." With that, the meeting ended—not having discussed for even a moment the critical negotiations issue that had brought us together in the first place.

We still had some difficult days ahead in these talks with both the AMPTP and AFTRA before the three network labor chiefs found a way forward. Despite the busted unity meeting, Dan's supporting our position, and Tisch and Wright individually backing their labor heads, contributed in its own bizarre way to a successful outcome.

We made a point of telling the AMPTP companies only that we had had a three-CEO meeting. Familiar with the fact that such a meeting was extremely rare and had not been called for decades, they immediately caught its significance. Because they presumed top-level solidarity had been achieved, this was all the leverage we needed to prevail in our internal squabble. With that point settled, we finally were able to move on to make the overall deal with AFTRA.

The three networks, the AMPTP, and AFTRA had Anita Hill, Clarence Thomas, and the US senate judiciary committee to thank.

Bob Wright's itchiness to catch just a few minutes and our being transfixed by what was happening on the screen won the day. As a nice footnote to this tale being written in 2021, President Joe Biden, when he was a US senator, chaired the judiciary committee hearing we were so intently watching that morning exactly 30 years ago.

1991 was significant in one other respect because it was the year I hired Marc Sandman. A decision of major consequence in the history of ABC, it's worthy of relating. I first met him a year or two earlier when I had an open staff position for which he applied but for some reason was not hired. There was a second meeting some time later that had destiny written all over it. By this time Marc had switched jobs and was working at a law firm that was representing ABC Sports' *Monday Night Football* announcer, Al Michaels. Al was in the middle of a dispute with Sports management that I had been brought into. Marc showed up as his lawyer.

Impressed by what I saw across the table, when later in '91 I was searching for another experienced lawyer on my staff, I was surprised to see Sandman's resume again come across my desk. It was apparent he really wanted to work for me. So, with his background and capabilities I had seen first-hand, I hired him. In his background, like mine, were several years of critical, NLRB experience.

He was soon to become, along with Olivia Cohen-Cutler, one of my two chief assistants. Sandman would take over from her as director of labor relations when she moved to Los Angeles in 1993 to run my West Coast team. In '97, Marc and his family would relocate to LA and take over again for her when she left labor relations and moved on to a senior position at the ABC Television Network. When I was to retire from the Company in 2009, it would be Sandman who would take my place as senior vice president in charge of ABC Labor Relations. He would be only the fourth person to head labor relations in the better than 75 year history of the Company.

Sandman was not to be part of my '92 NABET preparations and '93 bargaining team only because he was not yet conversant enough in all things NABET. It normally took under my watch considerably more than a year or two of seasoning. He would stay behind with my other lawyers in New York to attend to the multitude of our other labor relations matters with all our other unions while getting up to full speed on the intricacies and richness of that special contract. I needed him to become NABET-worthy. As I would tell my newly hired lawyers—

> "I don't care if you graduated number one in your class from Harvard Law and have been practicing labor law for 15, 20, or more years with New York's finest labor law firm. When you come to ABC you are totally broadcasting and union-contract ignorant. When a manager calls you for advice, particularly on a NABET matter, you won't have the foggiest idea of what he is asking and where to find the answer. It's a very long and steep labor relations learning curve in order to master the kind of labor law that we practice here at ABC, but in time I have no doubt you will."

Every one of the dozens of labor lawyers I hired can recite verbatim the stern admonition much better than I. Our labor law was far different from any other kind of law practiced in the ABC legal department where a new, experienced hire would be knowledgable in his or her specialty and be a valuable asset to the Company from day one.

As our preparation year 1992 progressed for the '93 NABET talks, the Company went ahead with another well-executed and costly strike training replacement program. Bader had retired. There was a new czar whom I found and Dan Burke appointed.

Also from Sports, he had served as Bader's chief assistant in '89 so he would know the ropes. Those of us involved in these decisions knew that the preparedness program's goals were twofold—a valuable shield in case the union was foolish enough to strike, and an invaluable sword in giving us projected strength at the bargaining table to prevent it from happening.

Traveling all around the country as we had the previous time, we met with station and network operators, listened to their concerns, and put together our lists. Olivia Cohen-Cutler joined me on most of these visits as did my main West Coast labor relations team member, Bob Key. Bob, although technically not a lawyer was better than most I had seen. He had been with me at the '89 table and would again serve a major role in the '93 talks since his knowledge of the NABET contract was deep, wide, and critical to our ultimate success.

The TV Station group was once more particularly active in seeking relief. Our three-legged stool, as I was to call it, of the contract's many inefficiencies, limitations, and restrictions, was still standing despite our '89 gains. In addition, we had to examine recent bargaining gains achieved by CBS and NBC in order to at least stay competitive. Our adapting to both business needs as well as fast-moving technological changes became paramount driving factors.

NABET sensed what was coming. It clearly was bracing for another assault on its 40-year old, carefully built but now beginning to show signs of stress fortress. Since '89 had been an awakening to new realities, the union's leaders were taking measures not just to re-build but also to fortify those walls.

Part of the membership was upset they had lost one-third of their ratification bonuses—amounting to thousands of dollars per person. A number of them, looking in from the outside, focused on previous gains surrendered while not much achieved in return. The union's negotiations the previous year with NBC had not gone any better. There was clearly a new dynamic let loose requiring some major changes. Long-considered and rejected, now it was timely. A merger is what their leaders believed they needed to become a more powerful force in taking on Murphy and Burke's ABC as well as the equally aggressive owners of NBC, General Electric, under its CEO, Jack Welch.

After some explorations with its two major broadcasting rivals, IATSE and the IBEW, NABET's Jim Nolan went outside of broadcasting. He found a new Big Brother to protect his perhaps 15,000 person-strong union. It was the union that had grown large and powerful by successfully dealing with the telephone companies—the Communication Workers of America, otherwise known as the CWA. With about 700,000 members, it was mostly in telecommunications. NABET's new, formal name would become NABET-CWA, but for purposes of this narrative we'll just continue calling it NABET.

As we were later to learn, 1993 was still the early days of the merger. Since there was a one-year waiting period during which either party could walk away, until that year passed, the merger would not be legally effective. What that meant was that Big Brother could participate only at some low levels at the '93 table while waiting in the wings. At the time though nothing about the trial period was known, so we had to assume the CWA would be helping to the maximum extent possible from the very start.

Dan Burke had taken over as CEO from Murphy when Tom reached the board's mandatory, age 65, retirement date for CEOs. Tom though had stayed on at the board's urging in a newly created position of chairman. But Burke, having long waited for this, was now fully in charge.

Once again I had prepared a strategic plan for the upcoming talks. In it I had laid out for Westin, Burke, Murphy, and the senior management involved in these talks, the scope, breadth, and estimated cost savings for what we meant to achieve, and our strategy for accomplishing those goals.

The seismic readings we had taken during our '92 preparation-year trips to our properties had revealed many things that needed major reform. Our goal once again was to regain more efficiency. Once bargained at the table, they would amount to several tens of millions of dollars in real operational savings during the term of the contract. My plan also included sizable Network staff reductions to be achieved through a voluntary buyout formula negotiated with the union. Since daily hire employment was becoming more normalized in our overall workforce and business model, and would continue to expand, the large numbers Dan Burke was interested in were entirely feasible.

At the very top of our list was a new proposal critical to our future. It was designed to gain significant computer flexibility by keeping keyboards—capable of giving operational commands to computers to operate equipment—out of NABET's exclusive hands. Helping us significantly to work our way through this concept and with appropriate contract language was one of my former lawyers who had gone over to work as a senior executive for BOE, Michael Lang.

Having decided with NABET's Nolan to start earlier to give ourselves more time to make a deal by the March 31 contract expiration, we chose mid-February to open talks. Nolan and I agreed to abandon San Diego and selected instead Orlando in central Florida. It was to be another month of six-day a week talks—away from family, home, and office. Orlando, not surprisingly, with its visions of Disney World, held even less appeal to Burke as a serious negotiating site than San Diego had in '89. Occasionally, he would still whimsically extoll the virtues of Alaska.

My team of operators and lawyers numbered the usual about 15 to 18. Senior representatives from Sports, News, Daytime, BOE, TV stations, radio stations, and the radio network, many of them veterans from '89, packed their bags and boarded planes.

Dan Burke accompanied by David Westin flew down to

Orlando for the opening day to make some remarks. In picking them up after they arrived on the Company plane, I promptly got lost on the way to the hotel due to my unfamiliarity with the interstate highway system. It turned out though to be an excellent turn of events because it gave me some quality time to brief Burke even further on a few the major issues. Dan joined us in our suite at the Peabody hotel before we headed over to the union hotel where the talks would be held.

By this time, Julie Barnathan was gone from BOE and his place had been taken a few years earlier by Bob Siegenthaler. Bob, who had come over from his senior executive position at ABC News, had little NABET background. Relying mostly on his chief lieutenant, Preston Davis, for guidance and table decision-making, Bob showed up that first day but did not appear often thereafter. And when he did, it was with very little across-the-table involvement.

Morty Bahr, the CWA's president, came that first day as we had anticipated. Sitting next to Nolan, he made an opening speech that included a reference to the broadband internet highway that Vice President Al Gore was designing. Not-so subtly mentioning that he and Gore were close friends, he ended his remarks by expressing hope that his NABET members would gain access to that highway under the terms of the new contract we were bargaining.

Burke and Bahr exchanged general pleasantries. Burke went on to make his brief speech anointing me and speaking the normal Cap Cities language of no-waste and maximum efficiency while holding out his hand in friendship. Westin made some comments about his father having worked in the auto factories of Flint, Michigan, and I made a few of my own. Tom Kennedy, again the union's chief negotiator, added his own remarks. After exchanging our mutually thick set of proposals, both sides adjourned to read and digest them for the rest of the day.

Our package of maybe 100 or more proposals covering the technicians and the other bargaining units was loaded, I was certain, with much of what NABET had been anticipating. It certainly was no surprise for them to hear repeated our mantra of no contract extension and no retroactivity. Their's was equally robust, and much of it, with its usual litany of improvements as well as rollbacks of what we had achieved at the '89 table, was what we had expected.

Talks were to go on in Orlando for close to four weeks. Our stay was to extend through the third week of March, with the contract due to expire on its usual last day of the month. Most of the time they had with them a middle-level CWA official but he hardly ever spoke. After our Orlando time, Nolan and I had agreed to a final week in New York before the March 31 expiration date.

About a week into the Orlando talks during some heated discussion, Tom Kennedy made some flip and unnecessary comments about Jews. It just seemed to come out of nowhere. Not apologizing when I objected, he actually doubled down. After I announced that we were leaving and not coming back to the table until he apologized, he swore he would never do that. Packing my bags, it was one of those moments when a chief negotiator hopes his people will be right behind him as he storms out of the room. Thankfully, mine were.

When we got back to our hotel suite, everyone anxiously gathered around and asked what our plan was. I have to admit I had absolutely no idea. My response though was that his anti-Semitic outburst was too important to have ignored and we were not returning to the table until we got an apology. After another day passed with no call, I decided to telephone Nolan and find out why Kennedy had not reached out to patch things up and resume talks. Because of the press-blackout we had agreed to, none of this had gotten out. I knew Kennedy was no anti-Semite but sometimes just said off-the-chart things. Nolan put me on the phone with Kennedy and we agreed to meet at a neutral site to talk things over.

Picking a Denny's restaurant about half-way between our two hotels, I drove over, sat on a bench outside, and waited for Tom.

When he arrived and sat next to me, he was full of apologies, which I quickly accepted. But he said he had ask me something really worrying him and Nolan, "Jeff, do you really expect to get everything in your proposal?" I replied, "Jeez Tom, not everything but a great deal of it, and you and Jimmy have to understand that and start preparing your committee." Hugely relieved by my reply, he added that Nolan would be appreciative, too.

The Denny's bench off-the-record meeting, I am positive to this day, created a mood that would make our ultimate deal possible. It was the closest the two parties had ever come to a true sidebar, even though we had not discussed a single specific issue. Absent Tom's earlier anti-Semitic remark, it might never have happened. Such is the unexpected strangeness of negotiations. It explains both the pleasures and frequent discomforts of labor pains that I experienced throughout my career. The next day we were back at the table— after the kicking, as if nothing had happened.

About half-way through the talks, Burke flew down to see how things were going and cheer us on. Showing the CEO flag is always vital, and Dan knew his visit to a group of stranded sailors would have an important impact on team spirit. After I gave my report, some operators spoke, he asked some questions, joined us for lunch, and flew home later that afternoon.

When our talks would finally settle months later, Bob Apter, once again our Laundry and Morale officer, presented me with a special wooden plaque he had specially ordered as a gift from the team. Complete with a little affixed plastic bench, it had an inscription on its front that read—"The Order of Denny's Award," with the 1993 date. I kept the bench displayed in my New York office until the day I retired. Nobody seeing it had the foggiest idea of what that little bench was doing on my office shelf except the '93 team members who would occasionally appear. Showing it once to Tom Kennedy when he visited, we both had a good laugh.

A few days after the Denny's bench episode was St. Patrick's

Day. Once again like San Diego I could not let the day pass. This time we needed festivities honoring a group that had now grown to four Irishmen—Nolan, Kennedy, Ray Taylor from Chicago taking Delaney's place since he had retired, and Kevin Wilson, the San Francisco local president. I surprised them with Irish, heraldic-crested, beer mugs adorned with their clan crests, that I had found in a downtown Orlando speciality shop.

Kennedy—ever the proud Irishman—wore the same, Kelly green, Irish cap and shirt combination that he had worn four years previous. At my invitation, he again joined me in the middle space of our hollow, rectangular table setup where I repeated the San Diego investiture ceremony and handed out the mugs. Their family crests were all interesting but Kennedy's was the best. It seemed so apt. His clan's heraldic crest prominently featured in its center a triangle of not one but three heads of medieval knights in heavy, armored helmets. When on subsequent occasions Tom and I would meet over drinks, I never failed to kid him about his helmet-headed DNA, which I had long suspected, and its apparent transference through the centuries.

Dan Burke once more arranged through Patti Matson the same thoughtful, Hermes scarf/tie gift for our spouses waiting at home for their sailors to return from the seas. Again, as in San Diego, he thoughtfully made sure our spouses and children were flown down half-way though our stay for a weekend visit. Most of us gratefully spent those two days with our families enjoying Walt Disney World.

Before the spouses and kids arrived, Kennedy repeated his by-now-famous "conjubial" visit remark that he had trademarked four years earlier. When I told him we could not work that specific weekend, a few of us San Diego veterans had been fully expecting that comment.

As normal with NABET, despite our winnowing down our package by withdrawals and making many modifications, they did what they did best—virtually nothing. As usual, they did not agree to any significant item in our package the entire time we were in Orlando—unless it somehow benefited them. The same, self-reducing wage retroactivity provision that had cost them dearly four years earlier again hung over their heads. While we were hoping they had learned a valuable lesson, their comments across the table revealed nothing.

Each day I cajoled them with our usual pitch about level playing fields, eliminating ancient provisions, curing inefficiencies, and establishing new jurisdictional boundaries. Most critical of what we were seeking was our computer keyboard proposal that was so important to our future.

A keyboard connected to a computer that was capable of performing operational functions, we argued, was not a piece of normal NABET "technical equipment" that only a NABET-represented technician under the contract could operate. It had no switches or buttons, other an on-off switch, or dials to turn. It was not like a camera or a tape playback machine. It stood to reason, we maintained, that the union should no longer have exclusive jurisdiction simply because the keyboard was connected to and operated a computer that performed certain functionality.

Our proposal gave the Company the absolute, unchallengeable right to decide when and to whom it could assign the operation of these computer keyboards. It could be a union or a non-union represented employee. But the unassailable right belonged to us to decide on any given occasion who that person would be. The exercise of creative judgment by the individual involved was to be the key factor in determining our assignment.

NABET fought our proposal at every turn. None of their resistance was surprising since we clearly understood a union's central mission is to preserve as much work as it can for its members. We were just looking at our futures from opposite sides of the same coin. We knew —with absolute resolution—we had to get this right.

Our ability to enter the computer age, and do so in the most sensible and efficient manner possible, depended upon this flexibility. We'd either get it right or pay the price forevermore in efficiency, cost, and wasted manpower. Technology had slammed into us hard like a speeding freight train and given us no room to maneuver.

Needing much and massive change, expanding our daily hire rights, fixing bad work rules, getting this computer technology right, ending restrictions and limitations—whatever we were seeking—it was all to no avail. Even the simplest and easiest to accept of our many dozens of proposals was rejected. Total denial again reigned supreme, as it had four years previous in San Diego. With us still doing all the work for both sides, withdrawing or modifying proposals along the way to get close to where we wanted our final proposal to be, finding some of their's that we could accept, their game plan never changed.

21
CHAPTER

The "Final Four" Saves Us at the Buzzer

It was back to New York to resume talks at the end of the month for a week just before the contract expired on March 31. They stayed at the Sheraton on Seventh Avenue and we were nearby at the Essex House. Walking over for meetings multiple times daily, with the union still giving us very little help or direction, we spent that week further winnowing down and modifying our proposals. As the week progressed we moved closer to our final proposal.

My plan all along had been to drop the final offer on Nolan and his committee the night the contract was expiring as the clock approached midnight. A day or two before, however, I came up with a new idea. Trying to avoid another 1989 situation where Nolan had run to first Burke and then Murphy at the very end to test our resolution, my brainstorm was to stash Dan Burke upstairs at the Sheraton. I would bring Nolan and Kennedy upstairs to see him at the witching hour. What a sobering message it would be to hear from the CEO himself that what Jeff had just said was final, was indeed final. Westin was to be there with Burke and he liked my idea. He asked if anything like this had ever been tried before and of course the answer was no.

Burke also thought it was a good plan. He just asked that we make sure the hotel suite would have a big screen TV so that they could watch ESPN's cablecast of the National Invitation Tournament's semi-finals (NIT) from Madison Square Garden to wile away the hours until our appearance. We arranged for the biggest set the hotel could find for Dan and David to watch the college basketball games. It would be another first—our "Final Offer" would be in play at the same time as the faux "Final Four."

We had agreed with Burke's blessing that our offer include a healthy wage increase in line with or exceeding other recent industry settlements. The package would also feature something both Burke and the union really wanted—a voluntary buyout program for our New York based, network engineers. There would be, however, a serious condition attached to the final offer. All five of their bargaining committee had to agree to accept and recommend the final deal or else no buyouts. Burke liked this idea too, and I reminded him of the condition that it had to be all five. Burke said he got it. "Jeff, don't worry—it's all five of them or no deal."

Our operations were poised for a possible strike at midnight on the 31st with many dozens of management personnel standing by at all locations. All of the signals were telling me that the union leadership knew it could not win and did not want a strike. Remembering the bitter '89 lesson where so much employee retroactivity money had been lost, it could not again risk the high probability, amounting to thousands of dollars per person, if talks dragged on for an extended period. It wanted and smelled a deal.

In a rare, private conversation I had out in the hallway that afternoon, I could see from Nolan that despite their official silence, he and his committee were close to accepting our modified final package, which I had just highlighted. The money part was fine. I went on to tell him we were preparing to deliver our final later that night and adding as a major sweetener, a voluntary and generous, up-to-two-years-of pay, buyout component that I knew Nolan and his members wanted. But it had to be all five accepting.

There we were at the Sheraton at about 11 P.M. and meeting in our separate rooms. Upstairs, Burke and Westin had been relaxing, enjoying room service, and watching NIT basketball. All of our facilities nationwide were ready. With our strategy seeming to be playing out, I had a few hours earlier dropped the final proposal on Nolan and the committee. When I did so, I had labeled it our "last, best, and final" so there would absolutely no doubt we meant to stand on it.

While their committee was locked in its room studying our package and wrestling with itself, I knocked on the door and asked Nolan and Kennedy to step outside. Headlining the various elements and the money, I repeated that the "final"—with its voluntary buyout component—was available only if the committee unanimously accepted and agreed to recommend it. Nolan and Kennedy nodded their understanding when I said it had do to be all five.

Both had been anxious for the buyout. Many of their senior members had been hoping for it so they could retire with up to two years pay and transition into their excellent NABET pensions. I was hoping that with this feature it would seal the deal that they were surely heatedly discussing. They clearly got that it was our last, best, and final—and its meaning—when I repeated that very purposeful phrase.

While appreciating the solemnity of the moment, it sunk in even more dramatically when I told them that Dan Burke was waiting upstairs to see them—and underscore our finality. Exchanging glances with one another as they absorbed the surprising news, it bordered on mild shock. All of us realized just how gigantic it really was. No CEO had ever shown up like this the final night in the long history of NABET. It might never have happened in any negotiations of this size and magnitude anywhere in the country.

Following me into the elevator, the two were in complete silence. As soon as we entered the suite upstairs and sat down, Nolan and Kennedy started in with Burke in their normal Irish-socializing way. Nolan somehow got into his emergency hernia surgery following ABC's *Belmont Stakes* a number of years earlier when he had to be rushed to the hospital. That reminded Burke of his own and he chimed in with his story.

After the exchange of hernia tales and other pleasantries, Nolan wasted no time and launched into the reason they were there. "Jeff has given me the final offer with the buyout package. I know it's final and all five have to accept." Burke agreed, "Yes Jim, it's the final offer as Jeff has said and nothing will change. And it's gotta be all five." Nolan said he accepted that but added he had a serious problem. With Kennedy nodding, Jim went on to explain he was fairly certain he could only get four of his five to accept and recommend the deal.

With that, Burke turned to me and Westin and said—"Well four out of five sounds pretty good fellas, doesn't it?" David and I looked at each other. Before either of us could answer, Nolan jumped in and said, "Don't do it Dan. It's all five or no deal. Jeff told me it's gotta be five. I'll go back and get you the five." With Dan quickly agreeing, the meeting ended and the three of us went downstairs to meet with our committees.

For Nolan, it was both a matter of honor and keeping his word as well as practicality. I had told him it had to be all five, he had accepted that condition, and was now bound and determined to make it happen. It also had to be that he and Kennedy needed five. The buyouts were far too important to the overall deal. They could not allow one committee member to destroy the deal contrary to the best interests of the overall membership.

More importantly, Nolan and Kennedy could not have one person hanging back to take shots at any offer the other four approved and would be recommending. With only four committee members in favor, it would adversely affect the ratification vote and would surely result in actual retroactivity losses if the deal was turned down. If it meant going back to the table and more weeks of futile negotiating, it again could mean, with ABC standing resolute after Dan had reinforced the chief negotiator's saying it was final, large losses from their members' pockets. Nolan couldn't risk another '89, or a strike.

On the way down in the elevator, Nolan shared with me that it was the Los Angeles representative who was the obstacle, which I had already suspected. Nolan and Kennedy disappeared into their caucus room, and I went into our's to tell my committee most of what had just transpired. The part about the four votes I left out of my report. There was a great deal of astonishment that our CEO Dan Burke was upstairs at that late hour and had just met with Nolan and Kennedy. Now after midnight, we settled in for a long wait. Some hit the carpeted floor or leaned back in our recliner chairs to grab some shut-eye.

Around 5 A.M. Nolan knocked on our door looking for me. He told me it took a lot of arm twisting but he and Kennedy finally got the Los Angeles official to go along with the deal in its totality and to recommend it. He had the five votes. There had to be a little sweetener though to secure her vote and that required offering the buyout also to the LA network engineers. I readily agreed, knowing Burke would gladly go along with even a bigger potential buyout to get this done.

With that happy news we shook hands. Clearly, Nolan and Kennedy understood just how significant this moment really was. NABET and ABC had never before in its half-century relationship made a deal the same day the contact expired. Of more significance, no CEO had ever been stashed away to confirm in a secret meeting with union leaders that the deal was final and would never be renegotiated.

Awakening my committee to the good news, I called upstairs to wake up the surely-catching-a bit-of-shuteye-themselves Burke and Westin. Ecstatic, they decided to come down and join us. Minutes later, everyone, including Dan and David, was walking around the conference room happily shaking hands. Officially, Nolan announced they had accepted the deal. The union committee was overjoyed with the package—as were Westin and Burke. Getting major operational adjustments, the dollar savings would be significant. On top of that, Burke finally was getting the chance to do a large staffing reduction—the kind he had been itching to do since he and Tom had bought the Company.

Someone on the union committee quickly went out and brought back a few six packs of cold bottled beer. We all sat there—with ABC's CEO and general counsel—25 or 30 of us, drinking beer at 5:30 A.M. Toasting each other, a few on the union team made little speeches about what a great moment this was in the history of the Company and the union. I, of course, echoed the same. One of the most ecstatic on their side proudly added it was truly a great company because, "Imagine a company that actually paid my tuition to take some labor relations courses at a local college." As dawn was breaking, Burke and Westin took off and we went back to our hotel rooms across the street to get some needed sleep.

Shortly after noon, I and a few of the lawyers were back in our Essex House suite wrapping up some final details and about to shut down the office when David Westin made a surprise appearance. Knowing we were more champagne than beer guys, he brought along a shopping bag full of cold champagne bottles. A couple were promptly popped so we could celebrate the moment with David more appropriately.

Typical of the NABET voting process, ratification followed six weeks later when Tom Kennedy called with the results. All 19 units had ratified, the most important being the nearly 2000-strong technicians group. The process had gone true to its expected and promised course with each of the five committee members, the heads of their locals, supporting the deal and recommending its passage.

But in Los Angeles something strange occurred. It seemed that while the local president officially recommended the deal, one of her senior officers had spoken out against it. A nasty, negative message went out that could have killed the vote. While there were fingerprints on it somewhere, we could never identify just whose those were. Yet we learned that despite this, even in Los Angeles the vote was positive.

Joy reigned supreme on the delivery table once again. A second celebration party was thrown by a pleased and thankful Dan Burke at the Rainbow Room. It was another gala dinner just as Tom and Dan had arranged after the 1989 San Diego negotiations, and it was attended largely by the same group. Once again the full bargaining committee, including administrative assistants, flew into New York from around the country. Division and group presidents responsible for our NABET operations, and senior corporate staff attended. Of course, everyone's spouse was also there.

It was another victory gathering of about 100 people, masterly managed once again by Patti Matson and her chief lieutenant, Julie Hoover. I made a speech, as did David Westin. It was then Dan's turn, thanking the whole team for our endurance, time away from our spouses, and success. One team member, KGO-TV GM's Jim Topping, put together a video. That evening was the CapitalCities/ABC way that milestone events were honored. Everybody on my team walked away feeling proud of their own efforts and Company's gracious response to our sacrifices and accomplishments.

The team had done it again, and this time we scored even bigger gains in achieving flexibility and ending restrictions than we had four years earlier. My lawyers did an outstanding job in working under great stress and continual pressure at each step along the way. Every proposal we achieved was masterfully thought through, skillfully drafted, well-argued, and resolutely nurtured to its final conclusion.

The NABET buyout proved to be a big success. Somewhere between 75 and 100 staff TV Network technicians on both coasts, representing several millions of dollars of annual overhead, ultimately raised their hands and left the Company with large severance payments. When they did, they moved into excellent ABC-NABET pensions. Their jobs were not replaced. Each person receiving the buyout received up to two years of regular salary as severance pay. Generous under anyone's definition, it was unprecedented in broadcasting. As Burke calculated it, we would begin our multi-million dollar payroll cost savings once those two years went by. That large staff and payroll reduction would be permanent, as Dan always said—it would last forever.

Hitting the road again on instructional tours, we began educating hundreds of managers how to apply the rule changes and flexibilities gained—with millions of dollars in operational savings waiting to be captured. As a consequence, managers were once more taking over without the "book" rigidly telling them what they could or could not do, using their own judgment. Our goals had been met—the workforce was being better managed, we were saving big money, and staff reductions were being achieved.

Burke's attention now turned to the TV Network's non-union staffing problem. John Sias had left the Company in '92 without ever properly addressing its inflated numbers. Burke now decided to take it on himself. Soon assembling a meeting in his office of the Network's major division and department heads, with myself, finance, and HR present, he threw out the kind of separation program he envisioned—an involuntary one.

Asking each Network division or department to look at their individual rosters, he wanted them to choose people by name and position, taking into consideration the importance of each individual to the continued success of the particular business unit.

Whether positions would have to be refilled was a major factor. All non-union jobs at Network locations in New York, Los Angeles, and Washington would be eligible for the buyout. Probably having a goal in mind, he did not say, but he was looking for a big number—in the several hundreds.

The severance amount was going to be the standard formula he and Tom had brought with them when they bought ABC—up to two years of pay—the same involved in the just completed NABET buyouts. It had been considered so generous over the years that it was famously said that the only thing better than being hired by Cap Cities was being fired by Cap Cities.

As soon as Dan finished laying out his concept, BOE chief Bob Siegenthaler pointed was that the buyout would be a lot more successful if it was voluntary. As Siegenthaler saw it, so long as a person volunteered, it did not matter what position that person held in the organization. High or low, senior with many years or new on the job, that non-union staff person should be approved and get the package. No one, he said, should be excluded, regardless of position, importance, or length of service if Dan really wanted to get a big response. A great many network people, he went on to say, had been waiting a long time for just this possibility.

Burke and Siegenthaler went back and forth for a while over the wisdom of a voluntary versus an involuntary plan. Burke opened it up for discussion and went around the room. Finally convinced, he changed his mind and agreed to make it a voluntary program. HR put the formal plan together and it soon went out to every non-union staff person at the entire ABC TV Network in its three cities of Washington, Los Angeles, and New York.

It was a surprise to many, surely to me and perhaps to Dan himself, that among the very first to submit his papers was Bob Siegenthaler. He had done such an excellent job in making the argument, he had apparently convinced himself. Siegenthaler soon retired to the seacoast in Maine. Many other senior Network officials of long service, including a number of important vice presidents, also raised their hands, collected their generous 2-year severance packages, and left. Some positions had to be replaced, but at the end of the day, the Network was thinned out considerably. A great many employees got a once in a lifetime chance to leave the Company, with a nice fat check, do something else in life, or just retire. The Network's payroll was cut by hundreds of jobs and millions in costs.

As an added footnote, when Siegenthaler took his buyout, Preston Davis was promoted by Burke to become president of BOE. Davis started out as a Washington bureau NABET maintenance technician in the '70s after serving in the US Army in Vietnam. He would go on to become my partner and closest colleague in every NABET negotiations and major NABET meeting from 1989 until the day I retired 20 years later in 2009. His achievements leading BOE during that challenging period were extraordinary.

When Preston a few years after his own retirement would sadly, and far too young, pass away in 2013, he had been, as BOE president, probably the highest-ranking African American executive in the entire Walt Disney Company. His funeral in Sarasota, FL., would be a sad occasion for the many of us who attended, and a great personal loss. When I looked into his face in the open coffin and realized all we had done together, through both great difficulty and joy, I could not help but shed a tear. When I stopped off at the Sarasota National Veteran's Cemetery in 2020 to visit his grave, it was another difficult moment as I thought back to the decades we had worked together.

But back in '93, as the management buyout program was drawing to a close, the ink was not yet dry on our new NABET agreement when the head of the Los Angeles local filed a grievance challenging our new and critically important keyboard computer language. Anticipating the possibility of just such a challenge, we had taken particular measures to draft our new language in a way that we believed it was as tight as a drum. It was "iron-clad," as we called it, harkening back to the famous Civil War naval battle between the first two iron-clad ships—the USS *Monitor* and the CSA *Merrimack.*

By encasing it in armor, we believed we had written a new provision that was absolutely clear and unambiguous on its face. As such, it would be impervious to any NABET attempt to use the grievance and arbitration machinery to gain what it had failed to achieve in negotiations. It had been our constant imperative to make it air-tight so that no arbitrator could ever find a way to rule in the union's favor. So, we steadfastly had rejected any counterproposals and stood absolutely firm on our language— refusing to alter even one word or punctuation mark, no matter how harmless each seemingly-innocent proposed change might appear on its face.

But now the Los Angeles president was filing a grievance and intending to take our iron-clad vessel to arbitration where a favorable outcome for us was expected but could not be guaranteed. Designed as unsinkable, our ship could still be torpedoed by an arbitrator in some strange and wholly unanticipated way.

Her grievance challenging the new language was a total shock. Most everyone on our side saw it as the highest form of bad faith. New BOE chief Preston Davis was particularly outraged. It had been unanimously accepted and recommended by the union, including this very representative, but now the essence of our new found flexibility to operate in this critical computer area was being challenged. Our Los Angeles attorneys prepared many hours for the upcoming battle royal. I personally flew out and took command at several days of hearing and remained deeply involved throughout every step and stage of the long and tortuous litigation process.

Jim Nolan and I had traveled around the country together after the 1993 ratification. Both of us had become concerned that our shared arbitration costs for our designated contract arbitrators were out of control. With an increasing number of cases everywhere, many of which were multiple day hearings, both of us felt the arbitrators started the sessions too late at 10 A.M. and ended them too early, at 4 P.M. We decided rather than write letters expressing our common desire for longer work days, we wanted to speak directly to each of the approximately ten arbitrators and look them in the eye.

In the course of travel, with so many hours spent sitting next to each other on multiple flights and at frequent meals, we bonded at an extraordinary level. Just two human beings, we found ourselves opening up after all these years of battling. The candor and closeness we experienced on that trip I never before, or since, encountered with another union leader.

Jim shared with me that he had come around during these past talks to respect me for my accomplishments with him and his union. He added that he thought he would never have been able to admit that when I had returned for my second tour in '87 when he disliked me, particularly after the Julie Barnathan episode. I told him I held the same deep respect for him. It had, I said, become a very tough job as leader of a union undergoing a vast sea change in technology, loss of power, influence, and control.

We told each other things—mostly personal things—that we trusted neither would reveal. I know I never did, and I believed he was such a man of honor and integrity he would do the same. I related stories about my family, and the Company, not the real secret things of course, nor the truly confidential things entrusted to me by virtue of my corporate position and lawyer's ethics. He did the same in some non-confidential stories, I am certain well-selected, about his family, as well as the union and its rich history.

Included in his comments were his feelings about the duplicity of the Los Angeles arbitration, knowing in his heart the claim was just wrong. He confided much else while we talked in very personal ways. Both of us walked away from those days together with a much deeper understanding of each other as human beings, and with warm feelings towards one another. Still today I often think about Jim, and I exchange messages with his widow, Frances.

Nolan retired as NABET president in late '93. Sadly, he was to pass away in the winter of '94, after a relatively short disabling illness, at the young age of 65. When Jim was at the NYU Medical Center in New York in his final days, I was there visiting one day with our colleague and mutual friend, Bob Apter. Nolan proudly told his chief nurse that the chairman of the board of that major hospital was his friend and CEO of CapitalCities/ABC, Tom Murphy. She was impressed. Tom had, without Jim's knowledge, actually spoken to the hospital's director about Jim's care and treatment after I related to Tom the serious nature of his illness.

Privately towards his end, he gave me some advice about a certain NABET official. "Jeff, never trust that fucking, little, lying cocksucker" Jim whispered to me on near his last day. The person attached to this warning shall remain anonymous, but of course Nolan's pronouncement proved to be entirely accurate.

Jim Nolan's funeral was well attended by both rank and file members as well as senior NABET officials. Many other high-ranking officials from a number of other unions came as well as numerous company officials including myself. It was replete that cold March day with police bagpipers playing his beloved Irish tunes and was a fine tribute to this great union leader. The Company sent along from Tom Murphy one of the largest floral arrangements at his service. Rebel at first, Jim led the very effective first NABET strike against ABC in 1967 and a second one ten years later. But by the time he passed away nearly 20 years further down the road, I think that Jim Nolan had mellowed in his outlook.

It was my feeling that in his final years he was much more believing that rationality and cooperation—not outright belligerence and hostility—were the keys to NABET's ultimate survival. Fighting us and NBC, I was certain he had come around to believe, was fruitless. It was only going to get his beloved union hurt and more seriously damaged. While he had positioned NABET well joining with the CWA, he didn't live long enough to judge its ultimate wisdom.

When Nolan had stepped down in '93, Tom Kennedy followed him out the door—like Johnny Carson and Ed McMahon. His place as chief negotiator would be taken by John Krieger. John Clark, the president of the NBC NABET local in New York, who I did not know well, succeeded Nolan as the new national NABET president. Clark, whose career had been at the NBC radio network, would complete the work Nolan had started by bringing it across the CWA finish line. Kennedy was also to pass away not too many years later.

In late 1993, David Westin moved over from general counsel to become head of a production unit at ABC Entertainment in Los Angeles. He was on his path within a few years to become first the TV Network president and later president of ABC News. Westin's place as general counsel was again taken, for a brief period, by Steve Weiswasser who had returned from ABC News. Upon resuming his general counsel role, Weiswasser brought in Alan Braverman to fill a new position of deputy general counsel. Alan came from the same Washington law firm—Wilmer Cutler & Pickering, the Company's chief outside counsel —as had Westin and Weiswasser before him.

Alan remained deputy general counsel for about six months in a newly constructed office directly adjacent to the labor relations suite. Its proximity allowed us to talk frequently. Promoted to GC upon Weiswasser's moving on to a new operating position, Braverman was to remain my boss for another 15 years—right up to my retirement in 2009.

Sometime in mid-'93, the New York NABET local went through its own transition. Its former head had developed a serious medical issue that affected his work and led to his being voted out of office. Losing his union position, he went into retirement from his ABC engineering job. Strangely enough, that's when I got to know him a bit better.

Coming across a possible treatment for his medical issue, I wanted to help this person's health and save his life. So I called his close friend, the recently retired Tom Kennedy, to pass on this information. Most fortunately, the treatment was a success, but a year or two later he died from another cause at a relatively young age. It was a sad day at his funeral which I attended to pay my respects. Needing my assistance with some ABC life insurance benefit issues, his widow contacted me and I was more than glad to help facilitate a solution to her and her family's concerns.

A new, more strident order came into power at some locals including New York's. The rhapsodic tones of the '93 negotiated settlement soon quickly dissipated. Some locals' leaders who had joyfully participated in that 5:30 A.M. toasting with cold beers were influenced by these new others and became negative if not radicalized. The new, emerging message became one of criticizing the unanimously recommended and easily ratified settlement. Nolan himself and Kennedy were called out by some for claimed leadership failures. The new leaders were promising a membership largely unfamiliar with the dynamics of the bargaining table and not attuned to the changing times, a new and better day.

It soon became clear what challenges lay ahead. While following what I am convinced these officials believed was the right path forward for their members, their extreme negativity and destructive behavior over the next half-decade would seriously damage the negotiating process and bring harsh, unforeseen consequences to their membership. For many of us watching the pot being stirred, it was painful to see a relationship deteriorate as we contemplated the harmful effect that unthoughtful words and immoderate actions would bring to both ourselves as well as our employees.

It was around this time that I got to know Alan Nesbitt so much better. I had first met Alan in 1989 when he managed our

Raleigh-Durham TV station and I had travelled to that North Carolina area on an unrelated *One Life to Live* remote pickup. Its executive producer, my friend Paul Rauch, was shooting one of his complicated story lines, so appealing to soap audiences, on the Duke University campus. It was a big remote with many performers and Paul had invited me down to see first hand the intricacies of soap opera remote production from both an AFTRA as well as a NABET labor relations perspective. Alan Nesbitt picked me up at the airport, and we soon became fast friends.

Later on, around the same time as changes in NABET leadership in '93, Alan had become the new president and general manager of our powerhouse KABC-TV in Los Angeles. He was, simply stated, the most gracious, smartest, most intuitive, and best broadcasting executive and general manager I ever encountered during my entire four-decade broadcasting career. And there were many greats. An old Cap Cities hand, Nesbitt had started out at its Buffalo radio and TV stations. Ironically, as his later relationship with the NABET would counterpoint, his first job was as a NABET-represented, on-air radio reporter.

While station news talent is normally represented by AFTRA, for some reason lost to history NABET held the contract at these Buffalo stations. He began, like so many before him, in radio and then moved to television. Over many drinks and meals together during our decades of friendship, he shared some of his mystifying moments as both a member of NABET and also serving on its bargaining committee.

That Buffalo on-air stint had been the end of Nesbitt's union career. Soon moved into management news positions, he rose along the way to the general manager post at Cap Cities' WTVD-TV in Raleigh- Durham where we first met. He later moved into the Philadelphia GM job at WPVI-TV before relocating once more a few years later to Los Angeles to take over as president and general manager at KABC-TV. Both Philadelphia and Los Angeles, at the time of Alan's management and still today, are among the most successful and profitable stations in the history of American broadcasting.

Alan Nesbitt joined us in Las Vegas in the spring of '94. Along with the other three TV station general managers and my usual five or six senior executives from Network News, Sports, Daytime, Radio, and BOE, we were there for our first "semi-annual" meeting with the NABET leadership. With my group of labor lawyers, it was our core NABET team of about 15. The union may have had as many as eight or ten on its side, including its five local presidents.

The semi-annual meeting was a feature from the CBS-IBEW engineering contract that I had imported into our NABET relationship during our most recently concluded talks in '93. Its essence was for the bargaining parties to meet twice a year, between contract negotiations, in a more casual setting. Both the IBEW and CBS felt that if issues, concerns, new initiatives, or prospective changes could be discussed more than once every four years at contract expiration time, built-up frustrations could be defused and strikes avoided. Both parties in the CBS-IBEW relationship, as I learned from discussions, believed it had improved the management of their shared destiny, which previously suffered some long work stoppages. Nolan signed on when I had proposed the idea at the '93 talks. We both saw its wisdom and thought it could be transported over to the ABC-NABET relationship. Perhaps, at least I was hoping, it could become as valuable a tool for us as it had been for CBS and the IBEW. But it was new to us as a concept as we sat down that morning at the Las Vegas table. Without any Nolan helping to guide it, it would take some period of adjustment if it had even a half-chance of being successful.

Nesbitt was in Las Vegas as the GM of his 300 or so KABC-TV technicians, news camerapersons, editors, and news writers. As the new general manager, and managing his first NABET station, Vegas was to be his initial exposure to this union in action since his own membership and bargaining committee days in Buffalo.

As Clark and I opened with our mutual greetings and expressions of hopes for a successful meeting, there was one union official sitting across from us drinking what looked from every appearance to be Bloody Mary's. From our table separated by only a few yards from their's, it sure looked like Bloody Mary's. The clear color of the vodka, as often happens in this alcoholic drink, was still sitting mostly at the top of a tall glass—not yet stirred into the tomato juice below. It had a swizzle stick in it. Even the union side seemed embarrassed at the disrespect drinking booze was showing all of us and the entire labor relations process.

Nobody drinks Bloody Mary's or any alcoholic drink at a negotiations or any other business meeting. It's not done at nine o'clock in the morning or two in the afternoon. In 40 years of business, I had never seen it. Not once in any of hundreds of labor negotiations and even more meetings in casual settings like this with dozens of unions officials. A drink at a restaurant during lunch or dinner, or at a bar after work is one thing—a negotiating table meeting like this is another— whether in Las Vegas or any other city. We weren't on vacation, this wasn't lunch, dinner or cocktail time, and we were working.

After the Bloody Mary was fairly quickly finished, the person got up, left the room, and soon brought back a second drink that looked very much like the first. Drinking it, soon becoming argumentative and then stridently attacking, it wasn't long before he walked out of the meeting and did not return until after lunch.

It was before the official abruptly left the table when we were attacked that most of us first saw what lay ahead. What we witnessed and heard from this individual was unsettling. I jumped right in and challenged some of the more outrageous comments as our side looked on in horror while the other side remained silent.

Going through all of our minds as we were watching this

performance were two overriding questions. How was the semi-annual meetings process going to function as a building block in our relationship if a union official could sit there drinking booze and bring disrespect and disruption to the very essence of what the meeting was designed to accomplish? The second question was even more telling. How was the entire relationship and the future of our negotiations going to develop if this individual's, abnormally aggressive and disrupting behavior became routine?

As we were seated there processing these questions while the attack was ongoing, from the end of our long table Nesbitt came onto the field. Novice as he was at the time in confronting NABET, it was a forceful rebuke of this official. My heart swelled with pride and joy as soon as I heard him speak. I knew immediately I had found another very strong ally among the operators in this articulate and thoughtful general manager. Like so many of the Cap Cities GMs who I knew, he was always for the people who worked for him—union or non-union. But, he would always speak out about bad, blustering, or misdirected union leadership adversely impacting his employees and affecting his business.

At the negotiating tables in the years ahead when he joined me, Nesbitt always took my chief negotiator's lead. He knew intuitively from the operator's point of view how to run downfield with the ball and always reinforce the contract points and arguments I'd been making. It just came so naturally. Partly, I think, it originated from his previous newsman's background. Not shy either about reciting and practicing the basic Tom Murphy and Dan Burke principles of proper workforce management, he was one of the Company's strongest assets throughout my career.

Despite Nesbitt's lack of specific knowledge that morning in Las Vegas about the NABET contract, he clearly smelled the evil concoction being brewed. Alan Nesbitt would take none of it that day, and he never did. All of us could smell it, too.

At CapitalCities/ABC's '94 annual management meeting at

the Arizona Biltmore, Dan Burke, reaching age 65, surprised all of us by announcing his retirement. After his long service to the Company and brief term as CEO, Dan was going to be leaving to devote his time to the minor league baseball team in Portland, Maine, he had recently bought. For the first three days, he led us in his normal inspirational manner. At the end of the third and last day, he made it absolutely clear that he wished to leave CapitalCities/ABC and the broadcasting business far behind. Burke's last line in his valedictory ended with, "Don't call me—think of me as dead."

A shock wave passed over the assembled room. There was a silence for a good five seconds as people absorbed the sharp and bewildering expression coming from the man everyone so admired. The 100 or maybe 125 of us simply did not know how to react properly— whether to laugh or cry. Finally, some nervous applause broke out that rapidly spread as we stood and applauded while looking at each other in total dismay. As the meeting ended with this thunderous applause, Dan silently walked off the stage and out the door, just as Jimmy Durante had done decades before each time his television variety show ended. There was from Burke, however, no goodnight to a mysterious Mrs. Calabash.

Dan was gone. Many of us chatting outside the room afterwards were totally mystified by his farewell comment. Saddened not only by his leaving, the starkness of his announcement was unsettling. Later that night there was a large fireworks show to celebrate Dan's retirement although many of us did not feel very much in a celebratory mood.

Dan, unlike Murphy when he stepped down the year or two before, really meant it. He was to remain gone even though he kept an office in the headquarters building for a short time. It was a sad occasion for me and most every executive to lose Dan as our leader. While I had heard he sometimes could be angry and harsh with people, he had never been that way with me. Monica loved baking him tins of chocolate chip cookies that I'd every now and then hand-deliver to his desk. There was always such a nice, hand-written note back to Monica thanking her for her thoughtfulness and delicious cookies. Or a note to me about something complimentary that someone had mentioned to him about something I had done. And his own well-dones. Those personal notes were part of his management style, and in those days before email, people so deeply appreciated receiving them from Dan.

When Dan stepped out of the Arizona Biltmore doors and disappeared, Tom Murphy came back to run the Company as our CEO once again.

22
CHAPTER

ABC News Hits the D-Day Beaches

June 6, 1944. The D-Day invasion. Normandy, France. It was the greatest amphibious assault in the history of warfare. ABC News along with the other networks was going to be covering the 50th celebration of this momentous event with several days of broadcasting that would culminate with the June 6, 1994 ceremonies at the American Military Cemetery overlooking the invasion beaches. President and Mrs. Clinton, Queen Elizabeth, and all the royalty and prime ministers of the Second World War allies were going to be there.

It was to be a very big event, with simulated landings, parachute drops, jet flyovers, and ceremonies at all cemeteries and landing sites. Military marching units and bands galore. The nuclear powered aircraft carrier, the USS *George Washington,* was to be anchored offshore Omaha and Utah Beaches, along with a small fleet of accompanying American warships. The Clintons would be staying in the admiral's suite on the carrier. Our star news anchors and many correspondents were going over, leading a very large ABC News presence of upwards of 100 or more NABET cameramen, technicians, and other ABC News production personnel.

Monica and I had been to Normandy several times over the previous 20 years on numerous trips to France, visiting not just the major museums, towns, and historical sites, but also the graves of our fallen heroes. We had no family member or friend buried under those crosses and Stars of David in the beautifully designed and maintained cemetery overlooking the Omaha invasion beach where our nearly 10,000 young boys laid. But this battle had been very meaningful to both of us in our understanding and knowledge of Second World War history. Writing my senior thesis at Lafayette College on Hitler and his generals, I had always considered myself a bit of a military history buff. Monica, with her MA degree in history, had been teaching the subject for many years in her junior high school classes.

There is nothing in the world quite so moving as standing at the headstones of former President Teddy Roosevelt's two sons, Teddy Jr. and Quentin, next to each other in the Omaha Beach cemetery. Teddy Jr. had been the deputy commander of the 4th Infantry Division and at 56-years old, he had been the oldest man in the invasion. Landing with his troops in the first wave at Utah Beach on June 6, General Roosevelt died from a heart attack in early July of 1944. His younger brother, Quentin, at age 20, was an American pilot shot down in 1918 in the First World War who had been buried where his plane had crashed in German-occupied France.

A decade after the Second World War ended, the Roosevelt family had Quentin's body exhumed from its lonely gravesite when he had been buried by German soldiers nearly 30 years earlier where his plane went down. It was relocated to Normandy where his brother Teddy Jr. had later died on the beaches. The two brothers in 1955 were laid to rest side-by-side in the peaceful setting of the American cemetery overlooking Omaha Beach. Teddy Jr.'s headstone has on it the gold-emblazoned seal and star of the Congressional Medal of Honor, of which he was a recipient. Standing there in awe on several occasions, each time it brought tears to our eyes and lumps to our throats.

We had planned this trip since the summer of '84 when we were in France right after Reagan's extraordinary Pointe du Hoc address on the occasion of D-Day's 40th anniversary. On that trip we had swung through Normandy on the way back to Paris with ours young sons, Josh and Alex. If the 40th was that exciting, we thought at the time, imagine what the 50th would be like. So we went ahead and secured reservations at an old chateau hotel not far from the invasion beaches. Of course, at the time we made those advance reservations I was with RKO and had absolutely no idea that ten years later I would be working for ABC.

Using vacation time I had coming, we took our two boys, now 15 and 13, out of school and shipped out to France on a 747 for the week of the commemorations. My colleagues at ABC News, particularly veep Bob Murphy in New York and those running the Paris Bureau, notably Pat Thompson, wife of our Paris-based ABC News correspondent, Jim Bittermann, were very helpful. We all got ABC News credentials and whatever assistance was needed. The boys at the time were just teenagers. Nevertheless, the photoed credentials they received showed them, as well as Monica and myself, as full-fledged, ABC News correspondents. That indulgence—often lent to ABC senior executives like myself at special events—was a product of its time. No way would that be possible in our post-9/11 world where tight security really matters.

The press credentials got us in everywhere. At each official ceremony or event featuring a VIP press seating section for real working journalists, we were the only ones sitting, and normally in prime locations. Our passes allowed us to drive anywhere on the jammed Normandy roads. Police and army barricades at key points would be lifted just by flipping our ABC News credentials. The shows' executive producers, several of whom I knew, like Rick

Kaplan, were gracious in inviting us to their production venues. Not wanting to get in the way of any operations, we were nevertheless interested to take in as much as we could of these historic events. With all the world's leaders attending, oftentimes kings, queens, prime ministers, and the US president himself, were sitting or standing just 50-feet distant from us.

Among the many events we attended was the parachute drop by elements of the 82nd and 101st Airborne Divisions on a large field outside of historic Sainte-Mère-Église. The drop was a reenactment of the real jump our boys had made 50 years earlier that D-Day morning. They were accompanied in their jump this day by former President George H. W. Bush, then in his 70s. It was a massive drop right out of *The Longest Day* as a never-ending column of C-17 troop transports appeared on the horizon, flew overhead, and filled the sky with hundreds of parachutes.

Our credentials not only got us through every checkpoint, they also earned us a parking spot right at the edge of the field itself. Tens of thousands of Frenchmen streamed to the site on the only access road after parking their vehicles as many as several miles away. It was a remarkable day as we almost got stuck while exiting on the overcrowded and narrow Normandy road system. Beating as we did the massive crowds surging back to their cars by quickly leaving the landing field just minutes before the final jumps took place, my sons were upset at dad's insistence that we depart as abruptly as we did. Leaving a few minutes early, however, saved us endless hours waiting in backed-up traffic on the over-crowded roads. Planning ahead like this for the best possible outcome had become ingrained in me.

Invited to the *This Week With David Brinkley* production that Sunday in an old chateau, we arrived early and chatted with hosts Cokie Roberts, Sam Donaldson, and George Will before they interviewed the American Ambassador to France, Pamela Harriman. We sat with Harriman in the "green room" and also spoke with her a bit before she went on. The widow of former diplomat and New York Governor Averell Harriman, before she married Harriman, during the Second World War she was famously Winston Churchill's daughter-in-law. Approaching 75 years of age, she was still a very engaging and formidable person.

We had dinner one night with some of our ABC News Radio managers and correspondents in the dining room of our hotel. Going to Normandy had many pleasant moments talking to any number of production people, correspondents, and technicians.

One evening during dinner at our hotel an extraordinary thing happened. We noticed another American couple sitting at the next table. They were older and we were soon to learn he was a returning veteran. Since it was impolite to talk between tables, we arranged to have coffee afterwards in the hotel bar once the boys went up to their room. After we introduced ourselves, we started with the usual who do you know, where are you from kind of talk. When he asked how long we had reserved at the hotel, I answered it was nearly ten years. Commenting how smart we had been to do it so far in advance, he offered that he had waited too long but had managed to get a spot on the waiting list. Much to his surprise, the hotel had called him just a month before to advise there had been a sudden cancellation and offered him the room.

That comment surprised me because we had just surrendered a third room we had earlier booked when we had planned to travel to France with another couple. They had recently gotten divorced and we had given their room back to the hotel just about four weeks previous. It was clear these new people had gotten the room we had just cancelled. The four of us had a good laugh over the incredible coincidence.

If that was not odd enough, we turned to our businesses. I told him I was with ABC in a senior executive role but just a visiting fireman with my family on this historic occasion. With his mentioning that he had been in the textile business for decades before retiring, Monica jumped in telling him that her father had also been in the textile business. Our new friend on what had to be lark asked what part of the business and she answered he was a small manufacturer who had invented some kind of velvet suede process. But, she added, he didn't make any money from it when he sold the business far too early.

Looking startled by what he had just heard, he asked for her father's name. When she told him, our new acquaintance said, "I bought your father's business, but don't worry, I sold it too early and didn't make much from it either." This was stunning. What had just happened that night, with a chance meeting between strangers in a small hotel on the French coast during a 50th anniversary war commemoration, was extraordinary. None of us had to be there, yet all of us had been drawn there—to the same hotel and adjacent tables. Two huge coincidences like this, it was something right out of the *The Twilight Zone*. Once again, destiny had called.

A couple of NABET technicians, again with Irish backgrounds, whom I had become friendly with had retired to Ireland a few years earlier. One was a D-Day veteran. We had stayed in touch, so when they had contacted me and told me they planned to be in Normandy for the celebrations and I told them we would be there too, we made arrangements to get together. We managed to meet for a few hours of chat and lifting elbows at a bar in Sainte-Mère-Église. It's the charming and historic town made famous in *The Longest Day* when the actor, Red Buttons, got his parachute caught on the church's steeple.

It turned out this was the last time I saw either before each passed on years later. One had an exciting career as an ABC Sports cameraman for decades in the Goodyear blimp. "Sully" had retired and bought what I was told was a small castle in Ireland. The other, a real character with huge eyebrows had the great Irish name of Finbar. With a brogue to match, he was a close friend of NABET's

Jim Nolan. I had seen him at Nolan's funeral earlier that year when the subject of Normandy had first come up. Oddly enough, I had met Finbar initially years before at a disciplinary proceeding that the Company had brought against him under the NABET contract for some minor infraction he had committed.

When I got back to the office, I found a mason jar of Omaha Beach sand that was dated June 6, 1994. Still sitting on a book shelf in my home library, it had been brought back from France by an ABC News executive producer who showed us around in Normandy. My friend, Pat Roddy, is still in the news productions business and we talk periodically.

It was shortly after this time that CapitalCities/ABC decided it should examine starting a 24-hour cable news network. A previous ABC News cable channel attempt under Goldenson in the mid-1980s had proven unsuccessful. CNN had earlier made history with its own '80 debut and had taken off providing the country and world with a successful all day-news outlet. Towards the end of that decade, NBC did a little of its own by starting a business news cable channel, CNBC. In 1991, CNN's coverage of the first Iraqi war put its channel and cable news on the map for good. ABC in the mid-'90s now thought the time was ripe to get into the cable news business, too.

After exhaustive research, it was found there was a market for another cable news channel and elaborate plans were undertaken before any formal announcement could be made. A new ABC News organization that would borrow parts and resources of the existing structure was put together to manage the new unit. The plan was that ABC News' on-air personalities would originate stories and host programs for both platforms. Peter Jennings, Diane Sawyer, Cokie Roberts, Charlie Gibson, Barbara Walters, Ted Koppel, and ABC's host of other anchors and correspondents would now be seen by the American viewing public, live and taped, 24/7. Additional on-air talent exclusively for the cable channel would be among the hundreds of production and technical operations jobs that would be added to the staff of the new venture.

Its head was selected, Jeff Gralnick, an experienced ABC News executive producer. Reporting to Arledge, he left his other producing duties behind and jumped in full-time. As the project moved forward, both were deeply involved in developing plans and putting together the new team that would be running the new operation. Editorially, it was expected the new cable news network would reflect the same mainstream reporting views as its older brother.

While still in the planning stages and not ready to be announced, the venture progressed under an imposed cone of silence. Possible sites for the new studios were investigated quietly before the search zeroed in on one particularly attractive parcel in the middle of New Jersey, about 35 miles and 45 minutes from our New York headquarters. An architectural firm was engaged to start drawing up design plans.

While this was happening, rumors were circulating that NBC was looking to start its own all-news cable channel and Rupert Murdoch was deep in planning for his own 24-hour Fox News Channel. It had been reported that CBS had looked at cable news possibilities a year or two earlier but had not jumped in. Perhaps, as some thought, it was thinking about it again. Cleary, beginning in the spring and summer of 1995, a lot of cable news dreaming was in the air.

I was engaged early-on in the project because if the idea was going to succeed, it had to be run to the largest extent possible on a non- union basis. CNN had been launched by Ted Turner in 1980 and had achieved its success operating in its union-free business model. Not just were its field crews and Atlanta headquarters' technicians, stagehands, and make-up artists not represented by any union, its on-air studio and field talent was not represented by AFTRA. Its writers did not belong to the WGA nor were its directors in the DGA. The IA was nowhere.

CNN's guiding philosophy from its very start had been to pay wages at least as good as the three established news networks, provide comparable benefits, and treat people fairly both in perception and practice. That was the open secret then, and still today, to being able to operate successfully a non-union company. 15 years after its founding, CNN in 1995 was still non-union, as it is in 2022. CNBC was also started by NBC in 1989 under that same, non-union business model, and so would later be MSNBC as well as Murdoch's Fox.

If both union-heavy NBC and union-free CNN could succeed in avoiding NABET and the other unions in their cable operations, we felt ABC could manage the same. Our ESPN had successfully since its inception operated on a non-union basis, so we had some experience in managing this result. For ABC though, it would be more difficult on the performing side than CNN because so many of our on-air talent who would be utilized in this project were already AFTRA represented. Plus we had other unions, too. It was an awesome challenge we faced in the months ahead as planning accelerated on the rumored $100 million plus investment.

The new 24-hour cable news service was formally revealed to the press in December of '95. That date just happened to be six months after Disney had announced it was acquiring CapitalCities/ABC. Its target date for launch was sometime in '97. Later in '96 while Disney's acquisition was still pending in Washington, the venture was not surprisingly put on hold for further study. We all knew from where that was coming. Some time subsequent that same year, after Disney's acquisition of ABC was approved, the cable channel idea was killed by the new parent. Not only would the cost have been huge, the Disney decision makers must have felt on re-evaluation that the timing to jump into the 24-hour cable news business had already passed.

Indeed it had. The cable news competitive landscape had shifted dramatically in that same year of 1996. In July NBC's launched its own 24-hour cable news channel, MSNBC, to add to its CNBC. Much-rumored and counter-programmed, the Fox News Channel finally made its cable debut in October. Cable news had become a very crowded space. Any new entrant, such as ABC's would have been, was not assured of any degree of success. The idea when dropped though was a crushing blow for many within ABC News and the larger Company who had seen for one of the few times a real opportunity for growth.

I had gotten the earlier news about Disney's takeover the same as everyone else. It was on July 31, 1995. Monica and I were in London. When we returned to our hotel room after a long day, we found a bunch of faxes shoved under our door. Worried that the faxes meant something serious had happened at home, it turned out that they were from Marc Sandman in New York. Marc was alerting me to the surprising news that CapitalCities/ABC had just been sold and we were now part of The Walt Disney Company.

After the initial shock wore off, I turned on the BBC to see the news. There was tape of Michael Eisner and Tom Murphy earlier that day standing in front of news cameras at our West 66 Street headquarters announcing the $19 billion deal. At the time it was the largest merger ever. Murphy had felt the time was right to sell the company to Eisner to maximize stockholder value. While called a merger, we were to find out it was much more of an acquisition.

There was much anguish at that night's dinner with our London friends and a very sleepless night. At the age of 54, I was concerned about the inevitable reorganization that normally follows any merger. I questioned whether my job managing ABC's labor relations and 14 people on both coasts would still exist. Why, I asked myself, would the newly combined company, particularly one based in Los Angeles, need to keep both of the fully-stocked ABC and Disney labor relations departments.

It was the normal question about redundancy and efficiency that most ask following any merger. There would always be a sudden quest for new-found synergies and cutbacks. If they were merged, I surely thought, the new head would most likely be either myself or my Disney counterpart, Robert Johnson. If merged under Johnson, which I saw as the more likely scenario because Disney was the "merger" and ABC was just the "mergee," there was a good chance my job would be eliminated. Many other senior ABC executives, including a number of senior lawyers, shared these same concerns about their own futures. Our London friends that night told me not to worry.

Of course we were all saddened to see the end of the Tom Murphy and Dan Burke era. In that one decade of ownership, they had taken a strong ABC and re-energized it into something truly special. Many of us felt, and still do, that there had never been a company like the one Murphy and Burke created and ran.

Since ABC was now to be a Disney subsidiary and no longer its own separate corporation, I would lose the word "corporate" from my title when the federal government approved the merger in '96. Still reporting to my boss Alan Braverman, until further notice of any reorganization I would continue being responsible for all of ABC's labor relations and labor law activities nationwide. Despite my initial fears that the acquisition would result in the ABC Labor Relations department and the Disney Labor Relations department becoming consolidated into one, managed by Disney, that never happened.

As an interesting footnote, many years into my retirement Robert Johnson and I talked about this. Having headed Disney's labor relations for about as long as I had been running ABC's, he shared that such a reorganization had actually been considered by Disney's acquisition team leader at the time. But Robert, who has remained a good friend to this day in 2021, maintained his normal cool head and displayed his usual excellent judgment when he recommended against any consolidation. Let ABC do its own thing, he wisely said. The idea never went any further.

Once the dust began to settle, my teams on both coasts were right back in the groove with all of our many union relationships. Staff or freelance talks were always going on somewhere. If it wasn't with AFTRA's announcers, soap opera performers, or Network news correspondents, it was the DGA, SAG, IATSE, the AFM, or the WGA. If we weren't physically yet at the table, we were busy setting the table for one or more of our next talks. My group had its experts in each contract. I had the fun of keeping my eye on everything and putting my hands on the ones I chose.

A few of us began our pivot to NABET '97 but what we began seeing all around us was not encouraging. The combination of the new NABET leaders and Big Brother CWA working together telegraphed we had dark days ahead. So my labor relations team began to prepare for wherever those days might take us in the enormously busy preparation year of 1996. Mark Sandman in New York and Olivia Cohen-Cutler with Bob Key out on the West Coast became my core team. From that point on, they joined me in hardly ever again getting enough undisturbed sleep.

Bob Iger kept running Capital Cities/ABC as president under Murphy while the merger went through all the necessary Washington regulatory approvals. After the early '96 approval, Murphy stepped down as CEO but remained with an office in the building and a seat for a while on the Disney board. The "Capital Cities" part would disappear from our new subsidiary name.

23
CHAPTER

Life, Labor, and Good Fortune Under Disney

Life gradually became noticeably different under Disney. It was not only the physical absence of Murphy and Burke's leadership in running the Company, but it was also learning to adapt to the new organizational structure. It was back to being just "ABC." We were now an important part but merely a subsidiary of The Walt Disney Company. But perhaps it also meant we were no longer responsible for much of our own destiny. No one—certainly at my level—knew the degree of control our new parent might choose to impose on its new subsidiary. While we were adjusting to the fact that it was an acquisition rather than the merger it had been called in the press, we also had to get our arms around our new culture—the Disney culture.

It was a relief to know that Michael Eisner had so much confidence in Bob Iger that he kept him as president and in charge of the American Broadcasting Company. Fortunately for all, Bob, along with the rest of ABC's headquarters, would continue to be based in New York. It was reassuring for the entire, senior executive cadre to know that there would no headquarters shift to Los Angeles as many had feared.

One of the first things that happened was a surge to find synergy. That would be the new term in vogue for a while. Creative ways of working together would have to be found within the newly combined companies that would result in greater efficiency. More efficiency would lead to better product flow, headcount reductions, and cost savings. The no-longer needed corporate jobs like the CFO and his large finance staff, treasurer, secretary, security chief, and shareholder relations veep would move to Disney. The people holding those ABC slots were not the ones who survived and were soon gone, as were their staffs. Publishing, with all the friends and colleagues I had acquired over the years, and work we had begun doing, did not fit the Disney entertainment model and was soon piecemeal-jettisoned.

The pressure was on in '96 to find more ways to reduce headcount and cut costs. Heavy ABC News costs in the US and around the world were among the ones targeted. Domestic and international bureaus were soon shut down. The 24-hour cable news channel and its expected $100 million investment that had been put on hold was now formally killed. From now on, ABC News would not be expanding but contracting and would need more reliance on new initiatives as well as partners around the globe.

I had become increasingly convinced that the next NABET negotiation was going to be intense and difficult. With Jim Nolan gone and the change in its top leadership, both national and local, I saw trouble on the horizon under the activated CWA umbrella. A hot, shooting war—like the ones the CWA periodically had with telephone companies—could easily result. Confrontation was in the air.

As the field commander of an army going off to fight that war, I was concerned about any possible uncertainty over whom my commander-in-chief would be. Would there be Disney involvement in our strategy, decision making, command, and battle plans? Or, would Eisner leave it to Bob Iger to be ABC's commanding general in much the same way that Tom and Dan had led the old ABC, as if we were still a self-standing company or self-governing subsidiary.

I talked this over with Alan Braverman who remained as ABC's general counsel reporting to Bob. I did not get a strong sense that he knew either to what degree, if any, Disney would want to get involved or actually take command or control. Other than I would be reporting to him as usual, I was instructed to start my planning, get the team assembled and begin moving preparations forward as we had in the past.

1996's annual Phoenix meeting for senior executives at the Biltmore introduced us to the new Disney management. Michael Eisner showed up on with a big and colorful production number on stage welcoming the former CapCities/ABC people into the Disney family. Featuring the M-I-C-K-E-Y-M-O-U-S-E song routine, it was warm, impressive, and I think most of us felt very good about it. Mickey and Minnie and a number of the other famous characters, including my personal favorite Goofy, were there in costume. Prancing around the stage to the familiar loud music, the characters were joined by Walt's nephew and vice-chair, Roy Disney, Eisner, his new COO, Michael Ovitz, and a few other senior Disney people. Eisner had appointed Ovitz as COO just a few months earlier for what was to be a short but costly stint.

With Dan Burke gone two years and now Murphy also retired, Phoenix was no longer a Murphy/Burke, or Murphy/Iger production. Bob Iger took over on stage for his first as our new leader. Eisner joined him and welcomed us into the Disney family as his newest "cast members." It was a term that Eisner had coined for Disney's employees that just did not seem to fit well with most of ABC's senior managers, including myself. I just never saw myself or any of my colleagues as "cast members." Donald, Mickey, Goofy, and some other performers—like Zoro, Davey Crockett, and the mouseketeers—were cast members, but not Ruthizer, Davis, Apter, or Nesbitt.

That night at the big cocktail party and dinner, in an Arab tent and dress motif, I walked over to and introduced myself to both Eisner and Ovitz. I will never forget how that went with Ovitz. "Hi Michael, I'm Jeff Ruthizer and I just wanted to say hello." Extending his hand for the shake, I continued, "I'm ABC's head of labor relations." Maybe he was in a playful mood or just tired by too much forced conversation—I have no idea. But I was taken aback when he said without a second's pause, in what sounded as a serious tone, "Nice to meet you, but Jeff, never call me. Labor relations gives me a big headache."

Although it often gave me a headache too, it came with my territory. It also, I had thought, came with his. Here he was, the number two executive in the entire Walt Disney Company, its brand-new, chief operations officer—its COO—telling me he wanted nothing to do with labor relations. Last I had heard, labor relations played a considerable role in operations. Strikes sometimes wipe out operations or have a serious impact. It would have been like Dan Burke telling me when he was COO never to get him involved. To the contrary, I constantly had Dan's jacket over my shoulders, and his keen interest.

I surmised immediately that if Ovitz was serious about my never reaching out, I would get no interest whatsoever from him in what was on ABC's operational horizon. Not just with NABET, that ban would extend to any union. It just reinforced the hope that Eisner would permit ABC to remain in charge of its own labor destiny and that Bob Iger would be the commanding general.

A part of me said Ovitz was just kidding, but I doubted it from his demeanor and could never be certain. Fortunately, I did not get the chance to find out. What made this all the more curious was because of what happened at the following February's Phoenix meeting that we both again attended. When I walked over and would go on to gently remind him of our conversation the year before, he, not surprisingly, had no recollection. But it had clearly stuck in my mind. Shortly after that '97 appearance, and with $100 million in severance pay from Eisner and the Disney Board in his pocket, cast member Michael Ovitz would be gone.

That year required a great deal of travel around the country. We visited all our stations and Network facilities, building support, listening to problems, and gaining an understanding of issues. Marc Sandman, who would be chiefly responsible for our contract proposal drafting, joined me on most of these visits as did my two other key assistants, West Coast veep Cohen-Cutler and Bob Key from her staff. Speaking with the many senior operators who managed our approximate 2300 or 2400 NABET staff and daily hire employees, we got a sense about operational problems they experienced and changes they deemed warranted. After the numerous meetings with senior executives, station GMs, news directors, sports managers, department heads, and engineering chiefs, we spent many days back in New York and Los Angeles doing our homework.

Ideas that germinated on those trips were synthesized, analyzed, and converted into proposed contract changes. What we learned was that despite the multitude of gains we had made in 1989 and '93, much still remained to get the contract normalized. Far too many inefficiencies and restrictions, built up over decades of too much giving to NABET, were still alive and well. Many wasteful work rules and excessive costs still dominated.

Among those issues that were raised to top priority, San Francisco's unique set of non-competitive circumstances bubbled to the surface and cried out for relief. Our arbitration-challenged, "iron-clad" computer keyboard language needed another foot or two of steel armor. We needed to make serious medical plan language revisions. In addition, both CBS and NBC had renegotiated their contracts, so those changes needed to be evaluated to see if they made sense for us, too.

After meeting with Bob Iger and Alan Braverman, Bob authorized another replacement strike training program. This time it was taken on for the Network by BOE's head, Preston Davis. The stations would be responsible for their own strike preparations. Once again, we would absolutely be ready for any strike that NABET might launch and come to the table with this great strength behind us. It would again be both our shield and our sword.

Larry Pollock's TV Station group was still the driving force in advocating further contract relief because it understood best the failings of the NABET contract. Its teachings had already made a powerful impact on BOE head Preston Davis' thinking, and this trend would only accelerate over time.

The TV Station group's new EVP was now my close colleague, Alan Nesbitt, formerly the KABC-TV general manager before his promotion and move back east. Alan, along with Preston Davis became my two strongest operational allies. Nesbitt joined my labor relations team in traveling around the country visiting the NABET-station properties and helped to flesh out the contract's flaws that needed correction.

Preparing largely as we had in the 1989 and '93 negotiations, I began developing my 1997 bargaining strategy and planned to submit it first to Alan Braverman. As his first negotiations as GC, there would be a great deal of background information for him to absorb and understand in order to get comfortable with the landscape and my recommendations. Over time as the plan developed and briefings continued, Alan would become attuned to its multiple nuanced parts and very supportive.

By the end of '96, the plan was completed. In the course of that year I had picked up through various methods and sources more information to confirm that the CWA now would play the dominant role we had expected in 1993. Consequently, our planning had to take that into account in much greater detail and develop a counterstrategy. Writing these pages in 2021, I am thumbing through a copy of what turned out to be a very prescient document. Sending it onto Iger and a handful of ABC's top executives, one of those was now Steve Burke.

Steve Burke had recently come over to ABC from Disney after running EuroDisney in Paris and then the Disney Stores. Iger now appointed him into a newly created position as president of Broadcasting. In that role, Burke would become Larry Pollock's boss as well as oversee the Radio Station and Radio Network groups. In his new job, he soon developed a great deal of interest in the upcoming talks that would so heavily involve his stations. After an extensive briefing, like his dad before him, Dan Burke, Steve got it intuitively. He soon became an enthusiast for the many contract reforms outlined in our plan. Steve was around for the start but not the finish when he would leave ABC in late 1998 to become president of Comcast. In 2010, he'd be back though with NABET when he became CEO of NBC.

At Braverman's suggestion, I also sent a copy of the plan to Disney's general counsel, Sandy Litwack. With Ovitz gone, Eisner had asked Sandy to assume some of Ovitz' former COO duties. Braverman and I met with Litwack at his offices in Burbank. Smart, thorough, and a quick take, it was clear he had read the plan and grasped both its big picture and myriad of details. But lacking any broadcasting background, Sandy had no real capacity to readily discern its many nuanced pages of intended operational reform. The clearer, more direct money saving items though were more easily understood. Excellent lawyer that he was, he commented favorably on the arbitration procedure reforms that we intended to seek.

After about an hour's meeting, Litwack gave his general approval and wished us well. Clearly though he left me with the distinct impression that he had no overriding interest in getting more intimately involved with us in these talks. Whether he ever had any further discussions on this subject with Iger or Braverman, he didn't with me.

When Braverman and I met with Iger to review the plan's major proposals, our path forward, and the union's probable strategy it was clear Bob was his usual well-prepared self. Familiar as he was with NABET from his years in studio operations and then ABC Sports management, he asked some questions and was clearly on board with our intended game plan to fix the many problems. When I suggested that he come to Washington and make opening day remarks, as Dan Burke always had, he responded with an immediate yes.

The Company team that assembled in Washington at our Hyatt Hotel headquarters in early February of '97 was largely the same group of mostly presidents or divisional vice presidents who had been at the table with me in our prior 1989 and '93 talks. With five of us from labor relations including myself, we had senior executives from the Network's ABC News, ABC Sports, and BOE divisions, the TV stations, the radio stations, and the radio network. All told, with a few new additions, there were around 20 of us on the core team.

My administrative assistant again set up a complete office suite equipped with high speed copying machines, telephones, an ample number of desk top computers for the whole group and a very large conference room for our planning seasons and caucuses. Our security team had for a year prior been brought in to do its job at our New York offices much as it had the previous time and now performed the same sweeps at the Hyatt.

Sandman, Cohen-Cutler, and Key were my chief lawyer lieutenants.

The several of us had just before these talks began first travelled around the country for a week negotiating with NABET over the other bargaining units covering the few hundred, non-engineering employees in the other units that were also part of this process. The largest of these groups were the three news writer contracts in Los Angeles, Chicago, and San Francisco. But it ran the full range of jobs from hair dressers and traffic coordinators to plumbers, painters, couriers, and publicists.

The plan I had worked out with NABET's John Clark was to meet in Washington beginning in February for about a month until early March. We would then adjourn for about a week and resume in New York for the final ten days leading up to the March 31 expiration. It was clear to me that the week's gap was intended by Clark to allow for strike votes in each of our five cities.

The score of people on my team was larger than previous talks because Larry Pollock wanted, for the first time, all four of his TV station GMs to be at the table throughout. In prior talks, the group had been represented, on a rotational basis, by just one GM. But their full presence as Larry wanted was fully embraced by me. All indications were that the union team would consist of about ten, made up of its five local presidents, Clark, his chief negotiator, John Krieger, and a few others. From time to time as subject matters changed or moved away from its normal engineering focus, the core group on both sides would expand or contract.

Iger flew down to Washington as promised for the opening round of talks accompanied by Alan Braverman. CWA president, Morty Bahr, was there with Clark. After first engaging in the expected pleasantries, Iger spoke from an outline of some bullet points I had suggested. His points were about efficiency, technology changes, and the need for working together cooperatively.

Bahr made his own opening remarks, more pointed than in 1993, largely about respect and mutuality at the bargaining table. Following my comments along my usual theme of hope, efficiency, and the need for reform, NABET's John Clark added some remarks about it being a new day for NABET. Clearly to me, Clark was referring to his CWA parent and the impact he believed it would play in these talks.

More important to me, however, than what Bahr and Clark said was the presence of several CWA veeps whom the CWA president had brought along and introduced. Their presence was designed, I was certain, to deliver a message that this was not going to be like last time. Nor would it be another 1989. Big Brother CWA was now on the scene full-time. "Make no mistake about it," its storyboard might have read—"No longer will our little brother be pushed around."

Most of us who'd been around in '93 sensed immediately that there had been a major shift from the final Jim Nolan days. When those talks ended on its high note as dawn was breaking, the NABET committee not only accepted but also unanimously recommended the final deal. We sat there in the wee small hours of the morning, with our CEO Dan Burke, bottles of beer raised high—for the first time in our joint history—happily toasting each other's success and hopes for the future. Those surrealistic days were now far-off and long-forgotten.

It was clear to me that Bahr came to the Washington table committed to do whatever his 700,000-strong and politically influential union could do to make certain NABET would never again have to agree to concessionary demands—sometimes referred to as "givebacks." To help ensure the result, he appointed one of his CWA officials, Carmine Turchi, as a permanent part of the NABET bargaining team. Turchi was a mid-level CWA representative from its New York operations and an experienced telephone company negotiator. He would prove to be a savvy, sometimes angry, but very worthy adversary throughout our time together.

After the speeches and exchange of our mutually thick sets of proposals that first morning, we adjourned and went back to our hotel. Iger joined us for a quick lunch meeting and then flew back to New York. Spending the rest of the day analyzing their proposals, we quickly saw they were replete with much that we had anticipated, including numerous deletions of our important gains over the past decade.

The next day before we resumed at the table, John Clark called me aside for a private conversation. It was even more unusual because it was only the first day of our talks. Clark brought Turchi and I had Marc Sandman. Turchi immediately launched into—"Hey Jeff, you got to be kidding. We've gone through your comic book. Pick maybe one or two things and we'll take a look at it. Everything else, forget about it." After quickly disabusing him of that ever happening, the brief meeting abruptly ended, but it set the tone for the days and months ahead. Maybe this was how it was done in telephone talks, but this was a new and unacceptable message for us. Never surprised at most anything, I left that brief meeting more convinced that with Turchi's expected prominence and their extreme negativity even before we sat down at the table, we were in for a very difficult time.

Pumped up in overconfidence with what they thought was the CWA secret sauce, it became readily apparent from the very start this bargaining committee was not going to conduct itself in any traditional manner. Not that we had expected them to come to the table and make it easy, but never in our wildest imaginations did we think it would degenerate into what it soon became.

It was largely the behavior of a few, but the NABET International president and its chief negotiator did nothing to discourage it. When the attacks came, they were often loud, foul, and abusive. Nearly every second or third word often out of one negotiator's mouth seemingly had a "fuck" in it somewhere. Personal threats across the table directed at me were many—including a warning from this same person not to stand too close to the edge of any subway platform. On another occasion, there was a break during a negotiating session in a warm hotel conference room where the air-conditioning had not been working properly and the windows had been wide-opened. As I stood at one to get a breath of fresh air, one of their committee members walked up and advised me not to get near any open window.

When I asked the same union negotiator some time later to

close the top of the open briefcase on the conference room table so I could see the official sitting behind it better, the response was— "Sure, but then you'll see the gun I have pointed at you." I ignored the insane comment and just moved on. At each such statement intended to intimidate and throw me off my game, I thought I could detect the tiniest of cringes from one or two on the other side, but the rest of the union committee sat there in silence.

Nobody had the courage—let alone the will—to try to shut down the unacceptable conduct. Never would I, or any other negotiator I ever knew, company or union, have ever before behaved or permitted behavior like this at any bargaining table. I had sat through more than a few tough talks in my lifetime with some really bad dudes, some of whom went to prison, but even the worst of them never carried on like this.

The union officials acting out like this—that the rest of us were getting to know better each day—would soon enough emerge more publicly. I kept waiting for the right moment when the darkest among them would reveal to all their true selves.

During that four-week stretch, we continued our practice of holding team dinners once or twice a week at nearby restaurants. Socialization for a group like this, thrown together and locked away for a month without spouses, kids and family, was always critical to our prior successes. Normal conversing with just not colleagues but friends, away from the stress and intimidation of our day jobs, was now more than ever needed to keep a team 20 high achievers together in mind and spirit—supporting each other in this assault on normalcy. Halfway though the talks our spouses and children were again brought down to Washington for the obligatory family R&R visit on the one weekend we didn't work.

Much as predicted, talks in Washington—mostly six days a week—went nowhere. We had no interest in their proposals to surrender gains we had achieved or grant them any new improvements except the most modest few that would not hamper us. They treated our proposals for relief and reform with nearly universal distain and ridicule. Like the great, tectonic plates I had imagined back in law school that labor relations would be, we were experiencing firsthand the constant grinding of management and union preparing for the inevitable earthquake.

It frustratingly went on like this for the four weeks we were in the nation's capitol. The Company again found itself having to negotiate with itself, getting no help whatsoever from the union. Reluctantly, we forged some necessary modifications and withdrawals. Over time, we searched for some of their's and began reducing our package down to its essential elements on which we intended to stand when that day came. The union, however, remained adamant throughout our weeks of futile bargaining that nothing we had proposed of any significance to us had any merit. Our moves to modify or withdraw proposals never induced any reciprocity.

Knowing our readiness and apparently realizing that the traditional strike weapon might get them nowhere, the union began employing a few different tools. Taken from a new labor movement resistance playbook, they launched what was called a "corporate campaign." It was a strategy designed to bring pressure on ABC by attempting to influence station and network advertisers, viewers and listeners, politicians and public officials, other ABC unions, the Disney board, and shareholders. The resistance handbook also called for various workplace initiatives including possible threats to refuse overtime assignments, work strictly according to the precise terms of the contract, and slow-walk assignments. We adjusted our own strategies to deal with all.

With no press blackout like the last time, NABET undertook an aggressive PR campaign of daily press releases and recorded telephone announcements to expose our claimed "union busting." It was, like any other propaganda machine—a faucet of one-sided and mostly inaccurate messaging intended to keep their members, and the public, as whipped up as possible. We answered with our own daily audio bulletins and written releases designed to tell the story from our point of view and in so doing defuse the spigot of highly inaccurate information and incendiary rhetoric.

In the meantime, strike preparations and replacement training at all locations were ramped up. Hundreds of management people everywhere had been trained, retrained, and were now ready. Much money was spent leasing outside technical facilities where most of this training had taken place. HR chief Jeff Rosen and his people developed another good strike pay bonus plan if that was needed. Security was substantially increased.

Taking a brief adjournment for each side to regroup after that four-week stretch of mutual futility, we resumed in New York for the last ten days of March. During the respite, NABET as expected held membership meetings and took strike votes that overwhelmingly passed in each of the five cities. It was a message intended to demonstrate determination and once again stoke fear.

24

Saying You Have an Open Mind Means Never Having to Admit It's Closed Like a Steel Trap

Basic NLRB law requires "good faith bargaining." One side or the other is free to reject as many of the other side's proposals as it wants, but they have to be discussed with an open mind. At some point every negotiations must end with a deal or no deal. Or a union can always strike when the contract expires. If no strike and there remains "irreconcilable differences" after a sufficient length of bargaining, the employer can declare at its risk a lawful impasse and then implement its final offer. The union's objective from day one was to prevent the "double i's" from ever happening. Our's, on the other hand, as in 1989 and '93, was to negotiate the best deal possible for the Company. If a negotiated deal, try as we might, would prove impossible to achieve, we were well aware of our other legal options.

In a perpetual state of total denial, the union committee had been playing for those four weeks, and would do so for long after, what can only be described as a cute game of attacking proposals but never definitively rejecting them. It's a defensive strategy sometimes engaged in by unions unwilling to strike who are facing unacceptable demands and unable to negotiate a deal with which it can live. In doing so, NABET thought they were developing a record for the NLRB that would demonstrate their open mindedness at some future point when ABC might attempt to end talks. It was the key, they had convinced themselves, to preventing us from ever being able to use the circumstances of the impasse they created to bring endless negotiations to a conclusion on our terms through a lawful implementation.

To accomplish this objective they employed a variety of artful dodges. Each was geared to show us how they really felt but at the same time trying to keep enough wiggle room so they could claim to the NLRB, when the time came, that they were never actually and definitively rejecting our proposals. Their goal was to be able to prove they had an open mind on everything they said they hated both across the table as well as in their constant flow of PR releases and telephone bulletins. It was disguises, camouflage, and lots of smoke. In so many words, comments such as "It's the worst thing we ever saw and totally detestable, but we're not saying no." Or, it could have been a loud rant like, "This despicable proposal will put us in our graves but we'll take another look at it."

Another might have been, "Hell no, you'll never, ever, get us to agree to this it, but maybe we can be convinced." It might have been simply the more vernacular, "You can shove it, but we're keeping and open mind." It was a giant a smokescreen, perpetual obfuscation, and complete sham bargaining. They thought they were immunizing themselves by creating some degree of ambiguity in their comments and could go on playing this game of avoiding "irreconcilable differences" forever. But we had taken some advanced courses ourselves in this tricky legal subject. The difference was that our classes had been taught by masters.

While the union continued engaging the entire time in Washington with this game of surface bargaining, the Company was busily preparing our defenses against the union's other possible and more immediate strategy. That was the potential nuclear bomb of a complete, nationwide strike at midnight on March 31 when the contract expired.

The ten days at New York's Empire hotel went by again in total futility as both sides continued to do their thing. We patiently went ahead, modifying or withdrawing where we could, arguing our positions and presenting our justifications—often over occasional shouting us down as we tried to persuade them. Finding a few of their's acceptable, we attempted to elicit some positive reactions and movement since our goal was always to get them to start bargaining.

Whether seniority, the whole host of separate San Francisco issues, keyboard access to computers, pension plan reform, jurisdictional issues, technical director duties, sports remotes, the full range of work rule changes, medical plan issues, grievance and arbitration relief, the lesser proposals—they remained in complete denial and accepted nothing. The entire time, as we were preparing our final proposal, they mostly held firm to their own demands, including desired rollbacks.

Most importantly, they were placing great faith in what support they thought they would get at the right time from what they saw as a pro-union NLRB. While we worried about that too, we were doing all we could to establish a clear, factual record for any fair trier of the facts.

Unable under law to make verbatim recordings of the proceedings, I kept two attorneys busy during the entire course of the negotiations taking careful, handwritten, contemporaneous notes of everything said across the table by both parties. We were dedicated to being able to demonstrate in a written record to the ultimate, unbiased reviewer of the facts, the NLRB, when the time came down the road, the true record of what had transpired. It would show they were just gaming the system with phony bargaining.

ABC's *69th Annual Academy Awards* from Hollywood, our biggest broadcast night of the year, and NABET's major production, went ahead as scheduled. As the Company did every four years when the contract was due to expire on March 31, we had made sure the show was produced prior to that date while we still had the protection of the no-strike provision. From our suite at the Pierre, a large group of us gathered to watch *The English Patient* sweep top honors. But I began thinking—in the back of my mind—about how next year's *Oscars* was going to be protected if we had no contract by then. On March 24 1997, however, the worse case scenario for a year down the road was still largely unfathomable.

Games, rants, raves, and body slams—we needed every now and then to get away from the combat zone and take a break in the safe R&R areas behind the front lines. One night that week the Cafe Carlyle, a few blocks north of our Pierre Hotel headquarters, beckoned. The star singer, Eartha Kitt, was performing. Eartha had been one of the three actresses who had played the famous Catwoman on ABC's popular '60's *Batman* television series.

Having dated for a period in the early '70s the most famous Catwoman of them all—the actress Julie Newmar—I was especially intrigued to see Julie's feline competition live and close-up. A few of us headed over and soon found ourselves at a table in the front of the room, right at the edge of the floor where Eartha and her pianist would be appearing.

Out she soon came in her shimmering gown to a big round of applause. As the lights went down, still glamorous at age 71, she launched into her routine after first engaging the audience with a few well-chosen, welcoming lines. "C'est si Bon" and "Santa Baby" were her signature numbers. Both songs performed by Kitt—in her well-known growl and with theatrical flare—needed a male member of the audience sitting nearby as her love interest. For some inexplicable reason known only to Bruce Wayne and the Gotham City police commissioner, as soon as the spotlight was turned on, it found me.

Before I knew what was happening, Eartha Kitt moved over in that cat-like way she had mastered. Standing just a foot or two away, she was purring those lyrics in her inimitable style directly at me. What a sexy song and famous routine it was the way she performed it. If there was any way of bottling that performance, I'd be taking a nip of that elixir every morning with my coffee just to brace myself for the expected discomfort and kicks at the negotiating table.

As those ten days came to an end on the contract's March 31 expiration, we presented our final package proposal. Just to ensure they would have no doubts before making their strike decision, we labelled it—as was my custom—our last, best, and final. The package importantly contained among its many dozens of features the self-reducing wage retroactivity provision we had been proposing from the start—just as we had in 1989 and 1993. My remarks and the proposal itself were received with the usual derision and attack. Leaving the Empire conference room after a particularly curt "we'll be in touch," we went back to our hotel to await further developments. When later that day arrived, the whole group ordered in room service in our Pierre suite but still had no clue if the union would call a nationwide strike at midnight.

Hunkered down in our suite for the remaining hours, the team was awaiting midnight. There was thick tension in the room. Normally reliable intelligence sources were telling us nothing. Teams of management employees had been brought in and stashed away in conference rooms and other secure waiting areas in all of our cities. Awaiting news like the rest of us, they were ready to take over operating positions on a moment's notice. All of the television station presidents were with me, but they had deputies back in their cities monitoring the situation and prepared to launch contingency plans. Alan Braverman was standing by at his home for my reports, and he was in close touch with Iger. The Company was ready for any eventuality. We were at DEFCON 1.

As the midnight moment of truth approached, all of us were on tinder-hooks. Television Station group president Larry Pollock had dropped by unexpectedly to give his support and show the flag. Appearances by senior executives like Larry at moments like this mean so much to negotiators, so he was very welcomed. Extemporaneously, he rose from his chair as we were sitting around idling and delivered a few comments. It was more inspirational than anything I had ever heard, before or since, and like one of George C. Scott's famous speeches in *Patton*. The room was in hushed silence as Larry spoke. Directed mainly at his four station GMs but intended I think for the whole room, he launched, in a slow and deliberative manner as only Larry could, pretty much into:

> "All of you have done an amazing job in getting us to this point and I am proud of you. Whatever the union decides to do in a few minutes your stations are perfectly ready. Whatever they do, whatever commercials get blown, don't worry about a thing. We'll fix it, we'll make it up. I'm telling you right now you can go can go out and hire whatever additional people you need to get through a strike. Don't worry. You've got to know that I, Steve Burke, Bob Iger and the entire Company stand right behind you as this marches forward no matter what happens."

What an electrifying moment it was. These written words don't express even the half of it. The awe and pride we all felt at that moment was enormous. The emotion could be cut with a knife. No one spoke in order to allow Larry's message to settle in, and then we sat back to await developments.

Normally when there's a strike, buildings quickly empty at the stroke of midnight. But that didn't happen. They stayed in place. The union, realizing the futility of defeating ABC and the Walt Disney Company in a traditional strike, had chosen another grand strategy from its economic warfare toolbox. Their path forward was to be a continuation of the same tactics they had practiced all along— deny, delay, and obfuscate. However, with the contracts' expiration and with it the demise of the no-strike clause, they could add new weapons to their arsenal—guerrilla job-actions and real strikes.

They would attack, but only when they felt the timing was right to impose maximum damage. In the meantime, they would play both the denial and the waiting games for as long as they could to try to wear us down. The promise of losing retroactivity for every week that went by without a deal seemed to have had no impact upon them whatsoever. Never was a word about it spoken.

Every ABC location nationwide, now operating without any protection against a strike, was susceptible to a work stoppage at any moment. As the cold war would continue, we would have to maintain a steady readiness for any eventuality, not knowing when and exactly how NABET would try to deliver a knockout blow to any of our operations and take us off the air. In the meantime, they would go on to flood the NLRB with dozens of unfair labor charges alleging many unlawful actions. It was just another way to stifle our bargaining demands and negotiation goals. In addition, they intensified the new artillery weapon they had rolled out earlier—an endless stream of information requests we'd have to answer.

Clark and I agreed to resume talks for about a week in mid-May and again it would be at the Empire hotel's big conference room. In that long and narrow room, the two tables that sat about 20 on each side had about ten feet of space separating us. It was the usual game. The Company would argue for the needed changes we had proposed and urged the union to stop being luddites and negotiate. The entire time the union stayed to its game plan of carefully camouflaged, total opposition to everything, downright belligerence, and often simple nastiness.

There was a specific exchange during one of those May days where the four-letter word was thrown around by one of their key disruptive characters in a particularly scurrilous way. In verbally attacking just not me but also other company officials present, including females, the "F-word" was used multiple times in an unusual syntax of verb, adjective and noun. When the notes of this vulgar and bullying exchange were circulated within the Company and specifically to Iger and Braverman, the Company's resolution became even stronger.

There had been another memorable exchange earlier in the talks. The morning session had just started. This time one of their chief disruptive characters was sitting at the bargaining table and seemingly disengaged. This individual sat there with the morning newspaper opened wide and appeared to be reading it. Discussion in respectful if not productive tones was going on all around us as the pages were turned. The performance and obvious disdain were shocking, but no one—on either side—ventured a comment. A few minutes into this pretend act of boredom and indifference, but more a display of disrespect for every one in the room and the process itself, this union bargainer folded the paper and put it down. Out of nowhere from this person's mouth came a foul-mouthed attack on me and the Company.

Arnie Kleiner, our Los Angeles KABC-TV president who had taken over from Alan Nesbitt as GM the previous year, just couldn't take it any more. He jumped in from his end of the long table with a resounding:

> "Hey, you sit there reading the morning paper, not paying any attention. And we're all getting along fine with each other. Then you open your mouth and get the nasty ball rolling."

Suddenly rising as if on cue and throwing back his chair, the individual just called-out pointed and yelled at Kleiner, "Outside in the hall, right now." Kleiner, standing up and pushing back his own chair, responded equally loudly with, "Yeah, but only one of us is coming back."

The confrontation in the hall didn't materialize as each unloaded their weapon and sat down. Kleiner later admitted to me that he was thinking to himself the entire time, "And it's not going to be me coming back." But the shout-out, coming from one of my strongest team members, was extremely effective in underscoring what we were up against. Others on the union team sat there in their usual silence to this kind of spectacle. But inner shame, at least by some, must have been felt.

Long gaps between talks dragged on for many months. We made efforts to get them back to the table every so often, but they usually declined. On the few occasions where we actually succeeded, it was about a week at a time and no progress was made. They came not to negotiate but rather to stonewall. The bad behavior, threats, and intimidation continued at many levels. It wasn't just threatening statements anymore telling me to watch where I stood on subway platforms or near open windows. Or the mad rush once by one member of their bargaining team around the table to try to come at me before one of my team members inserted his own body to block the lunge. It soon would become more than just certifiable comments about pointed guns.

Since the contract had expired, NABET was now free under law to strike. It could be the traditional long and protracted strike, or they could attempt, if they thought they could get away with it, hit and run guerrilla tactics. Unions in other industries had been trying those tactics. Of course, going the guerrilla-route was risky since ABC could always opt to lock them out. Having to navigate that possibility carefully, they had to choose their options wisely. But clearly our product was now vulnerable to attack, damage, and potential destruction. Our job number one ever since the contract expiration date had been to protect those valuable assets.

It became clearer as time went by that one of the most necessary assets worthy of protection was our annual *Academy Awards* broadcasts.

ABC and our NABET engineering-partner crews had produced this Hollywood broadcast together for decades. Unlike the annual *Daytime* and *Primetime Emmys*—where the networks rotated production—ABC had a long term, exclusive production and broadcast contract with the Academy of Motion Picture Arts and Sciences. The show each year had been a source of great pride not only to the Company but also to the union and the many dozen of Los Angeles-based, NABET-represented employees who annually worked on it. ABC Entertainment's biggest special event production, the *Oscars* broadcast made a huge amount of money for the Company, drew very large ratings, and was our top rated entertainment show of the year.

The *Oscars* broadcast that prior March had sneaked in unscathed just under the 1997 expiration wire. Early-stage discussions with the Academy and preparations for the next year's show had already begun. But as we approached the summer of '97, with no end in sight to our potentially volatile labor troubles with NABET, and understanding its game plan better, I began thinking more about the fate of the next year's broadcast.

One day I had an epiphany. If we had no contract by the time the show went into its major production phase later that year, which was looking increasingly likely, there'd be a gun to our head the following spring. If that happened, we'd be dead either at the table or with the broadcast. After Sandman and I discussed this with Braverman, he clearly understood we could never allow either to happen. We needed and came up with a Plan B.

Internal production under ABC's direction and control— where NABET's involvement, with or without a contract, would be required—was not vital. We could give that up if necessary. It was the broadcast itself that we had to protect. That meant negotiating a new arrangement with the Motion Picture Academy whereby we'd give back our *Academy Awards* production rights. The academy would produce the show for ABC's broadcast—in the same manner as all the other outside produced programs that appeared on ABC's air. But it would be done under whatever union arrangements the Academy would itself determine. Clearly, if the Academy was smart about protecting the production for ABC's broadcast, that was not going to be NABET.

The only other union that Hollywood producers had available was the union already very prominent in movie and prime time television production—IATSE. Although unquestionably more complicated to deal with because of the myriad of local unions involved in the production and not the one-stop shopping that dealing with NABET had allowed, that's the route the Academy selected with an IA production company.

The same path forward was chosen for other endangered species that we were producing for our own air. ABC's NABET crews had produced *Dick Clark's Rocking New Year's Eve* in New York's Times Square for many years. Those rights were renegotiated with Dick Clark. He took on the production with his own production company. That meant IATSE. ABC got what we needed—a safe broadcast. It also became the pattern with the Television Academy for our annual *Emmy* broadcasts, previously done NABET, when our turn in the network rotation would next be due. The Television Academy would produce the *Emmys* for ABC's air—engaging IATSE crews. IATSE's International president, Tom Short, received the news about all of these intended production changes with open arms.

ABC's NABET-represented technicians were the losers. The work would go away because of the union's scorched-earth strategy and sheer bargaining-table obstinacy. All of these production losses would be permanent—up to and including today in 2022.

NABET's refusal to face reality in the early stages of both the 1989 and '93 talks had not been not that surprising. In those two sets of talks, however, resistance had eventually led within months to negotiated deals. In '97 though, in their new suit of CWA armor, it was extreme, inflexible, and seemingly perpetual. In the earlier talks everything fell into place, but that was under the leadership of union officials who at the end proved to be more pragmatists than zealots. This time, with their CWA support and encouragement, the NABET leaders saw themselves as invincible. If the CWA, they thought, had the wherewithal to keep the telephone companies in check, they could certainly take on and help vanquish ABC the same way. After all, that had been the underlying promise of Nolan's merger.

I saw it as their version of Dan Burke's "jacket over my shoulders" routine a number of years before—their kevlar vest. They were confident in their strategy and girding for a major fight on the battlefield of their choice on the date they selected. It was much as my strategic plan, our blueprint for survival and victory, had predicted. We just did not know where, when, and how the cold war would turn into hot combat.

So constant vigilance and readiness were mandatory. The Network and local stations were continually evaluating and refreshing their strike contingency programs. And assuring me and senior management that replacements were both trained and ready. Whether I was at the table or in my labor relations command bunker watching over the scene, preparedness gave us great confidence.

While I felt supported by senior management and confident in managing the situation, there were moments when I felt the heavy load. Everything, in the final analysis, was on my shoulders. It was my strategy and my battle plan that Iger and the Company had adopted. In addition, it was essentially my negotiating skills on the line each time we met. Every chosen word and phrase. The union had made so many personal attacks against me and made it so clear it wanted my removal that it was only a matter of time before some senior executive might begin to get nervous. Then one day it happened.

The Television Network president's office called and asked me to come down for a meeting. The president was concerned about the effect the long-stalled talks was having on operations and asked a question about the prospects of my removing myself from the bargaining table. It was couched as just a simple suggestion. The point was made that it had become far too personal between myself and one or two of their key players. Would bargaining, I was asked, not be better served if I commanded from behind the front lines and left the actual table negotiating to others.

I took the comments trying to best protect network interests as nothing personal but just business. Many network executives—unfamiliar with the ebb and flow, and real lows, of true union combat—were getting more than a little war-weary. Long delays and constant churning always build anxieties. It was a grasp at an easy but an incomplete and bit naive solution. Stunned as I was, I answered it would be a major error and I would not do so unless Bob Iger himself so ordered. Demands for removal, I explained, are a normal weapon in an aggressive union's arsenal of personally attacking the messenger. Succumbing, I emphasized, only feeds the hungry tiger and serves the union's interests. I was positive that Iger, always supportive, had no knowledge this conversation was taking place. Moreover, he would not have approved had he been aware. Quickly backing off the suggestion as only a thought and probably not a good one, this was the last I ever heard of that idea from anyone.

The union leadership felt long delays between rounds was on its side. In no rush to make a bad deal, they committed every negotiating tactic in the book to permit the talks to drag on for months without any agreement or resolution. The serious, and ever-building, loss of retroactivity was never mentioned. It was something, I imagined, that they would try to muscle us out of at the very end if any deal could ever possibly be made.

So the likelihood of more sporadic and fruitless bargaining sessions continued as the charade went on. Months stretched on. The few meetings we managed to cajole them into scheduling, usually lasting several days or a week at a time at some remote location, occasionally attended by federal mediators, basically were useless.

As the bargaining standoff continued into the fall, Mike Tyson suddenly made a ringside appearance. There he was—the world heavyweight boxing champ—in the revolving entrance door of the Trump hotel where our team was staying during one round of futile New York talks. Entering the hotel one evening with his entourage just as a group of us was leaving, I waited a second or two for him to walk in. Tyson had a few months earlier made boxing news and lost the crown when he bit off more than he could chew in his attack on Evander Holyfield's ear. Instinct drove me to say something as we were standing face to face, blocking each other's way. What inexplicably came out was, "For me Mike you will always be the champ." Without missing a beat, Tyson responded by broadly smiling and swiftly placing his left hand—the size of a ham—on my right shoulder. Loudly thanking me, the force of his sudden, lethal paw on my body almost drove me through the hotel floor. Instantaneously, I wanted to borrow him for a few rounds at the table.

It was becoming a problem to continually horse-whip my committee members to fly in from out of town and return to the table. Frustrating for all, this was at least my job and that of my lawyers, even if we sat there and accomplished nothing. But their's was to be an operator. If they were back at their home bases and offices in Los Angeles, San Francisco, Washington, Chicago, and New York, they could at least be doing their day-job—some real and substantial managing of their people and their businesses.

NABET was at the same time fine-tuning its "corporate

campaign" designed to adversely affect us. Our viewership, reputation, Disney's board of directors, shareholders, advertisers, and ultimately our revenues were their targets. The CWA's political allies in Washington, the Democrats, were traditionally friends of any labor group—regardless of facts or underlying circumstances. At the request of union leadership, they were brought into the battle. Prominent Democratic congressional leaders and members of the Clinton administration complied by refusing to appear on our Sunday morning *This Week* hosted by Cokie Roberts and Sam Donaldson. ABC News, not happy, nevertheless soldiered on despite the pressure as the standoff continued.

We enlisted the efforts of the Federal Mediation Service to assist us in these stalled talks because federal mediation, with professional and experienced mediators, can often be helpful. The best ones can sometimes through force of personality alone or creativity shine light on overlooked proposals or come up with novel approaches. Occasionally, by the way they present an issue in private meetings with each side, they can reshape the playing field. In our case, however, where we were miles apart and operating basically in two different universes, separated by the vast ocean of our final proposal, it was a real reach to believe much could be accomplished.

Nevertheless that fall we tried. And it was not just for the positive PR benefit of telling our employees, and the world at large, that we were doing everything possible to try to reach a settlement. The union was resistant, as many usually are, when a company calls in the federal mediators. Once, however, the Mediation Service invited itself in after our initial approach, NABET's leadership had no choice but to agree.

We scheduled a week of talks at the Sheraton Hotel in Secaucus, NJ, near the Meadowlands stadium, a few miles across the Hudson River from our New York City offices. The same federal mediators, who had tried several months earlier in another futile effort, came again to assist.

Mediators generally do not care who is right or wrong on any particular issue. Their only concern is seeing if they can help with ideas in order to make a deal more possible. Their other job is to try to prevent strikes since mega-labor disruptions, such as our's could be, are never considered to be in the national interest. Mediators start by finding small areas of agreement and then move forward to build a larger consensus. Where, however, there is practically no agreement on anything, and we've already presented our last, best and final offer, it is not a very productive process.

The duo of federal mediators assigned to our case spent the better part of the first day in the Secaucus hotel's large conference room just observing. Sitting off to the side and watching our banter back and forth, they were busy taking notes. From seeing each side's behavior, they were learning more about issues and also studying our very different bargaining styles and personalities. From all of that, they would attempt to come up with some ideas to move the process forward.

We had our usual team from all over the country. It consisted of both my labor relations lawyers and—with the still-open whip marks on their backs—the operators. The union had its normal complement including its five local presidents. NABET president Clark, its chief negotiator Krieger, and the CWA's Turchi led their team.

Late in the day, the two mediators met privately with each side, shared their appraisal while trying to engender an air of optimism, and offered some suggestions. Seeing us in total disagreement on just about everything, and noting the tough and nasty talk the union was again displaying, they proposed a novel approach to calm the waters. It was to be a confidence building process.

"Let's meet," they said, "with five leaders from both sides in a separate small room." Both sides agreed, so I chose four others beside myself and NABET president John Clark chose his. We were asked to sit in a circle, with a company person alternating with a union person to complete the circle. The mediators standing outside the circle instructed us to hold hands and close our eyes, cleanse our minds, and think for a few moments without saying anything. Then, keeping our eyes closed, we were asked to go around the room and each say the first thing that popped into our minds.

Most of us, including the union side, said something like, "I hope we can get a deal," "let's finish these talks," or "can we try to get along better?" I think most of us, especially the management side, meant it. Surprising to all, and particularly the mediators, the president of the Washington local, Jim Harvey, stunned us. He said something that probably many of us were secretly thinking although he delivered it a little more graphically. When it came his turn, he blurted out, "I'm asking myself why the fuck am I sitting in a room in Secaucus, New Jersey, with my eyes closed and fucking holding hands with two company people." There may have been a third F-word in that sentence somewhere.

Not progressing exactly the way the mediators would have preferred, we broke up for the day. The next morning, they tried a different approach with the full teams on both sides. Bringing into the room a large easel and a blank paper flip chart, they said it was clear we needed some basic rules of proper conduct for the talks to continue and asked for suggestions. So, as ideas were thrown out by various people, mostly on the company side, one of the mediators wrote the most significant thoughts down with a Sharpie in big black letters on the chart.

It looked like this:

"1. No foul language
2. No cursing
3. No threats
4. No bad mouthing"

When the last comment was written on the board, one of the more troublesome union officials, well-known for outbursts and disruption, shouted out in all seriousness, "How am I going to represent my people if I can't curse, use foul language, make threats, or bad mouth?"

Such was the success of federal mediation. We spent the remainder of that week making our fruitless arguments and pressing our points. True to its course, the union continued to say, "no" or "fucking no, but we have an open mind," to just about everything. The mediators just observed and occasionally threw out a suggestion or two. As they shared with me later, it was even for them, used to all kinds of carnivals and sideshows, quite a shocking performance.

But for the NHL game that Alan Nesbitt and I went to at the nearby Meadowlands arena one night, the week was a complete bust. Everybody on my team left to go back to their home bases. Once again in total frustration, no one except my lawyers was eager to respond to my call to return when our next round would be scheduled. Who could blame them.

Large and loud NABET rallies became the norm, with hundreds of red-shirted, CWA members from nearby New York telephone company locals joining in to support their NABET brethren. Gathering often across the street from our ABC headquarters on West 66 Street, rallies, as they often do, got juices flowing. It just convinced them even more of the righteousness of their cause and their invincibility.

Recalcitrance and belligerence at the table, while not getting us the deal we wanted, was not resulting in our collapse either. To what had to be their dismay, we stood strong and showed no signs of weakening. Every week that passed without a deal was a promised loss of one more week's of wage retroactivity for each of their members. Having hurt themselves badly in 1989 to the tune of several thousand dollars per person, we had hoped that lesson, which they had remembered well in '93, would last forever. However, as the final few months of '97 approached, they had already lost half a year's wage increases. That 26-week loss already had climbed to over $1000 per person, and it was going north. For all the 2300-plus covered employees, it was lost wages already amounting to over $2 million.

But they continued to never raise it. Blind faith can lead to misguided conceptions and unforeseen consequences. Their thinking had to be that with the CWA not only at their side but firmly behind them, ABC would never again have the audacity or strength to insist on this loss of retroactivity. Or, that losing the wage increases, now only a half- year's worth, was a lot better than living under the Company's final package. As the stalemated talks stretched out into even more months with no apparent end in sight, we sensed the pressure was building for some job action. The pot was boiling. We just did not know when, where, and how the lid would blow.

25
CHAPTER

Hitting Our Way Out of a Sand Trap

The attack when it came was fierce and unexpected. It happened on Saturday, November 1, 1997, when NABET chose to flex its muscles in a new way intending to harm the Company and teach us a lesson. They took a live program off the air—for the first time in network broadcasting history. With this surprise pinpoint strike, the pot's lid we had been expecting to blow flew off. It happened at the Mercedes-Benz golf tournament in Houston, Texas.

An ABC Sports crew consisting of upwards of 75 daily hires was scheduled to produce the golf tournament live that day and the next. That same NABET crew had done the golf work the previous day for our sister ESPN's cablecast without any problems. Hundreds of thousands in advertising revenue was suddenly at stake if we lost the Saturday broadcast.

Called ostensibly as a 24-hour grievance strike over a New York employee's suspension months earlier for drawing and posting on a bulletin board a cartoon of Michael Eisner depicted as Scrooge McDuck, the Houston daily hire crew was ordered to strike. It complied by refusing to show up for their 6 A.M. scheduled call.

They'd give up their pay for that day but be back to do the Sunday show. All other NABETs nationwide continued working, but not that crew for that specific program. Bob Apter called me at home early that morning with the shocking news. I headed in to the offices and called in some of my chief labor people to help strategize.

ABC Sports and BOE quickly worked out a backup plan. Without a live golf tournament that day, they needed to fill the network's air. Because we had a few hours notice, we did the next best thing. Fortunately, some Sports executives went down to the video tape library in the basement and found suitable tapes from a previous year's golf tournament. At least ABC's air would not go black and we could recoup some if not most of the advertising revenue we otherwise would have lost.

ABC went on the air around noon that Saturday with an announcement from Sports announcer John Saunders that the scheduled golf tournament was not being broadcast due to a labor dispute in Houston. The announcer said a previous year's tournament was going to be replayed. To our surprise when the ratings later came in for that day's broadcast, the re-runs had an audience almost as high as the year before.

I was sitting at my desk when an agitated president of Mercedes-Benz of North America called the switchboard. Asking to speak with the highest ranking ABC official in the building on that Saturday afternoon, the switchboard operator knew I was in and connected us. Upset that the program for which Mercedes-Benz had surely paid a ton of money was not being broadcast, he demanded to know why he was watching a re-run of a different tournament. So I proceeded to explain it was a surprise strike in Houston over which we had no control and that the sales people would surely be calling to make amends.

Surprised like the rest of us when he heard the news, Bob Iger called an emergency meeting early that Sunday. ABC Sports was now being run by Steve Bornstein in his dual role of also heading up

ESPN, so Steve would have been been there live or on the call. SVP Bob Apter was there, plus some others from Sports such as probably Steve Anderson who had recently come over from ESPN. BOE's Preston Davis, my boss Alan Braverman, PR head Patti Matson, and I completed the group.

Iger wanted to know how we could have been knocked off the air by this sneak attack. But more importantly, he wanted to know how future sneak attacks on the full array of future sports programs could be prevented.

Bob Apter spoke up and said the only way was to double staff all sports remotes from that day until the day that a new contract was secured. It was, as Apter went on to explain, a very complex undertaking. Sports would have to find non-union vendors with trucks and crews. An entire shadow operation, complete with a separate, fenced-in compound, cameras, and mobile units would have to be set up. Cameras would have to positioned, manned, hot, and ready to go to air just in case of a walkout before, at, or during show time.

The shadow crew would need additional production personnel including producers, directors, ADs, PAs, and stage managers. The regular on-air talent team for each event though would be the same—they'd just shift over quickly to the nearby backup remote studio truck in the event the shadow crew had to go live on-air. For *Monday Night Football*, that would be Al Michaels, Dan Dierdorf, and Frank Gifford—calling his last season in the booth.

It was a huge logistical challenge starting with the next weekend's four college football games. The following week's *MNF* was coming up. Sports would have to make the same arrangements with reliable vendors for many dozens of sports events going forward. Clearly, we could not get this shadow setup ready for the next night's November 3 NFL game from Kansas City, but we viewed that *MNF* game as secure.

So, said Bob Apter, we'd have in the future two crews at each sports remote—consisting of the NABET broadcast crew and a complete, ready-to-go-live-to-air, shadow crew. For Saturday NCAA football, Sports said it would be necessary to protect only the two national games, taking a chance on the two regional games but being able to switch to the national games if either or both were struck. All our other unions, I was certain, such as AFTRA representing our sports announcers, and DGA representing our directors ADs and SMs, would work with the shadow crews.

The logistical and human demands would be enormous. Iger, with his deep sports background, knew this as well as if not better than anybody in the room. ABC Sports would first have to find non-union vendors with a ready supply of qualified, non-union technicians and equipment. Cameras would have to be leased, trucked in, set up in their final positions for game day, and manned—just feet away in many cases from where the regular cameras manned by NABETs would be positioned.

With as many as perhaps an extra 50, 60, or more technicians on the shadow crew, they'd also have to lay thousands of feet of cable, set up their own satellite dishes, and perform all the other technical work necessary for a separate broadcast. The ABC travel department would have to secure flight arrangements and hotel rooms—no easy task like this at the last minute. Sports would also have to arrange backup commercial integration from a neutral site for a broadcast that might never take place. And—of vital importance—take care to issue of all new identification cards.

It meant we had to hire scores of private guards to provide security throughout the shadow production's now about-to-be fenced-in facilities, cable runs, and camera set up locations. Virtually every foot of those cable runs would have to be observed to prevent some miscreant from thrusting an ice pick into the cable and taking us off the air— as once happened at a CBS sports event during a IBEW strike years before.

All these arrangements had to be put into place for the remainder of the *Monday Night Football* schedule, college football games, Bowl games, golf, basketball, thoroughbred and auto racing, and all other domestic sports broadcasts. It would be, in fact, every sports event in the United States where a NABET crew was normally assigned. Our pickups from Europe, such as skiing or ice skating, and around the world for *Wide World of Sports*—where there was no NABET jurisdiction and therefore no problem—would go on as normal.

With this shadow unit set up at each remote, with cameras manned, directors in their chairs, and production people in the second set of trucks all poised to go on-air with a flick of a switch if NABET pulled a strike at the site of that event, we'd be fully prepared. Bob Iger had the plan he wanted to protect our sports broadcasts against future NABET attacks.

Iger asked his old colleague from Sports, Bob Apter, two questions— "Can you get it ready by this weekend and are you confident it will work?" Apter, who had undoubtedly already given this a great deal of thought, responded in the affirmative. Iger, knowing just how expensive this venture was going to be, potentially costing millions if it went on for an extended period of time, said without hesitation, "Go for it."

Electrifying within the room when Bob said it, it was the greatest example of corporate leadership I ever witnessed. And Bob Iger did it with a certain calmness and certitude that would have made Murphy and Burke proud. I kept thanking the gods looking over us that it was Bob running the show—with his deep broadcasting and sports production background—and not someone from Disney far less knowledgeable and qualified making such a consequential decision.

What struck me most when the meeting was over was that not once did Iger or anyone ask, or even whisper, whether this enormous cost and effort were worth it. NABET had just flexed its muscles in this unprecedented, damaging manner and taken a live broadcast off the air, for the first time in broadcasting history. It had cost us revenue and we were facing huge, new expenditures in this massive undertaking. What I witnessed in that room, led by Bob but signed on by all, was a common shouldering of our negotiating load and strategic commitment.

There was not one microsecond of discussion given—then or later—to whether we should throw in the towel and back off our list of demands. Iger's demonstrated strength and clear resolution that we were going to stick with our game plan to achieve major reform and not meet their blackmail demands transmitted through me like electrical currents. The entire room must have felt Bob's strength the same way as I did and had to be equally proud.

With this expensive insurance policy in place for all future ABC Sports remotes, we could all sleep better at night. Yes, while it was costing ABC an enormous sum to protect its air, NABET could never strike again at any such future event in a way that would hurt us. NABET was checkmated with the plan that they thought they had so brilliantly devised to hurt and intimidate us, but it had just backfired. Rather than damaging or demoralizing us, the union's efforts had made Iger and the rest of the company even more dedicated to the correctness of our bargaining cause. And more resolute.

To help protect each event going forward where we had a shadow crew assigned, I sent along an ABC labor lawyer from either my New York or Los Angeles staffs. Rotating assignments each weekend, they were there to assist the event's management in whatever came up. With both the regular crew and their new adversary, the non-union shadow crew, in such close proximity to one another, tensions were likely to rise. Union officials would show up and stir the pot. My lawyers would be there to provide legal and labor relations guidance as well as interface with stadium officials and law enforcement authorities as circumstances required.

So my entire group of ABC labor lawyers, including myself occasionally, was on the road for the foreseeable future to provide this level of protection. Hot-headed saboteurs, local out of control union supporters, and other miscreants would be dealt with. Subsequently, a few arrests were made and prosecutions pursued. At least one lawyer did not have proper, midwest-necessary, cold weather gear in his closet. When he arrived in freezing Chicago the following weekend, he had to go out and buy the right storm coat after first borrowing one from WLS-TV GM Emily Barr's husband.

That Christmas, hundreds of unsigned holiday cards overflowed into my Westchester home's rural mailbox. It was a not-so-subtle signal they knew where I lived and wanted me to know it. In escalating their cause in what they saw as a clever way to now involve my home and family, they intended the new intimidation to stoke fear and cause me to back off at the table. A number of the cards we opened contained nasty messages. A new level of hooliganism had begun.

As 1997 bled into '98, the joyless but heated charade on the delivery table continued. We met periodically, with the Company pushing for our needed reforms and NABET doing everything in its power to reject any changes. The two-step to avoid an impasse went on. It was the old "I love you but I hate you" routine. It was the worst of bad faith bargaining, but under prevailing federal labor law, the union was allowed wide latitude to engage in difficult to prove acts of subterfuge and surface bargaining. Sooner or later though we knew their time would run out.

In the spring of 1998, following their Christmas card barrage a few months earlier, they came up with a new fear tactic. According to a neighbor's estimates, it was somewhere around 75 NABETs who showed up one day on the street outside my Westchester County residence. My wife was home alone.

Coming to picket with signs while I was at work, they noisily marched around at the bottom of the driveway. Living as we did far up the hill, Monica could not see or hear the racket. But she was alerted by alarmed neighbors who had called the local police. My brave wife told me afterwards, when she called me at the office, that she went out and got the garden hose ready to turn on full blast if they proceeded up the long driveway.

It was classic, union strong-arm tactics designed to embarrass a chief negotiator in his neighborhood and scare both him and his family. It had intimidation written all over it. A marked escalation beyond the stuffed mailbox, it was intended once more to force me to back off our demands. I wasn't so much concerned about my own physical safety, although I have to admit I was already by that time standing further back on subway platforms and far away from any open windows. It was more a worry for my wife and sons. While I was deeply troubled by what might happen next, it would have taken a great deal more pressure, broken bones, and inflicted pain before I would have ever even remotely thought about throwing the game.

It was about 700 feet from the street to our house atop a hill. Our home sat at the end on a circular driveway on a piece of pretty-much isolated property. It gave me serious concerns. Frustrated and growing more desperate people sometimes take desperate measures that they would otherwise never consider. This is particularly the case when they're led by characters who have issued wild warnings about other people's personal safety. It was not unimaginable to think about a brick, of something worse, being tossed one night from a speeding vehicle, through our windows while we were upstairs sleeping.

Braverman got the news of this new personal intimidation from a concerned outside lawyer with whom I had shared this level of escalation. Discussing it with Iger, those two also became concerned. This conduct was beyond the pale. Now the warnings to stand back at subway stations and away from open windows, coupled with the lunacy of the pointed gun comment and the Christmas card barrage, took on new meaning. Bob and Alan wanted me and my family safe, and feeling safe. Nothing could interfere with that safety or in any way hamper my focus on negotiations. The escalation in personal threats led Braverman to recommend and the Company to set up some unusual measures of security protection at my home.

For nearly the next year we had a team of big and tough-looking, non-uniformed, private security guards practically living with us. Parked in vans near the middle of our driveway hill, they were there 24/7. The property's hillside terrain made it accessible only up that driveway. A team of two sat in a big van that blocked foot or vehicular traffic coming to the house. It was three shifts a day. Occasionally they'd patrol the property. Positioned maybe 150 feet away from our front door, they'd stop all visitors, sinister-looking or not—even Alex's high school friends who came by after classes or on weekends. Then the guards would call the house for permission to let any visitor pass. They'd move the van, like a scene out of *The Godfather*, each time Monica would need to use her car or when I'd leave and return daily from my drive to the city.

Monica cooked for them a delicious Thanksgiving dinner. Special meals also were prepared and delivered hot to the van on Christmas Day. She'd carry freshly-baked muffins, homemade banana bread, and steaming-hot coffee just about every morning down the driveway to their eagerly awaiting hands. I'd do the same on weekends when not at work. Portable latrines that had been set up were too cold to use in the winter, so we allowed the guards to come up to the house to use our facilities. As the months went by, we got to know a few of our protectors fairly well.

The Company security department came and installed for an extra level of protection an elaborate, multi-camera and audio monitoring system all around the property. Our seven-foot tall, carved, wooden ornamental bear—originally intended to scare away deer—standing near where the van was parked and facing down the long driveway, was scoped out as an ideal place to install a hidden mini-camera. So one was embedded in its menacing jaws. Vans, guards, cameras, and the bear—all of it gave us a comforting blanket of protection. Another expense the union forced us into, its cost had to be enormous.

Through their political contacts in the Democratic Party and the Clinton administration, the union reached out for assistance from the US Secretary of Labor, Alexis Herman. She soon summoned ABC lawyers to her offices in Washington to explain our actions. Since it was such a high government official, our general counsel, Alan Braverman, flew down to meet with her himself. Nothing emerged.

Democratic politicians were always being asked to support the cause. US Senator Paul Wellstone showed up one day at an especially large and raucous CWA-NABET rally. Attended by several hundred NABET employees and their telephone local, red-shirted CWA allies, it was across the street from our West 66 Street headquarters. After the local NABET leader used his bullhorn to first whip up the crowd, Wellstone took it and directed the anger towards me in my 15th floor offices.

Shouting out, "Ruthizer we know you're up there hiding in your office and looking down on us," he was certainly correct I was up there monitoring the situation. But—as the cover to this book tells the story—I was far from hiding. Later during the same rally someone dressed as *Sesame Street's* Big Bird tried to storm our front doors and get into the building. There was an unconfirmed rumor that the yellow-feathered figure rebuffed by security had been the activist film maker, Michael Moore. We never knew.

Other Democratic politicians and left-leaning celebrities, without knowing any of the underlying facts and showing no interest in learning, continued in their normal, pro-labor, knee-jerk manner their boycott of appearing on ABC news programs. Many also increased their letter writing campaign to top Company officials as well as Disney board members.

Occasionally, NABET would invite officials from sister unions to join them at our infrequent bargaining table sessions in an attempt to show solidarity and sow fear. But it was more illusory than real when we'd occasionally see familiar WGA or AFTRA faces, normally no close friends of NABET, instructed not to smile, sitting silently—more as props.

At one session, they invited a few of their IBEW brethren from CBS as an additional show of unity. It backfired when I was able to get the IBEW officials, who I knew, to concede that they had the year before agreed to a number of the very same proposals we were seeking in their most recent round of CBS contract negotiations. The officials when gently prodded, acknowledged, with a slight smile I detected on their faces, that they had accepted a number of our other proposed changes many years previous. The IBEW guys were never invited back.

In Washington, our skilled VP and chief lobbyist, Billy Pitts, took on many visits to politicians' offices to try to calm with his very persuasive abilities the raging waters. Working closely with me during this trying, many month period, he became a great supporter and introduced me to some on the Washington scene he knew very well. In between his many governmental chores he'd regularly fly up to attend Braverman's weekly, vice president staff meetings.

One day I came in late to the conference room meeting because of all the balls in the air I was that morning juggling. When Billy saw me enter, he loudly proclaimed while getting up from his chair, "All rise, Jeff Ruthizer is entering the room." I'm not sure how many did, but it certainly felt good to hear Billy say that. Pitts was and remains a good friend despite our separation of a more than a decade and many miles.

NABET's daily disinformation campaign leveled more barrages against the Company on all internal and external platforms, including intensified propaganda efforts within our overall employee population. As the press, and lots of it unhelpful, was unfairly closing in on us, it became imperative we raise our PR game. The Company agreed after I pushed that we needed more professional help. Upon Patti Matson's recommendation, Braverman authorized engaging the experienced, national public relations firm, Fleishman-Hillard. Its involvement would go on to make a big difference in how ABC would be perceived both within ABC and the outside world.

Working very closely with me on the account, and traveling often with us, were two savvy PR guys. I had done a little investigating on my own before hiring the firm when one of their last names caught my eye. That name was Lansdale. After my deeper look, he turned out to be the son of the famed Vietnam War guerrilla warfare fighter and CIA agent, General Edward Lansdale. We hired the firm partly because we thought some of the general's anti-guerrilla DNA might have rubbed off on the son, also named Ed. We were, of course, proven exactly right. His partner, Peter McCue, was another talented public relations guy whom I had noticed, while going over his background, shared my Lafayette College roots. As a further coincidence, McCue had graduated the same year as and knew my younger brother, Ted.

On the legal front, the union accelerated the pace of unfair labor charges it was filing with the NLRB challenging actions we had taken. Our lead attorney from the Proskauer law firm was Joe Baumgarten. I had hired Joe in late '97 after that November's first sneak attack in Houston. Baumgarten worked closely with Marc Sandman and myself and handled all of the charges with great skills and enormous abilities. Never losing any of the charges, Joe's wisdom was instrumental in helping us plot our negotiating and legal strategies as the stalemate continued. With no other recourse possible to end these talks absent the unlikely scenario of them actually accepting our proposed offer, our only path forward was looking increasingly as if we had to get to a true impasse and then implement.

Olivia Cohen-Cutler, long my very close colleague, with me since 1983, first in my RKO days, who had gone out to California in '93 to take Novick's place as vice president of my West Coast labor relations unit, decided to make a career-changing move. She left labor relations for a high senior executive position at the Television Network. Having worked so closely together, and having spoken numerous times daily, live or on the phone, for a decade and half, both in pain and laughter, I was happy for her promotion. With her considerable lawyering talents though, her leaving and at particularly that juncture was both a personal as well as a Company loss.

Overcoming the temporary setback, I promoted Marc Sandman to vice president and moved him out to Los Angeles to take her place. Sandman had grown in enormous strides since he joined my team from an outside law firm in 1991. As my New York director of labor relations, he had become my major NABET planning and execution partner. Very sorry to lose his constant presence in the office next to mine, I would take comfort in knowing that he would be only a telephone call and three hours' time zone away. A day did not go by from that point on for a dozen years where we did not speak—often multiple times. Most fortunately, Marc would still be right next to me at the table every time we'd meet.

To take Sandman's place on my New York staff as director of labor relations, I recruited Sean Quinn from an outside law firm. Quinn had no broadcasting labor experience whatsoever. Both of us knew it was going to be a hard pull to get him up to speed quickly and become valuable as my new chief, New York lieutenant. But I saw in him a gritty tenacity and had confidence he would quickly rise to the occasion. He'd go on to conquer the normal very steep and long ABC labor relations learning curve in record time and soon became a valuable asset.

As 1998 moved along, ABC's studios remained in a state of constant strike preparedness while shadow-crewing did its deterrent job on remotes. After the previous season's college and NFL ended, ABC Sports launched into its normal late winter and spring schedule of college basketball, golf, Triple Crown thoroughbred racing, and then the Indy 500. Handled by NABET crews in the regular manner, our shadow crew peace-keepers were only feet away with their cameras poised and mobile units ready to roll.

The summer went by like this and soon we were into the fall. NCAA football and *Monday Night Football* returned. And with it the second year of shadow-crewing was upon us. The remote checkmate had worked. All remained peaceful. While the costs were huge and growing, they never rose to the level, despite NABET's wishful thinking, to cause even a shred of reconsidering our path forward. Whatever the tab throughout all of '98 was building to behind the bar, and it would be a huge one, we'd gladly pay it—but only when the joint closed.

That spring's recalculated *70th Annual Academy Awards* went off without a hitch. Of course, the LA NABET local made big noises to the press about having lost the work. Loudly demonstrating outside Hollywood's Shrine Auditorium—at a separate entrance set up just for this picketing purpose—nobody really cared. The house was packed with many hundreds of performers, writers, directors and technical or craft talent vying for their Oscars. The Motion Picture Academy did a very credible job in producing the show for ABC's air with its reliable, new IATSE crew. Billy Crystal hosted and over 57 million Americans watched—a gain of nearly ten million viewers from the previous year when ABC had produced it. Not only was the audience huge, it was one of the show's highest ratings ever. *Titanic* was the big winner with 11 awards, but the bigger winner was ABC.

Occasionally we'd corral the union into a meeting. But it was the same denial, resistance, belligerence, and stall. Their entire existence became nothing more than to drag out the talks long enough to wear us down and force ABC to back off at the table.

Tiring, they hoped, like governments, of the "forever war." But all the while they were dreaming up new guerrilla tactics. The union's own internal bulletins and messaging made that clear. Their focus had to be that the single or cumulative effect of new hit and run efforts, if they could find some, would be so damaging to the Company that we'd have no choice but to dramatically alter our final offer. At the same time, they continued assaulting us with new information requests, hoping we'd falter along the way and give them new opportunities to attack us in that murky legal arena. And the flow of new NLRB charges never ceased in the hopes of prevailing there, too.

Not willing to spend an eternity in this standoff, we spent many hours, like most companies engaged in long, drawn out labor talks, studying how we could put pressure on the union to settle on our terms. That meant imposing an offensive lockout at a time and place of our own choosing—and keeping them locked out for a good, long time. The Caterpillar corporation had just done this—with considerable national attention, to its many thousands of UAW-represented workers. Its chief lawyer and I had several conversations. After much study, we developed a foolproof lockout plan of our own that could be quickly implemented. But as we were getting closer, NABET preempted those efforts. It decided on a new sneak attack. The date chosen was November 2.

Accidental, or as some of us thought well-intended, that date was almost the exact anniversary of '97's Houston work stoppage. Designed to be a quick, 24-hour nationwide strike to inflict maximum pain and then a return to work, we had fortunately uncovered the plot the previous Saturday night. Preston Davis called me to pass on a tip that he had just received from a confidential source whom he considered to be 100% reliable. The attack would take place two days later sometime during the early morning hours of that upcoming Monday, November 2. Later on, I got a very-sorrowful, confirming warning of my own from another reliable

NABET source, who tearfully went on to tell me he feared grave consequences for the NABET membership.

As we processed what little little information we had, it became apparent its cover was to be a protest strike over a medical plan information request that they had convinced themselves we had not answered properly. If this secret plan to attack ABC was carried out successfully, it could have taken us down in many places and dramatically harmed the Company. With staggering costs, the economic losses from blown commercials and dead air time could have amounted to many millions.

It's a fairly complicated legal analysis. But in its essence, if they were factually correct about our failing to provide proper medical plan information, and striking over that alleged failure, prevailing NLRB law would have been barred ABC from responding with a lockout. Their game was an extremely high-risk strategy—for both of us.

Most fortunately, we had prepared for this exact information request scenario for quite some time. It was one area under wobbly NLRB law of which we had made ourselves very cognizant. Unions in heated labor battles loved to exploit unanswered information requests because it gave them, if carried out properly, impunity from employer lockouts in response to their guerrilla strikes. Specifically for this reason, I had put one of my senior and most experienced lawyers, Allen Frost, in charge of a system to record in a special ledger each individual information request received and our action taken. With well over 100 received, and many with multiple parts, Allen had made sure we had painstakingly recorded, researched, and timely responded to each with the best available information.

Many were frivolous, wacky, and mostly designed as a pure nuisance. Yet, we responded to all. And we had the proof to demonstrate to the Board how painstakingly we had handled each request—no matter how burdensome, trivial, or downright foolish each might have appeared to be. This one request in particular, although a bit tricky, and probably intended, like so many, for no other purpose than to trip us up, had been fully responded to with the best available information in the Company's possession.

Not to have been able to utilize our legal rights to lock out striking employees under these circumstances, if we had dropped the ball, would have been disastrous. But no matter how carefully we had responded to each of their voluminous requests, it would be up to the United States government's premier labor agency, the NLRB, to determine which of us was right and who was wrong.

26

The Battle Escalates After a Near Pearl Harbor

The day of the secretly planned, November 2, 24-hour strike coincided with the Network's regular broadcast that evening of *Monday Night Football*. That game would be coming from Philadelphia. The non-union shadow crew, standing by and near battle-ready from a year of practice, was already in town that Sunday and beginning its work. Also there and setting up alongside, with the normal tension close proximity brought, was the regular NABET *MNF* crew. Over the next two days both crews would be positioning cameras, installing other equipment, laying cable, and preparing for a broadcast that both crews—on that Sunday morning—still believed would be done, in the normal order of things, by the regular *MNF* crew.

Any actual broadcast performed by the shadow crew at a remote once the strike took place would undoubtedly be challenging and stressful. All experienced technicians, they had not yet worked as a unified team in producing an actual event. Now when they stepped into the main ring, it would be under strike circumstances.

The pressure would be on them and the supervising management team. Outside the stadium would be the regular crew picketing, surely joined by many loud and noisy CWA members from nearby telephone company locals. The New York NABET leaders would probably be there to help steer the fracas. Major attempts at both distraction and disruption could be expected.

Despite the high possibility of sabotage, with a plethora of extra guards to protect the cable runs and facilities, ABC Sports management had confidence that the broadcast by the experienced replacement workers, now out of the shadows, would be safe. A very decent 99% broadcast, if not exactly up to *Monday Night Football's* normal high quality standards, was expected. Rarely would ABC Sports accept under any other circumstances anything less than a perfect production.

While we were not privy to the exact time the strike would commence on November 2, we knew it was coming. By necessity, any 24-hour strike launched on November 2 would carry over to sometime the following day. That next day, Tuesday, November 3, was Election Day.

The union's plan to return to work, after 24 hours, at some hour on Election Day would mean technicians would normally be back performing some part of their regular duties before that evening's special Election Day studio broadcast coverages commenced. If however, we locked them out after they struck on November 2, Election Day—November 3—would be on us. We'd have to do it without them. Part of the union's strategy quite probably was that ABC would see Election Day as far too complicated and important a broadcast day to engage in a lockout. Would any company, they had to be asking themselves, voluntarily endanger its own critical broadcasts?

Election Day—even in non-presidential years such as this was— is always a huge deal for American broadcasters. Both ABC News and the news departments of our owned TV stations would be stretched thin and deeply committed. Lots of union and non-union personnel are normally involved in both special studio shows and remote coverages at polling places and candidate headquarters. Plans had long been formulated.

With no notice whatsoever and our only hearing unconfirmed rumors, ABC News and our owned TV stations would have to scramble to get their back up plans in place. And do so under the radar. Trained replacement personnel would have to be roused and assignments rearranged. Substitute ENG camera crews would have to be readied to hit the streets and satellite trucks reimagined.

Most probably, Network News and local station remote assignments at candidates' election headquarters and other planned coverage sites might have to be scaled back—or scrubbed. NABET picket lines outside these facilities could impact our intended replacement coverage and create tension with the candidates themselves, especially if Democratic. Non-union replacement crews could even cause some tussles with our rival broadcasters' own union crews.

Producing first-rate shows and maintaining audiences, ratings, and reputation during a strike or lockout while utilizing replacement workers are always critical. Especially in the early stages. Even the loss of one commercial, let alone several or many, could cost the Company potentially hundreds of thousands of dollars, or considerably more—potentially in the millions. Badly produced programs with shoddy camera or audio work could lead to turned-off audiences, critical press, and lower ratings. The reputational damage our stations and networks could suffer would be huge. If, on the other hand, Election Day coverage could be managed successfully—and from its start—it would be a huge morale booster.

Using the health care issue as a giant pretext in its war against ABC, if it could successfully hurt us with this sudden nationwide walkout, with real monetary loss, reasoned the union, we would be weakened. If weakened, their leaders surely surmised, the

Company's leaders would be more amenable to major changes in our negotiating positions. Unfortunately for the union and our 2300 employees it represented, the immunity blanket it thought it had wrapped itself in to protect against our responsive lockout would turn out to be illusory. The impact of NABET's flawed plan on the union itself, and on our thousands of employees, would prove to be calamitous.

Thanks to the call Preston Davis had received, the secret attack had been discovered. If the USS *Arizona* and the other battleships had been out to sea, and land-based anti-aircraft guns manned and trained to the sky at Pearl Harbor when the Japanese naval planes hit that December 7 morning, with our fighter planes airborne, it would have been an entirely different result. So it would be with us.

Calling Marc Sandman on the coast and alerting outside counsel Joe Baumgarten, I got my New York and Los Angeles staffs in early that Sunday morning to begin our planning. After I called Alan Braverman and gave him the news, we doubled and tripled-checked to make sure we had responded properly to the specific information request on which we believed NABET was relying. Several sets of eyes looked at it from every angle possible. Once it was three times confirmed, I then assigned a fourth set from outside counsel just to make sure NABET was dead wrong. Again, it was confirmed.

In that conversation with outside counsel, the three of us spent a great deal of time with Baumgarten on not just reviewing our facts but again on the complicated subject of lockouts. Some felt trying to worm confirming information about the rumored strike from the union was worth the effort so I decided to call its chief negotiator at his home. When I got John Krieger on the phone that Sunday morning, it first caught him a bit off-guard.

Initially acting coyly and stumbling when I mentioned strike rumors, he finally came around and mentioned around the edges there was one troublesome piece of information they had been seeking about health care benefits that had not been properly answered. We had our answer. Unless they changed their minds upon being detected, they were going out. Clever in its intention even though it was fundamentally flawed, the scheme fell apart once discovered. Most fortunately for us, they felt so confident they never called it off.

After my call to Braverman early that Sunday morning where we reviewed lockout rules, he notified Bob Iger. Bob called a summit meeting that afternoon in his New York office. Mostly live but also on the conference call were his television and radio division heads. David Westin was there running News, and Steve Bornstein for ABC Sports. Pat Fili-Krushel, the Network head, was there along with her EVP, Alex Wallau. Braverman and I were present, as was BOE's Preston Davis. Steve Burke would have also been there as head of broadcasting. TV station head Larry Pollock either drove up from Philadelphia, as I think he did, or was on the phone. Patti Matson was another in the room, and probably Bob Apter. Maybe there were a dozen of us. Joe Baumgarten was standing by at his home in case I needed him.

After my situational briefing about the discovered 24-hour strike-plot, Iger went around the room to make sure all ships at sea were ready to carry on in the event of the surprise attack. *Monday Night Football* and Election Day coverages were his major concerns. After he got assurances that all business units would be ready to mount their necessary broadcasts, and not just for the next day but also going forward, he then asked about a lockout. Eyes turned to me as I advised that either an offensive or defensive lockout would be legal. Turning to Braverman, his general counsel, Bob asked him if he agreed and Alan, who had gone over this with us in detail earlier, said he did.

Iger asked how confident we were about that conclusion. I responded that we were very confident - on both the law and facts. So Bob made that fateful mega-decision—a lockout it would be.

Going around the room on his next question about timing, there was differing opinion. A few reminded the group about the Houston strike the year before, as if any of us needed any reminding. Some felt our lockout should be immediate now that we knew they were about to strike. Their reasoning was solid. We had a chance at that moment which we might not have again. If we waited, they could change their minds now that they knew their plot had been uncovered. Since we had our operational plans in place to carry on without them, and we could gain bargaining pressure at the table if they were locked out, these few saw this as our "striking" while the iron was hot.

Everyone of course realized that by choosing a lockout, whether immediate or delayed until after they struck, our Election Day coverages across the Company would be severely challenged. That was the acceptable price we'd choose to pay.

It was then my turn. While it's never easy to disagree with others of more senior rank in a meeting such as this, I knew that Braverman and Iger, indeed all in the room, would want me to give, as I always had, my independent thinking and best judgment. I said that we should wait. It would be so much easier logistically just to lock the door behind them once they were out of our buildings, as we fully expected would be the case within maybe another 12 hours. Although we didn't know the exact timing of the November 2 strike, my gut told me it would be in the early morning hours. The union's going out, I said, was an unexpected gift we should thankfully accept. If they changed their mind, we had a plan ready to lock them out later at a moment of our own choosing. Alex Wallau, Iger's longtime colleague from his days at ABC Sports, chimed in with his agreement on waiting until NABET struck the first blow.

Iger made an instantaneous decision that the lockout would wait until they struck. It was another inspirational moment. Everybody quickly left the meeting with adrenaline racing to quietly get operations ready. All knew the next 24 hours and few days would present some extraordinary challenges to get ramped up to full strike-replacement capacity. Everyone took extreme comfort from knowing that the Network under Preston Davis' leadership, and the TV stations, under Larry Pollock's, had prepared well and long for just this eventuality. As had radio. Everything and everyone was ready—as we had been since 18 months earlier, March 31, 1997. All we needed was for the opposing army to blow the whistle and climb out of the trenches. Then we'd begin executing our well-oiled plan.

Iger had urged all to keep our plans secret to the greatest extent possible while preparing our properties for the attack and our counter-offensive. Another example of Iger's decisiveness and strong leadership—brave and bold—this lockout was like his Houston shadow-crew decision the year earlier. As I had felt at the time, only he and no Disney official could have made that wise lockout call.

Getting back to my office, I called Sandman and Baumgarten. My entire labor relations staff of 14 lawyers on both coasts was in our offices, poised for action. Our bargaining team from around the country were all confidentially briefed. All of us were also working off our own extra doses of adrenaline. Implementing our own battle plans, I handed out the specific assignments for the next 24 hours. Quinn started getting ready his computer-printed, "Locked Out" signs that he would personally tape the next day to the big front doors and all entrances into our New York buildings once they walked. We'd make certain the same would be done throughout the Company. I kept asking myself and the others, "what is that one more thing we may have forgotten?"

The next day, Monday, November 2, the union announced and implemented its nationwide, 24-hour strike at 5 A.M. Eastern Time. The few overnight shift NABET employees working in our buildings at that early hour in all five cities began to exit and set up loud and raucous picket lines outside our entrances. Some not quite believing they were being ordered out held back a bit before leaving the buildings. It turned out the union had not done a particularly good job in getting the 5 A.M. word out and some of our managers had to help spread their message. A number left with tears in their eyes that it had come to this. The incoming day shifts that were gathering outside put on the picket signs and began their loud marching routine.

Washington—always more pro-company in its labor relations attitudes—was not anxious to walk. So one of the more bellicose leaders from another city flew in to help push them out the door. Chicago would go out but also reluctantly. The Philadelphia *Monday Night Football* crew showed up at the stadium but now they were loud and raucous picketers while the shadow crew, standing on the sidelines for a year now, prepared to spring into action. Later that morning the shadow crew walked into the stadium through the jeering picket line to complete their set up for the game they now knew they would later that day actually broadcast. Stadium security was put on high alert for striking employees who might attempt to infiltrate with their press credentials to create a little mayhem.

I was already in my office monitoring developments when the strike began. The official notice from NABET's Clark arrived by fax advising us the strike would start at 5 A.M. and end 24 hours later on Tuesday. The letter cited as the reason for the strike the same as Krieger had intimated earlier—their protest over our not having properly answered their request for medical plan information. Waves of calls shortly began coming in from all locations nationwide confirming the walkouts.

Later that day Sean Quinn went down to the main lobby and taped the "Locked Out" notices to the now heavily guarded front doors. The signs in bold, black letters basically said:

LOCKED OUT
NO NABET REPRESENTED EMPLOYEE IS
ALLOWED INTO THIS BUILDING FOR ANY
REASON UNTIL FURTHER NOTICE FROM
THE COMPANY.

Watching through the plate-glass windows was the crowd of massed pickets on the street—undoubtedly shocked at the message he was affixing to the doors. Making his way to all the other doors in all the other ABC buildings in the complex, Quinn did the same. Getting on the phone with me and Sandman, we made certain the locked-out message was posted at all other ABC locations.

I sent the official Company letter to Clark around that same hour advising the union they were locked out and would not be allowed back in until the union signed an attached return to work agreement. The attachment laid out the strict conditions that would be required before we would end the lockout and permit our employees to return to work.

When the 5 A.M. strike began, the management replacement work force that had been standing by discretely inside conference rooms and offices at all locations swiftly moved in and took over the vacated operating positions. *Good Morning America* was preparing to go on the air. WABC-TV was about to start its early morning local news show. Later that morning, it would be the network *Live with Regis and Kathie Lee* show from its normal, next door Channel 7 studio. The soaps would soon be getting ready for setups, rehearsals, and tapings. All of our stations and the Network would carry on that Monday with its regular programming schedules. There was hardly a hiccup.

The crew on the floor of all Network and local station new shows that first day might have looked a little different to the anchors from their anchor chairs, but those shows looked no different to viewing audiences in their living rooms. Nobody sitting at home could tell a strike was taking place other than from the top-of-the-show headline announcing our own news that Peter Jennings on his *World News Tonight* set and all other anchors delivered.

For those filling in behind cameras or in studio control rooms, remembering or hearing the legend of the last NABET strike in '77 and the rich strike bonuses many had received, visions of swimming pools and fancy sports cars again surely danced in their heads. Under HR chief Jeff Rosen's direction, we had put together an exemplary strike bonus plan that top management had approved.

The *Monday Night Football* game produced that night by the no longer bored shadow crew in Philadelphia went off smoothly as the show's regular executive producer and director slid into their normal chairs in the back-up mobile unit. A host of extra security guards employed to protect against possible sabotage from overly enthusiastic picketers who might infiltrate the stadium's premises swarmed the facility with a huge, protective blanket. Despite the fact that only 10 or 12 cameras were used instead of the normal complement in excess of 20, it was said that very few if any viewers sitting in their living rooms, watching, and listening to Al Michaels, Dan Dierdorf, and Boomer Esiason call the game, would be able to discern the slightest difference.

ABC News carried on that Monday with some reduced plans for Jennings' *World News Tonight* The next day's election coverage would be shifted around a bit. A few show elements may have been moved to our London bureau, and more would soon follow.

The TV stations, and the radio stations carrying news along with the four radio networks, went on with their Monday newscasts and Election Day coverages as normal. Some election headquarters remotes were indeed cut back or scrubbed. Guards were sent along with replacement ENG crews to protect against roaming NABET pickets. As was to be expected in a surprise situation like this, there were initially several small, on-air glitches that caused at first much and overblown union glee but in the big scheme of things were terribly inconsequential.

A support team built in advance jumped in. Patti Matson began her daily conference calls with dozens of key management people providing a steady flow of necessary information to all ships at sea. Our ABC litigation lawyers led by their chief, Henry Hoberman, went to court to enjoin successfully Election Day NABET interferences with our new coverages and managed our outside counsels' involvement. The head of security activated his plan to bring in many extra guards, secure all doors, and issue new ID's to all Company employees.

Clearly, for the chanting picketers on the street outside having seen Quinn tape locked out notices on the doors, this was not what they had been promised by their NABET leadership. "It will be over in 24 hours," they had surely been lead to believe. "They will never lock us out on Election Day," is probably what they had believed.

Some locations had more sound and fury. San Francisco, where the traditional animosity against the Company that had been stoked by union officials for many years ran deep, was particularly fervent. Los Angeles pickets at our Prospect lot were extremely unruly. As the news of our surprise lockout and the reality that the workforce was not coming back anytime soon was settling in everywhere, both sides began gearing up for a long battle. The NABET PR efforts went into immediate overdrive as news of the lockout spread.

The Fleishman-Hillard anti-guerilla PR squad led by Peter McCue and Ed Lansdale sprang into action with a counter-offensive that would have made Ed's dad, the CIA general, very proud. Our story got out quickly and effectively to all bases and ships at sea, in home waters and abroad. Media interviews were scheduled for some of our key players. I normally preferred to stay behind the curtain and leave these interviews to our press spokesperson, Julie

Hoover—much to our amusement referred to by the union as the "pirate's parrot."

But this time Patti Matson, Julie, and the Fleishman-Hillard boys felt it was too important. So I myself went on to grant a few choice interviews that I was told were successful with trade magazines and dailies. Stories appeared on local TV as well as in newspapers such as *The New York Times, The Washington Post,* and many other outlets throughout the country.

Sean Quinn and our head of security proceeded to the local New York police precinct for a sit-down with the captain. Much had to be discussed. Quinn did his best to ensure there were enough police present on West 66 Street to keep intimidating picket lines as far away as possible from entrances to ensure safe and unimpeded passage for the rest of ABC's workforce passing through the noisy picket lines. But there was no getting away from the fact that hoots and hollers, horns, whistles, and chants were to be our steady welcome for months to follow.

Preston Davis, the BOE chief, soon called. "Come over," he said, "there's not a NAB in the place for the first time ever, and there's something I want to show you in the basement I think you'll be interested in seeing." So I headed over to his offices in the next-door building and met him downstairs. Preston, a former NABET-represented employee himself at the time of the last ABC strike in 1977, was both sad and ecstatic. I understood that completely simply because I had those same mixed emotions. The Rubicon had been crossed. "Come with me," he said, as I followed him into the basement area where I had been many times before. The hallways normally teeming with NABET engineers were nearly deserted.

It was an eerie feeling. There was a room in the basement called the NABET lounge that Preston was taking me to see. Normally strictly off limits to anyone but NABET-represented employees as their break room, it was their inner sanctum for relaxing and socializing during down time. He opened the door with the security code, feeling perfectly comfortable as the landlord of that property to do so. As we walked in, he shared with me he had been in there a few minutes earlier.

The room was dark and the lighting not so great. But he wanted to show me that on the walls of this, the holy of holies, hung all kinds of photos, posters, caricatures, and foul messages about the Company, him, and "that bastard Ruthizer." Included among the photos was a doctored one of me with ABC News head Roone Arledge, with me on his arm, as his date at an event, wearing an evening dress. I had seen this scurrilous photo earlier when the union had distributed it as part of its normal, vicious attack. From looking at the sacred newly discovered walls I knew how the first Egyptologists must have felt on opening the tomb of King Tut.

With my formal letter to NABET advising of the nationwide lockout in response to their sneak attack, we let them know they were not coming back until they signed an agreement requiring the union to give us two weeks notice before ever again striking the Company at a remote event and one week's notice of a strike in the studio.

A joint creation with our outside labor counsel, Joe Baumgarten, he had found in his deep research a relatively obscure but highly relevant legal doctrine permitting us to demand this advance strike notice. The doctrine only applied if a company had a so-called "perishable product" that needed protection against unannounced strikes. In our case, broadcasts and advertising were clearly highly perishable products.

If our programs that cost millions to produce were knocked off the air by a sudden attack or damaged, the considerable revenue from lost commercials for those hours would be gone forever. So would also be viewers' eyes and ratings. Nothing could be more perishable than those broadcast hours, the commercials, and our audiences. Millions of dollars of revenue were at risk. Under the string of prevailing NLRB cases which Joe found and was still good law, we were entitled to receive such notice.

The proffered agreement stipulated very strict money penalties for breach. It was potentially many millions for both NABET and its parent, the CWA. Surely they would have been bankrupted if they violated the advance notice commitment, should they agree to sign the agreement and return to work. As expected, the NABET and CWA leaders made it much easier for us by quickly responding they would never agree to such onerous terms. Giving notice of a strike was anathema, they said, to any self-respecting union. With their deciding this would disembowel them if they had to give us notice, we settled in and prepared for a long and difficult war ahead.

The only other lockout going on at that time in America was the NBA's lockout of its million dollar players.

Bob Iger sent a rousing letter to all Company employees. It called for extra efforts in the trying weeks ahead and explained the circumstances that required the lockout. Steve Burke, Larry Pollock, and Radio's Bob Callahan visited their stations to show the flag. The generous bonus pay plan from Jeff Rosen's HR for management replacement workers was activated. From that day forward, people working their regular jobs who also were working extra hours as replacement technicians received substantial additional pay. It proved once again to be a great motivator.

When my lawyers and I touched bases with all of our other unions once the strike took place and after the lockout began, the reaction we received was most often a simple thank you for the advisory. With a few, however, it was refreshingly favorable. Every union honored their no-strike clauses and their members continued working with all of the temporary replacements, and getting paid. In certain instances, such as with Tommy O'Donnell's Teamsters, special arrangements for our serials had to be made for off-site scenery drops.

Our guard force at all buildings everywhere was immediately tripled or quadrupled to provide maximum security at all entrances.

Special photo ID's to gain access and bar the locked-out NABETs from entering were issued.

Just as we had expected, the union lost no time in filing new unfair labor charges with the NLRB over the lockout. They zeroed in on both the information request response that had been the subject of the protest strike as well as the lockout itself and its proffered return to work agreement. The NLRB's New York regional office, headed by Regional Director Dan Silverman, because this was such a major and visible national labor dispute, promised a thorough but quick investigation and a fast decision. We were told it would be a matter of weeks and not months.

The union quickly set up a large, nasty looking, inflatable, dark gray rat on the street outside of our ABC headquarters complex at the Columbus Avenue entrance. The rat, to this day in 2022, is often used by unions during heated labor disputes as a symbol of animosity towards employers.

The mean, poisonous, and treacherous-looking, 20-foot high rodent had a large sign on its side that read in foot-high bold, white letters:

"THE FOUR MOST HATED PEOPLE IN THE WORLD:

Saddam Hussein
Michael Eisner
Bob Iger
Jeff Ruthizer"

Breathing a sigh of relief that I made the list, even at the number four slot, I would have been disappointed if I had not been included in this grouping. I never received more calls from people whom I had not heard from in 20 or 30 years than I did during the following few days. The callers all said the same thing—they either walked by and saw my name on the Columbus Avenue rodent or caught the rat live on the evening's news. At that moment and for the rest of my career, I became the Company's legal expert on the Law of the Rat.

ABC Sports management would go on to do an incredible job under huge logistical challenges producing the remainder of its *MNF* and NCAA football seasons, the Bowl games, the college football BCS championships, and then go on with '99's normal remote schedule. The replacement engineers were largely the same personnel who had manned the shadow crews for nearly a year, but they were now out in the sunlight, well-paid, and working. Many actually were IBEW or IATSE members but working non-union for our vendors, which had no trouble finding additional workers. As expected, we had no problems with our other AFTRA and DGA-represented personnel in the announce booth or director's chair. All the productions, at least to the viewer's eyes, were flawless.

Crowds of chanting NABET and CWA local pickets, controlled to the extent possible by police and barricades, assisted by our enhanced private security guard force, showed up at the sports remotes. They had anger in their hearts and some had interference on their minds. A steady stream of ABC labor lawyers at each event helped ensure things ran as well as could be expected in the face of stiff NABET resistance and occasional attempts at sabotage. Sean Quinn was particularly effective at one serious confrontation with attempted saboteurs in Boston that resulted in arrests and discharges.

All of the TV network shows that were produced live or on tape from our studios on both coasts and Washington, including *Good Morning America,* Peter Jennings' *World News Tonight,* and Ted Koppel's *Nightline* were managed with a minimum of problems by replacement personnel. Our afternoon soap operas—*All My Children, One Life to Live,* and *General Hospital* on both coasts carried on with only some minor and largely unnoticeable production issues, after first utilizing a short inventory of pre-taped shows. Some ABC News programs, elements and inserts were moved across the Atlantic to our London Bureau where production and broadcast back to America would be easier.

Our local TV stations in New York, Chicago, Los Angeles, and San Francisco, well prepared for months, managed close to perfection. Larry Pollock, as he had promised that March 31 evening in his *Patton* speech at the Pierre, authorized hiring extra staff that his stations needed. Some management personnel came into the stations from our other owned TV properties in Philadelphia, Houston, Fresno, and Raleigh-Durham to help their sister stations weather the storm. News gathering in the field for ABC News and the stations was more difficult but not compromised with replacement camera crews protected by lots of beefed-up security guards. Network and local stations ratings remained unaffected.

Radio stations and network operations had it easier than TV. They didn't miss a beat because a decade earlier we had eliminated NABET's operational jurisdiction and with it about 150 engineering jobs. All that the radio managers had to worry about was studio and transmitter maintenance. For years, DJs and news people had been operating their own control panels and running the board.

Now we were in a shooting war. As the lockout went on, because of our deep war preparedness, every part of the Company was involved and functioning well. It had to be a demoralizer for the pickets walking those endless elliptical circles, for hours-long shifts, in front our buildings, particularly as the weather was turning colder with winter approaching. As the lockout continued and we managed on in our war footing, a typical comment we often heard from many replacements everywhere, as they were becoming more proficient and confident in what they were doing while earning their strike bonuses, was just how easy many of these high paid NABET jobs really were.

In the middle of November, Dan Silverman, the NLRB's New York regional director and highly respected among labor practitioners on both sides of the table, issued his decision in the lockout charges the union had brought against ABC. Agreeing completely with our arguments about the applicable law, he found we were acting to protect our "perishable product" in the return to work agreement and had every right to insist on advance notice for future strikes.

He further found that we had supplied the proper response to the union's medical information request and our lockout therefore had been an appropriate reaction to their unprotected striking. In effect, the NLRB decision meant that both their strike and their attempt at immunizing themselves from our lockout had failed. Much relieved, we waited to hear from the other side about some possible negotiations breakthrough.

Dismayed and unhappy at the Board's decision, the union still had no interest in accepting our final offer. Instead, it filed an immediate appeal with the general counsel in Washington. Both sides knew this could take several months before a decision would be issued. NABET was putting its faith in a hope the Washington headquarters of this US governmental agency—headed by a Democratic, Clinton administration-appointed official, its GC, would view their case favorably and come to the union's rescue by overruling Regional Director Silverman.

So the lockout and picketing continued. After about a month, and with no end in sight, the Company made a decision to stop paying medical benefit coverage for the locked-out employees. We acted no differently from many other companies involved in irreconcilable strikes and lockouts. From that point, the full cost of medical coverage would have to be borne by the employees themselves if they wanted to keep insurance protection for themselves and their families. It was a difficult decision to reach that we knew would cause much discontent. But we felt, considering the circumstances of total obstinacy and no possible light at the end of the tunnel, it was our only choice. Just as pay had stopped for employees no longer working, so would benefits cease.

The pressure was building on the union to make some dramatic decisions about ending the standoff. Around the same time, we began to get word that a few of the smaller bargaining units locked out were unhappy with the union's leadership and looking to leave their NABET affiliation. Representing only a handful though of the 2300-plus NABET-represented employees, a few units left, as they were permitted under NLRB law, and became non-union. A small number of locked out employees in both the news writer and engineering units were upset with their union leadership, resigned their union membership, crossed the picket lines, and returned to work. Resignations were first necessary in order to avoid stiff union fines, but when these brave employees began to think for themselves and chose to do this, we allowed them back in to work.

It's a heart-wrenching phenomenon that occasionally occurs during major labor strife when some employees on the street begin to think for themselves more clearly about what is in their own best interests—and that of their families. As time went on, more did the same. When individuals made these choices, it was much to the unhappiness and near certain, eternal hatred of their former union brothers and sisters who were suffering serious economic distress while marching on the wet, cold, and getting colder picket lines.

New York's winter of 1998-'99 was a bad one. The second half of December had particularly low temperatures and a bit of snow around Christmas. An Arctic chill descended in early January. Chicago was hit with the blizzard of '99 that brought 22 inches of snow. The pickets outside our buildings in our colder cities of New York, Washington, and Chicago—the several hundreds of them assigned picket-line duty—marched round the clock and often in freezing rain and snow. In a scene right out of *Rocky,* some union guys started a fire in a steel barrel outside of our Manhattan headquarters building on West 66 Street to help keep marching picketers' hands warm.

Loud and noisy chanting resounded throughout our

neighborhoods. It was particularly raucous outside of our buildings in New York City. Many hundreds of residents in the surrounding high-rises angrily called NABET—or the police—to complain about the constant racket. Who could blame them after being kept awake at night by loud whistles, horns, the banging of steel garbage can covers, and other ear-shattering noises.

When the West 66 Street residents unable to sleep at night because of the din called the union, they were told, "Call Ruthizer at his home." They then were given my unpublished home telephone number to harass me further. So we'd get crazy calls in the middle of the night. With the police powerless to do anything about the loud pickets, many neighbors on West 66 Street were upset at ABC and remained so for a long while.

There is often no accounting for what happens to peoples' decency, humanity, and just common sense when they find themselves deeply trapped in desperate situations of their own, foolish making. Fortunately, my home and family in Westchester was under 24 hour protection.

As one example of lost decency, my valued administrative assistant was expecting a baby. One day that winter in about her seventh month while sitting at her desk preparing some documents, she experienced some serious labor difficulties. After our calling an ambulance which quickly arrived, the medical techs rushed up in the elevators to our 15th floor to take her down on a gurney to nearby Roosevelt Hospital's emergency room. I accompanied her to the hospital. As she was being taken out of the building and a path cleared to put her into the ambulance, the picketing NABETs saw me with her and started loudly jeering. They later suggested in their daily propaganda that I had physically assaulted her and was taking her to the hospital. Nothing was too low.

Her's were true labor pains in the normal meaning of the term. Mine during that period were of the different variety and while not nearly as serious, they are nevertheless discomforting. The lockout's great stress on everybody continued. I and some of my staff were spending a lot of overnight-time at local hotels after very long days in our offices managing crisis after crisis because we had to stay as close as possible to our command center. Early in the lockout there was one brief Federal Mediation effort to get the parties together where Bahr and Braverman participated. It went nowhere, however, and quickly ended after the union showed no interest in negotiating off of any of its previously announced positions.

27
CHAPTER

It Gets Cold and Lonely in New York During the Winter

After 11 weeks out on the street, in the cold and nasty winter weather, with no pay and many millions of dollars in lost salaries, bills building up, rent, mortgages and college tuitions payments overdue, medical benefits suspended and their paying their own full-freight for medical coverage, no advertiser abandonment, no viewer diminishment, no NLRB or other government ruling in their favor, the latest NLRB case dismissed but on appeal, few if any blown commercials, the Democratic politicians in Washington not helping, every ABC operation performing well if not perfectly, several of the bargaining units decertifying from the NABET orbit out of dismay and disgust, some brave striking workers resigning from NABET and coming back to work non-union, their CWA Big Brother apparently neutered in its ability to protect them, it was clear that NABET'S entire game plan had not worked out as they had expected. For many of us seeing our employees hurting so unnecessarily, it was sad and painful.

The abandonment by their imagined friends at the NLRB's

New York's offices, although the dismissal was under appeal to their other-imagined, more important friends in Washington, must have hurt them as they had never thought possible. The clever, November strategy of harming ABC by a sudden strike and getting inoculated against any possible lockout was poorly conceived. And it totally backfired. Nothing was working for them.

With their circumstances so dismal, the union's top leadership had to find a way to get their members back to work and start earning real money again. The locked out workers were getting some small stipend but it was recent and not much more than a token. Peoples' financial circumstances were in many cases quite desperate. We wanted them back. But we had been resolute with the the NABET and CWA leadership about what coming back to work would necessitate. What we really preferred was a signed agreement and then their coming back to work. But we saw no chance of that happening.

Finally, the two union leaders, John Clark and Morty Bahr, called in mid-January 1999 and announced they were prepared to sign the much-hated return to work agreement. Three months earlier when it was presented, they had found it far too onerous, and laughable, to even consider. But now, with their backs up against the wall and absolutely nowhere to go, they had a change of heart. They held their noses, agreed to give us the required notices if they ever again wanted to go out on strike, and signed. And they did so knowing that a breach of the strictly enforceable promises to give notice would indisputably subject them to many millions of dollars in damages. Doing so would surely bankrupt both unions. So they were well aware this contractual commitment was being undertaken at their peril, had to be taken seriously, and was strictly enforceable.

Our employees came back to work. Sullen and depressed, they were nevertheless eager to start earning some money again, pay off some of bills that had accumulated, and get back their valuable medical insurance coverage. With many understandably angry at their union as well as the Company, each locked out employee had lost at a minimum between $12,000 and $15,000 in wages during those 11 fruitless weeks. Some, and particularly the heavy overtime and higher classification earners, had lost considerably more. No spin doctor could sugar-coat these devastating facts.

The jobs they had voluntarily walked away from on orders of their top leadership were excellent paying ones. Like most American workers—even among the highest earners—many lived from paycheck to paycheck. With little savings, some sadly had to exhaust college funds and delay mortgage payments. Homes were put at risk while they walked the winter pavement. In New York at least they had received some unemployment stipend, but it was small and hardly came close to their normal wages.

With the protection the Company now had from the strict two-week advance notice requirement of the return to work agreement, it was now safe to bring back the regular NABET crews to ABC Sports remotes. The use of shadow crews that we had been employing since November of 1997 was discontinued.

All the while, the union continued to use the Board for its own purposes. But the NLRB refused to play along. The New York Board office kept investigating and dismissing every charge the union filed. While its Washington chiefs kept listening and perhaps squirming a bit, they continued to follow the law and denied all of the union's appeals for lacking any merit whatsoever. Of the over 100 unfair labor practice charges that had been filed, all had been dismissed by the New York region—with dismissals sustained on appeal.

To no avail, we held more bargaining sessions in the ensuing month to break the logjam. Trying it both with and without federal mediators, in both big team and small team formats, nothing seemed to work. Alan Nesbitt, Preston Davis, and I would take the subway daily down to the World Trade Center for endless hours of talks over a three- weeks span with a trio of union leaders in continued attempts for a breakthrough.

Held under the auspices of the federal mediators at their offices in an adjacent building to the towers that would later be destroyed as the result of the terrorist 9/11 attack, we had many memorable moments. But denial and across-the-board resistance continued to reign supreme. Never did they even try to say, "Okay, we'll agree to these six or seven major items, but not to these other things." Or select even a solitary item or two. Maybe they sensed the futility because we had said, and meant, our offer was indeed final. But their attitude remained the same—total, across the board rejection of everything.

In the early winter of '99, Braverman, Baumgarten, Sandman, and I travelled to Washington to meet with the Board's general counsel and his senior officials regarding the union's appeal of the New York office's dismissal of their lockout charges. Joe Baumgarten did a brilliant job in making our "perishable product" argument and responding to their questions. We left Washington optimistic but uncertain—awaiting a decision that we suspected might take another month or two.

When that day came a month of two later, we were again vindicated. That denial of the union's appeal re-energized us and put us on a clearer trajectory. Still batting .000, NABET was once again stymied. The best it could come up with was to take ABC's unchanged final package proposal to its nationwide membership for a quick vote. It had to be thinking a sound rejection by the membership would demonstrate to ABC once again just how detestable our proposals still were and force us to drastically modify our ways if we ever wanted a resolution.

We knew it had little chance of being ratified by the membership, and particularly by the overwhelming number of engineering technicians among the nearly 2400 staff and daily hires voting. This was the group most impacted by the proposed changes. As expected, the union bargaining committee recommended against approval. When it was resoundingly rejected by 80% of the union's overall membership, there were nevertheless some welcome surprises. Seven of the smaller groups of the now 12 remaining bargaining units—anxious to get back to work despite their leaders' recommendations—found our final offer acceptable and voted in favor.

Disappointing to us, the union refused to permit these seven, small units, totaling no more than 100 or so employees who accepted the offer, to get the benefits of the deal they had just ratified. It had to be, according to their rules, all or none. So, the employees in these unlucky seven groups who wanted the offered contract had to continue to lose wage increases and other monetary improvements for even longer. NABET continued on with its denial and resistance in its efforts to wear us down.

Finally, after another day or two of futile bargaining, we stood once more on our "Final Offer" from nearly two years previous. It was still our "last, best, and final"—so the union heard it loud and clear once again we were holding on all the points that we had long been arguing. It was considerable—including every minor and major point that NABET from the very outset had detested.

Contained in the offer as it had been from the start was the same, self -reducing wage retroactivity clause that had been triggered on April 1, 1997. It would extend to whatever future date the contract would be fully ratified. It was the very same provision we had headlined since we first sat down with them in February of '97. A bitter pill indeed, it now amounted to essentially two years of lost wage increases—thousands of dollars for each employee. And well over $5 million for the entire group of 2300 employees. That loss, while tragic, was irrevocable.

The rejection of our offer that followed by words and conduct was consistent with their behavior over the prior two years. When they did that, we made a legal judgment. Finally we could now, with a very clear bargaining record, establish to a virtual certainty under governing law that we were at an impasse on all the major and less important issues. Once we were at an impasse, as the law allowed, we could implement. The day had arrived.

We and our outside lawyers felt certain that the more than two-year bargaining record would prove that their numerous protestations of good faith and continual attempts to show open-mindedness were total shams. The union leaders' minds on these critical issues were as closed on that February of 1999 day as they had been the day we had opened talks—and throughout the ensuing 24 months. We had, unquestionably, serious "irreconcilable differences."

So we acted. Declaring an impasse, we implemented our Final Offer. We were confident that the Board, examining closely the facts of the two years of fruitless bargaining, would have no option but to find the parties had truly reached an impasse and that ABC was entirely correct when it implemented its final offer.

However, what we chose to implement in our Final Offer, as the law permitted, were only the many dozens of proposals favorable to the Company. It was a wide range of proposals that we chose to implement that were geared to lift or modify the gaggle of the contract's remaining inefficiencies, inflexibilities, and restrictions. The list included the further tightening of our previously attained "iron-clad" computer language. When we did that, we made it even more impervious to any possible future NABET attack through their beloved grievance and arbitration procedure. The items in the final offer that were good for employees—like future pay increases and other monetary improvements—were withheld from implementation.

Sandman, Quinn, Key, and I traveled to all locations to have quick meetings with all management explaining in detail the new contract terms being implemented. Operating management was pleased that this day had finally arrived. Our NABET-represented population, however, since they now clearly understood nothing good for them was being put into effect, were angry.

What ensued with NABET was more denial. Like Pavlov's favorite animal, the union's reaction—their only card left since their time to bargain with us a better deal had long run out—was to file yet another unfair labor charge. As expected, they were claiming, with a straight face, that the bargaining parties had not yet arrived at a true impasse and the Company was barred from implementing our final offer. Incredibly, they were contending they still had an open mind on many if not all issues. There were not, they said, any irreconcilable differences between the parties that justified our declaring an impasse.

After New York NLRB's office once again did an expedited investigation, a few weeks later regional director Silverman issued another dismissal of the union's latest charges. Looking at the overwhelming evidence, he found the conclusion inescapable that the parties had been at a true impasse when the Company implemented its final proposal a few weeks earlier. There were indeed, said Silverman, irreconcilable differences between the parties.

Suddenly, their carefully-laid smokescreen had been blown away by a rush of US government fresh air. Those many yards of camouflage fabric had been wasted. It was another staggering loss for the union that had counted for so long on a strategy that was now indisputably proven totally flawed. Clearly ineffective, they had failed to pull the wool over the Board's eyes that had just barely covered their own.

Still not content to salvage what they could and cut their losses, it was again groundhog day. The union took another immediate appeal to the NLRB's general counsel's office in Washington. In a last gasp hope that finally the Clinton administration's high officials would perform miracles for them, they argued that New York Regional Director Silverman was mistaken in not recognizing their true open-mindedness when he found there was an impasse. Incredibly, the union was still alleging there were no irreconcilable differences.

Bound by the terms of return to work agreement, the union was not free to strike without the requisite one or two week notices or face bankruptcy if they did. Striking thus was no longer a realistic weapon. Even with the requisite notice, it would have been an act of economic and organizational suicide. Exactly how many of their employees would have actually gone out on strike again if ordered was largely unknown. But the leaders had to know it might have been very few. It could easily have destroyed the union. Boxed by themselves into their little corner, all they had left was this last, "Hail Mary," Washington NLRB challenge.

This is where the final battle of the epic two-year struggle would be waged. Both parties would be standing on the sidelines while the NLRB's head Washington official, its GC, reviewed the latest dismissal.

It was during the time of relative calm while awaiting the Board's decision that the ABC Television Network worked out with Air France a special deal that included several sets of promotional tickets on its *Concorde* flight to Paris. The supersonic jet that cut travel time across the Atlantic to three and a half hours was still flying. Someone at the Network thought it might be a nice gesture if those tickets could be given to a few of ABC's chief bargainers and their spouses as a special thank you. Alan Braverman selected Preston Davis, Alan Nesbitt, and myself.

It was a welcomed respite at a relatively safe moment when none of us had to worry about another sneak attack. I had not really had any real vacation since the contract's expiration in March of '97 when we had gone on full DEFCON 1 alert. Paris was easily one of Monica's and my favorite destinations and springtime was its most glorious season. Flying over on separate flights, the Davises and Nesbitts joined us for dinner at two of Paris' finest restaurants.

Raising our glasses high, how could we not have toasted our good *Concorde* fortune. After hanging out in Paris for a week, it was back to New York and the reality of waiting for the NLRB to deliver what we hoped would be another crippling decision against the union.

After New York's regional office had carefully investigated the facts and applied the law in its decision to dismiss, a real question remained about their Washington bosses. We kept asking ourselves one question. Would they, the top NLRB officials appointed by the Democratic Clinton administration and known in management circles for its leaning towards unions, have the character, fortitude, professionalism, and devotion to the law to stand by Dan Silverman's well-reasoned decision.

28
CHAPTER

A Lost and Wandering
Battalion Gets Rescued

It was late in the spring of 1999. For almost two and one-half years we had gone through a process that now, looking back from more than 20 years later, was totally surrealistic.

We had sustained many months of useless and mostly nasty bargaining sessions, intimidation, attempted sabotage, picketing in front of our buildings and once outside my home, near violence at the bargaining table, and death threats. We had home security bodyguards 24/7, unruly demonstrations, news programming boycotts by Democrats, intervention by Democratic US senators, federal mediation, and meetings with the Secretary of Labor. Upwards of 100 unfair labor practice charges had been filed, and scores of mostly ridiculous information requests made. A huge inflated rat had taken up permanent residence outside on Columbus Avenue. We had sustained two strikes and delivered an 11-week lockout. The union had suffered universal rejection by the NLRB at every turn of the road when its voluminous legal challenges had been investigated and dismissed. All of these actions and activities have been carefully described earlier.

As of that spring, while none of the previous charges had stuck, we were waiting for this final legal challenge to be determined. It was easily the most consequential. Dan Silverman, its respected New York regional director, had agreed with us, but would Washington's Board chief agree with his dismissal? If Washington would agree, the union's legal fate would be sealed. What its leaders would choose to do at that point on the negotiations front, however, was anyone's guess. But when one is locked in a sealed room with the water level rising, there aren't too many choices available.

On that late spring day for which we had all been waiting for months, the NLRB put the last nail into NABET's legal coffin. You could hear the pop of the nail gun fired from the nation's capital all up and down the east coast and echoing its way out to California. These last charges that the union had filed in March were fully and finally rejected by the Board's general counsel when he denied their appeal. It was, as we had argued, a legitimate impasse and a lawful implementation. While over 100 charges had been dismissed earlier, this sustained dismissal would prove to be by far the most consequential. And we hoped definitive.

The defeat that day would force the union to do something it never thought would be possible. It could either cash in its few remaining chips and accept defeat or continue down its ever-more suicidal path. No longer with any viable strike option in their arsenal, as many were asking, for what purpose would they persist in their pride, animosity, and sheer stubbornness? How much longer would they allow their members to be hurt? We all felt the pain our employees were experiencing, but we had been helpless to bring this saga to a close on our own—only the union had the power do that. It seemed to be the end of the long road, but we kept asking ourselves would the voices of reason finally prevail.

So this day was truly one of those "wow" moments in ABC history. We had won and won big. Decided by the senior ranking NLRB official in Washington—its general counsel—who many felt was too-union leaning to be able to deliver a fair and unbiased decision in a case of this magnitude in favor of a company, his action had proven that perception totally wrong. The NLRB—my old, neutral employer from more than three decades earlier—had done its professional job.

Prevailing because we had carefully bargained and thoughtfully behaved, we had excellent lawyers both—inside and out, great facts, and very good arguments. In addition, we had the additional benefit of the prevailing law on our side. All of this together made for an unbeatable combination. So at the end of the day, the Board, perhaps reluctantly but nevertheless fulfilling its obligation under federal law, agreed it had to rule against the union and sustain the dismissal of the charges.

When the shot was fired that day from Washington and we heard its ring in New York, CWA President Morty Bahr, not too far from the NLRB at his CWA offices in Washington, heard it, too. Loud and clear. As disappointed as he undoubtedly was, he picked up the phone and called Bob Iger in his office at ABC headquarters in New York City. Saying to Bob from what I can piece together 23 years later that the time had come to make a deal, Bahr said he wanted to come to see Bob. Iger thought for a moment and pretty much replied, "No Morty, call Jeff Ruthizer." That was it—just "call Jeff Ruthizer."

Knowing Bob Iger as I do for now over three decades, I am sure that there was a bit more pleasantry and diplomacy wrapped around his reply. But the clear message to Bahr, as Morty later related to me, was for him to deal with me. When I learned this, I felt Bob's jacket inherited from Dan Burke fitting better than ever around my shoulders. Alan Braverman called me on Bob's behalf and told me to expect Morty's call. Alan's message was clear—meet, listen to what he had to say, and using my best judgment try to make the deal happen.

Bahr must have been in shock that Iger had turned him down. As he told me later, he was used to making closing deals at final moments in difficult talks like this directly with major company CEOs—not the head labor guy. He added that no CEO had ever turned him down. So having to meet with me and not Bob must have been somewhat humiliating for him, the International president of one of the largest and most powerful unions in America—700,000 strong. While Morty was used to closing deals with titans, I was not yet even a senior vice president—something that would have probably made it a bit more palatable.

Immediately calling Marc Sandman in Los Angeles and Joe Baumgarten to alert them confidentially to this development, I asked Sean Quinn to join us in my office. As we talked it through, none of us were quite sure what it meant.

As expected, Bahr soon called and we agreed to meet as early as possible on the first available date a few days later in early June. With both of us wanting it off-campus to preserve strict confidentiality, I suggested and he agreed to meet at the Essex House hotel. Meeting in a small conference room which I had reserved, we started with some pleasantries before ordering sandwiches from room service. Morty jumped into what was on his mind.

Sharing with me that NABET's senior officials had come to him for his help after the disastrous NLRB decision, he emphasized that he could be very helpful for both sides in finally settling the stalemate. Not sure whether to take him at his word that it was NABET's idea rather than his own to intervene and save NABET from drowning, I nevertheless listened closely. Bahr continued by telling me about the SPRINT and US Air CEOs with whom he usually closed deals and his surprise that Iger had turned him down. Between bites of probably tuna or roast beef, he went on to say he had the power under the CWA constitution and by-laws to make any deal and overrule the five person NABET bargaining committee on anything and everything.

The time had come, he emphasized, to end this, and of course I nodded my head in agreement. Before I could comment, he went on to say that he was prepared to agree to ABC's entire final offer—including every point that NABET had been fighting over for more than two years. Pausing for a moment to let this sink in, he continued that there was only one thing he needed in return to make this deal happen—complete pay retroactivity for everyone back to April 1, 1997.

By that time in June of '99, we were talking about over two years of lost pay increases that added up to roughly $5,000 or more per employee.

There were about 2300 or 2400 workers who would be eligible for what he was asking. With that plea, Morty was trying to salvage for his members, as the clock had finally run out for NABET, the millions of dollars in wage increases they had lost because of his junior partner's stubbornness and miscues. As Morty was talking, I was reviewing in my head just how many millions we had saved in NABET salaries and benefits, and how much this request would cost. The rough math, I remembered from some numbers I had seen a few days earlier, added up to over $10 million. It was a huge ask.

Of course, in the back of my mind I was recalling that NABET's late president, Jim Nolan, ten years earlier had tried the same, last minute gambit with Tom Murphy. When he attempted to salvage retroactivity in the '89 talks, Tom on my advice had turned him down and the deal came together anyway. Credibility on our "no retroactivity" pledge a decade earlier had been the critical factor in Tom's and my thinking. Remaining the pillar of every NABET negotiations since, maintaining that credibility was now even more important.

Immediately jumping in, I replied that while we were appreciative he was accepting everything in the final package, his ask was absolutely out of the question. Never, I said, were we ever going to reward the bad conduct we had experienced for more than two years. Further, I reminded Bahr, we had consistently delivered our stern warning to the bargaining committee about losing wage retroactivity from day one of our talks 28 months earlier.

"We meant what we said at the time and we still mean it," I told Morty. "If the NABET leaders had only listened, they could have had this same deal, or even a much better deal, many months or a year or more ago." More importantly, their members, for whom we all felt great sympathy, could have been receiving their higher salaries, with the two solid wage increases under their belt, which they lost because of the union's poor decisions.

Voicing surprise at my reaction, Bahr went on to say that the CEOs of SPRINT or US Air, if he was dealing with them, would certainly see the major benefit of what he was offering. Since it was such a gigantic move he was making in agreeing to everything, he said, there could be no doubt they would grant retroactivity. They would also do it in a flash out of respect for his position as CWA president. He went on to say that if Bob Iger was in the room, he was certain Bob would do the same.

Responding that he was completely wrong about Bob, I knew that as a fact because I had discussed our firm "no retroactivity" commitment with Braverman on numerous occasions. Each time Alan had told me Bob was completely on board. But in any event, as I told Morty, Bob was not in the room and I had complete authority from him to make the deal I thought best. No way, I knew deep within myself, was I going to sweeten the Company's offer by his asking price of $10 million—let alone even by one penny.

Persisting, he backed off but came back with some kind of partial retroactivity—maybe for even half of the 26-month period since March 31 of 1997. Knowing the leverage we had after the NLRB decision, and remembering Tom's stern retroactivity message to Nolan a decade earlier, I remained with my best game face and strong voice just as adamant in repeating it was going to be nothing. Zero. Again, he voiced shock at my rejection of any retroactivity.

On the spot though, quickly recalling that it took about six weeks for NABET to complete its formal ratification process, I told Morty that I would be willing to do one thing and one thing only. "Six weeks of retroactivity—not a day or cent more," I said. But he would have to give me his word right then and there that we had a deal based upon what he said earlier about accepting our complete Final Offer, and we'd handshake on it. If he would so agree, I would make the first wage increase of any ratified deal effective as of that very day we were meeting in the Essex House. That would mean, I said, about six weeks of retroactivity, and I would not agree to anything more. Six weeks, of course, paled in comparison with Bahr's huge ask for 113 weeks, but at least it was something with which he could walk away.

I knew I was a bit out on the limb. However, I felt this was certainly within my authority as chief negotiator and that Braverman and Iger would approve. Further, I told Bahr he had to agree that he and the CWA would publicly and in writing recommend the deal to the members and he would get NABET president John Clark to do the same. In addition, he would have to get the identical commitment from the five local presidents on the bargaining committee, or at least get their pledge not to speak out or work against the deal in any way—directly or indirectly.

Considering my partial face-saving offer for a brief moment and obviously realizing it was not going to get any better, he said—"You are the toughest SOB I ever met." With a kind of half-smile, knowing he had no choice and had to bring this to a close, he extended his hand for the shake and agreed to all of these conditions. Finishing our sandwiches quickly, we soon departed, thanking each other on the way out.

The deal was done. With that one handshake, all of the heavy labor pains and stress of the previous two and one-half years, since talks began, started to lift from my shoulders. The extreme discomfort and all the kicking were about to end. I was confident that Morty Bahr, the International president of the big and powerful CWA, and NABET's boss in their merged relationship, would have the influence to get this across the finish line.

We had suffered a lot of pain and sustained a great deal of never-expected cost. Many millions had been spent on extra security, shadow crews, strike training, and replacements. There had been an enormous amount of wear and tear on the Company at many locations. Many executives had become war-weary.

Yet the union and its members had seriously suffered, and much of it needlessly. It had gone on far too long. If only the NABET leadership had not pursued such a misguided strategy and not been so stubborn. What a heavy message it would be to lose, on top of their other heavy monetary losses during the lockout, two years of solid pay increases. As I was leaving the hotel, I was thinking that Morty, deep down, surely shared that same opinion of what had transpired. He knew serious mistakes had been made. Having done all that he and the CWA could have done to help NABET from the very outset, he now understood that ABC was no telephone company.

Now because of Morty's intervention, riding in as he did to rescue his surrounded troops at the last minute, it was all about to end. But it surely was not as he set out to accomplish in the winter of '97 when we first sat down at the negotiations table. Undoubtedly, he hated every moment of being there with me, but the NLRB, and NABET's consistently bad choices, had given him no option.

Significantly, for its members on the eve of voting whether to accept the final offer, they would be facing several grim realties. First, was the realization that they were effectively barred from launching any strike that might hurt the Company since the notice requirements of the return to work agreement still applied. Secondly, our implementation had just been approved by the NLRB. Lastly, the Company was already reaping the financial and operational advantages of the contract changes, but the employees weren't. Seven bargaining groups had earlier accepted the final offer that the NABET leadership had rejected and recommended against. Now the NABET leaders unanimously, and CWA-head Bahr himself, would be recommending that everybody vote yes on ABC's Final Offer. These were overwhelming factors in our favor.

Calling Alan Braverman on the way back to the office to give him the headlines, I went upstairs to see him as soon as I returned. Equally thrilled, he enthusiastically complimented me and said I made the right call—telling me he would let Bob Iger know immediately. Bob later telephoned with his own congratulations.

Bahr as I had expected was true to his word. The CWA president would go on in the weeks ahead to send out a few letters, emails, and messages reflecting the realities of the situation and strongly recommending the deal. In his words, it was the best possible outcome that NABET could hope to achieve under very difficult circumstances. While there was much grousing in the ranks about the loss of over two years of pay increases as well as the previously lost 11 weeks of lockout pay, the members when voting would have to face this sobering truth about their dire circumstances. The NABET leaders in all five of our cities were surely working behind the scene to secure the deal.

Six weeks later I got the call. Krieger delivered the news that all bargaining units had basically held their noses but ratified the deal. Seven had previously. Apparently enough of the members who voted in favor had become realists and recognized the necessity to stop the bleeding. Six weeks of retroactivity instead of risking even more pay losses—on top of the $5000 in retroactivity alone each had already suffered—was the far better choice. Anxious to get their first wage increase since 1996, they were ready to put the sorry story behind them.

Going on to congratulate me, Krieger was actually buoyant

that our shared odyssey had finally come to an end. It was classic Krieger—an individual I had known for many years and whom I had always considered a decent person. I knew he believed deep down that much of what we had achieved was deserved. More importantly, although he never used these terms, I am certain he felt much of what they had tried to do to us was wrong, unwise, and counterproductive. In later years over dinners or drinks he as much as admitted this.

Like so many of the other NABET leaders, he had been swept away by the promise of the CWA's invincible support, the over-exuberance of some on his side, and the false narrative they had convinced themselves into believing was a winning strategy. Having shared with me confidentially on several occasions that he was embarrassed by the behavior of a few, he though had done nothing to stop it.

Thus ended the biggest, most complicated, and most difficult labor dispute in ABC's 75 year history. It had been stressful and exhausting for so many people in so many ways for so long, but at the end we got our deal and made the peace. It was and remained the biggest of the many labor pains that I had endured in my entire 45-year labor relations career. But also, in a bizarre way, it was—despite all the stress and worry—the most major of my labor satisfactions. Overcoming during that two and a half-year period numerous sand traps, torpedoes, trip wires, and mine fields, achieving an end like this was the ultimate joy of my decades-long stay on the broadcasting delivery table.

With this deal finally done and job routines back to normal throughout the Company, there was a feeling of calmness again. Except, quite understandably, in the NABET ranks. So much of what our employees had suffered was unnecessary. I kept wondering what would have happened had Jim Nolan and Tom Kennedy still been in charge. But now at least the long 1997-'99 NABET War was over.

We had prevailed under very stressful circumstances. But our victory was especially sweet because we had achieved the many highly consequential operational and financial objectives we had set out to accomplish years earlier. When I thought back to what the CWA bargainer, Carmine Turchi, had said to me that day in the late winter of '97 when negotiations began—that I should pick out one or two things from our package of 100 and maybe they would take a look at those—I could not help but break out into a smile.

Oddly enough, when Turchi and I were to meet in Washington a few years later at some major CWA dinner, we gave each other a warm, and I think, genuine embrace. It was reminiscent of the photos I've seen of Confederate and Union Civil War veterans—formerly bitter enemies—shaking hands over stone walls at their reunions decades after the war had ended.

To honor the team's efforts, my wife, Monica, and I decided to host a celebratory party at our home in Westchester County later that summer. Maybe 75 attended, including outside counsel, consultants and my entire legal staff. Other New York headquarters colleagues who had worked on this venture were invited. It was ironically the same home where NABET pickets had come to intimidate me and where guards for nearly a year had protected my family.

Largely everyone invited from the New York area showed up. And many of the out of town crew, too. I was especially pleased that our chief Washington lobbyist, Billy Pitts, who had become a good friend and had given me so much personal support during this ordeal, found his way to our door. Mike Norman, a valuable team member from Los Angeles for many years, and always an inspiration, also managed to be there.

Shortly after these events took place, I received a very nice congratulatory note from Disney CEO, Michael Eisner. Having been advised by Bob Iger that we made the deal, he expressed his appreciation for our accomplishments and my personal efforts.

It was rewarding to get a note from the Boss acknowledging my team's success after our arduous journey.

Bob Iger, having started many years before in a Network studio position before moving into operations at ABC Sports, had known the difficulties of the NABET situation first-hand. His stirring decisions during the two strikes and the 11-week lockout were instrumental in our ultimate success. When Bob called and we met in his office, he was very kind in his praise and enthusiastic in expressing his appreciation.

Alan Braverman knew better than most exactly what we had gone through and accomplished. I had kept him closely apprised along the way, starting at the very beginning as we began our planning in 1996. Working closely with Marc Sandman and myself in fashioning the initial set of proposals, he supported my bargaining plan and immersed himself in our legal strategizing. Particularly involved during the lockout in meetings with the federal mediators, Bahr, and the Secretary of Labor, Alan—the smartest and longest serving of all of the ABC general counsels for whom I worked—gave us strong backing and encouragement throughout.

Showing his pride in us by telling so many within the Company that his labor lawyers had beaten back successfully over 100 unfair labor practice charges, his praise and commendation—both publicly and in private—for my leadership and lawyering were substantial. He was also very high on our entire labor relations team on both coasts and our outside counsel from the Proskauer firm, Joe Baumgarten.

Morty Bahr and I saw each other again only once after our '99 Essex House meeting. It was at the 2003 talks' opening day table. We spoke over the phone a few times on other matters before we both retired, but we never again discussed that 1999 day or the negotiations.

Morty would pass away at age 93 in the fall of 2019. Not learning of his death for several weeks, I missed his funeral services that I very much would've liked to attend. Later in November of that same year, a CWA memorial service for Morty was held in Washington. Many hundreds of family members, labor officials, rank and file workers, politicians, and company executives attended to pay their respects to this distinguished labor leader.

At the time of his memorial service, I was on the West Coast and regrettably unable to attend. I had wanted to pay my personal respects to the man who had saved NABET and its members from certain destruction with that handshake 20 years earlier. Realizing I could not be there, I sent a condolence note to NABET president, Charlie Braico. Out of the ABC Chicago local and a former TD, Charlie and I had gotten to know each other quite well over the intervening decades. He was kind enough to respond, thanking me for my note.

29
CHAPTER

The Millennium Arrives for Disney

The ABC TV Network closed out 1999 by following the world's time zones sequentially as the centuries changed hands. Our millennium coverage was a splendid, audience-shattering, unprecedented broadcast by ABC News called *ABC 2000 Today.* Probably its proudest moment ever, 175 million Americans watched at least part.

I had not realized until I read Bob Iger's 2019 book, *The Ride of a Lifetime,* that it had been Bob's idea. He had passed his suggestion along to Roone Arledge, his old boss, who was now ABC News' chairman. It was a new position that Iger had created for Roone a few years earlier as Bob was developing the next generation of News leadership. David Westin, one of my old bosses, had become its president at that time.

Iger had seen his unique concept for welcoming the new century as the perfect project for Roone's visionary skills. It was to be his last big show sitting in the executive producer's chair. But the showman—who had produced decades of stellar ABC sports and news events and been responsible for producing political conventions, presidential debates and inaugurations, *Super Bowls,* and *Olympic Games*—still had some prime juice left in him. It was probably his greatest production ever. Two years later, Roone would sadly be dead from cancer.

Peter Jennings anchored the 24-hour broadcast, as only Peter could, from ABC's Times Square Studios in New York. Tuxedo-clad for the festivities when the time would come halfway through the show for the ball drop in Times Square, he had only short breaks for nutrition, a change of clothes, and maybe to catch a wink every now and then. A host of producers, crews, anchors, and correspondents had been dispatched to major capitals to give the American viewing audience the show of their lifetimes as the new century was ushered in at many locations around the globe. Dozens of others were working in the studio and control rooms.

The marathon coverage began on a South Pacific island as midnight approached and ended in Los Angeles the following evening—many hours and time zones apart. In between were numerous live remotes from such places as Sydney, Moscow, China, Rio de Janeiro, London, Walt Disney World, and Paris. The City of Light—Paris—was where Monica and I had planned to be at this time for a brief vacation.

Figuring out a year or two earlier that there would be no better place to celebrate the millennium than Paris, Monica and I had booked at our favorite hotel on the Left Bank. So when I learned that Paris would be a major stop in David and Roone's worldwide coverage plans and we'd be there, I decided we would drop by the anchor site. When we did, it was in the most unobtrusive way possible so as not to disturb the production's frenetic efforts. Barbara Walters was anchoring our coverage from near the Eiffel Tower. It was another of Barbara's outstanding broadcasts as part of a great performance by ABC News people all around the world.

Paris was going nuts. Restaurants were flooded with reservations. Elaborate menus had been prepared. The better restaurants charging nose bleed prices would expect their dining guests for this special evening to be in tuxedos and evening wear. The hotel was finally able to book us a last minute reservation at a nearby place called Alcazar. Really more of a nightclub than a restaurant, it dated back at that site to the 19th century. Designed originally with very high ceilings so that acrobats could hang from a flying trapeze high above the audience, dining below, that's what they were doing the night we were there.

Not was it just a trapeze act to celebrate the 21st century and entertain us, there were also also jugglers and magicians. Snake handlers, not exactly our most favorite dinner-time companions, worked the narrow spaces between tables. It would have been a performance worthy of Roone Arledge's showmanship. After an average dinner at absurd prices and the extravagant show, we headed out into the teeming streets to see the midnight fireworks over the Seine that ABC's cameras would be broadcasting.

The French capital was experiencing extremely mild weather that winter evening. It was so mild, in fact, that neither of us—like all the teeming party-goers—needed warm jackets. We just wandered the streets for hours in jeans and sweaters. In a scene like none other we had ever witnessed, massive, joyous, singing crowds were surging through the streets—shoulder to shoulder and often arm in arm. It reminded me of what the exuberant crowds in Paris would have been like more than two centuries earlier on their way to witness the guillotining of the aristocrats. This time though, many were carrying champagne bottles and offering gulps to total strangers. Millions of highly spirited but peaceful Parisians were thronging the streets and happily celebrating the millennium–much as people were doing that night all around the world.

The city had been hit a few days earlier by a historic wind and rain storm. The Seine had overflowed it banks but by now had receded. Hundreds of thousands of Paris' beautiful trees had been blown down but by now massive removal efforts were nearly finished and the streets were mostly passable.

We had dinner one night with my old friend and former head of the DGA, Glen Gumpel. Glen and his wife along with young son flew into Paris for the same reason as we had. We had been both close friends for nearly 30 years since my NBC days and had done many deals together. Glen had gone on after the DGA to work for Universal and had run its giant amusement park in Osaka, Japan, for over a decade. It was soon to be owned by Glen himself and a consortium of Japanese business leaders after it was sold by Universal and it went private, with him in charge. It was later sold back to Comcast. Glen retired. A guest at our wedding in 1976, Glen remains a friend today, nearly a half-century later.

The millennium did not destroy the world's computer systems as many had feared. Once that was established to our satisfaction, we could safely fly back to the US. It had been a peaceful, calming, and restorative ten days in Paris—particularly after the intensity of the last two and a half years in the NABET arena. Once I flew home, I could resume living in my real world of just the ordinary kicking and discomfort on the broadcasting delivery table. And sometimes even experience again a little joy.

The months following our striking the NABET deal the previous summer had brought back some normalcy, such as it was, to ABC and all of our lives in labor relations. Preparations for, or the actual negotiations themselves, with our many other unions in our five cities handled by my lawyers were always going on somewhere. Just as they always had, issues and disputes that needed my attention were constantly popping up. NABET grievances and arbitrations had slowed down but were still considerable and the lawyers involved, as I wanted it, often sought my involvement and guidance. Something significant was always happening that required my presence. It was problem-solving at the highest level.

In that half-year following my '99 handshake with Morty Bahr we had taken on a broad, instructional role within the Company. It became even more of our job to ensure that all of our network and station operations were taking full advantage of the dozens of tools gained in those marathons talks. Numerous and often complicated, the changes had to be not only fully taught but also carefully monitored. The myriad of modifications and additions had to be explained in their many details to the operators who would administer them and be understood by all if the Company was to reap the significant savings.

Alex Wallau, the Network's EVP, led its efforts. Keen on maximizing the new tools just negotiated, he would hold regular, periodic meetings in the months following the deal. With us and his key BOE and finance people, he had to be satisfied for his bottom line that all we had gained was being exercised—and dollars achieved.

The TV station group undertook the same monitoring process under EVP Alan Nesbitt's guidance. In traveling around with him to our television stations and doing a dozen or more presentations, we quickly learned the GMs needed little prodding to jump at their new opportunities. We did much the same with our radio operations although its gains were fewer and guidance less necessary. It was personally satisfying because past experience had taught that all too frequently major labor gains from hard fought wars could easily go unused, underutilized, or just forgotten.

Computer flexibility—after we kevlar-vested the old, iron-clad contract language—was undoubtedly our greatest gain. The additional armor we had added was intended to wipeout any possibility of loss from NABET's ill-considered West Coast arbitration pursuits. The new layers of steel were highly consequential and resulted in the withdrawal of the grievance. It was now even more clear—beyond any possibility that an arbitrator might interpose a contrary interpretation. Non-NABET-represented employees, mainly producers involved in the news editing process, at our indisputable assignment, could perform a wide range of computer keyboard functions.

Considerably expanding our daily hire capabilities was another major gain. With this ability to dramatically hire more people on a non-staff basis for only the days we needed them, it would enable over time considerable staff reductions.

Larry Pollock and the San Francisco station people had been particularly pleased with the results attained for KGO. After 40 years, we had finally broken out of NABET's hammer-hold. No longer would the much smaller-ranked and far less profitable San Francisco TV station, and its KGO-AM sibling, have to stay in a complete contract- lockstep arrangement with ABC's big market stations. The expensive set of terms and conditions—far above those applicable to other commercial local San Francisco stations—were substantially modified. Significant cost savings followed. Many had said this restructuring could never be achieved, but firm resolution had proven them wrong.

Major reforms had been achieved in the critical grievance and arbitration areas. We limited both how grievances could be filed and in some instances, where we felt the terms were excessive, we modified the authority of arbitrators. Virtually unprecedented in any labor contract across America, some of the arbitrators themselves expressed some degree of disbelief. Again, many people had said it could never be done, but we did it.

Numerous work rules were changed or eliminated. Once again, more than several onerous arbitration decisions and adverse grievance resolutions were nullified. The net result was that there was now less to grieve over. It would be just a short time before we would see the number of grievances beginning to fall dramatically everywhere—the start of a trend that only accelerated over time.

Once more there was a sense of personal satisfaction. Finally, my old friend Hammurabi was being sidelined. Thousands of hours of managers' collective time no longer would have to be spent laboring at the looms of the grievance machine, cottage industry. Managers could now spend more time on their main jobs of actually managing. As the number of grievances and arbitrations began to subside because there was a lot less to grieve over, I could look at my own staff reductions because NABET was no longer monopolizing the time of the ABC Labor Relations department. It was refreshing that managers could now walk into a studio and say "good morning" without somehow violating the contract.

NABET's New York local leadership was now more quiet and would not change hands for another two years. Its president had been re-elected by his membership in early '99 just before the NLRB brought down the final curtain on NABET's failed strategy. Inexplicable to many, some surmised it had been largely a show of loyalty by an ever-faithful membership. But during the ensuing months as greater awareness set in, the person's popularity sank and defeat would follow at the next election in 2001.

The Los Angeles NABET leader announced she, too, was leaving her post. Imagine our shock when we learned that she had become a lawyer and was accepting a position with a law firm. It seemed she had for several years secretly been attending law school at night. Even her fellow local union officials apparently did not know it. This was, of course, in addition to the free legal education she had been receiving across the broadcasting delivery table.

Sad for many, the Company's headquarters, after five years of Disney ownership, finally shifted to Los Angeles in 2000. After Ovitz' unsuccessful days as COO and Sandy Litwack's time performing some part-time COO duties, Eisner decided he needed a full-time COO and promoted Bob Iger to be Disney's president and COO. The entire ABC organization was overjoyed for Bob and only hoped the day would arrive that he would take the top job, too.

Bob's ascendancy to the number two Disney job though meant the ABC organizational structure would dramatically change. No longer would there be an overall ABC president. The subsidiary going forward would exist as just a group of various media units. All of these, and the other Disney media units in cable, such as ESPN and the Disney Channel, would report to Bob in his new role as president and COO of the Walt Disney Company.

Disney's new structure required that Bob would relocate to the West Coast. He'd keep a New York office for occasional visits, but he would be based in Burbank at Disney headquarters. Bob's move meant New York would no longer be the center of ABC's universe. Much of the senior staff structure and what was left of ABC headquarters would also be shifted to Burbank. It also meant that the Television Network would move west to a new building to be constructed on the Disney lot.

Many hundreds of executive and administrative jobs were affected. New York-based executives whose positions would shift to the West Coast were offered relocation packages or the option to leave the Company with healthy severance. Those who chose not to relocate for personal reasons, such as the TV Network president and its CFO, soon resigned.

The move also meant that Alan Braverman, as ABC's general counsel, was moving west with Bob and the rest of Bob's staff. Alan spoke with his staff of six or seven legal department vice presidents about our relocation with him. One or two who were asked declined, took their generous severance, and resigned. With my major New York-based, clients of ABC News, ABC Sports, BOE, and the ESPN work I was doing, Alan agreed it made the most sense for me to remain with my East Coast group. Some other vice presidents on Alan's staff, like my colleague and friend, Henry Hoberman, the head of litigation, were also allowed to remain on the East Coast.

But the consequences of the Westward Ho movement created for the rest of my time with the Company a certain distance from the seat of power. And one not measurable in miles alone. It was a sense of disquietude. So much in my successful practice of labor relations was up-front and personal, dealing with senior colleagues and major clients face to face. Here I was, the Company's head of labor relations, but I could no longer just pop upstairs and see my boss for a few minutes, assured of his undivided attention. Hopping an elevator for meetings with my peers among the senior staff or Network officials, when critical matters dictated, was no longer possible.

Most of the other senior officials at or above my level and department heads with whom I had always interfaced were shifting 2500 miles and three time zones away to the West Coast. Sure, there were telephones, video conference calls, and email, and I had Marc Sandman out there to run my office. He would be my deputy on the ground in Burbank, but it was not close to the same. Much of our important collegially would be gone—or substantially dissipated.

While I remained the overall labor relations chief for all of ABC's operations nationwide, I began to feel slowly but increasingly marginalized within the greater Company despite my frequent trips out to Burbank to meet with Marc and his staff, Braverman, as well as other Company officials.

This shift of power to California, delayed as it had been for five years, reversed what had been the underlying organizational structure at ABC since its Leonard Goldenson birth many decades earlier. Los Angeles had always been the satellite. Now, in the much diminished in importance and depopulated New York, we had become the satellite. And starting to experience how the Los Angeles people must have felt all those years at not being at the center of the ABC universe.

A great deal of the vacated space was soon taken over by ESPN as it consolidated its previous real estate around town. With some senior executives moving down from Bristol to have second offices, George Bodenheimer, its president, took over Iger's vacated office that had once belonged to Dan Burke.

The move to the West Coast also meant the death of certain

ABC institutions such as the 22nd floor executive dining room. Once Murphy and Burke's grand experiment in corporate dining egalitarianism, it was no longer deemed important. That decision made sense since New York's vice president population had been seriously denuded. In addition, the space on that floor was needed to build out new executive offices for Eisner, Iger, Braverman, and other Disney executives for their periodic visits to the new, satellite city.

September 11, 2001. 9/11. More than 20 years ago it was like yesterday. Monica and I were on vacation out of the country on a long-planned, Mediterranean cruise. Sailing calmly somewhere off the coast of Sicily, it was shortly before 3 P.M. local time when the news hit the ship that the World Trade Towers had been attacked. About 300 of us—mostly Americans—crowded into the ship's lounge as word spread and soon saw on the giant screen's CNN broadcast, as many screamed, the fall of one and then the second tower. Scared not just for the country and our families back home, we were concerned if the cruise would even continue as well as the safety of the ship itself so long as we were in what was sometimes referred to as *Achille Lauro* waters. So was the captain. He immediately announced he was putting into place some extreme security measures to protect the vessel against any possible terrorist attack.

Our older son, Josh, was in New York at the time studying at Columbia Law School and our other son, Alex, was a sophomore at the University of Michigan in Ann Arbor. Reaching both, we learned while they were rattled just as the rest of us, they were safe and coping—like all in America. But they concerned, as we were, about our isolated situation in European waters and uncertainty about returning to the States now that all international air space had been shut down. I reached out to my office and staff and learned they were all safe.

The morning of the attack the ship's satellite system had been taking down as news channels only the CNN and Al Jazeera cable networks. Using my best negotiating skills, and a lot of luck, wearing my ABC-logo'ed fleece and maybe hat, I convinced the ship's captain to also take down the ABC Television Network. 9/11 was day five of a 12 day cruise that began in Venice and was to end in Athens. For the next week our ship sailed close to warships of the US Navy Sixth Fleet that we later learned had been placed on maximum alert. When we arrived at our remaining ports of call, small police boats encircled and created a safe perimeter around the berthed ship. Police vehicles escorted our tour buses, both front and rear, on all excursions.

Back on the ship, we were riveted to the screen for hours in our cabin watching our star anchor, the superb Peter Jennings, hold America's hand during his endless shifts over many days. Numerous others on board, as we were to discover, were also watching ABC and Peter.

It was incredible seeing Jennings do his long shifts and only occasionally leave the set to take short breaks. It was very reminiscent of the prior year's millennium coverage, minus the tuxedo. Then he would be back a few hours later, seemingly refreshed, with a new shirt and carefully coifed. Peter was an important link for the 900 of us on the ship who were not big Al Jazeera or even CNN fans.

With the passengers mostly Americans, he and the entire ABC News organization kept us tuned in to the unspeakable drama taking place back home for the next five days. Whether it was the smoldering ruins of lower Manhattan, the burning Pentagon, the nervous White House, or the anxious nation at large, we felt attuned to the horror taking place. As I proudly walked around the ship in my ABC News logo'ed fleece during those remaining days at sea, people would see it, catch my eye, and tell me what a great job Peter and ABC News were doing. While I stood ready the entire time to be engaged as a ship-board stringer for ABC News to recount our special circumstances at sea, the assignment desk never called.

It wasn't just Peter of course. ABC News was working on overdrive—camera operators, producers, correspondents, editors, TDs, graphic artists, writers, directors, managers, stagehands, desk assistants, PA's—everybody. Employees represented by our eight or nine different unions, even the people who coifed Peter's hair and did a touch of makeup—ABC News' normal union complement—and our large, non-union management and producing team. And all were doing a magnificent job under very trying circumstances in helping Peter, and the other anchors who occasionally sat in his chair, tell the story non-stop. For a considerable length of time, it was without any commercial interruptions. Americans in their homes or anywhere they might be temporarily stationed or stranded around the globe—like us at sea—were deep into soaking up everything transpiring back home.

The ship's captain held a nonsectarian memorial service, and most everyone showed up in our universal grief. Then we went back to our cabins for more of Jennings' collective-hand holding.

Like other major news anchors, Jennings had never come to the negotiations table with his union, AFTRA. His multi-million dollar deal that some reports said it was in excess of $10 million had put him so far above union-negotiated, news correspondents scale that his presence with his bargaining representatives would have made no difference. I had been in Peter's studio many times in my career and met him of several occasions. He may have known who I was, or recognized my name, but that was of little consequence. Those days at sea though, I felt a huge, almost personal connection. And I was not alone. In fact, I dropped him a few emails—that I knew for certain would never get answered—expressing our pride and relating conditions we Americans stranded on a Mediterranean cruise were experiencing. Like all at ABC and throughout America,

I was tremendously saddened when he passed away from cancer a few short years later.

In another footnote, my son, Alex, is friends with Peter's second wife, Kati Marton, herself a former ABC journalist. They have worked together on a documentary film project that Alex is producing on the life of Raoul Wallenberg, the great holocaust hero.

Our return home from Greece after nearly a week's forced-stay was itself eventful. It only happened with the assistance of ABC's head of travel, Alda Garone, who used all of her influence to get us re-ticketed once the planes started flying. The old Athens airport's security system had been at the very top of the world's list of those most vulnerable to terrorism. Even that day security seemed little better as every passenger arrived and boarded aircraft in great fear. Pilots that day—and for months after until cockpits were retrofitted and fully secured—would announce that we were their last line of defense. Throw shoes, laptops—anything we had, they would say, if there was an attack.

Only after we returned home did I learn of the death of an ABC employee at the World Trade Center that terrible day. A NABET-represented engineer, he had been assigned that fateful morning to his one-day-a-week WABC-TV transmitter work on the top floor of one of the towers. Unable to descend after the plane hit, he cell-phoned in, bravely climbed to the roof, and was never seen again. A well-attended memorial service was later conducted by the station's GM in its lobby where a plaque in his memory to this day still rests.

On that ship sailing through Mediterranean waters on our way to Athens and sharing that terrible experience had been the singer and noted Broadway and television actor, Jerry Orbach. Having seen Jerry at our hotel dining room in Venice just before we boarded the ship, my wife and I had wondered if he was going to be on our cruise. Fate had it that he would. I shared a hot tub on the ship with Jerry, and we chatted a bit about our common business. For the next few years before he passed away, we would run into each other at industry New York black-tie dinners that Jerry frequented. I'd remind him who I was by tossing out our shared hot tub experience on our 9/11 adventure.

When not taking a Mediterranean cruises and sharing hot tubs with actors, occasionally I would go out to the West Coast for some meetings with the AMPTP leaders preparing for major industry-wide talks. It was usually only in the initial preparation phases of serious union negotiations when only a smaller group of a dozen or so of the most senior people would attend and not the entire gaggle of 40, 50, or more. Collegial with all my fellow senior heads, and longtime friends with many, we'd toss around ideas and come up with the outline of a game plan we could all agree upon. Then, I'd beat a hasty retreat back east.

Over time though, I left most of the hectic Hollywood scene to Marc Sandman and his key people. They were the most knowledgable among us who daily dealt with the West Coast based unions and guilds whose members were most directly involved in our prime time production. A few years after the 1995 Disney merger, ABC had joined the AMPTP and had another seat at the table alongside our Disney partner. Going forward at that table, all the talks with the DGA, AFM, WGA, SAG, and IATSE, would be handled, AMPTP-style, by my West Coast group that Marc headed.

In many ways when I attended that handful of AMPTP summit meetings I understood so much better what Michael Ovitz must have meant. That unforgettable comment about labor relations giving him a headache had to be reflective of his talent agent experiences in Los Angeles—with so many of his clients deeply affected by the outcome of those perpetual talks. Many others felt it, too. It was no wonder, with the constant state of Hollywood negotiations.

One major contract or another was expiring and up for renewal. There was the ritualistic preparing for and then the actual talks themselves. It was almost groundhog day—always one guild or union needed this, wanted that, or hated something. It was the constant similarity of issues but with different players, the frequent noises about going out on strike, and attacks on the industry for one reason or another. All of this would give most sane people a severe headache.

This headache, thankfully, was for Marc Sandman and his people to sort out with the AMPTP colleagues and its president. He did an excellent job working with our senior Network business and financial people—particularly since it was often a difficult challenge to get their undivided attention and force some understanding. I trusted Marc to keep me in the loop when he felt necessary.

At serious moments, he'd bounce things off me while keeping me informed. It was always fascinating to hear what other companies or Disney's representative, my good friend and colleague, Robert Johnson, wanted or had to say. Marc had exceeded my expectations when I had moved him to the West Coast and had grown tremendously in his leadership role. I had perfect confidence in his judgment to manage our situations properly.

When on occasion he'd bestow upon me the ultimate compliment of saying he knew exactly what to do because, "that is what Jeff Ruthizer would've done," I always had an enormous sense of pride in him. If I had to fly out for a quick AMPTP summit meeting with Marc, I would, but thankfully with Sandman out there representing our interests and doing as I would have done, there was little need.

The Hollywood talks were long, often emotional, and always serious. Reflecting the complexities of the contracts and the personalities of the key players on both sides, they were downright grueling. It might have been the WGA periodically thumping its chest about more respect for its movie script writers and their product, and striking every ten years or so to prove it. Or, perhaps it was the DGA holding the carriage reins more steadily so that the industry wouldn't crash into a state of chaos. Maybe it was SAG demanding more and better compensation because of new, emerging distribution platforms and reruns. It might have been IATSE pressing for increasingly more producer money to maintain its excellent health and welfare plans.

When temperatures really got raised, there was always plenty going on to cause that headache. Sandman and the people who worked for and with him must have kept a steady supply of headache medication in their office desk drawers and bedroom nightstand tables.

The only industry-wide talks where I preferred to stay directly involved at the table were our two major AFTRA Network television negotiations. One set of talks covered network programs' freelance performers—in the so called "Network Code of Fair Practice." Sometimes referred to as the "Network Code," it was most often called just the "Code." The other AFTRA national contract involved our network staff newspersons—correspondents and anchors such as Jennings, Rather, or Brokaw, even though those mega-stars never showed. It covered them and dozens of on-air journalists employed by ABC News, CBS News, and NBC News in the US and around the globe.

This was the contract that had been involved in the decades-earlier, 1967 news correspondents strike. Every three years we'd prepare for and then sit down in New York to do this one. New issues arose periodically—like correspondents being able to shoot news stories in very limited circumstances—where access was restricted—with the new small cameras. We had wrested this ability away from NABET in our recent talks, and now AFTRA and our newspeople had to be convinced to accept the work. We managed that change—and used it.

There was another AFTRA agreement covering the original three networks' announcers that once had been much more important. Each of the ABC, CBS, and NBC networks had employed a group of individuals—dating back to the 1940s and '50s—who performed exclusive on-air but off-camera announcing duties. Called the "staff announcers," they, and only they, could deliver the necessary station and network ID's, program messages, station breaks, and other off-camera program announcements. Once a powerful and influential group in both AFTRA politics and at the negotiating table, the staff announcers had been performing these announcements from their network announce booths since the three companies' earliest radio days.

When one heard a voice say, "This is the ABC Television Network," "Stay tuned to the Columbia Broadcasting System," or, in the really old television days, "You are watching the *NBC News Caravan With John Cameron Swayze,* it had to be one of these staff announcers. It was an all-male group. The men were blessed with deep, penetrating, silky voices that were intended to hold viewers' attention and listeners' interest—between and during program breaks—with each syllable or word spoken and every phrase carefully enunciated.

The announcing groups that worked for ABC, CBS and NBC had many famous voices and names familiar to millions of Americans. ABC's Fred Foy announcing decades earlier for *The Lone Ranger* was one. NBC's Don Pardo from its *Saturday Night Life* for many decades became perhaps the most famous—maybe the last who was still working before he died in 2014 after a 70-year tenure.

Once upon a time the announcements had to be delivered not only exclusively by this group but also performed live. From network sign-on to sign-off, one of these staff announcers had to be sitting in the network announce booth to deliver these periodic messages. But beginning in 1968, the year I started, as the networks discovered they needed a mix of other voices and people to do it, the exclusive duties and live requirements were negotiated away in return for lifetime employment guarantees—until each announcer on the special list of about 25 at each network died or retired at age 65. Recording and playback equipment technology dramatically changed how these announcements were made and broadcast. By the early 2000s, only a handful of these men at each network were still employed.

New staff or freelance voices were added and for the first time, female announcers were engaged. The freelance announcing community became more important as the networks turned increasingly to freelance voices to deliver program announcements instead of the diminishing group of staff announcers.

By the time I had returned to the networks in 1987, AFTRA's former head, Bud Wolff, my old friend from my first tour of duty days and fellow '71 Detroit-combatant, had retired. Bud's assistant, John Hall, once a high official with the IA, had taken his place. Hall led the three-network AFTRA talks for a number of years in the '90s before a new generation of AFTRA leaders emerged. First Bruce York, it was now Greg Hessinger who was greeting us at our next set of AFTRA Code freelance negotiations at the 2001 table.

Most of its covered work involved soap operas, sports events, talk shows, and late night programing. It covered the once popular but now nearly extinct genre of the weekly prime time variety shows—*Milton Berle, Bob Hope, Tom Jones, The Ed Sullivan Show, Dean Martin, Sonny & Cher,* and perhaps the last ever—in its short, ABC 1988 run—*The Dolly Parton Show.* Formerly a large source of AFTRA network employment, now in 2001 audience tastes had changed considerably. New forms of programs had come along—like reality shows. Game and quiz shows, as had been hosted by my old friend, Gene Rayburn for *The Match Game,* were still legion and hot—*Jeopardy, Wheel of Fortune,* and *the Price is Right.* Also covered by the AFTRA agreement were the annual award specials—The *Oscars, Emmys, Grammys, Tonys,* and *Country Music Awards*—employing lots of dancers and singers in big production numbers. But the three networks' nearly dozen soaps—employing hundreds of principal actors and many hundreds more extras, perhaps thousands—were the major subject of our Code talks.

The three networks, now having been joined at the table for a number of years by Fox after it became the fourth network, remained in charge of the AFTRA negotiations. The AMPTP companies sat with us as partners when these talks took place. Usually however, they left the central bargaining to us and normally deferred to our more experienced judgments because we were the major Code producers and employers of AFTRA talent. ABC—because of our daytime serials that we uniquely produced ourselves—was the largest employer of AFTRA talent.

I took over as the co-chair of these negotiations at the request of my NBC, Fox and CBS counterparts around the time when CBS' Jim Sirmons, its longtime labor relations head and consistent chair of these Code talks, retired. Being the management-side chair in any of these industry-wide negotiations brought with it a whole range of bargaining challenges and leadership skills.

Reaching consensus across a broad front over a panoply of issues just on our management side sometimes took twists and turns. And then convincing the union committee to accept our joint positions was the much bigger challenge. I took on this role in three successive Code talks over about a decade. It was only because the AFTRA leaders were as good as they were that we managed each time—despite temporary disruptions and some periodic across the table skirmishes—to get unanimously recommended deals. Ratified contracts followed.

On three year cycles, the networks prepared for and then went through the extended period for these freelance negotiations. The bargaining process with our three-network team of maybe a dozen normally began with a week on the West Coast for the benefit of the performers on television shows based there. Then we'd shift to New York where the bulk of the shows were based for several additional weeks. We'd get a large attendance of observers from the acting community on both coasts—mostly from the hundreds of soap opera actors.

At the special freelance announcers' sessions, a number of the America's best known voices would fly in to protect their speaking interests. A few of the truly most successful even used their own planes.

Once during talks on the West Coast in the mid-'90s, a few of us ran into the popular actor, Telly Savalas. It was in the lobby of a major hotel in Hollywood that someone recognized Telly because of his unique bald head. A celebrated television and movie star from a number of hits including CBS's cop-drama, *Kojak,* and *The Dirty Dozen* movie, he was exuberantly friendly. He really began engaging with us when we told him we were network negotiators in town to bargain with one of his unions, AFTRA.

Giving off a big laugh, he went on with a bit of a pep talk about how we looked like tough bargainers. Coming from Theo Kojak himself, it was a big compliment. We only wished we had him on our side, sucking on his near-trademarked lollipops. Every time over the years that I would return to Los Angeles for another set of AFTRA Code talks, I thought of Telly—the one "who loves ya, baby."

Later on, as I was researching Savalas in preparation for this writing, I found out Telly ironically died in the very same hotel where we had met him, the Sheraton Universal. Even more of a coincidence, I discovered that he had in the 1950s worked, before his acting career began, as a producer and director at ABC News and then became involved in our sports production. After his rise to the position of executive producer of ABC's legendary *Gillette Cavalcade of Sports,* he gave Howard Cosell, ABC's famous sports commentator, his first announcing job. You can't make this stuff up—Howard Cosell *and* Telly Savalas. Can anyone familiar with both of these unique personalities picture *that pair* in the studio together?

Soaps—despite their gradual decline to ratings beginning to approach half of what they were 20 years previous—were still big in 2001. The daily dozen still employed in their totality probably a few thousand principles, minor characters, and multitudes of extras. Their production issues about length of workday, rest periods, and remotes, plus foreign and domestic residual issues, usually dominated the talks. Daytime drama acting jobs were hard and stressful. Normally for many it was at least three and maybe five days a week. Memorizing lines—with script changes sometimes put into actors' hands just hours and sometimes even minutes before taping—frequently made for very difficult circumstances.

It was well-known for decades that serials—with its many thousands of cast members since network television daytime dramas had started in the 1950s and '60s, after the migration from radio—was the fertile breeding ground for the Hollywood movie industry. It was like having a baseball minor league farm system. Starting their careers in relatively minor roles before moving to ultimate film stardom were a countless number of actors. Lawrence Fishburne, Julianne Moore, Josh Duhamel, Alec Baldwin, Morgan Freeman, Demi Moore, and Mark Hamill were just a few. Others were Leonardo DiCaprio, Ray Liotta, Brad Pitt, Meg Ryan, Kevin Bacon, Kathy Bates, Robin Wright, and Tom Selleck. Even Bryan Cranston, Melissa Leo, and Tommie Lee Jones started in television soap operas. Dozens more.

Hugely popular and profitable in their prime, soaps had been the mainstay of the ABC Television Network's financial success for many years. At one point before my 1968 arrival—in the golden era of daytime drama—there were as many as 16 on the three networks' air. ABC had as many as six. But by the fall of '01, soap operas had been slipping badly in the ratings—and profits—and not just at ABC but for the other two legacy networks as well. People's viewing tastes had been rapidly changing. The once slavishly-loyal soap audiences were disappearing not just because of cable penetration and channel proliferation but also because of new forms of entertainment—the internet, home computers, and video games. DVD's had already done their damage. Social media would within a few more years take away even more daytime eyeballs.

In fact, soap ratings and profitability were to slip so rapidly that daytime serials would nearly completely die within another decade. By the beginning of the next decade—in 2010, after I had retired—there were only a few left across all the networks. And most of those would later crash and burn in the succeeding year or two as the networks finally faced up to their fate. By 2022, ABC would have standing only a largely diminished *General Hospital*—having lasted an incredible 59 years.

AFTRA and its performers meeting with us at the 2001 table had serious concerns. First among the worries that the acting community shared with the producers was most certainly the genre's remaining longevity. But that was something we couldn't bargain let alone predict. ABC had cancelled by this time years before its two less popular half-hours—*Ryan's Hope* and *Loving*. It still had its trio of the more successful, one-hour soaps—*General Hospital, One Life to Live, and All My Children*.

When the AFTRA negotiations after the Los Angeles week shifted to the East Coast, another group of the daytime actors from all of New York's produced serials would populate our talks whenever their busy schedules allowed. Susan Lucci—despite her 18 Emmy nominations—was a frequent no-show, but other major stars over the years sometimes came. Once, I had been roundly chewed out by Ruth Warrick—the longtime cast member of *All My Children*. Ruth's career had gone the other way—a film star decades earlier when she had a major role in Orson Welles' 1941 classic for RKO Pictures, *Citizen Kane*. We'd all hang out a bit chatting during breaks in the hallway outside of the big CBS conference room. Often from just mingling, the actors would find out that the network labor chiefs were not really such horrible people after all.

Beth Holland, still a friend today in her 90s, had been the president of the New York local of AFTRA. New York was the biggest and most influential of all the AFTRA locals. Beth, an accomplished dramatic stage and TV performer in her acting days, always had an elegant, theatrical-air about her. The presidents of AFTRA's two major locals in New York and Los Angeles sat on its bargaining committee. There, she'd be seated next to the union's chief negotiator—maybe John Hall or Bruce York in those days—playing a prominent role in the talks.

Outside in the hallway during a break, we happened to be at the coffee pot and danish tray at the same time the day we first met. And we just started talking. Later on, Beth confided in me, and still repeats the story to this day, that she was chided by one of her hardliners for talking to a member of "management." Never shy in responding to anyone, she answered that she thought ABC's head labor guy was not "that bad." High praise indeed from this lovely and highly talented performer—whom I back then and still today hugely adore.

On AFTRA's central bargaining committee at every three year interval since I had returned to ABC in the late '80s sat the distinguished serial actor, Don Hastings. Don was a longtime star from the CBS soap opera, *As the World Turns*. But as I was to discover, he had been one of my childhood heroes. As a teenager, he had played the role of the Video Ranger on the early '50's drama on the defunct Dumont television network—*Captain Video and His Video Rangers*. As a kid growing up during that era, I was one of Captain Video's biggest fans—a video ranger sitting at home and watching the program in my family's basement on our tiny 10 inch, GE black and white screen.

At the end of every show the staff announcer would recite—typical of the time—the major cast credits. He'd say in his deepest of tones, "The role of the video ranger was played by Don Hastings." For some reason, that phrase and name stuck in my mind for over 30 years. When we first met across the AFTRA table in 1988 and I heard his name mentioned, it was instant recognition. Outside in the hall during a break, I started chatting with Don and told him of our shared Dumont history. Every three years—well into the first decade of the 21st century—we'd engage in warm conversation on the sidelines out in the hallways of the CBS building's labor relations floor during breaks. A lovely gentleman, always in the most handsome of tweedy sports jackets each time we met, he was barely older than I was at the time I first saw him on Dumont as the Ranger.

Another hero of mine growing up on Long Island and listening to rock 'n roll radio in its early days was the noted disc jockey from the old *Music Radio WABC 77* Top 40 days, Dan Ingram. Now he was now a featured performer on AFTRA's central bargaining committee every three years. I just loved to hear Dan's deep, penetrating DJ voice and distinctive inflection when he said my name, "Jeffrey," while commenting on something or asking a question across the table.

AFTRA's bargainers in 2001 led by Hessinger, who would go on in a few years to head SAG, were once again knowledgable and wise. Committed to industry peace, after many weeks of stressful talks and some late and near all-night sessions, the final deal would be reached in November. The few months earlier September 9/11 terrorist attacks on the World Trade Center had temporarily disrupted talks. But after a brief postponement, we resumed, overcame that obstacle, and made the deal. Not feeling the need to go to its membership for a strike vote, unlike some of its sibling unions and guilds who routinely took premature and often incendiary strike tallies, AFTRA's philosophy did not believe threats through early strike votes were necessary when reason at the bargaining table had normally proven successful.

In fact, only once in 75 years of bargaining did AFTRA and its performers ever find it necessary to go out on strike against the three networks. That happened, as previously outlined in these pages, in 1967. And it was over a dispute having nothing to do with actors but rather network news correspondents. It's often just smart leadership that makes the difference between settlements and work stoppages. This was once again the case in 2001.

Over the decades, AFTRA and its rival actors' union, SAG, periodically flirted with each other in talks over a possible merger. The early 2000s were no exception. The stars though would not align for another decade—in 2012. When that merger process would finally materialize, AFTRA, as a distinct labor organization representing both radio DJs and television performers as well as broadcast journalists, after its rich history, would virtually drop off the face of the planet.

It was around this time that even more pressure was building on ABC News from corporate management to find new ways to reduce both union and non-union staffing and costs. Bureaus in the US and around the world had been shuttered. Now more bureau locations followed suit—like Miami, where I accompanied News' Bob Murphy on his closing mission. Different ways of covering news with far fewer people, and new combinations, were being examined. There were a few painful, non-union staff reductions amounting to hundreds of jobs each time as ABC cut back and learned to live with a smaller work force.

At that stage, no one was sure if there was a solution to the constantly escalating network news costs. Neither revenues nor profits from our more profitable *Good Morning America* as well as our other news programs were growing sufficiently to cover ABC's necessary news footprint both domestically and around the world. Sending producers, correspondents, and crews was expensive. One of the major problems ABC News faced was not having any 24-hour cable news outlet, like NBC's, on which it could lay off some of its production costs.

One day I got a call to come over to ABC News president David Westin's office. Westin wanted to give me a heads-up on a future meeting he was planning with CNN. A handful of senior executives from both companies were going to sit down secretly off-campus to explore various ways to combine news crews or other operations to gain some real savings. David wanted me there to assist in the search to find any possible way to make it happen. Non-union CNN, which brought along its own labor relations expert, was extremely wary of any combination for fear it could contaminate its union-free status. Although it turned out to be an interesting and robust conversation, it was, as most of us thought going in, a mission impossible.

Some press reports later surfaced that CBS News, like us without any cable news channel to help amortize its steadily rising news gathering costs, was also courting CNN for the same purpose. Since CBS was union with its IBEW, any possible combination with non-union CNN died there, too, for the same reasons that our's had gone nowhere.

What developed months later was another round of even more intriguing talks. David Westin invited me to a highly confidential meeting at CBS among a handful of top ABC News and CBS News executives to explore, as each of us had separately done with CNN, some possible news combinations of our own. Two fierce competitors meeting like this, searching for a possible joint working structure, was truly extraordinary.

Although we shared other news room unions such as the WGA, our NABET structure and CBS's IBEW could not possibly be mixed. These secret talks died, too. A leaked story that later appeared in one of New York's tabloids upset some senior ABC News' officials who by necessity had been left in the dark—and many others within both news organizations.

CBS News had its famous *60 Minutes*. Roone Arledge's answer when he took over ABC News was its weekly *20/20*. Since its 1978 debut, many hundreds of stories had been produced and broadcast. Hosted by Barbara Walters and Hugh Downs, *20/20* features were produced by a myriad of non-union producers. However, their writing services were covered under the WGA freelance agreement. For every story they wrote that was broadcast or re-run, they were entitled to certain WGA-mandated minimum fee compensation that was most often credited against their high producing salaries. ABC News, however, was required to make actual dollar contributions to the WGA pension plan for each story written by each such individual and subsequently broadcast or rebroadcast.

For some reason lost to history, network finance people had since nearly the program's inception neglected to do so. A WGA pension plan auditor caught the error. Years went by as we arm-wrestled over the audit findings with the WGA's head official in New York, Mona Mangan.

Mona, one of the entertainment industry's few female union leaders, for years had shared with me many moments of high tension and explosive drama across the bargaining table. Once in my frustrations I had committed the unpardonable sin—much to her delight—of calling her Monica. Quickly correcting myself, she never let me forget this slip of tongue. Over the decades together, depending upon the particular season in which we found ourselves, we alternated between being friendly and not-so friendly adversaries.

Our battle over proper pension contributions, and appropriate interest during this two-decade absence, was just another example of our tenuous relationship. Lunches to make and keep the peace— even nice ones—usually didn't help. The venue normally suggested by Mona was her favorite New York restaurant, Le Bernardin. The Company, of course in situations like this where we were looking for some accommodation, was expected to pick up the tab. And this place was not cheap. Usually pleasant-enough experiences—especially after our obligatory second glass of wine—the better Le Bernardin moments were not sufficiently remembered to change our underlying karma.

It became a giant chess match that took years to research properly and finally resolve. During that period, I drove a few of ABC News' best and busiest producers more than a little nuts in the pursuit of reconstructing a complete and accurate set of records, dating back over 20 years. Every *20/20* show ever produced had to be found from paper records that had long before been put into the warehouse, and then analyzed. Potentially, we were talking millions of dollars in liability. Mona ultimately corralled me into flying out to a WGA pension plan meeting in Los Angeles on a special mission with a virtual $1 million settlement check locked away in my briefcase. It pained me deeply to turn it over into her gleefully-awaiting hands.

30
CHAPTER

Planning for More Olympic Gold

It was as Bob Iger had said to me years before, "Jeff, this is your Olympics." It would be six years since we had started the last set of NABET talks but four since they had been settled. So once again, as the end of the four-year cycle was approaching for another negotiations with this union, we had to go deep into our best training mode. I had to assemble another outstanding team and make sure all of us, and the Company-at-large, were prepared for one more strenuous competition. The 2003 games were just over the horizon. Our 2002 training routine had to be intense because the arena in which we would be competing allowed for neither errors nor do-overs.

With Alan Nesbitt and Sean Quinn, and frequently Marc Sandman joining us, we travelled the country on another listening tour taking our normal seismic readings. What we learned was that after so many changes had taken place over the past near decade and a half, so much more still bubbled to the surface. Too many hampering vestiges of the old, pre-Cap Cities contract still existed— too many defiances of just common sense, operating efficiency, and sound business practices. And we were not operating in a vacuum— NBC and CBS's most recent gains were all too real and had to be considered. Moreover, technology's march was relentless and affected everything. In many ways I was sorry to face this reality because I had hoped that our stressful days from the previous decade would be over.

I started with a belief that the NABET which would appear before us would be a different creature from the one we had battled so fiercely during the previous NABET War. Something told me valuable lessons had been learned. Semi-annual meetings had resumed and had contributed to a better labor relations atmosphere. Grievances were way down and there was starting to be far fewer arbitrations.

Some of the change was attitudinal, but much stemmed from the downsized contract itself and the disappearance of so many gopher holes. Helping greatly to bring about this new attitude was the fact that most of the spoilers were gone. Those few local leaders who had been the most difficult and unreasonable to deal with were no longer around. They had been replaced by elected officials who appeared to be more moderate in both substance and tone. While the air was not nearly as toxic and belligerence as a currency seemed to be gone, some on my side though felt it was lurking just beneath the surface.

We soon learned that the union bargaining committee that we would be dealing with at our next talks would be different. One or two would be from the ranks and not be the still-around local presidents who were part of the major chaos at the 1997-'99 table. That was a hopeful sign that perhaps memberships were awakening. After all, this was their Olympiad too. They had the same right as we did to change their competing athletes to bring back the most gold. The Clark and Krieger committee with whom we would be dealing was a mix of the old, the new, and the unknown.

Clark must have guessed we would be coming in again with another sizable set of meaty proposals. Trying to avoid another donnybrook and attempting to optimize his own hand, he approached me with a novel idea. Suggesting that each side come in with only ten proposals and start our talks not only early but also meet for a limited two week span, it wasn't at all what we wanted. So I said no.

Preparing my usual strategic plan, copies went to Braverman, Iger, and the other senior leaders for their understanding and approval, which soon came. In that plan I presented not only our own needs but also an analysis of what we hoped would be a new NABET. No way, we thought, could it allow its membership to suffer financially so badly again from its own miscues.

My strong hunch was that the loud displays of anger and nasty tactics—unprecedented in the industry and so counterproductive—would be banished from the table. The failed bargaining strategy of stall, delay, disrupt, deny, and obfuscate probably would not be repeated. In the back of my mind, I had this feeling that they had finally figured out they could do far better if they actually bargained and not force an impasse. But, of course this was just idle speculation.

Talks would go ahead as originally planned beginning in late February for five weeks and scheduled to end March 31. Again, we chose the Washington area. But this time it would be in Virginia—outside of the capital—in Tyson's Corner, not far from Dulles Airport. It was shortly after the infamous "Washington sniper" killing spree. For a while before the terrorists were apprehended, these shootings had thrown both sides into doubt over whether the Washington area would be wise choice for our meetings.

Because of the recent financial crisis resulting from the Dotcom bubble meltdown, there was suddenly a lot of hotel rooms and good meeting space available at extremely attractive rates. We needed a large area that we could secure to set up our offices. The local

Sheraton was ideal. They stayed nearby at an Embassy Suites and we'd do our normal drive over for multiple-times-a-day, six days-a-week, sessions.

My administrative assistant, Jacqueline Greco, and her team arrived a few days early to convert the space into what was necessary for our month's stay. It actually was quite an elaborate logistical undertaking that Jacqueline supervised. Leased high speed and volume printers, big conference room tables, secretarial desks, refrigerators, telephones, couches, lots of desk top computers, and most importantly an industrial-sized coffee maker, had to be arranged from local vendors. As we were now typically doing, the offices had to be swept for any possible listening devices before we moved in, and repeated several times during our stay.

While Clark and chief negotiator Krieger's team had a new composition, our nearly a score remained largely the same. Now mostly veterans from the prior three sets of talks over the past decade and a half but with a few key substitutions, it was senior operating executives and my several lawyers. Larry Pollock had retired as head of the TV Station group a year or two earlier and Water Liss had taken over.

Like Larry before him, Walter wanted his EVP, Alan Nesbitt, and all of his station presidents present and participating throughout. Their involvement was again welcomed by me. BOE's chief Preston Davis, my strong, right negotiating arm from the operational side, brought one or two senior lieutenants. We had a radio representative, a senior Sports executive and a pair of ABC News vice presidents from New York and Washington. Our Television Station group engineering vice presidents—Dave Converse and Jim Casabella—were first timers. Others would float in and out as needed.

It was in totality a good group of my most savvy NABET-contract people and smart broadcasting executives. Most of them had by now become familiar to the ebb and flow of the bargaining process, and while once reticent to speak up were now much more comfortable and adept in doing so.

Preston Davis and Alan Nesbitt were again my key operational allies—as they had been in our preparations. We three later became the sidebar committee after Clark raised the subject. Even though newly-found, it was little used until the later, Chicago phases. NABET's previous negotiating style for decades had been everything had to be on-the-record and at the table. Exploring "what-ifs," as other unions commonly did, had been avoided. It was encouraging when Clark first approached me. Again, what it was saying was that the NABET leaders, after the disastrous last round, had decided it needed to re-invent itself. Starting to explore side-barring, it was putting its toes into the informal negotiations waters to test the temperature.

Marc Sandman and Sean Quinn, my two chief labor lieutenants, had worked closely with me and a few other of my lawyers for months to produce our set of proposals. Marc had been with me now for 12 years, had become an extremely good negotiator and was very NABET-worthy. Sean had grown tremendously since joining me five years earlier—having mastered that long and steep labor relations learning curve. The three of us did a fast trip across the country with the NABET leaders to do a first round of the non-engineering unit negotiations before we arrived in Virginia.

What greeted the NABET committee that first day in Virginia was another package of well over 100 proposals. Their Olympic team presented us with its own thick set. If the mutually-challenging packages did not present a gloomy enough picture for the month ahead, we'd soon experience a particularly harsh winter of snow, ice, and deep cold. It was as if Dan Burke's wishes for the harshness of Alaska had suddenly materialized.

Alex Wallau had become Network president in 2000 after the former president had resigned because she did not want to relocate to the West Coast. Flying in from Los Angeles, he delivered his opening comments in the tradition of Dan Burke and Bob Iger. It was a good speech about competition and restrictions. Coming out of ABC Sports management where he also did some on-air boxing commentary, he knew the NABET situation from the ground level. Morty Bahr came that first morning and made his own speech. From its mild tone and the fact that he was not accompanied by CWA vice presidents, it was another sign that perhaps the union side was going to chart a new course.

This time I had asked TV Network financial vice president, Steve Sommer, to join my team. A trustee along with me on the ABC-NABET pension plan and well-respected by both sides, his presence was vital so we could explain and hopefully better realize certain pension fund changes that were among our top proposals. His help and expertise, along with that of consulting actuaries and benefits attorneys we also brought in, would be enormously helpful in bringing about our ultimate negotiated resolution.

Despite our once again healthy agenda, talks started off just as I had been hoping—a lot more smoothly than last time. The nastiness and belligerence seemed to be gone. As we kept pressing for changes with our usual litany of argued inefficiencies, limitations, and restrictions, and it was all resisted, it was not met with the vehemence and high tension from the time previous. Meeting technological advances and matching competitive changes, as we were seeking, while not embraced, were not viciously attacked.

We were actually hearing comments from one or two committee members that we should not expect to get all the contract fixes we were seeking in just one negotiations. While daily propaganda releases and telephone bulletins were still going out daily, they were relatively mild in both tone and tenor in comparison with the previous talks. Despite not agreeing to much and even with some heated moments, discussions were by and large proceeding normally—much as they would have with any other union involved in a difficult set of talks.

Despite everyone's best efforts, bargaining was not completed in Tysons Corners by the March 31 expiration date. War intervened. America went to war. A real war of "shock and awe," live bullets, and potentially heavy casualties. On March 20, 2003, George W. Bush's American military invaded Iraq to drive Saddam Hussein from power and rid the country of weapons of mass destruction. The Iraqi leader had been number one on the 1998 NABET rat's most hated list when I had only managed to gain the number four slot.

Negotiations had to be suspended because our Network and stations were sending their reporters and NABET news crews overseas to cover the war. It was in the national interest, one could say our patriotic duty, that we suspend talks during the crisis. Some on my team had to depart immediately after Bush spoke to get their houses in order. Clark and I quickly agreed, broke off talks, and signed a six-week extension agreement. We then issued a joint press release that basically said NABET and ABC had joined forces to help the US go to war. Call it our patriotic duty. By necessity, that extension to mid-May guaranteed retroactivity to March 31 in return for continued protection against strikes.

When talks resumed in May after America's lightning victory, we met in Chicago for two weeks. When no deal was made despite real bargaining over issues big and small, and the beginning of what some saw as progress, we broke off again amicably and scheduled another round in Chicago for later that summer.

Our second round of Chicago talks in early August yielded the desired result. Following an intense five days of off-the-record bargaining. Deep in the sub-basement of the Hyatt hotel, many escalators down, Preston Davis, Alan Nesbitt and I did much shuttling back and forth between rooms to meet with Clark's three-person sidebar committee to work out the last details. Once again, loss of retroactivity was staring them in the face.

The NABET committee apparently well-remembered the failed

process and resulting pain from the decade previous. They knew full- well they could not possibly win a strike or risk another huge loss of retroactivity. This time they accepted our final offer and agreed to unanimously recommend it to the membership. All groups nationwide ratified six weeks later, so no retroactivity was lost.

It had been a topsy-turvy type of negotiations. But it was accomplished without the histrionics from the previous time. Reason, but more important, practicality had prevailed. Having stuck their toes in the side-barring waters, they had actually bargained. With it all, the Company achieved enough of what we had initially set out to accomplish. Compromises in our positions had been made, and their's. The result was a peaceful settlement.

Our package was much like previous ones in that it resulted in tens of millions of dollars in projected operational savings over the four year term of that contract from the many efficiencies gained. The union once more got a healthy buyout for which many had been hoping—helping to seal the deal by securing many votes. After ratification, we travelled the country once again giving tutorials to management so that all properties could take full advantage of the various changes and capture the savings.

Voiding grievance resolutions and arbitration decisions were again among our gains along with another round of removing or modifying restrictive and inefficient work rules and jurisdictional requirements. Visions of far fewer grievances and wasted lawyer and management time constantly were racing through my head. That trend which already started would only accelerate as more contractual tripping clauses were lifted.

Probably the biggest battle waged was over "Parkervision." In its simplest definition, it was a new computer automation system in our TV station news studios that allowed the pre-setting of many show elements that previously had been done manually during the show. Once operational, the new technology would permit stations to downsize a number of camera operators and other studio technicians —resulting in a significant payroll savings.

Our two TV Station group engineering chiefs, Dave Converse and Jim Casabella, had spent a year devoted to the Parkervision project. Affectionately referred to by us as the Smith Brothers because of their remarkable resemblance to the famed, cough-drop, bearded duo, the pair were engineering gurus and helped us in very great measures. Jim was once a NABET engineer himself at KGO-TV in San Francisco where we had first met in 1987, before his coming over to management. A former US Navy atomic-vessel submariner, he knew how to navigate silently and deep under both the uncharted North Pole as well as through the churning NABET waters.

Our contest with NABET was not over the system itself, now permitted under our flexible computer language. It was rather over who the Parkervision operator would be. The two possible choices were either the technical director (TD), as NABET wanted, or the program director. In the past, these two individuals had sat next to one another in the control room where the director called the camera shots and various show elements and the TD "punched up" his calls on the control panel. Now with Parkervision loaded and calling the preset shots, the question was which of these two would be programming the system that would run the show.

Convinced that the computer operation work presetting the show was not technical in nature but instead creative, we decided it should be in hands of the show's director and not the TD. At our operations that meant the DGA—representing the director—would get the work. Upsetting to NABET because of its consequential impact on TD's, the highest paid and most signifiant of NABET positions, we nevertheless held firm that it had to be the show director. Fighting hard, the union reluctantly but finally agreed.

When we instituted Parkervision at all our stations, we did so largely as a pioneer among group broadcasters. It was a huge shift in the dynamics of studio operations. The net effect, with technology having changed so much as the result of automation, computers, robotic cameras, and now this new system, was that our TV studios and control rooms would have fewer NABET technicians and costs would be substantially reduced. Parkervision would soon also be introduced in our Network studios.

Having promised the union we would attempt to find some path forward whereby both unions could meet and perhaps reach some accommodations with each other based upon the jurisdictional change we had just negotiated, we set up a tripartite summit. Before meeting at DGA's New York headquarters a few weeks after the deal was done, ABC made it clear we would have to sign off on any arrangement that might be reached between the two unions. However, the all-day discussions went nowhere when the DGA rejected compromises NABET demanded which the DGA saw as encroaching upon its newly granted Parkervision jurisdiction.

The other major Company gain in this negotiations was the beginning of fixing the Company's pension plan liability problem. NABET was unique among ABC's many unions in having its own defined benefit pension plan. Dated in its origins to the union's bargaining gain in the early 1960s, the ABC-NABET plan was under joint trustee management. Providing excellent pensions, it was widely recognized they were among the very best for technicians in the industry.

The way the plan was structured, benefit formulas and changes were determined by the plan's trustees rather than by the bargaining parties. ABC over the years had contributed large amounts into the plan, starting at a rate of about $10 million annually. Assets had grown enormously under wise trustee management and by 2003 probably were worth, despite recent big drops attributable to the Dotcom crash, somewhere around $500 million. In 2022, its asset base, despite paying many tens of millions in benefits each year, has probably grown to just south of $1billion, prior to the recent losses.

Without getting overly technical, the stock market's crash following '02's Dotcom bubble had been a wakeup call to the Walt Disney Company's senior financial people. It forced them, and then us, the labor negotiators, to focus on the serious liability the Walt Disney Company would face if the plan continued to sustain huge, non-recoverable losses in major stock market drops. We were looking at potentially hundreds of millions. Normally a risk shared by all contributing employers, in this plan there were no others—it was only ABC/Disney contributing. We therefore proposed ending the defined benefit nature of the plan and substituting another formula that would best protect the Walt Disney Company from any such future financial jeopardy. NABET, not surprisingly, was vehemently opposed.

Many days were devoted to this subject—with endless presentations from differing actuaries. Finally, the union convinced us to drop our proposal to end the defined benefit plan. We came up with and settled on a different approach. One of the key ways to help fix the stratospheric, future potential liability issue was to make the bargaining parties—the union and the Company—rather than the plan's trustees, responsible for future benefit changes.

Going forward, future changes in retirement benefits would be managed only at the bargaining table. The change was negotiated only after actuarial experts in which the Company and union had confidence, including the union's own expert plan trustees, helped us establish the new contract formulas. Steve Sommer's presence was instrumental. As were some expert Proskauer benefits lawyers. From 2003 forward, the subject of pension benefits, like every other term and condition of employment, would be in the hands of the union and Company together and dealt with as part of our overall negotiations.

A nice perk of my senior executive status over the years continued to be attending various entertainment industry, black tie events. Normally held at New York's finest hotels such as the

Waldorf Astoria, the Pierre, or the Hilton, there was always an industry or union celebration of one kind or another.

One of New York's major unions was IATSE Local 52. It was big, powerful, and did most of the production work on theatrical films and TV or cable productions shot in the New York City metropolitan area. Celebrating its 75th anniversary, it threw a gala dinner in the grand ballroom at the Waldorf-Astoria for its members and invited guests. Casts and crews from many of its TV shows shot in the New York area were expected to be there as were executives from many entertainment companies. The Local 52 boys put the arm on me for ABC to buy a table and I was glad to comply.

Before the dinner was the usual cocktail hour in the ballroom's outer reception rooms. Running into Jerry Orbach, a habitué at these industry black tie events, then starring in *Law and Order,* we laughed when I reminded him about the hot tub incident on the infamous 9/11 cruise a few years before. I had used that secret code as my triggering remark three or four times previous to get him to remember that we once met on that fateful Mediterranean journey.

Monica went off to the ladies room. I was standing at one of the bars with my drink awaiting her return when a celebrated actor and major thug whom I immediately recognized from HBO's hit, *The Sopranos,* came up next to me. While he was ordering his drink, I had glanced over and sure enough it was Paulie Walnuts. Played so well by the actor Tony Sirico, Paulie was one of our favorite gangsters on the series. I proceeded to say hello, introduced myself of course as an ABC executive, and told him of our great love for the show and admiration of him personally. I added how disappointed my wife, off at the ladies, would be when she found out she had blown the opportunity to meet her favorite character.

At that moment the lights dimmed to advise the throng that the cocktail party was over and we should proceed into the ballroom for dinner. Sirico, in his true Paulie Walnuts accent and voice, after getting his drink and about to depart, said, "Hey Jeff, stop by at

Table 'XX' and bring your wife so I can meet her. We're all there."
Having related the story to a thrilled Monica about meeting Sirico
upon her return to me at the bar, later about halfway through the
dinner we went over to Table 'XX' to visit. Recognizing me as we
approached, he got up from his seat to greet us.

It turned out as he had intimated that this was *The Sopranos*
cast table. They were all there—Tony himself, played by James
Gandolfini, Uncle Junior, the son, the daughter, Lorraine Bracco
who played Tony's shrink, Dr. Melfi, Tony's wife Carmela—played
so deliciously by Edie Falco—and my new best friend, Paulie
Walnuts. I introduced Monica to Sirico, who then graciously took
us around the table and introduced us to the entire group. It was all
those fascinating characters who had been our closest companions
every Sunday on HBO at 9 P.M. for nearly ten years.

Tony Soprano was the first. He rose from his chair as Paulie
Walnuts introduced him to Monica, reached for her offered hand,
and proceeded, in a very Italian, romantic style from another era, to
kiss it. A kiss on the hand from Tony Soprano. It could have been a
lot worse. We chatted for a few minutes and then completed our trip
around the table saying hello to them all as they stood to greet us.

Going back to our very envious table for dessert, what a way
it was to finish the evening. First Jerry Orbach, my fellow 9/11
sailor and tough cop, then the thug Paulie Walnuts, and last it
was Tony Soprano himself–the world's number one hoodlum—
followed by the whole cast. It was all thanks to Local 52's bending
but fortunately not breaking my arm. In the parking garage after
the dinner we ran into Lorraine Bracco's Dr. Melfi again for a final
goodbye. It was a suitable ending for one of the best evenings we
ever had.

31
CHAPTER

Bob Iger Assumes Command

In the spring of 2005 there was a thunderous upheaval at Disney when Michael Eisner was forced out as CEO and the job given to COO Bob Iger. It had been widely reported in the press for some time that members of the board had grown increasingly unhappy with Eisner's running the Company. Now they finally acted to remove him. I can tell you there was great joy in our Mudville when this Casey went down at the plate. For one reason, there was a feeling among many that he had been grossly overpaid. The Disney board back in the late 1990s had one year given him a $500 million stock grant that just struck many people of all ranks as absurd and just plain wrong. It was more than the entire profit of the ABC Network that year.

Aside from press releases and letters to shareholders at annual meeting time, after a decade, New York's senior executive cadre at my vice presidential level hardly knew him. Of course, everyone in the Company had heard much in our early days about his highly publicized battle with Jeffrey Katzenberg and his giant error in hiring, and then firing, Michael Ovitz. Both of these were embarrassing episodes that wound up costing the Walt Disney Company hundreds of millions of dollars. The payments were also the subject of much razzing from unions at the bargaining table during moments I was busy fighting off their big wage increase demands.

Many were comparing his distance and aloofness to the closeness and warmth we were all so fortunate to have experienced with Bob Iger and our prior leaders—Tom Murphy and Dan Burke. His first appearance before ABC senior executives had been on the Phoenix stage in 1996 when he pranced around with costumed Disney characters in the impressive M-I-C-K-E-Y-M-O-U-S-E routine. I had managed a few words with him later that night—the only time we ever exchanged words. He showed up again with Bob Iger at our next, and last, Phoenix meeting the following year.

There was one more sighting for me though in the soon-to-be-shuttered 22nd floor executive dining room. That was early-on after the acquisition. On that occasion he just ignored us—not saying hello to any of us sitting at the tables, or even giving a smile or wave. He just chose to go through the buffet line, take his food, and eat by himself in one of the small private rooms down the hall rather than join in and sit with any of the vice presidents at one of our communal tables. That aloofness was a pretty good clue for many veeps in the room what Eisner the man would be like as our leader. Despite his many trips to New York over the ensuing decade, he never felt the need to call a meeting of the New York senior executive cadre, or visit with any of us. I had always found that strange.

Back in 1999, he had sent me a nice email note congratulating me after our NABET victory. That that was it for me personally—one note, a single brief social conversation, and three visuals in ten years. There was, of course, also his "cast member" thing that was such a turnoff to so many. So no one I knew among New York's senior executive staff, and many in Los Angeles, too, to whom I spoke, had any warm and fuzzy feelings for Eisner—or any notion of regret whatsoever—when the board ousted him and promoted Bob.

I remember that giant stock grant well because we were in the midst of heated NABET bargaining in Washington when it was announced. There we were, deep in the strife and tension of negotiations at our '97 table. I was probably telling the union why a big pay increase was totally out of the question because the Company was doing so badly. When the news of the $500 million grant came across the wire, the union's chief bargainer, John Krieger, smugly read it aloud to us across the table. But it was always my job to defend the Company's CEO against any attack, justified or not. "What are you talking about," I said in my deepest voice and angriest tone.

I pretty much went on to say:

> "Eisner is the head of a cruise line, a movie studio, several cable networks including ESPN, a major television network, three or four giant amusement parks, many radio stations, a radio network, the most successful group of TV stations in the United States, foreign broadcasting assets, a publishing company, a record company, and several major sports teams. He probably deserves more than $500 million."

When I finished, what I got was an extra dose of the usual hoots and jeers. Outside the room after a quickly called break, some of my cohorts, including I think Alan Nesbitt, came over with a big smile on their faces and asked what had come over me to defend him so. I have to admit, it was a damn fine speech—one of my best ever.

All of us at ABC were tremendously elated when Bob Iger took over as head of Disney. I know I sent him a note, but so did thousands of others. He probably responded because that's the way Bob always is. At last there was a person at the very top who had a personality, warmth, great interpersonal skills, strong leadership abilities, and was well-liked by everyone. From my personal point of view, it was great he knew something about labor relations as well as my name. My boss, Alan Braverman, who had become GC of the Walt Disney Company a few years earlier, now reported to Bob. We all wished Bob the best of success.

Iger had gained in the 1970s his first broadcasting experience and initial exposure to unions—IATSE's stagehands and NABET's technicians—when supervising ABC's New York soap opera and game shows studios. Then he moved over into operational jobs with ABC Sports. It was a time when ABC Sports—under Roone Arledge's leadership—was considered the world's premiere television sports producing organization. During Roone's time and that of his successors—with its team of talented producers and famous announcers—ABC Sports had set the gold standard.

Saturday afternoon's *Wide World of Sports* was legendary. Its "spanning the globe" coverage brought many sports other than the traditional football, baseball, and basketball into American homes. Beginning the weekly Saturday afternoon show with an unrecognizable ski jumper agonizedly flying off the side of a mountain into life-saving bales of hay, *Wide World of Sports* and ABC Sports had consistently been there for the American viewing public. Dominating the Olympics scene for two decades with its close-up and personal coverage, it had become an American broadcasting institution. Its *Monday Night Football* was the first sports program regularly telecast in prime time. In cracking the top ten in ratings week in and week out, *MNF* was hugely popular and very successful.

Sports crews including many NABET cameramen and other engineers had travelled the world. They worked hard, had fun, and got paid good money. Many had retired directly into excellent NABET pensions.

Covering these ABC sports events was an outstanding stable of famous announcers who all belonged to AFTRA. The esteemed group of giants included Chris Schenkel, Frank Gifford, Bud Palmer, Don Meredith, Jim McKay, Howard Cosell, Keith Jackson, Bill Flemming, Curt Gowdy, Brent Musburger, Al Michaels, John Madden and Bob Griese. Even future felon O.J. Simpson once served time at ABC Sports on *Monday Night Football*. So had comedian Dennis Miller—and former New York Jets star quarterback, Joe Namath.

But for the ABC TV network, except for Olympics and multi-game championship events like the World Series, or spread-out special sports events like the World Cup, sports broadcasts were mostly a part-time and usually just a weekend thing.

Its high audience ratings and excellent profitability had over the decades served its parent, the ABC Television Network, extremely well. In fact, ABC Sports' popularity and dramatic growth had played a significant role in the Network's losing its "Almost Broadcasting Company" status back in the late '60s.

Sports was the first part of the Network that I had gotten to know well and felt closest to after joining the Company for my first tour of duty in '68. That continued and grew stronger with my second tour. Tickets and access to many events were a special perk. Personal highlights included going through the players' raucous picket lines in 1987 at Meadowlands Stadium when the NFL was on strike and replacement players were brought in. Of course, top memories also included our 1997-'99 NABET War when ABC Sports' executives set the modern day standards for perseverance and excellence in sports broadcasting. Done under Force 10 storm conditions, if an Emmy or ESPY could have been awarded in this category, or a lifetime achievement award granted, the hands-down winner would have been ABC Sports.

I own another recollection way back as a rookie ABC lawyer in 1970. It was when I reached up to give an attaboy pat to 6'9"

Willis Reed's rear end as he raced by me outside the Madison Square Garden dressing room. That pat was in the excitement that erupted over the Knicks having just won the NBA championship. Reed was big, but ABC Sports then and for many years thereafter was gigantic.

As gigantic as it was though, its days were numbered. Like Rome and all great empires before or since, ABC Sports' slide at first was slight and unnoticeable. But as the pace quickened, its decline became more obvious and its ultimate fate more certain. Just like the Roman empire, it was to fall to an invader from the north. But this invader was not a Visigoth barbarian from a distant Germania clothed in animal skins and carrying long spears. The invader came from neighboring Connecticut. And it was wrapped instead in cable—and carrying a satellite dish. The invader was ESPN.

ESPN had started as a small, New England regional cable sports network during the '70s in the days of cable TV's infancy. Headquartered in Bristol, CT., about two hours north of New York City, it changed substantially when a couple of former NBC Sports executives, who I knew from my NBC days, took over its management.

These visionaries saw the huge potential of delivering a steady stream of sports events and news about sports into American homes through a cable connection and not over-the-air. It grew exponentially over the years as cable penetration widely expanded and cable networks offering a wide variety of programming became the norm. Sports-hungry America became hooked on its new 24/7 sports format. And the response was a widening and seemingly never-ending stream of subscription revenue and advertising dollars.

Its leadership changed when ABC, under Leonard Goldenson, became the 80% owner. As America's thirst for sports coverage could never be satisfied, audience ratings exploded. Its dual revenue stream from subscribers and commercials allowed it a rich and guaranteed profitability—which traditional over-the-air broadcasters like ABC, CBS, and NBC could only dream of while quietly crying themselves to sleep. *SportsCenter*—with my old RKO colleague Charlie Steiner—was huge. Ratings, profitability, and ESPN's place in the television sports world grew even more substantially after it acquired the new Sunday night part of the NFL schedule in '87. In fact, ESPN's success was so substantial that it had been one of the major reasons why Tom Murphy had decided to buy ABC in 1985.

When later multiple ownership of cable channels became possible, ESPN's rocket really took off, with ultimately three new sports platforms in addition to the original. The company was developing its sprawling Bristol campus with a host of new buildings and studios, hiring a slew of people, and buying up all kinds of sports rights. As its cable footprint was growing with an ever-increasing viewership, it was a huge, expanding empire—spreading in all directions and constantly on the move.

As ESPN's rocket ship was reeling off into outer space, ABC Sports' star, on the other hand, was glowing increasingly dimmer. After its '88 Calgary Olympics and apparent exit from Olympics' broadcasting, despite all the rights packages it still owned, its limited presence and part-time, weekend future was viewed even within the ranks of its senior executives with ever-increasing doubt and considerable frustration if not outright fear. Many had to see what what was coming down the line.

Neither CapitalCities/ABC before, nor Disney after the 1996 merger, needed or wanted two different sports brands. The normal rules of American business efficiency cried out against two co-owned brands sitting side-by-side and doing mostly the same thing. A reorganization was desperately required. Courses at the Harvard Business School would have taught it—professors demanding it. It was clear that the lesser ABC brand, catering only part-time to a mainly weekend broadcast audience, needed to be jettisoned and its slice of the sports television production market absorbed by the other.

In the normal ring of athletic competition, it would have been no contest between the 24/7, 800-pound contender and its scraggly, part-time, weekend opponent. But one thing, and one thing only, kept that exhausted boxer on his feet and still fighting in the arena. And that one thing propping up the athlete was unions— particularly ABC's NABET union.

ESPN's operations, whether at its Bristol studios or at its many remotes, whether in front of or behind the camera, were entirely non-union. All of its presidents since its founding in the late '70s had been dedicated to maintaining that status. Built on that premise, it was a major reason for its success. Much had been done over the years, including some of my own and my department's involvement, and also with outside counsel, to keep it non-union. Its smart management vigilantly took care of its employees to ensure that this guiding principle would never be compromised.

Deeply aware of the risks a reorganization or mixture with heavily-union ABC Sports could bring, there was no way ESPN would expose itself to any possible ABC-union involvement. There could be no merger with, or absorption of the heavily unionized ABC Sports product intended for the ABC Network's air.

What operating non-union meant to ESPN was that unlike ABC, NBC, CBS, or most every other sports broadcasting competitor, it had no third party telling it how it could manage its business. With no unions or labor contracts, it was free of negotiated work rules, seniority provisions, and detailed clauses that limited its freedom to operate as it, from its years of operating experience, knew was best for itself. It was like my old lawyer friend, Al DeMaria, preaching decades earlier to RKO's non-union Pepsi Cola bottling management about union avoidance, used to say—"Why do you want them, why do you need them?"

ESPN's leaders were very familiar with the restrictions, limitations, and challenges its sibling-company ABC Sports faced under its NABET contract. They were very mindful of the overriding grievance and arbitration culture. Not wanting any part of it, they had observed from the sidelines the stress and strain on ABC Sports from the previous decade's ABC-NABET War. And they were very cognizant of the same challenge NBC Sports or CBS Sports dealt with under their labor agreements.

Paying good, competitive wages, providing excellent benefits, and knowing how to treat employees fairly—both in fact and perception— went a very long way. Just as it did at CNN, Fox News and other non-union cable television operations. Maybe even paying better than its over-the-air unionized competition. Because of this, employees—whether behind the mic or operating a camera, never felt the need to bring in a union. Why pay pay hefty initiation fees and dues for the privilege of joining and keeping union membership in a totally unnecessary organization? That was ESPN's culture.

ESPN's overriding interest in maintaining its non-union status had been shared by CapitalCities/ABC management and now also by the Walt Disney Company. It became part of my responsibility as head of ABC Labor Relations, and part time consigliere to its CEO, George Bodenheimer, that my job had morphed into, to help keep ESPN non-union. It wasn't in my official job description—but it just kept happening.

By this time George was wearing two hats—his presidency of both ESPN and ABC Sports. Painfully aware that deeper integration or consolidation of operations was impossible, Bodenheimer though, as well as his key ESPN executives, were always pressing on the outer edges of functional combinations between the two entities to maximize efficiency. So, targeted synergy became the goal. The major example of that effort was Bodenheimer's combining his two separate sales teams into one distinct sales force under ESPN's management—selling advertising time on both platforms.

So long as this greater concern about union contamination dominated ESPN and the greater Company's thinking, ABC Sports would continue to survive. But it did so in a diminished, increasingly dead-man-walking-status that went on for the better part of a decade. As Bob Apter, my close friend and colleague at ABC Sports for many years would say—"Ruthizer kept ABC Sports alive for a lot longer than most thought possible" after its ultimate fate became clear to many within. It was not really me, as I would explain to Bob, who retired from the Company around 2004—it was more concerns over the NABET contract.

There's an expression in not just labor relations but also in life itself that a solution to a problem is sometimes just too obvious and staring one in the face. In late '05, a simple solution suddenly popped into my head that would allow the desired consolidation without exposing ESPN to any NABET consequences. We just needed a simple understanding with NABET to clarify the status-quo arrangement of continuing to use NABET-represented employees on any ABC broadcast product to be produced by ESPN.

Thus would be born the concept of what was initially called *ESPN on ABC*. ESPN management would produce ABC's sports broadcasts in its outside producer capacity. But the technicians it would be hiring would be NABET-represented and covered by all the terms of ABC's NABET contract. Just as they had done this broadcast work for the entire existence of ABC Sports, NABET-represented technicians would continue doing it.

The only difference was that now—in the age of freelance employment and daily hire engagement—the individuals would entirely be members of the sports freelance community. They would be engaged for the day under the ABC-NABET contract. Many hundreds, probably thousands, already held membership in all three broadcasting technical unions—the IBEW, IATSE and NABET. They did that in order to accept assignments from any union-represented employer. Now they'd be employed and paid as NABETs when they worked these ABC broadcast events.

I went to George and his senior executives and laid out my plan to allow Bodenheimer to do what ESPN and the Walt Disney Company had long wanted—reorganize and shut down ABC Sports. Bodenheimer was pleased there was at long last a solution. And Bob Iger later sent me an attaboy. Entering into a series of talks with top NABET leadership on the mechanics of how this would play out, NABET's John Clark liked the protected broadcast work to which his members would continue to be assigned. The deal was done.

To show his thanks, George Bodenheimer promised tickets to every Super Bowl from that day until the day I would pass from this earth. February '06 was the first. Unfortunately for my timing, *Super Bowl XL* between Seattle and Pittsburgh, called by Al Michaels and John Madden, was in a cold and snowy Detroit. Monica and I went as George's personal guests. We had excellent, mid-field seats under the thankfully covered dome and stayed at the Ritz Carlton in nearby Dearborn along with the rest of the ESPN and ABC executive entourage. Detroit was the last Super Bowl produced by ABC Sports before it was folded into ESPN. 91 million viewers watched that game and the Rolling Stones half-time show—the last Super Bowl to be broadcast on the ABC Television Network.

It was there on the field in Detroit where I first met "Duke" Fakir and his fellow vocalists from the Four Tops. The legendary group was performing during the pre-game "MoTown" extravaganza. Duke is and remains the leader and the only original member from the group's glory days decades earlier. We just happened to run into each other at his rehearsal the day before game day while I was wandering the field, checking out camera locations, and talking with some NABET crew members.

Chatting with Duke briefly about the old Detroit I had known in my WXYZ-TV days decades earlier, somehow I had the temerity to ask for his email address. We stayed in touch. Later on after my retirement in 2009, when the Four Tops would come to the Kravis Center in West Palm Beach to perform, and we'd be in the audience, Duke would give me and Monica a shout out from the stage. On one occasion we visited him and the group backstage. On both occasions people in the audience sitting around us asked incredulously, after we sat down following his shoutout and the spotlight on us in the darkened concert hall, how we knew the Four Tops so well. My reply was simply, "The group was once called the Five Tops."

Later in the fall of 2006, ESPN took over *Monday Night Football* from ABC under a new cable rights package negotiated with the NFL. ABC's former *MNF* announce team of Al Michaels and John Madden flipped to NBC Sports with its Sunday night NFL broadcast package. It was also the year of ABC Sports' obituary that ended in sadness for its few remaining executives, production personnel, and talent.

It was tough to attend the last meeting George Bodenheimer called to inform the remaining ABC Sports staff of its closure. And even more impactful watching the faces of friends and colleagues while they listened to the dreaded news they had long expected. The realization that the decision affecting so many lives and careers had only come about through my labor imagination troubled me for some time after.

A few from ABC Sports management were offered positions with ESPN in Bristol, but it was only a handful. It was unsettling to see so many I had gotten to know over the years of its proud existence just disappear. ABC Sports and its rich history—made famous for decades by the great showman, Roone Arledge, and his team of creative executive producers, top on-air talent, and smart executives, just vanished from the face of the earth. There was never a film made documenting its storied past. Nor is there an

ABC Sports museum anywhere, or even a small public collection. It was all swept into the dustbin of history and became just another Ozymandias.

It was around this same time that we encountered some serious negotiating issues in an extended set of talks with the Writers Guild East at our New York and Washington news operations. It was, in fact, the same contract that had resulted in a strike my first day on the job when I had returned to ABC in '87 and walked through the WGA picket line. Not able to get us to back off of our major demands for better efficiency in the 250-person Network News and WABC-TV staff news writers unit, the union's leader, Mona Mangan, or one of her lieutenants, decided on some new pressure tactics to advance their cause.

Bob Iger was arriving in New York City to hold an open town hall meeting for all of Disney's New York-based employees. It was to be at Disney's spacious, New Amsterdam theater on 42nd Street where the famed Disney musical, *The Lion King,* was being nightly performed. Unlike anything Eisner had ever done, Iger was going to address an expected crowd of over 1000 that was to include many ABC employees who were being given time off from work. After Bob's remarks, he intended to open the floor to questions.

A few of us took the iron horse downtown to see Bob speak. As we were approaching the theater, I could see people—some I recognized as disgruntled WGA members involved in our stalled news talks— handing out leaflets. Securing one, while continuing to walk I quickly read through its complaints about the negotiations I was leading.

As I entered the theater, there was Bob Iger just inside the entrance—leaflet in one hand and cellphone in the other. Seeing me, he motioned me over and said he had been trying to reach me. "What's this all about," he asked. I went on to brief him in about a two-minute drill on the complex issues. Nodding, he said he got it, thanked me, and proceeded a few minutes later to walk onto the stage. About an hour into his presentation, as he began taking questions, there came the one for which I had been waiting. The person speaking was one of the union members I had recognized from our talks.

Clearly directed at me, the questioner asked Bob why the Company was taking such a tough stand in bargaining with the WGA. Two minutes is all that Bob had needed. His answer was perfect. Having absorbed what I had told him in that flash briefing, Bob went on to explain the dynamics driving the television business and motivating the proposed changes.

The WGA person sat down disarmed and Bob went on to the next question. The potentially dangerous situation was skillfully defused. Later thanking me, Bob instinctively knew how to handle and unpack explosive labor questions. It was just pure luck I had at the last minute decided to attend the New Amsterdam theater meeting.

Discussions over this contract, often heated, would go on with the WGA for quite some time, with some interesting twists and turns, before resolution was ultimately reached in late 2007.

It was around this same time that Iger and the Disney board decided to get out of the radio business. Rumored for a while, it finally came to fruition. It was a blow to everyone in radio and sad for us on the Company staff who had worked closely with the managers and stations for so long. Radio had been an important part of ABC's history and mine for 40 years—at ABC, NBC, RKO, and now Disney. ABC's very beginnings in the 1940s were in radio. Going back to my earliest 1968 broadcasting days, some radio GMs and even a few performer DJs and newsmen had become friends. There had been scores of challenging negotiations over talent, engineers, and even some decades ago with AFM record spinners. Mostly still popular and enjoying relatively good profitability, radio's revenues and profit margins though were nothing even remotely approaching those from television.

But now, with its relatively small and shrinking business size, coupled with technology and the expected explosive growth of satellite radio, the decision was made to jettison radio. As difficult as that might have been for the many radio employees receiving the news, Iger decided radio really did not fit any longer into Disney's future business plans. It was painful working with local management and dealing with the affected unions at our unionized stations where AFTRA represented performers and NABET or the IBEW represented the technicians. Disney insisted as part of the sales transaction that the new owners take over the existing union contracts. Radio was soon to be gone except for a small piece involving our radio network news operations in New York.

The last NABET negotiations in which I participated as chief of ABC's bargaining team took place in the late winter of '07. My seventh set of network talks with NABET, counting both my earlier ABC service and NBC days, it was my fifth Olympics since returning to ABC in 1987. It might have been another Olympiad for both parties, but it was an odd feeling going into this athletic arena without ABC Sports as an active player at my side. Radio's absence would be felt, too.

The relationship had improved considerably over the intervening years with more reasonable local leaders and a reliable if not always loving but always rational International president. I partially attributed that improvement in our doing business together not only to the removal of the bomb-throwers but also to our more or less regular stream of semi-annual meetings. Their initial '93 purpose had been to bring the parties together between contracts to talk in more civilized tones about issues and initiatives. It had been re-instituted after the 1997-'99 breakdown and seemed to be working effectively if not perfectly each time we met.

A sense of normalcy, as we had with all of our other unions, seemed to have become more standard. A great many fewer grievances and arbitrations, due to a much shrunken contract, had played a large role in that. The recent ESPN deal had also contributed to a more trusting attitude.

The ABC Network NABET staff size by now everywhere had been reduced to about 1200 employees in what had become the remaining eight bargaining units. The shrinkage in our engineering base had been helped along dramatically by using so many—in fact now routinely many hundreds of daily hires—representing annually many tens of thousands of work days, aided by huge technological advances.

Northern Virginia outside of Washington was again chosen as our '07 bargaining location. Talks were scheduled to begin in late February in Tyson's Corners, but this time the Company group stayed at the Hilton. We'd drive over to their same union hotel for multiple daily sessions largely as we had in '03. Their team was to be basically the same as last time but with more local presidents participating. Jacqueline Greco, my experienced administrative assistant, was again in charge of setting up and running our office, a major logistical undertaking, but she was now an experienced hand.

Our return to Virginia was with a somewhat smaller than usual team because ABC Sports and Radio were gone. But it again consisted of experienced senior executives from Network News— both New York and Washington—and BOE along with TV station GM's and their group's chief engineers. Plus, of course, my lawyers. Station group engineering executives Converse, Casabella, and Mike Norman were also back. Most of the group were returning veterans from the past several of our quadrennial battles. It was virtually the same assemblage as '03, minus radio and Sports, except Alan Nesbitt had retired.

The TV station GM's were all there once again at Walter Liss's insistence—and with my hearty approval. Dave Davis was now on the bargaining committee. He had come up to New York from managing WPVI-TV in Philadelphia and was now running WABC-TV. Dave's roots, like Nesbitt's, had been in news, beginning with his days as a cameraman. But Dave unlike Nesbitt had never been in NABET. He would be a great asset at the table not just in NABET but also in WGA talks. Valari Staab returned. She had brought years earlier a new vitality and dimension to running KGO-TV in San Francisco—as she would bring to NBC when a few years later she headed its TV station group. Emily Barr had taken over at WLS-TV a decade earlier and had been with me at the NABET table since '97. Like Valari, she was a great asset and would go on in a few years to head the Post-Newsweek TV station group. I remain friends with all three.

With Nesbitt's retirement, KABC-TV's head, Arnie Kleiner, formerly of near-pugilistic fame at the 1997-'99 table, had now taken Alan's place in our sidebar committee. Along with returning all-pro Preston Davis, these two were my two principal operating partners.

We prepared for the talks much as we had for any other negotiations by first doing a listening tour. Sandman, Quinn, and I travelled the country for months preceding the talks putting together our list of needed changes and getting the company ready for any contingency. Both we and the union knew the package would again be considerable. This time though there would be two blockbuster proposals that originated not from operating management but rather from labor relations and senior financial management.

BOE's president Preston Davis would once more bring with him to Virginia one or two of his most senior managers. Preston was again in charge of the Network's training and strike preparedness program, so we—on both sides of the table—knew the Company would be well protected. The stations, carefully watched over by Walter Liss and his engineering chiefs, would be responsible for their own.

Anne Sweeney was now the president of the TV Network and

Jim Hedges her CFO. When I flew out to Los Angeles to meet with both, it became clear that Anne, great executive that she was at a whole bunch of other things that got her the job, was not used to the dynamics of unions or the bargaining process. Not different in that sense from other Network chiefs who would succeed her, she was busy running major businesses and simply had other priorities. CFO Jim Hedges, however, took an active interest from the start and was deeply engaged with us every step of the way.

While she promised to come to Virginia and deliver the always important, opening-day comments that I would help her prepare, in the tradition of Dan Burke, Bob Iger, and Alex Wallau before her, I was far from confident she would be able to find the time. Much as I thought might happen, at the last minute she would notify me she could not be there and asked Preston Davis, her direct report whom she knew was on my team, to make the Network's opening comments in her place.

The strategic bargaining plan I had prepared, now my fifth, contained the usual analysis. The focus was once again on our needs and plannings as well as NABET's anticipated goals and possible strategies. All laid out in a carefully balanced framework with financial estimates on savings and projected costs of any settlement, it was sent confidentially to a few senior executives with the need to know in addition to Anne Sweeney. I also sent it to Alan Braverman who, after our discussion, once again signed on, as well as to my new immediate boss—deputy general counsel Scott Fain. I doubted that Bob Iger in his Disney CEO chair saw it this time but I left that to Braverman.

Vigorous athletic competition had taken place at our four previous Olympiads—'89 San Diego/New York, '93 Orlando/New York, '97-'99 Washington/New York, and '03 Northern Virginia/Chicago. But there were no guarantees that the upcoming 2007 table games would make it a "five-peat." We had to be constantly thinking about whether another Pearl Harbor—a throwback to a time only a decade earlier— was even remotely possible.

A month or two before we arrived in Virginia I had gotten a call from John Clark. He proposed, as he had four years earlier, a limited set of proposals and the same shortened time frame. For the reasons we had rejected it in '03—that none of this was in the Company's best interests—I did so again.

Negotiations in Virginia initially followed the same path as four years previous. But most importantly, as in '03, the vitriol, abuse and disruption from the previous decade's war did not resurface.

While we did not think they were there to surprise us with sneak attacks or to throw bombs, neither did they come to toss bouquets. The union came smarter—displaying a willingness to discuss and consider, as reluctant as that effort might have initially been. In fact, it was a real attempt once again, like '03, at bargaining. They had to know by now that strikes were no longer a practical weapon, not even the "new" strikes rolled out during the prior decade's NABET War. Too much economic pain on their members had resulted. Accommodating our demands to the extent they could while trying to talk us out of as much as possible was their only path forward. It had to be a hard realization for this union that had so freely struck ABC and NBC on six separate occasions only years earlier.

Starting out initially for its first few weeks to resemble 2003 in both process and substance, the Virginia delivery table kept discussions going amicably but produced very little real progress. Friendly discussion, however, abruptly ended on March 27 when the NABET committee angrily walked out and flew home. They were disturbed by our holding onto in our comprehensive package proposal two specific items. Detested from the outset, these were our proposals for dramatic seniority change as well as significant pension reform. Phrases were tossed out that last morning as they were leaving—such as, "You're throwing down the gauntlet," and "this is a declaration of war. We're going home to prepare for it."

The impending loss of retroactivity post-March 31, and its severe consequences, seemed to be have no impact on them whatsoever.

The NABET committee that went back to their home cities called membership meetings and took strike votes after the contract expired. The tallies were overwhelmingly in favor of going out on strike at some unspecified future date as the committee in its wisdom would determine. With that news, our strike preparedness teams at all locations ramped up their training and went into a state of perpetual readiness—but nothing changed our strategic direction.

Meeting again some time in late May, it was Chicago once again for another two weeks. Those talks narrowed the issues on a number of the lesser Company proposals. But at their conclusion, no progress was made on an overall deal because our two mega-proposals were still on the table. Chicago was when we were joined one June day by the new CWA president, Larry Cohen, who had taken Morty Bahr's place a year or two earlier. Clearly there to support his NABET members, Cohen engaged with me in some lively but still amicable dialogue.

But NABET throughout those two weeks had remained neither nasty nor threatening despite the tension and the announced positive strike vote. A few of us saw just a brief flicker of light on the horizon, but it was very faint. Only those with "Chuck Yeager-eyes" could see it. I felt a bit optimistic though it might just be a matter of time before we would be able to reach a negotiated settlement.

First, we had to reach accord on our two major proposals for seniority changes and freezing the pension plan. Much everything else seemed to be or would be falling into place. The loss of a dramatic amount of wage retroactivity, although never raised, we believed still had some legs as a disincentive for those many who remembered the serious wage losses of the late '90s. We hoped it would still be a major factor in determining the union's ultimate actions.

Although Marc Sandman was my chief lieutenant when the '07 talks started, and for part of the Chicago summer, other storm clouds gathering on the West Coast involving the WGA freelance movie and television agreement— and threatened strike talk—required his presence there. Fortunately Sean Quinn, now my chief New York lieutenant for a decade and very NABET-knowledgeable in all form and fashion, already working closely with me, took on both his job and Marc's. Assisted by several other Company lawyers on the team, Sean became my chief assistant for the balance of the talks.

Marc would be on the end of the phone when needed, as was our Proskauer outside counsel, Joe Baumgarten. Our PR person, Julie Hoover, was constantly at the ready in her New York offices to deal with both bulletins and releases as well as the media. Strike preparation team leaders were always assuring me of their complete readiness, so we felt confident if NABET were to decide to strike.

A second round of Chicago meetings a month or two later for another two weeks resulted in no further progress. But all indications were that NABET was not thinking about any job action. Like '03— and in total contrast to its strategy the decade previous—there were no NLRB charges, nor any raft of information requests. It just wasn't feeling as if they were bracing for another stalemate or secret attack. Nor were we on our side anywhere near to even begin thinking about getting to an impasse stage as we had in '99 with our implementation. None of this appeared necessary because NABET was this time actually again negotiating—trying to make a bargained-for deal— and not just stonewalling. Another round was scheduled.

For a period that fall, NABET tried a new tack and teamed up with the WGA's Mona Mangan to exert pressure on us. Her news writer contract that had caused such a flutter at Iger's New Amsterdam theater meeting was still open. So, the two unions dreamed up a temporary alliance that each thought would benefit both by bringing common pressure on ABC at the bargaining table.

But at the end of the day, their attempts to join forces went nowhere and made little difference in either of their separate resolutions.

It was only when the NABET talks resumed and moved—for the first time ever—to the ABC building in New York in the late fall that side-barring and deal-making really began to pay off. Making compromises and dropping proposals because the union was bargaining, we were nevertheless still getting much of what we had set out to accomplish. Decent and very competitive wage increases were again offered. New, union-proposed wage classification upgrades were agreed to as well as some other of its proposals. Things were coming together.

Still with a few tough nuts to crack, the contract's very strict seniority clause that we had proposed modifying back in Virginia, and over which they had walked out, was by far the biggest obstacle to a bargained deal. The term "LIFO" means "last in, first out." Contained in most industrial-type labor contracts in America such as NABET's, the clause made it impossible for any unionized employer—facing a layoff, as we might well in the future—to do so in a reasonably intelligent manner to protect not only its remaining workforce but also its underlying business.

Special skills, abilities, knowledge, or any other factor do not matter in a straight "LIFO" situation when a layoff is contemplated because all employees are presumed equal. Starting at the bottom and going up the seniority list, the rule might have worked in an earlier era when all workers and most jobs were basically the same. But that was no longer the case. Most positions and skills in television engineering had become much more specialized. People's skills—and jobs— were not uniform. Our need was particularly intense at a time when we were facing potential downsizings everywhere as the result of huge shifts in technology and business models.

We had begun fixing the antiquated and unwieldy union-layoff seniority system in other important but less significant ways to protect our businesses years earlier at our 1989 and '93 negotiations.

But while those were major changes, they were no longer sufficient. Resisted mightily by the union at the time, in '89 we had first separated television from radio in each city. In 1993, we had gone further and separated local television and radio from network television and radio. But it was still the strict inverse order "LIFO" formula governing television layoffs in those two remaining local and network television seniority lists in each city. The time, we felt, was ripe to fix the failings of the "LIFO" provision itself.

At the same time, we had another critical proposal on the table. Equally hated by the union, this would have modified the NABET pension formula. Intended to reduce the Walt Disney Company's massive pension fund liability, the union had argued strenuously about this back in Virginia when it had been the other cause of the union committee walkout from the talks. With the ABC-NABET pension formula better than most in the industry, we clearly understood the union's institutional need to keep pension benefits strong. While we had negotiated in '03 the ability of the parties themselves to bargain over the pension formula—and no longer leave it in the hands of the fund's trustees—now that we were attempting to do so left their bargaining committee in considerable distress.

While the union was fighting the pair of blockbusters with equal zeal, we still wanted both. When it became obvious over time that there was no reasonable chance to achieve both, it was time to compromise. I made it absolutely clear to John Clark that no deal would ever be possible without at least one of these two proposals. I knew which one I and senior management preferred. I felt confident—and so must have Clark—we would achieve it one way or the other. NABET ultimately came around to the same choice after more conversations with Clark and his sidebar committee.

It was a joint decision therefore to keep pensions untouched and strong. But we succeeded in changing dramatically the "LIFO" seniority proposal to give the Company great latitude in each separate business unit in the event of a future layoff. NABET managed to bargain some constraints on our ability to layoff out of seniority, but we achieved essentially in the restructured provision what we needed. New, enhanced severance arrangements were also negotiated when the modified "LIFO" would be triggered.

Everything else fell into place and a new deal was reached. Ironically, it happened on December 7, 2007—the real Pearl Harbor day. In mid-January, following unanimous recommendation after their normal, six-week ratification process, we were notified all eight units had ratified.

It brought envy from competitors when they learned what ABC had accomplished in better managing its workforce in these technologically challenging times. So ABC now stood unique among broadcasters with an intelligent downsizing tool we could use wisely in the years ahead when staff layoffs would be necessary, as we knew they would. Once again, there was a hefty number of buyouts. Some nine months of wage retroactivity would be lost when the new pay rates went into effect as of mid-December rather than March 31, but it could have been a great deal worse for our employees.

Much else in our Final Offer was of considerable value to the Company by easing remaining restrictions and limitations that for decades had hurt us. Tens of millions of dollars in further efficiency gains over the term of the four-year contract were once more the result.

As this negotiations drew to a close, there was little truly painful that we saw remaining in the contract I first encountered as a young lawyer in '68. Or the even worse book I inherited when I became chief labor relations officer in '87. With this degree of normalization, I saw little left of significant consequence that would need change in future talks.

It was now a fair and reasonable document—not the lopsided one it had once been. And one as good as if not better than our broadcast competitors in so many ways. Operational changes were legion. What Tom and Dan had imagined when they bought ABC in 1985 and commissioned me to fix had now been realized.

When I had returned to ABC in '87, the NABET staff workforce was near 2500. By the mid-2000s it had been reduced by well over half. It's probably much smaller now in 2021 as I write these pages. Grievances were dramatically down and arbitrations had become rare. They were to become even more rare in years to come. The total number of NABET bargaining units had also been reduced by well over half as disenchanted union members bailed out or groups just faded away because of changing technology, or like radio—sales of businesses.

Daily hire employment skyrocketed. All of the better efficiencies the agreement allowed were now a matter of routine and not the exception. It was now many thousands of daily hire work days. Used much more effectively, as in our *ESPN on ABC* sports presentations, and in far greater numbers, we could more easily reduce excessive staff. When staff reductions would be needed, absent buyouts, it would be done much more efficiently in accordance with our modified "LIFO" seniority clause that provided a large and extra kick of severance pay.

We had firmly in place robotic cameras, automation, computer flexibility, and Parkervision. Another very significant concept called "hubbing" that I had bargained in the 2000s was just sitting there—waiting to be utilized. It would later enable the ABC TV Network to consolidate its master control operations out of town in a combined non-union setting with Disney's multiple cable channel operations.

Buyouts had been a blessing for both Company and union. Begun under Jim Nolan, many hundreds of staff engineers had voluntarily left over the decades with substantial severance payments. When they did, they moved into very significant ABC-NABET pensions—among the highest in the entertainment industry. In its totality, the NABET landscape by '09 had become a far different one from the one I encountered when I crossed the AFM picket line my first day on the job 41 years earlier in 1968.

32
CHAPTER

The Truly Last, Best, and Final Contract

Arnie Kleiner had run KABC-TV in Los Angeles ever since he had taken over as its president and GM in the late '90s from Alan Nesbitt. Carrying on in Alan's tradition, Arnie made the powerhouse station even better. Driven by its very high news ratings, it was one of the most profitable and best run stations in America.

With funding from Disney's deep pockets, Kleiner had completed the effort that Nesbitt had started to move the station out of its old, rabbit warren on the ABC Prospect lot. A splendid new facility was built off of a major freeway that came complete with a landing pad for Channel 7's news helicopter. Morale was sky-high with the new building. Everybody felt that way—the entire station.

Arnie and his program director came to me shortly after the '07 NABET talks were completed with a highly unusual idea. They had a concept for an entirely new KABC-TV morning program. If it was successful, maybe they could syndicate it. It was to be a two-hour daily show designed for the LA lifestyle—with lots of talk and action that envisioned plenty of remotes. There'd be multiple daily short features about restaurants, theaters, night clubs, openings, high school or college sports, community involvement of any sort, and anything else imaginable relevant to the LA youth and nightlife scene.

The challenge was that he wanted to hire a group of young and attractive people right out of college or communication schools with skills and duties that would run the gamut—both in front of and behind the camera. They'd have to be able to rotate into all jobs with equal skill and have engaging personalities—a very tall order indeed.

The way Kleiner saw it was that one of these young people would for a day be a studio host, another day a reporter in the field on a segment, or a cameraperson shooting a story. On a third day, he or she could be an editor in the edit booth in the morning cutting a piece and a producer in the afternoon supervising some inserts. Or possibly direct some studio interviews, field segments, or entire programs. Highly unusual people—if they existed—they would all have to be competent in all areas when hired or be trained once on board to do everything. If they had at the minimum the basic on-air personality he needed to garner viewer interest, he was confident they could be taught the rest. An extension of the perfect, one-man band, the group would have to be equally adept at sequentially playing all the band's possible instruments. Total multi-functionality was required.

All the contemplated work, except the producing of course, would be covered work under the station's labor contracts. It would normally be DGA, AFTRA, or NABET. There was very fortunately no WGA-covered work to worry about for this particular program. Arnie's question threw me for a loop. He wanted to know which of the three unions could we approach to negotiate a deal covering everything and how such a deal would be structured.

I was used to tough questions from Arnie, but this one was really unusual. I told him quite frankly that I did not have a clue. In fact, it was the toughest union question I had ever been asked. I was not sure there was any solution—other than dumping the program concept. Since that was a non-starter, I promised I would get back to him after I gave it considerably more consideration.

For a while, I was completely stumped. I saw no solution. Nothing like this existed—not in entertainment, not in any industry or any union contract—not anywhere. Contracts everywhere and in the entertainment business were for a distinct group of covered employees and normally with one specific skill set. Period. Acting, directing, operating technical equipment—they were all separate. There was no such thing as cross pollination of different functionalities under one tent the way Arnie envisioned for his group of two dozen or so people. He needed total flexibility of assignment, complete interchangeability, plus the unlimited freedom to easily get rid of anyone who proved incapable of performing any or all of these intended varied tasks requiring the many different skill sets. I saw no happy ending for Arnie.

I consulted with some of my key inside lawyers and a few of the most prominent outside labor lawyers with whom I was most familiar, all solid pros. Like me, nobody had a clue. Nor could anyone offer any suggestions whatsoever other than have separate contracts with each of the unions covering the specific people that each union traditionally represented. However, this was no solution for the program Arnie wanted to produce under his novel concept of total interchangeability. While ideas were rolling around in my head, nothing had yet jelled.

One night at dinner in Los Angeles with the head of the DGA, Jay Roth, on an entirely different subject, I broached Arnie's idea. At the time, Jay and I often dined on my West Coast trips and were close. Never having met Arnie and hardly knowing his name, Jay did not usually deal with any labor matter unless it had the words *Major Network Show* or *Spielberg Production* written all over it. Local television station matters such as this were usually left to his other competent guild officials on his staff. Probably at the time

Jay had the most creative head of any labor leader in Hollywood, or perhaps anywhere. He wasn't referred to as "the General" for nothing.

As I laid it out, Jay found the whole idea deeply fascinating as a challenging intellectual exercise for any practical-minded union leader. Hosting a show or doing field pieces one morning and directing the next day? Maybe a little camera or editing work in between, or producing,—and then repeating? What a great idea for a show and why couldn't this work? Before he had taken over at the DGA from my old pal Glen Gumpel, Jay had an active law practice and represented a number of major unions, which included both the Directors Guild and the Airline Pilots Association. As well as anyone, he knew there was no precedent for this kind of combined job contract not just in Hollywood but probably in any other industry. Maybe nowhere in America.

Union jobs were traditionally silo'ed into separate unions representing the specific skills, trades, or crafts each union represented. There was no contract we could find like this anywhere. Rubber workers were in one union, steelworkers in a second, and airline pilots in a third. Television performers were in AFTRA or SAG, but not cameramen, editors or directors. No company ever hired employees under one labor agreement on the basis of making steel in the morning, molding automobile tires in the afternoon, and the following day flying an airplane. There were no union combo jobs like this in America. No multi-union contract. But the two of us kept asking, why not? "One contract for three different crafts or trades? Maybe with three different unions," I asked? "Why can't we create that?" Jay said, "Let's go for it."

We both knew that night this would be very difficult to accomplish. Intrigued, he said he would put the weight of the Directors Guild behind it. Roth soon turned it over into the very able and creative hands of his deputy head and chief assistant, Warren Adler—who would go to work tirelessly with us in the succeeding weeks to help structure a common format. With the entire prestige and influence of the DGA behind it, the plan began to get fleshed out. We had to get these three unions that usually never dealt with each other into the same room and entice each to do something it had never seen or done before—make one common deal covering all.

Jay Roth became dedicated to making this happen. He was doing this, I thought, for a number of reasons. My friendship with him mattered, but not really that much. At his suggestion, I had introduced him earlier to Bob Iger, but this certainly was not payback. It had to be, for Jay, the steep intellectual challenge of coming up with a solution to Arnie's conundrum. It was like an Einstein, or Oppenheimer with the atomic bomb Manhattan Project. Or today, Jeff Bezos with his space shots. I have to believe this was the motivator. He had never met Arnie Kleiner, probably never would, and could care less about Channel 7's business even though he had a few directors and stage managers working there. Yes, some of the new people would join his DGA when they directed a show segment or the program itself, but the few dollars of dues and initiation fee money coming out of this deal was certainly not the motivator.

What followed were several months of sporadic talks with the NABET, AFTRA, and DGA officials. We first talked to each separately and explained the concept. Voicing interest, we then got them sitting in the same room and bargaining a common contract. The logistics alone were enormous. Sometimes I would just scratch my head as I looked around the unique space we had created out of whole cloth. It was to be a new day in contract creation and show production. A camera-person one minute and an actor or host the next? Directing in between or editing a story after producing? It was a startling concept.

Arnie and his key managers joined Marc Sandman and myself and the group of maybe 15 or more different union officials from three unions over multiple sessions trying to work this out. Just getting the other two unions interested enough to even meet with the DGA and ourselves initially was a feat in itself. Finding a conference room for a group this large to meet—with necessary breakout rooms—was no simple task. Kim Roberts, the head of AFTRA, participated pretty much throughout, along with Warren Adler and NABET's John Clark. Each of these other leaders also became enamored with the show's unique concept.

Everything was new, strange—and hard to accomplish. But the more I got into it myself, the more the challenge of making it happen made my juices flow. Marc Sandman's, too. Obstacles and challenges were everywhere. But we had to find a four-way accord on each and every issue—every proposed word, phrase, and sentence. Where to even begin? Which union would the person join? What health plan and pensions would apply? Seniority? How much would the pay be for the different functions? What discipline rules if any would apply? Which severance pay, workday, vacations, split days and meal period provisions would govern. It was the whole range of normal contact issues—but now four layers deep, and with many examining eyes.

Each union, of course, was a business. So each wanted to know to whom dues and initiation fee monies would be paid. We worked that out, too. It was the most intellectually challenging set of negotiations any of us had—or would ever face. All of us were doing it together, a group of one employer and three unions. Sidebars with each, or a duo or sometimes even the trio, happened with some frequency as we tried to get four square pegs to fit the one, round hole. The normally-to-be-expected frequent suspicions had to be allayed—among the unions, between the players, and with ourselves.

Finally—after maybe 25 or 30 separate days of live bargaining stretched out over three or four months, numerous telephone calls, many traded back and forth sheets of paper, and multiple plane trips to LA, we managed to resolve all issues. Warren Adler, with Jay's backing, played a huge role in making it all happen. Drafting acceptable language went though many hands and under numerous green eyeshades. We had our common contract.

Looking back, it was the special relationships we had built up over the years with both the DGA and AFTRA that allowed this to germinate and finally bud. The new modus operandi we had developed with NABET also helped after the barriers and bitterness of 1997-'99 had been broken down. We had made the '03, the ESPN, and finally the '07 deal. The bad feelings over Parkervision seemed to be behind us. We had our semi-annual meetings and broken bread together. Learning to get along with each other, we had bargained and accomplished things. Good faith—if not exactly love—was in the air.

The new, four-party deal, to be called the "Multi-Function" agreement, was an example of labor-management cooperation at its finest. All of us made it happen because it was in all of our separate but also mutual interests. Maybe, some thought, it could be the prototype for other such industry deals.

The new agreement was a highly technical document. It's far too detailed—and frankly boring—to break down in these pages. But we worked out a deal that satisfied all of the union officials and their committees. Everyone was happy. Ratified by their three separate memberships and their governing boards, it was signed several weeks later. It had no specific start or expiration date but was designed to go into effect for three years only when the show's production began. Arnie Kleiner had anticipated a start time in three or four months and an on-air debut shortly later.

This was the *Oscars, Emmys,* and *Grammys* all rolled into one. Maybe even the *Tonys.* It surely would have earned the "Best of Everything Labor Pains" award that year at any academy ceremony.

But, at the end of the day, that award never came. After so much hard work, to my disappointment and dismay, and that of the three sets of union officials who had spent cumulatively many hundreds of hours on this unique idea, Kleiner decided to pull the plug. He just reconsidered one day after the rush of excitement and decided the program concept just did not have any real legs.

Yet the highly unique Multi-Function contract remains today, nearly a decade and half later, in its originally negotiated form, ready to be rolled out if and when any ABC GM decides to adopt this highly unusual programming format. Since it had no start date, it's ready to make its debut anytime. The lucky station manager need not worry about royalties. No deal like this has been done since.

At Walter Liss' annual Television Station group meeting that year in New York, he and Bob Iger gave me a shoutout for coming up with this unique concept and making the highly unusual contract happen.

Hollywood in 2007 and '08 saw its biggest labor turmoil in decades. In November of '07, the normally always-itching-to-strike Writers Guild West decided, after many months of bargaining, to flex its freelance entertainment muscles and go out against all of the AMPTP companies and networks. It had been about 20 years since their last Hollywood disruption. Two decades was a record for keeping the peace. During that period of calm, the Guild had stable leadership, including six years of being led by a former CBS labor relations West Coast veep who moved over to the union-side—my old friend, John McLean. But he was kicked out by a new, activist board that over time had become dissatisfied by what they misconstrued as his lack of aggression.

This time the strike was over pay for residuals and streaming on "new media" platforms. The strike was to last 100 days—about 15 weeks. At the same time, I was engaged in an extended and difficult set of talks with their WGA East branch over entirely separate, staff news writer issues under a different WGA contract. Sometimes there would be an intimation of this group's striking in support of their freelance WGA entertainment brethren. But the most we ever saw were some New York demonstrations outside our building and picket signs with nasty caricatures of Mickey.

Hollywood film production came to a grinding halt. Work on television prime time and other covered product was suspended—including the freelance writing for the networks' daytime soaps. With no writers writing, no new Hollywood or daytime serial product was possible. Once again, Hollywood film and prime time television actors stopped working, directors ceased directing, and the many IATSE workers on these productions were no longer performing their variety of jobs. Shooting cameras, hanging lights, building sets, fixing hair and makeup, editing, or special effects—everything they normally did for the AMPTP companies involved in these productions ended. Where work ceased, paychecks ended for these many tens of thousands across the entire film and television production industry. Ancillary businesses were once again deeply affected.

Hollywood-town again shut down because the West Coast WGA had reverted to its old habit of striking. Marc Sandman was involved for us with his AMPTP counterparts throughout these talks, the ensuing strike, and the final settlement. He did his normally good job in this tough, industry-wide bargaining environment—keeping me advised at each breathless turn. The extended talks, and then the strike, is what kept him away from a great deal of our NABET negotiations beginning that 2007 Chicago summer. After nearly four months on the picket lines, the chaos ended. The town sprang back to life when a deal was finally reached with the AMPTP companies in early February of 2008.

After the WGA strike was settled and work resumed, all eyes were focused on the next two sets of upcoming Hollywood talks with the DGA and SAG later in '08 when their contracts would expire. A feeling of discontent was growing—with much fear of another calamitous walkout. It was clearly another headache moment. First amongst the malcontents was a group of SAG film and TV actors. Again, these talks would be handled by Sandman and his team.

Part of '08's SAG talks for television product would also involve its sibling performers' union, AFTRA, now led by Kim Roberts, under its own prime time contract with television producers. But AFTRA's agenda was different from SAG's and they would go on to have sharp differences. In the head AFTRA job for two years now following Hessinger's departure, Roberts had just played a major role with me in the recently completed 2007 four-network and AMPTP AFTRA Code talks. She had also been influential in fashioning the KABC-TV Multi-Function agreement. Years later, she would play an instrumental role in bringing the AFTRA-SAG merger across the finish line.

The DGA negotiations came in first. With Jay Roth's normal creativity and leadership, another crisis was averted. A deal was reached with the AMPTP that many in the industry thought would once again set the pattern with SAG. But a new SAG president, supported by his board, had taken control. Actor Alan Rosenberg and his board no longer found it acceptable that the DGA would lead the way and lock the actors into its just negotiated settlement. Wanting more and better than the DGA had achieved, it seemed to be building up for another ruinous, industry-wide strike.

Since the AMPTP and network companies were not about to relent and upset the DGA deal, the SAG talks dragged on for many more months as the war clouds darkened. AFTRA stayed out of the fray by moving in its own direction and picking up more production work from nervous producers. The feeling was pervasive that Hollywood-town was on the verge of another industry shutdown.

As months went by with no progress and SAG strike-talk building, the DGA's Jay Roth must have picked up the phone and called Bob Iger. I had introduced the two several years earlier, at Jay's request, soon after Bob had assumed top Disney command. It turns out both had grown up and attended schools around the same time in the town of Oceanside on Long Island. A relationship had developed from that initial meeting that could be useful at moments like the one fast approaching.

Suddenly, Bob, the CEO of one of the nation's largest companies, with a huge agenda on his plate running his worldwide empire involving far more than Hollywood entertainment product, found himself enmeshed in the fine details of the SAG labor talks. It happened more by default than by design. There was no else in the Disney entertainment high executive suite—neither its studio head nor television head—who were conversant enough in labor matters to be able to rise to the occasion.

Marc Sandman, Disney's labor chief Robert Johnson, and I had earlier met with Iger and those same studio and TV heads when there was a serious AMPTP organizational issue over its top command. Since the head of the AMPTP reported to the Hollywood CEOs, only they could resolve the issue. Bob brought us together seeking our collective wisdom about whom we thought should succeed its then current head if the change some were advocating took place. It was a highly nuanced situation with no easy answer.

There was some talk at the meeting that day about delay and doing an outside search. I felt strongly this was not a watch and wait situation, a search was not necessary, and the present head should be replaced immediately. I spoke up in favor of its number-two person. When the smoke cleared some time later and the CEOs finally made their decision, my choice, Carol Lombardini, emerged as the new AMPTP head. She was the first female to ever lead the AMPTP. Still running the outfit 13 years later, she's managing her very difficult job with continued success.

It was only after Bob Iger got involved with Lombardini and some of the union heads that order began to take hold. On the SAG side, prominent actors Tom Hanks and George Clooney jumped in and preached within their acting ranks that after 100 days of industry shut down, the last thing Hollywood needed was another bitter strike. So with Bob directly involved and getting into some of the negotiations' finer contract points with Marc Sandman's help, peace rather than war ultimately prevailed. The wisdom preached by Hanks and Clooney triumphed over the pitchforks and barricades others advocated when it came to the ratification vote. SAG's Rosenberg was soon thereafter relieved of command and re-entered the acting community.

The simple truth was that Bob's entire career working with labor relations executives and union leaders in tough situations had made him the right person at the right time to help get Hollywood back to its senses. Once before, decades earlier, the legendary Hollywood-strongman—Universal's Lew Wasserman—had stepped in like Bob at a crisis-moment, even more decidedly so, and engineered labor peace to save Hollywood from itself.

Sandman tried to keep me in the loop as best as he could, but frankly the bullets were being fired so fast and furiously that it was better he relied upon his own judgment and deal directly with Iger, Lombardini, and his colleagues at the AMPTP. Having been Marc's mentor all those years, rather than feeling marginalized, I had confidence that he would do things as I would if I were present—the highest of compliments one can pay to any subordinate.

As '08 rolled on to its end, it was my 40th year of working in the broadcasting industry. Four decades after first being hired by ABC and walking my initial day of work with Howard Cosell through an AFM picket line, it was also my 67th year on the planet. I had the pleasure of serving in what easily could be one of the most stressful jobs ever created in corporate America. Still enjoying, strangely enough, nearly every challenging moment of the accompanying labor pains, I was deeply appreciative of the little bit of success and slight prominence I may have achieved as an industry negotiator and chief labor relations officer. Despite the attendant joy, with so many of my former colleagues retiring or leaving the Company, plus getting a little war-weary, I felt a major change was getting closer.

The labor pains had been coming less frequently. While they had slowed down considerably from the late '90s fever pitch of death threats, bodyguards, insane profanity, and vicious middle of the night calls from unhappy residents on West 66 Street, the events of 2007 and '08 had begun to bring them back. While my health was still excellent, as was my wife's, Monica and I had always travelled as much as we could—mostly in Europe on our short breaks and longer holidays. There were still many regions and countries around the globe we had not yet visited—like Africa, India, China, Japan, and South America. Even Israel beckoned. When Alan Braverman offered me a deal I could not refuse, to retire in mid-2009 with a nice package, and allow Marc Sandman to succeed me, plus I would become a consultant to the Walt Disney Company, I was ready to accept.

Before my retirement was announced, however, Bob Iger graciously invited Monica and myself to come out to California in February for 2009's *81st Annual Academy Awards*.The *Oscars* were to be broadcast once again by ABC as part of our virtually perpetual deal. For a decade now following our deal with the Motion Picture Academy, it was no longer an ABC and NABET production. In all my years with ABC and Disney, I had never gone to the *Oscars*. I thought this would be a nice part of my farewell and Bob readily agreed.

It was the year of *Slumdog Millionaire*. Monica got her gorgeous formal gown off the bargain rack at Saks Fifth Avenue and we flew out to Hollywood to walk the famous "red carpet" along with the real celebrities. As we were making our way into the Kodak Theater, fans were shouting out to us—with absolutely no idea who we were. Monica was blowing kisses back to those few screaming loudly, "I love your gown."

At the event and the Governor's Ball afterwards catered by Wolfgang Puck of Spago fame, we were shoulder to shoulder with a myriad of stars and Hollywood luminaries. I greeted Iger and huddled with my old friend—fellow labor lawyer, Jerry Hathaway.

Jerry is the father of the actress, Anne Hathaway, who was up for her own Academy Award that night in *Rachel Getting Married*. While Jerry and I spoke to Anne, Monica chatted with the very talented Viola Davis, nominated for her own best supporting actress role in *Doubt*.

Hosted by Hugh Jackman, the show this year was being directed by my old colleague from ABC News and Sports now busy in the freelance directing community, Emmy award-winning Roger Goodman. Goodman had directed over his many years some of ABC's great Super Bowls, political conventions, the Millennium's *ABC 2000 Today*, and election night coverages. Later that night I ran into Roger at the party.

As the Governor's Ball ended, Monica and I shared the elevator down to the garage with the actor, Michael Nouri. Michael was escorting the mother of his dear friend, Sean Penn, the Oscar winner that night for his role in *Harvey Milk*. Also in that elevator were Heidi Klum and her husband, Seal. It was just the six of us, but the oxygen was sucked out the moment Heidi entered. Nearly fatal for both Nouri and myself, we arranged to meet the next day in the hotel's bar to have a drink, catch our breath, and regain our equilibrium. We stayed in touch for a time thereafter, with Heidi as our link. And then we chatted once again—shortly before this book went to the printing presses.

My retirement for later that year was announced by Alan Braverman shortly after my return to New York just after I met with my staff to break the news. The next few months proved to be a bit odd. As things were winding down, I had little to do as the mantle of authority was being passed to Marc. I watched the stock market collapse, finished up some projects, took many calls, and enjoyed a number of lunches with colleagues and many union leaders. Planning for Marc's transition, I also finally had time to begin to think about my retirement. Exactly where Monica and I would be living in a post-Disney world was central.

With a large reception in the ABC building, followed by a smaller, private dinner, both brilliantly managed by my administrative assistant, Jaqueline Greco, and my staff, that last June night of '09 was very special. I was deeply touched that my old boss and former CapitalCities/ABC CEO, Tom Murphy, stopped by to wish me well. There were several speeches by Company colleagues and high union officials.

Among the most eloquent was from the DGA's Bill Brady. Bill was its longtime New York president and chief negotiator in our three-network staff talks. He had frequently been my respected and very worthy bargaining partner across the table in many DGA negotiations, an absolute gentleman, and a skilled, valuable director for CBS News. Brady caught me and probably the room off guard when he graciously said, "Jeff Ruthizer is superman." Wow, I thought—if I had only known I had those special powers I would have used them more effectively to fly even higher and faster. Some senior NABET officials, I believe John Clark among them, spoke kind words. Deep down though they had to be glad I was leaving, but surely not about to be forgotten. AFTRA's top people with whom I was most friendly also made it a point to be there.

At the small, private dinner following the reception for just my closest company colleagues, staff and immediate family, my boss now for nearly 16 years, Alan Braverman, spoke first. He very graciously referred to how I had broken new ground with ideas, leadership, and tenacity. Walter Liss and Larry Pollock—current and past presidents of the Television Station group—both sang my praises. My close friend, Alan Nesbitt, revealed some interesting stories from our past times together deep in the trenches. So did my other foxhole partners—Bob Apter and Preston Davis. My Disney labor relations colleague and still today good friend, Robert Johnson, flew in from the West Coast, as did Marc Sandman who was about to take my place. I was very pleased that Olivia Cohen-Cutler, who had been with me at both RKO and ABC for 15 years as both close colleague and friend, was able to fly in from California.

One of my lawyers, Kevin Casey, spoke about how I had hired him without his knowing that he would be attending seven years of graduate study at the "Jeff Ruthizer university of labor relations." He had to throw in for extra emphasis one of my favorite and oft-used expressions—my warning at the time I hired all my lawyers, about the need to "master the very long and steep labor relations learning curve." Having mastered that curve backwards, forwards, and blindfolded, Kevin shortly after my retirement left ABC to become labor relations vice president at the Fox TV stations group. He became one more of my extraordinary hires over the decades to have achieved senior leadership rank in the broadcasting and entertainment industry.

It was the night of Michael Jackson's death. Because of that supervening event, several ABC News executives, including its president and my old boss, David Westin, could not attend. Once again some major news story had collided with an aspect of my life and career. There was one of those clever videos, produced by Sean Quinn, on which Bob Iger in Burbank sent along some heartfelt comments about my career that brought a tear to my eye as I watched Bob speak.

Several *Eyewitness News* anchors from our New York, Los Angeles, San Francisco, and Chicago TV stations put together headline stories about my career and retirement. Many other company officials I had known best but who were unable to fly in sent along their video greetings. After some excellent roasting and ribbing, I made some remarks thanking everyone attending, tying together my career and numerous people I had known in a special poem I had written. It was a kind of "Thanks for the Memories" moment.

I was extremely happy that my two sons, Josh and Alex, now successful in their careers, were there, as was, of course, my wife, Monica. She sat next to me at the dinner tightly holding my hand to help me control the emotions of the evening swelling up inside of me. Since that evening I had taken her to the IATSE dinner 36 years earlier on our first date, she had experienced many of these moments by proxy—multiple times over.

The dinner was held in the private room at one of my favorite restaurants in the Lincoln Center area of the Upper West Side near ABC headquarters, Fiorello's. Over the years I had enjoyed many a meal there while conducting company business. On some days, it had been meetings with union or company officials at breakfast, lunch, and dinner. The restaurant manager considered me one of his best customers and later put up a name plaque on the wall of my regular booth—which still resides there today in 2022.

Feeling very good that the Company, my closest colleagues, and union officials were honoring me for my career, I was proud of what I had accomplished and the new territory I had pioneered in the industry. Those live on, over a decade later, not only in the text of many union contracts—most prominently in the multiple pages of the NABET agreement—but also in ABC's and Disney's bottom line. They also live on in the senior labor relations suites and executive offices of several major American companies that I had helped populate. That June 2009 evening, I had joyfully passed the leadership gavel to Marc Sandman. Hired by me in '91, he took over as only the fourth head of labor relations in the storied history of ABC.

Happily ending my stressful and challenging broadcasting career, I was proud it had presented opportunities and allowed success for me and my family. I had brought change to my Company and industry where needed and made my mark. In balance, I had to admit that it turned out considerably better than what Mohawk Airlines and the airline business would have offered. The heavy burden of labor pains began to be lifted entirely from my shoulders as soon as I left Fiorello's with Monica for the car ride to White Plains. Kicking and discomfort were gone. The trip home gave the term "joy ride" a whole new meaning.

EPILOGUE

It's called *Labor Pains* for a reason. In its purest form, it recounts a voyage that started in the still and innocent waters of a well-sheltered harbor but soon encountered strong winds. As the velocity picked up, sea conditions worsened, and turbulent waves sometimes reached staggering heights. Lifeboat drills became the norm as we rigged our vessel for rough sailing and possible combat. When the call came to "beat to quarters"—our man-of-war would be ready.

During those four decades of seamanship, there were untold adventures and numerous, unexpected encounters. As the reader has learned, kicking and discomforting pains normally associated with a different kind of labor frequently tore through my mind and body as our warship sailed on through many storms. Sometimes, those swells were stunning. But the reader has also discerned that voyages calmed themselves enough so that there were also intermittent lulls, and yes, some joys. Life sustaining, nurturing moments, they were pleasurable episodes vital to counter the perilous threats from the roiling seas and bring peace of mind to a weary labor relations sailor.

Thus *Labor Pains* is not so subtly subtitled "A Tale of Kicking, Discomfort, and Joy on the Broadcasting Delivery Table." It also contains other related stories. These collected tales are my sea-log of both the occasional battles as well as the more frequent calms.

Where did I develop that sense to look out over the horizon to reimagine our labor contracts? To do it not just once but in a continuum? How was I able to steer our vessel through numerous storms, around shoals, and make landfall safely many thousands of miles away? I surely did not gain this seamanship studying history at Lafayette College or in my Columbia Law School days—even when I was learning other lessons of the sea from my course in admiralty law.

For over four decades my life in broadcasting was imagining, strategizing, dealing, and negotiating. Depending upon the season and the challenge, it could be either detente, cold war, or hot combat. Sometimes it was all. Facing a constant new day in technology, changing competition, and post-Ronald Reagan thinking after his '81 taking on of the air traffic controllers, my own pilgrimage was hastened.

As I grew in both confidence and skills while learning the businesses in which I was working, my position and stature changed. When that happened, I became more a businessman with legal skills, labor instincts, and negotiating abilities. That also meant I would be more influential and effective within my companies in finding and dealing with long-negotiated business restrictions that no longer made sense.

Writing this memoir 12 years after my 2009 retirement from a far more mature and commercially successful ABC than the one I had joined 50 years earlier, it's been a joy to remember, refresh, and get down on paper a few of the people I knew and experiences I encountered.

I was encouraged over the years by the many who have listened patiently to my stories and advised I should get the best down on paper. This memoir though was kick-started by 2019's book and movie about Jimmy Hoffa and my one time adversary—Teamster official Chuckie O'Brien. So, to Jimmy, Chuckie, Martin Scorsese, and the book's author, Jack Goldsmith—a big thank you.

Looking back, I had the good fortune to have had a number of strong influences in my career. Starting with my first broadcasting labor bosses at ABC and NBC where I was developing my own thinking about unions and began sharpening my labor relations skills, they were the two Dicks—Dick Freund and Dick Goldstein. Both strong mentors, I learned much from observing, absorbing, discerning, and distilling the better labor lessons I saw unfolding around me.

My dozen RKO years taught me a great deal both inside and out of my chosen field of labor relations. It was much of the good, some of the bad, and sadly more than I wanted about the ugly. Its leaders and Bob Glaser in particular, its television head, helped me mostly by trusting my judgment and giving me unqualified support. His contributions also revolved around lessons in high character, the importance of relationships, and life itself. While working in a company— sent to its premature grave by a politically influenced FCC—I was given complete freedom. With that grant of authority, I developed my own set of values and priorities in establishing labor policies, handling bigger responsibilities, dealing with people, and learning leadership.

Tom Murphy and Dan Burke gave me at the right moment in my career the opportunity to translate their operational aspirations and basic business instincts into major labor contract reform. Not only was it their constant inspiration, it was also their humility and unqualified support. Commendation and unabashed praise always pushed me to work harder and strive for ever better results—for myself, them, and the Company. Dan Burke's kevlar jacket over my shoulders kept me more than warm and safe—it served as my kryptonite shield. Their high ethical standards only made my own sense of integrity even stronger.

Both were inspirational in a way I had never seen before. Tom leading the way and Dan, as he was fond of so modestly saying, carrying Tom's golf bag. But all the time he was hitting his own holes-in-one. For a few years before he made his swift exit, Dan went on to carry his own bag, and very effectively. The scene of our toasting with beer at 5:30 A.M. that 1993 day could have been a Frans Hals or even a Rembrandt, *The Night Watch,* canvas.

My annual winter luncheons in Florida this past decade with Tom were unexpected, post-retirement bonuses. His reintroducing me to Warren Buffett at a Berkshire Hathaway shareholder meeting in Omaha a few years ago, with my son Alex joshing Warren about my solving the NetJets pilots' picketing then taking place outside the arena, was an unforgettable moment.

When deals were struck that labeled me by the beholders as a "Cap Cities person," I had no greater joy than to be inducted into that elite group. In fact, that appellation got me invited by Phil Beuth to a reunion of the old Cap Cities hands in New York about eight years ago, which Tom Murphy attended—where I was the only non-original, Cap Cities executive present in the room. As many of us felt, there was never any better company for which to work than the one Tom and Dan put together.

When Bob Iger took over high command, he inherited from Tom and Dan all of their best parts and added them onto his own. He gave me the support, encouragement, and much latitude to deal with the many issues bubbling up from below that my vision from the bridge told me needed correction. His leadership moments during the 1997-'99 NABET War were the best I ever witnessed of any corporate leader.

On those few occasions since my retirement this past decade when I drop him a line, this incredibly busy, industry titan takes a minute to respond to me, just one of his many former stewards—remembering our time together. It's a warm feeling of respect and gratitude that I feel for what we went through for decades. And appreciation for his outstanding Disney leadership these many years.

My three general counsel bosses at ABC over two decades—Steve

Weiswasser, David Westin, and Alan Braverman—all treated me with far more reverence than I deserved in just about everything I ever brought to them. Steve, it must be admitted, displayed enormous wisdom when he hired me from RKO in 1987. He gave me his complete confidence in a job both us knew was bigger and had more moving parts than anything on my resume to that point in my career. But he must have seen the tenacity and deeper person within me— the Cap Cities guy just awaiting to emerge. And then three decades later he offered me encouragement after reading through some chapters I had begun to write.

David initially referred to me as "the Doctor." He allowed me great latitude in our many strategies together. Included in that was the extraordinary night in '93 that he permitted me to stash him and Dan Burke upstairs at the Sheraton. At that unforgettable moment, we were getting ready to ever so nicely drop the final package on the union while the two of them wiled way the hours watching NIT basketball awaiting my midnight appearance. The next day, David showered us with both champagne and praise while extending the strong hand of friendship for a job well done. And then working with me so effectively when he was president of ABC News.

Alan helped me navigate the tricky Disney waters after the 1995 acquisition. That assistance continued up through the next decade when Eisner was removed from the bridge and Bob Iger assumed command. He had earlier stood shoulder to shoulder with me as the worst storm in ABC's history was washing up on our shores. Massive litigation, political and governmental intervention, strikes, death threats, lockouts, and a huge inflated rat ruled the day for over two and a half years before the ship was safely brought into harbor. That was only possible after the port's entrance had been swept clean of mines and other threatening devices—with Alan's expert help. Support in all endeavors for the next ten years followed.

His reading advance pages of this book after more than a decade's absence played an instrumental role in its publishing.

The full roster of my labor relations teammates over the years and particularly the key players gets a loud shout-out. They are too numerous to name but they were sharp in their analyses and conclusions, strong-willed, up to the challenge, and superb practitioners of the art, science, and indeed sometimes even just the pure luck of good labor relations. These excellent lawyers were always there besides me and rose even higher when the occasion demanded. My several administrative assistants over the years going back to my NLRB days—loyal, and willing to put up with me, especially during the many hot negotiating seasons—get a shout-out, too.

It's a particular big round of applause for my chief lieutenants over the two decades of my second tour of duty at ABC—Olivia Cohen-Cutler, Marc Sandman, and Sean Quinn. Many thanks for the creativity, diligence, and superhuman endurance they displayed in their critical roles. It's not so easy following a steady flow of fast changing orders from the bridge when it is constantly under simultaneous, long range land, air, and torpedo attack. At the same time we were engaging, they were preparing for the peace—or the next war over the horizon.

I learned much from many union leaders I've known in my career, and most of it admirable. Most obviously, the very first to be mentioned is Chuckie O'Brien. Without his bursting into the Northland Inn hotel room that day in 1971, there would never have been this memoir.

Bud Wolff, the head of AFTRA when I joined the industry in the late '60s, taught me the value of always keeping bridges open, striving in new ways to make deals, making peace with once bitter enemies, and never using the term "strike" in vain. Our time together, after he left his Louisville convention—with Chuckie in that Detroit hotel— should one day be made into a movie. A succession of other AFTRA leaders who kept the many decades-long peace with ABC were among the best union officials I ever knew.

Jim Nolan, the longtime head of NABET before its merger with the CWA, showed me many things over the years we knew each other. Most of all was his strength, devotion to members, incredible honesty, but especially his pragmatism. Among the most valuable of my remembrances is hearing the teaching of never trusting some of your own internal enemies. Fortunately, I never had any on my team. It didn't start off all that well between us. But the mutual respect grew and reached considerable heights before he passed away, much too young, in 1994. I learned much of the same good teaching, plus a bit of the odd notion of "conjubiality," from his longtime chief assistant, Tom Kennedy.

The CWA's Morty Bahr showed me that great labor leaders—like great companies—also know when to throw in the towel at the end of epic battles they cannot win. Bizarrely, he bestowed upon me the greatest compliment of my career when he called me, "The toughest SOB" he ever met.

Over the years, IATSE leaders impressed me with many things. The list begins with their internal use of unbridled power to re-organize and accomplish milestone goals within their own organization that by necessity would go on to have consequential impacts on the industry. My deep respect extends to friendships with a number of them in the face of both personal and company danger when I occasionally stepped out into traffic. One of those occasions was an unsolicited handgun offered to protect my family and myself in the face of serious threats. While deeply appreciated, it was summarily rejected—with tears in my eyes.

Teamster Tommy O'Donnell extended the hand of friendship while hoisting with the other many a drink we had at lengthy lunches in New York's best steakhouses and saloons. I regret, Tommy, that we never went up in your plane together. Another Teamster leader, together with an RKO Pepsi plant manager, taught me the lesson a law school never could—about the necessity of replacing shattered plate glass windows during major labor disputes.

The head of the DGA, Jay Roth, showed me and the entire industry how creativity, influence, careful planning, and good "generalship" cannot just keep the peace but can also work miracles in Hollywood.

I have to tip my hat to one other labor leader not mentioned throughout—the AFM's Ray Hair. I always told him of my regret we never shared joy across the broadcasting delivery table. We met on a different playing field—the AFM Pension plan—where I sat after my retirement for another decade to complete 30 years. As matters later developed, it became clear he had one of the most difficult jobs in the union world. And his challenges were totally unique— because they weren't brought about by anything that happened at the bargaining table. It was rather the dramatically changed nature of the music business itself that had heavily impacted his musicians. Never quite knowing what to make of me, once he found out we shared a Hattiesburg dorm background one summer in the 1970s in Mississippi during my JAG army reserve days, I went up a notch or two in his estimation. Thanks brother.

I've spoken at considerable length in the pages of this memoir about a few of the major operational players I was fortunate to have besides me on my bargaining teams. But it's worth repeating the names of the standout stars and outstanding executives—Alan Nesbitt and Preston Davis.

Alan gets a particular credit for remaining a true friend up to and including this day in 2022. It's been over 25 years since we first met in North Carolina when he picked me up at the airport. Our 2014 Normandy invasion for the 70th anniversary of D-Day and our sailing up a French canal—at somewhat less than ramming speed— are priceless. Preston's efforts, help, friendship, and contributions to success over two decades were enormous. His taking me into the inner sanctum on November 2, 1998, for my Egyptology tour will live in history. Our five-hour dinner together with our wives in Paris is unforgettable.

Along with my friend Bob Apter, famous in my mind for his award in sports management excellence during the 1997-1999 NABET War and earlier in '89 his taking me for a little R&R to San Diego's *Top Gun* bar, Alan Nesbitt read some of these pages. As this writing project labored along, both made some excellent suggestions. I know that Preston Davis—from the Sarasota National Veterans Cemetery—offered his advice, too.

There's some colleagues over the years at the four companies where I worked, outside of my labor relations comfort zone, in legal, PR, finance, HR, operations, and travel—far too many to list, whose encouragement, support, assistance, and friendship helped me immeasurably. A few are mentioned in these pages. The several who always laughed as if on cue at my stock lines of "first tour of duty" and "iron horse" know who they are. We worked our "Disney magic" together before we even knew what it meant.

Getting closer to the end, there's the outside labor lawyers I engaged throughout my career when I needed to call in the real cavalry of the Nathan Brittles variety. They were the finest legal minds around who knew labor law inside out and whose guidance I needed in serious moments of imminent crisis.

Starting and ending with the Proskauer firm, there's Bob Batterman from my early NBC and RKO days and Joe Baumgarten in the last decade of my ABC and Disney career. Both brilliant lawyers, their assistance and advice were nothing short of incredible. Bob offered me encouragement with this book—reading many pages. So did Joe. Their actions through real time experiences not only helped me write it, they ensured there would be a happy ending. They're joined for high praise by their benefits partners, Rory Albert and Rob Projansky. For their advice in both my bargaining as well as my pension trustee days, these two solved deep and complicated problems from which most others would have run.

Among the other first-rate labor lawyers who stood out for their superb guidance over the years are Al DeMaria and Jerry Kauff. Both had their own New York boutique labor firms. Al played an instrumental role in my RKO bottling and broadcasting days. He also read some of this book. Jerry stepped in with vital assistance at many important times throughout the broadcasting years in numerous difficult and complex situations. Both remain friends today.

All of the lawyers mentioned provided not just excellent legal advice and out of the box thinking but also strategic guidance. It was though more—the hand of friendship—when the going got more than tough, and long after, that was so very special.

My Columbia Law School professor, and later to be dean of the school and president of the university, Mike Sovern, deserves a curtain call. It's not just because of his theater days with the Shubert Organization. Mike inspired me back in 1964 by opening up the intricacies of what labor law could really be. When I discovered the vast possibilities of the rubber of the law meeting the reality of the road—a wide interstate built and maintained by union construction workers—I knew it was for me.

There's the NLRB. It taught me how to deal with and talk to union leaders—and begin to understand their thinking. The presiding NLRB judge helped a struggling government lawyer that 1967 winter day of my first trial in an Arkansas rural courthouse.

Long-gone Mohawk Airlines gets an attaboy, too. My ABC career was the beneficiary when Mohawk did not make an extraordinary enough offer to convince me to take a job in the wrong city with a soon-disappearing airline in a constantly struggling industry. That beats the trifecta. Thankfully, all roads did not lead to that Rome.

My good friend and Lafayette College fraternity brother, Martin Greenwald, with his vast experience in the publishing industry, was of enormous help in holding my hand as *Labor Pains* made its way through the endless editing and publishing processes this past year.

Finally there's Monica. Monica was always there. From the moment we met in the elevator. It extended to all of the IA gala dinners, including our first date, our Pan Am 747 *Clipper* RKO gift honeymoon flight to London, and my weeklong, snowbound adventure at the Ohio Ramada Inn during 1978's blizzard winter where I was stranded during Pepsi negotiations and she was home alone. It continued into our several D-Day landings, our *Concorde* flight to Paris, her cooking Thanksgiving and Christmas dinners for our bodyguards at our Armonk home, and our living behind moats when we were under siege those many months.

It extended to when she introduced herself to the famous actor, Zero Mostel, at a Vladimir Horowitz, Carnegie Hall piano recital (and said, "I've seen your movie *The Producers* a dozen times" and he replied, "Good, little girl. Call me when you've seen it 100 times,"), or when she got autographs from Academy Award nominee Peter O'Toole at the Pierre Hotel *Lawrence of Arabia* dinner. After meeting Emmy award-winning Tony Soprano, she showed no hesitancy in allowing that thug to kiss her hand.

She charmed Dan Burke sitting next to her at a Waldorf-Astoria dinner and then baked him many a tin of her excellent chocolate chip cookies. Monica—once herself a proud union member of the United Federation of Teachers—was indispensable at every twist and turn of my long labor road. It's now approaching a half-century since we met on the elevator in a building that was very appropriately called Time-Life.

During the darkest days of our longest labor winters, when she fielded late night conspiratorial calls from secret allies and senior management, or just giving me good, sound advice when I was needing some uplifting, she was always there providing comfort and strength. When I was away in the trenches of the front lines for large chunks of Josh and Alex' upbringing, she was a rock on the home front.

Standing there with a running water garden hose in hand as the union pickets were about to surge up our driveway, I would have been very nervous if I had been in their shoes. Reading through these mega- pages numerous times, often blurry-eyed—with fixes and suggestions—she was of enormous help in the writing, polishing, and perfecting of this tome as I was sitting at the computer those two years of the pandemic shutdown. Monica cannot be thanked enough for her support, tolerance, and love.

INDEX

Lightning Source UK Ltd.
Milton Keynes UK
UKHW012232060223
416577UK00003B/275/J